D1422413

5 050 082 1

Memories, Thoughts, and Emotions:

*Essays in Honor of
George Mandler*

GEORGE MANDLER

Memories, Thoughts, and Emotions:
Essays in Honor of
George Mandler

Edited by

William Kessen
Yale University

Andrew Ortony
Northwestern University

Fergus Craik
University of Toronto

 LAWRENCE ERLBAUM ASSOCIATES, PUBLISHERS
1991   Hillsdale, New Jersey   Hove and London

Lawrence Erlbaum Associates, Inc., Publishers
365 Broadway
Hillsdale, New Jersey 07642

Library of Congress Cataloging-in-Publication Data

Memories, thoughts, and emotions : essays in honor of George Mandler /
   edited by William Kessen, Andrew Ortony, Fergus Craik.
        p.   cm.
   Includes bibliographical references.
     ISBN 0-8058-0869-8
     1. Cognition. 2. Emotions and cognition. 3. Memory. 4. Mandler,
George. I. Mandler, George. II. Kessen, William. III. Ortony,
Andrew, 1942-   . IV. Craik, Fergus I. M.
BF311.M445   1991
153--dc20   91-8792
                                                      CIP

Printed in the United States of America
10 9 8 7 6 5 4 3 2 1

CONTENTS

PART III: MEMORY

PART IV: CONSCIOUSNESS

PART V: EMOTION

Preface

This book is about our memories, our thoughts, and our emotions about George Mandler. As the title of the book suggests, this collection of essays was compiled by Bill Kessen and ourselves as a Festschrift to honor our friend and colleague George Mandler on the occasion of his (more-or-less) retirement from the hurly-burly of an active teaching and research career. Manuscripts were solicited from the contributors at dead of night and by means of elaborately coded signals so that the finished book could be presented as a surprise to a suitably astonished George at a party in his honor held in Los Angeles in March 1991.

George is not the easiest person in the world to keep a secret from, since he takes—let us say—a "lively interest" in the doings of his colleagues, often with a view toward providing anecdotes for the later amusement of his friends. So it was particularly gratifying that we should, for once, know something that George did not, and this feeling added to the pleasure of preparing a tribute that we hope he will like.

The book was organized around people rather than around a specific theme, although the topics addressed all fit within the general area of cognition and emotion. We have grouped the chapters into four Mandlerian areas: From Association to Structure; Memory; Consciousness; and Emotion, in addition to a more personal introductory section of Recollections. But it is George Mandler himself—or his influence at least—that pervades the book and holds it together. George's ideas and findings have, of course, been extremely influential throughout the whole field of experimental psychology for the past 40 years, but in addition to this public influence he has been a rich source of stimulation, criticism, and encouragement in a more personal way to his many friends in the profession. Each contributor to this volume has his or her store of recollections of George's kindness and concern over the years.

Two other characteristics of George's interactions with people in the field are, first, that many of his friends either work in Europe or (like himself indeed) are of European origin. The blend of European theorizing and American empiricism in his work is, in our view, one of its great strengths. The second characteristic is that George has made a point of being particularly helpful and encouraging to young

PREFACE

researchers; we would like to place on record our personal gratitude for his interest in our own earlier work.

We also wish to thank Jean Mandler for her helpful collusion in preparing this gift for George; we hope that she does not get into too much trouble at home! Also, we all owe a great debt of gratitude to Judi Amsel, Larry Erlbaum, and Art Lizza of LEA for their tireless efforts and support; Larry Erlbaum, in particular, was immediately enthusiastic and saw to it that the book was quietly assembled and produced in record time.

So, George, here it is, a Festschrift for you after all! We hope you enjoy it, despite your earlier protestations that you did not wish a fuss to be made. It is, after all, just a small gift from some of your friends, presented to you with fond memories, thoughts, and emotions.

Fergus Craik
Andrew Ortony

RECOLLECTIONS

1 George

Jean Matter Mandler
University of California, San Diego

William Kessen
Yale University

We know him better than any other two people but it is still not easy to distill a life into a few pages. We want to tell his professional story, but our love and esteem bias our narration toward a more personal telling—the anecdote or reminiscence that hints at the man and makes us smile in remembrance of the event. We may not describe his career as others would do, but our account provides a sampler from our intertwined lives.

We did not know him, of course, in the early days. George was born in Vienna in 1924, and lived a normal child's life there until the *Anschluss*. The changes were small at first—he no longer got As on his papers at school because, as he was told, Jews could not understand German culture. But as the restrictions gathered momentum and became increasingly ominous, his parents decided to send him to safety in England. So at 14, alone and with a passport of uncertain usefulness, he began his passage out of Austria through Germany to a new world. There were Dickensian overtones to his stay at a boarding school in Bournemouth, where he lived for a year and a half. His memories of this time are about such matters as being hungry and of haunting embassies to find a sponsor in the United States who would provide the precious financial guarantee that would enable his parents and younger sister to emigrate from Austria. But he must have worked academically as well because, before the first year was over, he had taken and passed his Oxford School Certificate (the equivalent of today's O levels) in what was a still quite foreign tongue. Reminiscing about this achievement, George says this was his most impressive intellectual accomplishment and it has been downhill ever since! Here perhaps, began George's lifelong lamenting query: "When will they find me out?"

The sponsor was finally found, and the family was reunited in the United

States. Shortly thereafter, war was declared and, when he was 18, George joined the Army. He was in boot camp in Abilene, Texas, when his naturalization papers came through, and he was assigned Texas citizenship (this surely makes him one of the few Texans who has a paper to prove the authenticity of his status). During his stay there, he applied for military intelligence training, but in the way of the Army, he was assigned instead to the Pacific sector. A long train trip back to New York to say goodbye once again to his family, another long train trip to California, and only upon his arrival did his reassignment to military intelligence catch up with him. Back on the train to Camp Ritchie, Maryland and his first taste of higher education—in this case, learning how to interrogate German prisoners of war, a training program that virtually mirrored what he later experienced when actually doing the job in France and Germany.

After the war George entered New York University and toyed with the idea of becoming a journalist. A year studying philosophy at the University of Berne in Switzerland, however, turned him on to more academic pursuits, and by the time he graduated from NYU he had decided to become a clinical psychologist. He was accepted at the University of Pennsylvania, but a quirk of fate sent him to Yale instead. It seems that Seymour Sarason and Frank Beach (Sarason tells the story on p. 14), looking over his rather unusual application file, decided they should take a chance on this maverick young man, who might just turn out to be an unusual psychologist. Indeed!

Bill: Our first encounter was minipolitical. I had arrived at Yale in 1950 as Kimble's protegé and as another older student (like George, I had done my stint in the Army); lo, and for long-forgotten reasons, I found myself facing George as opponent in the contest for chairmanship of the colloquium. He won, as justice required, but it was a tense moment—a trueblue teapot tempest! But, the curious occasion brought us together across the great gulfs that separated the clinical students from the experimental, the advanced students from us first-year folk, my history of narrow waspy South from George's European and New Yorker breadth. Who knows what made us friends? My best guesses are that we shared, unknowingly, a sense of being Outsiders, a passion for politics, a profound skepticism, and, withal, a buried conviction that, somehow, the Truth would win.

I was one of George's practice clients when he was learning the Rorschach (for me, sitting for a projective test was only part of the insanity of Yale; people there took *everything* seriously) but we were soon engaged in more important business. Together, we attended Peter Hempel's courses in logic and in the foundations of science, courses that set our standards for teaching and for seriousness of scholarship. Peter remains a friend of great moment for George. We were moved, as were almost all of our colleagues, by the brilliance and the restraint of Carl Hovland. We stood, stunned by awe, in the presence of Clark Hull. Frank Beach and Seymour Sarason were maturing friends.

For George, Sarason was a protector and a guide. They developed the test anxiety scales together, they sought out a dissertation project that would satisfy them both (it did not work; George finally carried out a study that was the envy of the experimentalists), they wrestled with being Jews at Yale.

George and I had talked about writing a book on the philosophy of psychology (my wife maintains that we spent 6 months inventing a title) and, incredibly after George went to Harvard, we continued our plans. The first half of *The Language of Psychology* is of George's first design, the second half of mine; the order of authors was determined precisely as the preface describes. The book for all its enthusiasms, shook out of us the last of the remaining positivism we possessed. When we survived the completion of the book and when we decided to go to the Center in Palo Alto in 1959–1960 (we had been invited as younger members of the first class of 1954), we had become locked together as friends forever.

Jean: I first met George at the Psychological Clinic at Harvard, where many of the psychologists in the Social Relations department were posted. I was a graduate student and he a supersmart assistant professor, so I did not learn much about him the first year he was there. My first real contact came during my dissertation qualifying examinations in 1954. Jerry Bruner, who was my adviser, had recommended that George be on my committee, but before the examination I had mostly seen him from afar. During the examination, he laid into my overly intricate proposal with gusto. Because he was the only faculty member who was critical, I asked Jerry as we walked out the door, "Who is this guy, Mandler, and why did he give me such a hard time?" Jerry replied to the effect that he was just a new assistant professor, still wet behind the ears, and I shouldn't worry about it. Worry I did not, until some months later I was in all the trouble that George had predicted. So one day I knocked at his door to ask his advice, and got my first dose of Mandler troubleshooting. George has always had a superb experimental nose: sensing potential trouble and confounds, and especially sniffing at fashionable hypotheses that fly in the face of common sense. It was my first experience of the forthrightness and wisdom on which I have relied so extensively over the years.

He must have found some merit in my work as well, because the following fall George asked me to become his research assistant on his new NIMH grant to study emotion. Our first task was to develop a polygraph to measure various ANS responses while subjects were taking stressful tests. George knew the measures he wanted but we were both ignorant of the technology. He chose as expert adviser Albert Grass, whose company in nearby Quincy was already well known for EKG recording. There followed many trips to Quincy, working out the prototypes for recording GSR, muscle tension, blood flow, and respiration, in addition to heart rate. Finally, the multiple-channel polygraph was a reality—full of preamps engraved with the numbers 001. Some years later when we moved to the University of Toronto, Harvard insisted that he leave this beautiful machine behind.

During the Harvard years George worked on three of the topics that have engaged him during much of his career: the effects of organization on memory, the development of a theory of emotion, particularly the effects of interruption on emotional arousal, and reflections on the nature of psychology as a science. The work on emotion proceeded apace in the lab, and in the interstices George worked with Bill on what would become their book *The Language of Psychology*.

I finished my degree in 1956, and George took a sabbatical semester back to Yale to work on the book with Bill. But love had bloomed amidst the polygraph tracings and trips to Quincy, and George and I were married early in 1957. Our first son Peter was born a year later, and we settled into the life of young parents, not thinking too much of what would come after Harvard. Then George decided to go to the Center for Advanced Studies in the Behavioral Sciences in Stanford in 1959, as did Bill, and it seemed time to leave Cambridge behind.

Bill: The year at the Stanford Center was exhilarating in many ways—the new minds, the glories of California scenery, the chance to talk and to work both seriously and leisurely—but it was a troublesome time too. Both George and I were without tenure and we probably spent as much time worrying about that issue of eternity as we did playing three-handed poker with David Lykken.

Jean: Two job feelers came through while we were at the Center, one at the new addition to the University of California campuses, Santa Barbara, the other at the University of Toronto. Santa Barbara did not seem to have a lot to offer at that time beyond the splendid view, and although we (certainly I) had become enamored of California, the job at Toronto seemed much more promising. Roger Myers, who was chair of the Psychology Department, was making a concerted effort to upgrade the department from a rather traditional provincial one to a department that would have international stature. He was instrumental in hiring George, Dan Berlyne, and Abe Amsel. The department appeared on the point of blossoming into a forward-looking, vibrant place, as did the city itself. So we decided to emigrate and took up our new lives in Canada in 1960.

George met Endel Tulving, who was a young assistant professor there, and thought him a man of uncommon talent. They soon joined forces in what came to be known as the Ebbinghaus Empire, holding forth in the basement of Sidney Smith Hall. There they worked on the notions of availability and accessibility, and advanced their ideas on organization and memory. Endel published his paper on subjective organization and George his paper "From association to structure." These works made clear that the mind does not passively lay down traces from whatever information is presented, but instead actively organizes even unrelated materials—the new cognitive psychology, as yet unnamed, was in the air. George and I worked together on some cognitive history—putting together a book of readings on thinking, translating selections from the Wurzburg school, Otto Selz, and the Gestalt psychologists, many of which were not available in English (it is surprising how modern some of that work still sounds when translated into current terminology).

Bill: The Mandlers' book was part of a series, *Perspectives in Psychology,* for which George and I had high expectations; the books represented, first, our shared desire to write history and to influence psychology by reminding folks about the past. Second, *Perspectives* was one of the marks of our long affiliation with Gordon Ierardi, the genius-editor of John Wiley who shaped the field at least as much as many of our academic colleagues and who would now weep with the rest of us in the cemetery of most contemporary commercial publishing. Finally, both the series and the work with Ierardi measure George's obsession with the making and selling of books—his persistent and mad conviction that, somewhere in the chaos, there is a grain of order.

These were the years when we saw one another most often at professional meetings or at the gatherings of the Psychological Round Table; we would never again be in the same place for more than a few days, but the working together would continue.

Jean: We spent 5 wonderful years in Toronto. George met and taught many fine students—Rochel Gelman among them—whom he encouraged to go professional and to explore the wider world of psychology beyond Canada's boundaries. Our second son, Michael, was born in 1960. We bought our first home and threw ourselves into the life of the city. Toronto changed beyond recognition during the time we lived there—from a provincial town to a cosmopolitan city. New buildings, restaurants, outdoor cafés sprang up, theater and music blossomed. We made friends in many professions and expanded our acquaintances far beyond the university's borders. It was an exciting place to live and we were content to be part of it. But in late 1963 Keith Bruckner, vice-chancellor at the new University of California, San Diego campus, came to see George to persuade him to come to La Jolla to start a psychology department there. It was an enticing offer: to be handed the opportunity to build a new department from scratch, with the encouragement and backing to find the best minds available in psychology and to lure them to southern California. Of course, we had to be lured to southern California as well. We look back now and laugh at the hours we spent discussing the possible dangers of lotus-land, that subtropical paradise of surfers and strange political sects. Would we be sucked into a pleasure-seeking mode of life that would sap our energy and destroy our will to work? It is hard to believe how naive we were about that exotic place we knew so little. Still, the notion of a dream department was almost irresistible. George started laying the groundwork, talking to people he most wanted to form the backbone of his ideal department. Bill McGill, Norman Anderson, and John Lacey were interested—although eventually John Lacey did not come—but of the initial group of people he talked to, only Bill Kessen decided against leaving Yale, a heavy disappointment. Nevertheless, when it became clear that the dream department was possible, we came out to La Jolla to visit in 1964. The excitement in the air, the enthusiastic recruiting, the sense of adventure, all were heady experiences. George accepted the offer.

We sold our house, sent our belongings to La Jolla, and headed for California via Europe in the summer of 1965. We spent 6 weeks in Cambridge at the Applied Psychology Unit, where we met John Morton and Donald Broadbent. George became a fledgling member of the English contingent of the new cognitive psychology (which did not seem so new to those who had escaped the ravages of behaviorism in the States, but logogens and information filters were still not the stuff of ordinary psychological conversation back home).

It was our first trip together to Europe and I discovered something about George that I did not know. I was living with a man at the height of his career, who worked incredibly long hours and whose life was devoted to his profession. We thought that was only right and proper. But in Europe I found a man who liked to sit in a coffee house reading *Le Monde* or talking politics with friends—a more leisurely, slower paced man than I had seen before. That summer was the start of an increasing number of trips to Europe and George's gradual realization that he was still influenced by the world he thought he had left forever. So even before arriving in California, the newest of new worlds, the pull of the old world began to exert its influence.

It is hard to summarize the building of a department, the work and pleasure of it. Certainly the work loomed large; there were endless recruiting endeavors (not only for Psychology because we all had to participate in other departments' recruiting efforts as well), planning a building, seeking funds, planning undergraduate and graduate programs. George, Bill McGill, and Norman Anderson were the first to arrive. Their first year was mercifully teaching-free, so the most important business of filling slots could be realized. And a stellar cast it was that was recruited that year: Don Norman and Dave Green were enticed away from Harvard, and a new assistant professor, Peter Lindsay, joined the group too. The next year, among others, David Rumelhart was hired, and so the foundations of a thriving cognitive group were well and truly laid down, with George's laboratory concentration on memory and organization and what became the LNR (Lindsay, Norman, and Rumelhart) laboratory concentrating on semantic networks, language, and the formal representation of knowledge. Lynn Cooper joined the department a few years later, then Jay McClelland and Elissa Newport. But although George's heart was in cognitive psychology, he wanted a well-rounded department, and there was recruitment across the range of experimental, social, and developmental psychology. Still, I believe that the international recognition that the department received over the next two decades was chargeable in large part to its becoming a major center for cognitive psychology.

The Center for Human Information Processing (CHIP) was founded, and George went to Washington to seek federal funds for a building for it. Getting the buildings up was a trying and time-consuming business, and it took 5 years before Psychology and CHIP had their new homes. Let me tell you a small sample of the bureaucracy involved in such endeavors. Sound-proofing was vitally important to a building that was to house laboratories and offices mingled together. By far the cheapest (and most pleasing) solution was to carpet the floors. But the State bureaucracy insisted that that was conspicuous consumption, and expensive double flooring should be built instead. Only George's threats to "go public" over this unnecessary expenditure of several hundred thousand dollars finally obtained the cheaper, more livable carpeting.

Amidst department building, George managed to get psychology done. Much of his experimental work during this period concentrated on organization and memory. For some time he had been part of a group of "verbal learners," who met annually at Lake Arrowhead in California to have a vacation, read their latest papers, and keep up on the newest in the field. But it was not until he was released from being chair in 1970 that he could turn his full efforts again to his field. The experience of the chairmanship taught George an important truth for his life: being good at something does not mean you have to like it. He was a superb administrator, timely, far-seeing, able to cut through endless red tape to get things done, and always concerned for the health and happiness of the department as a whole. But it took its toll in worries and sleepless nights, fretting over this person's troubles or that person's lack of responsibility. It was a relief to both of us when he was finally freed.

Bill: Our families were together briefly in Kent in 1971 when some philosophers and some psychologists had a common belief (George would later think it a delusion) that the two professional clubs were transclubbable. No way. But George was happy in England; it was both more absurd and more humane than La Jolla, a combination that gave George a platform from which he could see (and reconstruct) the world.

Jean: The department became established and so he turned to what would become a major theoretical preoccupation for the next decade—developing a new theory of emotion. A Guggenheim Fellowship and an invitation from Larry Weiskrantz allowed us to spend a year in Oxford, where George began work on the first of two books on this topic; *Mind and Emotion* appeared in 1975 and almost 10 years later its successor *Mind and Body*. I will not try to estimate the impact of this work—it won him the William James Award from APA and several chapters in this volume testify to its influence. I will share with you one anecdote, however. In a review in *Contemporary Psychology* of a textbook on emotion that appeared during this time, Ellen Berscheid complained that the text was too brief in its discussion of Mandler's theory of emotion. She said that it was like visiting Paris and only being able to catch a glimpse of Notre Dame through the windshield of a rainswept bus! I remember thinking that if I ever received an accolade like that, I would be forever satisfied.

During the 1970s, George also continued work on memory and organization, developing the theory of recognition that led to his increasing interest in consciousness and its role in psychological processing. And he had to suffer the effects of being a good administrator—he become increasingly in demand to work for APA, the Psychonomic Society, and other national organizations. By the end of the decade he was president first of the Division of Experimental Psychology and then of the Division of General Psychology. Next came a stint on the Psychonomic Society Governing Board, serving as chair in 1983 and also as chairman of the Society of Experimental Psychologists (although it must be confessed that the last two posts were more honorary than time-consuming). Editorial work, on the other hand, was extremely time-consuming, especially George's being editor of the *Psychological Review* for 6 years.

It is hard to capture the spirit of more than two decades at La Jolla. Vignettes fill my mind: George working behind the scenes to contain the disruptive effects of the unrest of the late 1960s while maintaining the goal of everyone's freedom of speech, and his great sympathy with their cause, perhaps especially because of its welcome contrast to the conservative nature of southern California politics. The legacy of his early experience had long since made him a person of the Left, deeply committed to improving the lot of society's dispossessed and ignored. George "adopting" young psychologists who came to La Jolla, recognizing the brilliance of an Elissa Newport or Lynn Cooper, a Dave Rumelhart or Geoff Hinton, always ready to talk psychology, give advice, and help in the encouragement of their careers. The nurturance of graduate students and postdoctoral fellows and the joy of the chase that research allowed. The annual parties held in our garden for the students from our two laboratories. The many informal therapeutic sessions with students and young colleagues—George may have left clinical for experimental psychology, but he remained a wise and sensitive counselor. His interest in books and their making: advisory work first for Gordon Ierardi at Wiley, then for Larry Erlbaum, and always working on what he called his rug-trading skills in the service of teaching academics how to write more advantageous book contracts. The many trips to Washington to serve on the Council of APA and to help found the Federation of Behavioral, Psychological, and Cognitive Sciences. George and I watching over our sons, and our pleasure as they bypassed the surf and took up academics—our even greater pleasure as they became friends with each other and with us.

Our increasingly frequent trips to Europe, first with our sons and then as liberated parents, made our attachment to England grow and produced a widening circle of psychologist friends there: Tony Marcel, Elizabeth Warrington, Tim Shallice, Annette Karmiloff-Smith, and Kara and Roy Patterson. George had been Kara's graduate advisor at UCSD (as Dave Green had been Roy's). They were now settled at the APU in Cambridge, and the mentor–student relationship changed to colleague–friends. We bought a house in Hampstead, London, and began to spend part of each year there, soaking up the theater, opera, bookstores, and great newspapers that were still scarce in San Diego. The ties to La Jolla began to loosen.

Because of the University of California's benign policy of phased retirement, we can now spend half of our time in London, freeing us to work in new domains. George is at last able to read at leisure in anthropology, history, sociology, philosophy, and biology, all in the service of his next book, on human nature. He has time to nurture his collection of first editions, searching for the volumes of Shaw or Traven he does not have. Peter and his wife, Ruth, recently had a son, Benjamin, who has proved to be an ideal grandchild, clearly much taken with a grandfather who is teaching him a dirty laugh. And now, good friends and colleagues have written this book for him. It will please him more than he will be able to express.

Bill: Jean thoroughly, and I at a distance, have seen George in his historical form—the being who is all at once and through time ennobling, richly wise, amusing, provocative, deeply feeling, profound, skeptical, and irritating. The chapters that follow testify to only some of that kaleidosopic variety but the chapters are uniform in the expression of two qualities that George will consider splendid birthday presents—affection and respect.

2 Luck Was a Lady That Day

Seymour B. Sarason
Yale University

Predicting the course of a person's development—his or her achievement, vocation, scope of impact, personal style—may not be a ridiculous indulgence of arrogance, but it comes awfully close. Understanding retrospectively a person's development is, on the surface, a more reasonable and doable task, but deceptively so. For such understanding we start with a sample of facts from which we deduce other facts and events, concluding from them plausible truths. And in doing so we paint what we think is an explanatory picture of why a person became what he or she is. The reason why there is more than one biography of an historical figure is that each biographer starts with a somewhat different sample of facts or interprets existing facts differently. Biographers differ about what are causes and what are effects.

Let me make my point by current events, which I hope to show is not a pathological clang association. No one predicted what is happening today in Russia and eastern Europe, certainly not its timing, speed, or lack of violence. If all the reporters, including the experts, are surprised, they nevertheless are not lacking explanations. They seek "causes." What I find both amusing and puzzling is that no one has focussed on events that can be subsumed in the categories of "luck" or good fortune. Put in the form of a question: If Brezhnev had not died when he did, if Chernenko and Andropov did not quickly depart from this earth, would we be witnessing today what we are? A good case can be made that if they, especially Brezhnev, had not died, the momentous upheavals would have been at least postponed. There is a kernel of truth to the position that the military and economic strength of the west was a factor in what has happened. But it was strength (among other things) interacting with fortuitous factors.

And now to George Mandler, his career, and the role of luck. In the years immediately following World War II every member of the Yale department read every application for our graduate programs. And all of us met for a good part of a day to get a consensus slate of new students. Those were times when everything (size of faculty, number of applicants) was smaller than today. If those admissions meetings had been transcribed, you would agree that they were more like clinical case conferences than "objective" discussions. Applications were read as if they were ink blots. Everyone was a clinician. Everyone began with facts: college transcripts, GRE, letters of recommendation, (sometimes) Miller Analogies scores, and so on. If the facts were unassailable, different people arrived at different truths because everyone read on and between the lines.

When I read George's folder, I had several reactions. First, he had a very high grade average at NYU. Second, how would Yale snobbery view such a record from the NYU of those days? I was a relatively new, lowly assistant professor from Brooklyn-Manhattan-Newark but I had quickly learned that an applicant from NYU would not be viewed as favorably as one from Harvard, Stanford, and similar "prestigious" universities. Third, his GRE was well above our cut-off point. Fourth, he was applying for the clinical program and said all the "right" things about a research career. Fifth, he was from a refugee family and had some schooling in England (I think). Clearly he was Jewish. And I was Jewish, facts that were quite important to me. I put him on my admit slate.

When his name came up for discussion I indicated that I was in favor of his admission. No one else had rated him as highly as I. Sitting around the table with the likes of Walter Miles, Carl Hovland, Neal Miller, Leonard Doob, and similar notables, I was not about to pound the table for George. Who was inexperienced I to argue with the judgments of them, people who already had a niche in 20th century psychology? (I cannot recall if Clark Hull was there.) But they were gentlemen (no women then!): They listened to me respectfully and agreed to postpone a decision until after it became more clear how large a slate of top candidates we had. That meant, I concluded, that George's chances were near zero because there were many superb candidates from all the right places.

Frank Beach was at the meeting but had left it during the discussion of George. When he returned, toward the end of the meeting, he looked at the names of admits on the blackboard, studied a sheet on which he had written his list of admits, frowned, and then said something like: "What did you decide about Mandler from NYU? I had him high on my list." I was more intimate with Frank than with anyone else in the department. But I cannot say why he rated George as highly as I did. Frank had recently come to Yale after years in New York at the Museum of Natural History. He knew New York, NYU, and he was a very good friend of Schneirla. And, I think it important to note, when Yale convinced him to join the department as Sterling Professor, Frank told me that he had made it clear that he was not really a psychologist, certainly not the usual one, his Harvard training to the contrary notwithstanding. And Frank was from Kansas, "a hick who made it into the big time." So when Frank read George's folder, his judgment was not a relative but an absolute one. George sounded *good*.

Well, when Frank Beach asked his question in his usual direct way, it elicited a degree of attention that my mild comments had not. The long and short of it is that George was admitted. My friendship with Frank really took off! It was not long after that *Guys and Dolls* opened on Broadway, curtaining that marvelous Frank Loesser song: "Luck be a lady tonite." Damon Runyon had it right. When I hear that song, I think of George as well as similar stories in my own life.

What if Cleopatra had a long nose? What if George Mandler had not been admitted to Yale? Having said what I did at the start of this paper, I am not about to answer such a question. I could say that if he had gone elsewhere, his career would probably have been different. I could say that regardless of where he went, the chances that his gifts would have been demonstrated were very high. These are fruitless speculations, operationally meaningless. Let's just say that for George and psychology luck was a lady that day.

George was my first research assistant. That is a fact: The truth is we were colleagues (we are not that far apart in age!). Several things were immediately clear. George was a budding theorist and experimentalist. I was quite the opposite. He was at home in the "hard" part of psychology to a degree that I never was or am. We were opposites who willingly exploited each other. I was a blend of clinical and social psychologist. George was already then moving step-by-step into the information processing era. What was distinctive were not these characteristics but his persistence and creativity. He was a systems builder who also knew how to build programs and departments.

Psychology today is a vast, sprawling field that seems to have no conceptual center. It is hard to avoid the conclusion that it is a Tower of Babel. Fortunately, there are some psychologists who have sought such a center. George has been one of them. He is not one of those psychologists who knows the intellectual price of everything and the value of nothing. He knows the ball game and the score. All else is commentary.

3 Questions and Answers

Donald A. Norman
University of California, San Diego

INTRODUCTION

It Would All Be Illegal, Today

I joined the Department of Psychology at the University of California, San Diego in 1966, the year after the three founding fathers—George Mandler, Norman Anderson, and Bill McGill—had set things up. Recruiting in those days was dramatically different from the way it is today. In 1965, at a meeting of the Psychological Round Table, the east coast secret society of psychologists who had proclaimed themselves "the young Turks," I told David Green that the University of California campus at Irvine was being established and that they were asking if I were interested in joining them. Dave said "don't go to Irvine, go to La Jolla." I responded that I hadn't been asked. A few days later I was asked.

I visited, was treated to lunch overlooking the beach, and was driven about the housing areas where everyone laughed about how outrageously high the housing costs were (today those 1965 prices seem outrageously low). Then I was asked to stand outside, alone on the balcony of the Department's temporary home while Anderson, McGill, and Mandler conferred. "OK," said McGill, and that was that. No job talks, no lengthy reviews. It would all be illegal today.

Six folks were hired that first year, so when I arrived in 1966, there were nine of us in the department. I set up a laboratory jointly with Dave Green and Peter Lindsay, and got to work. I went to George asking for his advice: "Oh," he said offhandedly, "go write a book or something." Young faculty take even the most offhanded comments seriously, so off I went to write a book, the result being

Memory and Attention. And of course George just happened to be an editor of a series for Wiley, in those days, the publishing house for psychology, so publishing the book meant handing the manuscript to him. Life has certainly changed.

One thing has not changed: George's penchant for offhanded comments that I take seriously. Two were important enough that they changed my career and therefore, seem fitting to serve as the basis for the rest of this chapter. But first, some more history.

On Asking the Right Questions

Once upon a time I was an experimental psychologist. I started off in auditory psychophysics, where one had very precise notions about data: a single psychometric function might have a dozen points, each based on at least 2,000 observations. Then I moved to the study of memory, but still trying to emulate those psychometric functions, with lots of careful, elaborate collections of observations on each data point, except that in memory research one does not get the kind of consistency one gets in psychoacoustics.

In psychoacoustics, subjects were treated with special care. In fact, they weren't "subjects," they were "observers." It took a long time to train an observer how to behave properly, so you could not afford to use too many, and once you found good ones, you were loath to discard them. Observers were hired on semipermanently (when von Békésy moved from Harvard to Hawaii, he took his subjects with him). Experimenters often served as one of their own observers, and if an observer had an "off" day or session, you simply threw the data away. Many experiments used only three observers: one would be too few, two might lead to discrepancy, but three, well, that was enough to generalize to all human beings.

Memory research has a different set of standards. There really are subjects, and each new experiment uses a different set. One wants many subjects, and the concept of an off day violates the canons of statistical wisdom. Statistical demands control the memory experiments, as opposed to the psychophysical experiments, where common sense and a feeling for elegant and clean phenomena dominate. In memory research, the experimenter is kept at a suitable professional distance from the subjects, the data analyses are more formal, and the data are a lot messier.

Moving from psychoacoustics to memory was the start of my downfall. The rest I blame on Mandler: He kept asking me questions.

The importance of the scientific question was first pounded into me at Harvard by the psychophysicist Georg von Békésy. Békésy worked in the basement of Memorial Hall where he was noted for careful precise experiments, for working alone without students, for his collection of prehistoric statues, for his Nobel prize, and for his gentle advice to budding young scientists. The one that stuck with me was his continual admonition, "The most important thing in research is to learn to ask the right questions."

Békésy's advice has stayed with me. Modern experimental psychology is often neat and orderly, with various experimental paradigms that dominate much of the research. But does the research matter? The question is seldom asked, and for most of the published work I suspect the research matters very little. The experiments are all precisely carried out according to the best of experimental traditions, and statistical significance is carefully computed, but the significance for our eventual understanding of human behavior is seldom questioned. Experimental psychologists are masters at designing experiments. But more important than the experiments are the questions they are meant to address. What are we trying to understand? Why are we studying these issues? What questions should we ask?

Mandler and I talk about Science surprisingly little. We talk scientific and academic politics, and gossip. We worry about university matters and trends. He calls me a Philistine, and keeps reminding me of the sacred intellectual function of a university. I tell him that this sacred intellectual function never existed, thank goodness. He calls me an engineer. I smile. But he helps me win the university battles for space, for appointments, for students.

We also observe phenomena. And two of George's observations of psychological phenomena have caused me to look beyond the simple experimental issues toward the larger issues. These observations stimulated me to consider significant problems that had not been addressed previously, problems that seem fundamental to human behavior. Both led to published papers, which are in fact two of my favorite papers. I can think of no better tribute for George than these two papers. And so, in the rest of this chapter, I provide short excerpts from the papers, along with a special introduction that tells their history: first, his observations and then, the work that resulted.

MEMORY, KNOWLEDGE, AND THE ANSWERING OF QUESTIONS

"You know the Soviet psychologist Luria?" asked George one day. "What is his telephone number?"

"Huh," said I, "how would I know? Besides, he's dead."

"How did you know so quickly?" replied George. "How do you know so readily that you don't know?"

This not-so-innocent question of George's forced me to rethink the meaning of memory. What is memory for? Certainly not to learn lists of nonsense syllables or words. It is to get around in life, to let current activities benefit from one's experiences, and to allow one to answer questions. But how? And, how is it that we know whether or not we know? This is not just the tip-of-the-tongue phenomenon: We know whether we know something way before it reaches the tip of the tongue. Do you know Beethoven's birthday? Do you know any of the Eskimo words for "snow"? How do you know whether you know?

Here is what I made of George's question in 1973, right at the flowering age of semantic memory, when psychologists rediscovered the importance of meaning, or knowledge, and knowledge representation.

In the actual paper, I spent a good deal of time discussing how to represent knowledge—the semantic networks that were being developed with David Rumelhart and Peter Lindsay (Norman, Rumelhart, & The LNR Research Group, 1975; Rumelhart, Lindsay, & Norman, 1972). But for the purposes of this chapter, let me only reprint the important parts, the places where the question itself is addressed.

The paper itself was presented at the Loyola Symposium on Cognitive Psychology and published in the resulting volume (Norman, 1973).

The paradigm question, the one that started my interest,[1] is this: "What is the telephone number of Charles Dickens, the novelist?"

According to what is usually assumed about the retrieval of information, this question should be answered by searching for the information in memory about Charles Dickens and telephone numbers—it is a simple paired-associate task. Because no such association will exist, the subject should immediately respond, "I don't know." No one says "I don't know" to this question. Rather, people claim not even to bother to search for the answer; they simply reject the question as illegitimate. In fact, by examining a set of questions of this nature, it becomes clear that considerable preprocessing precedes question answering. Similarly, there are other stages of processing, including search, deduction, and, then, various levels of postprocessing. In order to know how people attempt to answer questions, we need to know how people store information and how they combine general information about the world with information about the question to derive an appropriate answer—in short, how people think. Moreover, we see that in order to answer questions, people must use:

- Simple inference
- Knowledge of causality
- Their understanding of physical laws

---

[1]George Mandler is responsible for first demonstrating to me the importance of preprocessing by devising the question, "What is Professor Luria's telephone number?" The answer, "Why on earth would I know his phone number?" proved to be a central influence in developing the sets of queries and analyses presented in this chapter.

- General knowledge of the world
- Their understanding of what the person asking the question already knows

QUESTION ANSWERING BY SIMPLE RETRIEVAL

Just how do questions get answered? Let us start our studies by examining the difficulties encountered with a strategy of simple retrieval.

The Telephone Number Problem

Consider the following set of questions:

What is X's telephone number? Where X is:
    John Happenstance
    Charles Dickens
    The President
    A local restaurant
    A friend
    You

If these questions could be answered by simple retrieval from memory, the algorithm would look something like this:

1. Search memory for the structure equivalent to "the telephone number of A is B."
2. If successful, then B is the number.
3. If not, then the answer is "I don't know."

This algorithm has one immediate difficulty, that caused by what has come to be known as the *paraphrase problem*. That is, the information may actually exist in memory, but in a different format from that of the question. We might have the telephone number of X's home, or of his spouse or roommate, or we may not encode the number with the relation *the-tele-phone-number-of* but rather with *phone-number,* or *extension,* or simply as *his-number-is.* All these variations on the information require expansion of the simple algorithm: If the first search fails, it is necessary to consider variations on the question.

But even the most casual thought about these questions indicates that it is the basic philosophy of the algorithm that is wrong. For some of the questions, we do not even bother checking in memory for the relevant information. With the request for the telephone number of John Happenstance, the typical response is something like "Who on earth is he?" With the requests about the numbers of Charles Dickens and of the President, it is clear that we determine that the phone number was never learned (or could not even have existed), so again the response is either explanation or an incredulous return question, not a simple "I don't know." In the situation where the correct answer is actually known, such as when asked for the number of an infrequently called telephone, then the answer is likely to take a long time to be retrieved. This is in fact just the opposite of the prediction from the simple search algorithm: The algorithm should produce the fastest response time when the number is actually known.

•   •   •

FINDING THE SUITABLE ANSWERS TO QUESTIONS

One last stage remains in our study of how questions get answered. Just as the acquisition and the search through the knowledge contained in memory is a more complex task than originally thought, so too is the way that knowledge gets used when it is finally found more complex than is immediately obvious. The construction of a proper answer to a question is not performed simply by describing the relevant information that has been found. A number of different issues arise in the development of a suitable answer to a question. Let me examine only one of these issues here.

The Empire State Building Problem

The most straightforward situation occurs when the question is found to have an answer. Except in the most simple psychological experiments on memory, however, we would not expect that the answer be describable by a single word or phase. Usually we can expect that a large body of information is found relevant to the question, perhaps with several different possible interpretations. What then should the respondent do?

Suppose we consider a question with a reasonably unambiguous answer:[2]

"Where is the Empire State Building?"

To answer this question properly requires that the respondent understand the requirement of the person who asked the question. If I were asked this question in Russia, I might well respond "In the United States." If I were asked by an adult in Europe, I would probably respond "In New York City." In the United States—especially in New York City, I would respond "On 34th Street." Finally, if asked in the New York subway system, I would not answer with a location, but rather with instructions on how to get there.

---

[2]The subtleties involved in answering questions of this sort and the Empire State Building example were pointed out to me by Marc Eisenstadt and Yaakov Kareev.

In order to answer a question appropriately, it is necessary to have a model of the knowledge of the listener, including knowledge of why the question was asked. Full exploration of this issue leads to the development of a major set of experimental and theoretical issues, so I only touch on a few now. Basically, a person who is giving a serious answer to a question must consider the developing network of information owned by his listener and attempt to fill the gaps. To do this well requires reasonable depth of knowledge about the listener, or perhaps a sophisticated understanding of the reason that certain questions get asked. A humorous, yet insightful demonstration of the difficulties involved in answering questions without any appreciation for the knowledge base of the listener occurs at any cocktail party where strangers from a wide variety of occupations meet and ask "What do you do?" If the question is taken seriously, then it may require a good deal of conversation to establish sufficient common ground that it can be answered at an appropriate level.

Piaget has studied a highly related problem in the *egocentric* behavior of a young child. As is easily imagined, learning to consider another person's knowledge in answering a question is not a simple task. Piaget suggests that children of 7 years or less are unable to do this. Young children are egocentric in their behavior, describing everything from their own point of view. Thus, they frequently use pronouns in their speech without any understanding that the referent may not be intelligible to the bewildered adult to whom they are speaking.

As far as I can determine, all of the existing computer-based information retrieval systems are egocentric: Their designers are usually so pleased that they can sometimes find the information requested of them that they deluge the inquirer with more information than can be used, as well as information that may already be known. According to my interpretation of Piaget's stages of intellectual development, we would have to say that these systems had just barely started the acquisition of intelligent behavior.

To answer a question intelligently requires a large body of specific knowledge about the area being questioned, including general knowledge about the world and its causal and physical laws, and also an understanding of the knowledge and behavior of other people. Those of us trying to model the human use of memory have just barely gotten used to the fact that we must add knowledge of the world to the model, so it comes as a surprising and new challenge that we must also incorporate a person's understanding of other people into the model.

SLIPS OF THE MIND AND OUTLINE
FOR A THEORY OF ACTION

"I must be getting old," said George to me one day. *"The other day, I went to pour myself a glass of scotch, but after I had poured the drink, I put the glass in the cupboard and walked away with the bottle."*

"You aren't getting old," I said. *"Hell, I make those sorts of errors all the time."*

There is a large literature on slips of the tongue and speech errors, but surprisingly little on how people accomplish actions, let alone on how they fail to accomplish desired actions. George's observation did not lead to any readily available response. I could argue that slips of the sort that he had just described for himself were relatively common, but all I had was my own faulty memory of my own actions to guide me: I knew of no experimental literature on the topic. The German linguist Meringer had collected a large corpus of action errors in the early 1900s, but I was initially quite unaware of this collection. All I knew about was Freud, and although he is always fun to read, his analyses are too clever by far and lack any means of confirming their scientific authenticity. Moreover, Freud concentrated on verbal slips, although he did occasionally delve into action slips, mainly from Meringer's corpus.

In 1978, when George made his observation, the existing psychological literature on slips of action was very sparse indeed. Since then I have come to discover others who were working at the same time: Donald Mackay at the University of California Los Angeles, Bernie Baars, then also at Los Angeles, and Jim Reason at Manchester. Fitts and Jones had done a masterful analysis of pilot errors in military accidents that helped lead to the field of Human Factors. But when I started, I knew only of Fitts and Jones (and since only Reason and Fitts and Jones had published their work before 1978, I couldn't have known). So off I went to collect my own corpus of errors, enlisting all my friends, colleagues, and students in the endeavor.

I collected a fascinating collection of events. As I pondered, analyzed, and classified them, I discovered that they could be divided into a small number of classifications that could be understood by relatively simple information processing mechanisms, plus activation values and "trigger" conditions. The interesting part, however, was that to understand error, one had to know a person's intention and goal. "Intention" was a relatively foreign concept to cognitive psychology, for intention is only of importance when one analyzes action and most of experimental psychology had concentrated upon perception, memory, and reasoning, where behavior is driven by the external materials presented by the experimenter. But when one thinks about action, one is talking about behavior that originates inside the head, from the person's internal goals and intentions.

Action errors can occur in two different ways: in the carrying out of the intention or in the initial formation of the intention. These are two quite different errors. The former, where the intention is improperly carried out, is a *slip*. The latter, where the intention is faulty, is a *mistake*. Slips are more common than mistakes and they are the focus of the work reported here. Slips are relatively easy to discover because one has only to compare the actual action with the intended one to see the discrepancy. But mistakes are the more serious error, for when intention is wrong, the error can be difficult or impossible to detect: After all, the action matches one's intention.

The classification of slips has led to a number of new directions. It was the start toward a theory of action, and more important, the start toward my realization that any analysis of actions required equal consideration of both the execution and evaluation sides of that action. That is, we must consider the entire feedback loop, with actions continually being executed and evaluated for their effects. But enough: I wander. Suffice it to say that I consider the slips paper to be the starting point for almost all of my more recent work, most especially work on applications of cognitive science to design (e.g., Norman, 1988; Norman & Draper, 1986).

Here I reprint part of my original paper, the technical report on slips printed as a CHIP report. The Center for Human Information Processing was George's invention and creation. It housed the early work on information processing at UCSD and helped make the department a major contributor to the development of modern research on cognition. It also provided a comfortable administrative home for Michael Cole's Laboratory for Comparative Human Cognition and for the Institute for Cognitive Science (which later became the Department of Cognitive Science).

The CHIP report series was an extremely important part of life at UCSD. It led a long and healthy life, one that still continues. Most of my papers first appeared as CHIP reports. I consider the CHIP report version of the slips paper more fun than the version published in the *Psychological Review* [The editor of the *Psychological Review,* (properly) pronounced the CHIP version much too informal for inclusion in that august, serious publication, so I had to revise it].

In these excerpts, I concentrate on the two themes that owe most to George's influence on me: the role of Freud in the analysis of behavior, and then, the interpretation of the underlying meaning of slips. I shy away from interpretation. In fact, a major theme of the paper is that most slips are readily explained through simple information processing glitches: They may not have any meaningful interpretation. George always smiles when I tell him that, for his position is that information processing analyses can only tell part of the story, namely, why an error occurred, but that a deeper, more psychoanalytic analysis is required to understand why it was that *particular error* that occurred (see, e.g., footnote 3). A third theme is present in the paper, but deleted from these excerpts—the role of consciousness. I owe much of my understanding of consciousness to George's considerable output on the topic, but we never could reconcile our different views on this topic, so for this occasion, it is most seemly to skip over them. But in a latter paper, Tim Shallice and I did build directly upon George's analysis of the purposes of consciousness (Norman & Shallice, 1986).

The paper to follow was originally published as *Slips of Mind and an Outline for a Theory of Action* (Norman, 1979) and then, after revision, as *Categorization of Action Slips* (Norman, 1981).

PROLOGUE

I was touring in Europe several years ago, wandering through streets, camera on its strap around my neck. This particular camera had a built in exposure meter, with a small button near the center of the camera top that was both the on–off switch for the meter and the indicator that signalled that the meter was on. As I was walking, I glanced idly down at the camera and noted that the exposure meter was on. Without paying much attention I reached down with my right hand to turn off the exposure meter and instead put my finger on the shutter release button and took a picture. The resulting click caused me to stop, look down at my camera and ask "Why did I do that?" I thought the mistake interesting enough that I immediately wrote down what had happened, and started to think about its implications.

This incident started me off on a series of studies and observations. One direction led me to think about the nature of a processing system that could make errors of this sort. This investigation is still continuing, but it has led directly to a conceptualization of the role of a description in the retrieval of information from memory (Norman & Bobrow, 1979). A second direction was to lead me to the study of human motor control. The third direction was to continue the study of slips, especially slips of performance and actions (as opposed to slips of the tongue). All three of these lines of research are intimately related, as this paper will show.

For a year I have collected performance slips. Whenever I observed one, I immediately wrote down what happened, usually asking the people who made the slip to provide additional information, such as what they were thinking, and if they themselves noticed the error, how they came to notice and what their explanation would be (I do not necessarily believe their explanation). I enlisted my students and colleagues into the act, and my collection reached reasonable proportions.

One of my students started his car engine in the daytime and then intended to put it in gear: instead he discovered that he had turned on the lights. I was in a hotel restaurant when the check came. I signed my name to it, but couldn't remember the number of my hotel room. So I looked at my watch. The incidents go on and on. Some are amusing, such as the person who put the salad into the oven and the cake into the refrigerator and didn't discover the errors for several hours. Some slips are tragic. A performance slip in an aircraft can—and does—lead to aircraft crashes. Pilots have noted a problem in one engine and then, when meaning to shut it off, shut off the healthy engine instead. Fitts and Jones (1947a, 1947b) record 730 such errors, some of them fatal. Reason has recorded others (Reason, 1977, 1979). And I have talked with flight instructors and experienced pilots, many of whom have told me about incidents that either they themselves took part in or that they have seen others make: push the throttle instead of pulling it;

retract the flaps instead of the landing gear; turn a switch on instead of off; navigate from the wrong map; land on the taxi strip of an airport instead of the landing strip, or at the wrong airport. Slips can be serious business.

Slips: Window to the Mind

A slip occurs when someone performs an action that is not intended. Slips do not occur randomly. They often result from conflict among several possible actions or thoughts, or by intermixing the components of a single action sequence, or by performing an appropriate ate act in some inappropriate way. It is my belief that errors can be interpreted by a suitable understanding of how people come to their intentions, and how that intent then becomes translated into action. Freud knew this, and from his analyses of errors, Freud made important contributions to our understanding of the mind. Freud's contributions have been severely under valued by contemporary scientists, possibly as a reaction to his apparent overinterpretation of slips.

Freud's contributions can be reinterpreted. I believe Freud confused two different aspects of cognitive machinery: mechanism and knowledge. Freud believed that slips resulted from competition among underlying mechanisms, often working in parallel with one another, almost always beneath the consciousness of the owner. The resulting notions were of mental operations controlled by a quasi-hierarchical control structure, with parallel activation of thoughts and memories, with conscious access to only a limited amount of this activity. The ideas are sophisticated even for today's theorists who only recently have introduced the differences between conscious and subconscious processing into their models of cognitive functioning (we still do not know how a layered system of independently operating computational units might work). Freud also was concerned with the particular knowledge contents of the memories and beliefs of his patients. I believe that it is this aspect of Freud that is most controversial, for like most of my colleagues, I believe he went far beyond reasonable bounds in attributing vast influence from hypothesized belief structures.

Slips are indeed compelling sources of data. To Freud, the interpretation of some was clear, "for the meaning in them is unmistakable, even to the dullest intelligence, and strong enough to impress even the most critical judgment" (Freud, 1924). The examination of any large collection of slips reveals that they are not random occurrences. They can be categorized. They fall into patterns. Moreover, if one attempts to determine what possible mechanism could lead to such patterns of errors, the result requires autonomous, subconscious processing, with intentions, past habits, thoughts, and memories all playing some role in corrupting the intended behavior.

On the Interpretation of Slips

Consider the following slip. I was the discussant on a paper by a distinguished psychologist. I had no advance notice about the contents of the paper, and so was forced to prepare remarks as the paper was presented and to continue planning the latter part of my remarks even as I started to say the first part. The conference was on the topic of knowledge representation, and the speaker had presented us with some observations from experiments in visual perception, along with some theoretical interpretations. His interpretations are well-known, and quite controversial, at least within this audience. I deliberately wished to downplay the controversy and to emphasize the positive contributions of the talk to the issues of the conference. At one point, however, I said, ". . . this tells us nothing of the reputation (pause) *representation* of the information" (and one of my colleagues in the audience gleefully recorded the slip for my files).[3]

Freud would have nodded wisely and stated that my slip revealed my underlying concern about the "reputation" of the speaker (and another of my colleagues, afterwards presented such an interpretation to me). That may very well be so, but note that the slip itself didn't occur at a random time: the hidden intent must have been sitting around waiting for just the right opportunity to reveal itself, a situation where the syntax and phonological components would match properly. The words "reputation" and "representation" share a common ending, a common beginning, and a common part of speech. These different aspects of a slip point out an important point: *most slips have multiple causes.* Freudian forces may indeed operate, but they do so in conjunction with other underlying forces, so that the resulting slip is multipli-determined, consistent with a number of constraints and explanations.

Analyses of verbal slips—and hundreds have been analyzed by other investigators (see Fromkin 1973, 1979)—indicate that the pronunciation of words is not a unitary concept associated with the words. Otherwise, once having started a word, we should go all the way through with it. But people say such things as "canpakes" for "pancakes" and "relevation" for "revelation." Or they interchange sounds among several words as in the "the sweeter hitch" instead of "the heater switch." And then there are blends, when in indecision between two words, out comes a mixture, as in "momentaneous" for the mix of "momentary" and "instantaneous" (all these examples come from Fromkin, 1973, Appendix). There appears to be the notion of individual parts of an action or of an utterance, perhaps differentially activated, waiting to be picked up and executed. My slip of "reputation" for "representation" probably had several contributing causes, with the actual word selection

---

[3]Added footnote: Now it can be told. The "colleague in the audience" was, of course, George Mandler, most gleeful at having discovered my true opinion of the speaker. I still deny that interpretation.

influenced by a combination of syntactical considerations, meaning, and phonological selection from the set of possible words, and perhaps other factors such as Freudian-like activation of my underlying motives and plans for the commentary. None of these things individually would suffice to cause this particular error. It took the whole ensemble of reasons.

Some slips seem to result from the triggering of a well-formed habit in inappropriate circumstances, as in the report by William James that "very absent-minded persons in going to their bedroom to dress for dinner have been known to take off one garment after another and finally to get into bed, merely because that was the habitual issue of the first few movements when performed at a later hour" (James, 1890, p. 115). Other slips seem to result from "activation" of thoughts that are not intended to be said or performed. Sometimes these thoughts get done, with verbal slips leading to embarrassment and action slips to difficulties. Sometimes the complementary error occurs. Having thought about the need to do some action or to say some utterance, the deed is not done, but the person believes that it has been done (or, at least, later remembers it to have been done). If the former slip can be called "thoughts cause actions," the latter can be called "thoughts replace actions."

• ● ●

SUMMARY

Slips of word and deed cry out for interpretation. The errors are revealing of hidden intentions and mechanisms. In this paper, I have attempted to draw from a reasonable collection of slips sufficient components and constraints for a theory of action and its essential cohort, a cybernetic theory of monitoring. The nature of the errors seems such that simple serial buffer models will not suffice, but rather the individual components of an action must compete for their turn to be executed. Each activated component is a sensori-motor schema, with conditions that specify when it is to be triggered into action. Were this all there was to the theory, the only errors that could occur would be errors of ordering, in which a relevant component missed its triggering situation, or an erroneous one was mistriggered when the existing situation provided a sufficient match for its trigger conditions.

• ● ●

Conscious awareness of the schemas is not necessary for performance. The general idea is that well-learned action sequences need only be specified at the highest level. It is only with poorly learned acts or with novel rearrangements of well-learned components that conscious awareness of lower level components is required. When an action sequence is modified, however, then there is a critical junction point at which the modification must occur, and if the required schema is not activated at that time, the regular, unmodified act will continue. Some errors occur when there is loss of components from memory. Depending on what is lost, the error may simply be a missed action, or an erroneous sequence, or reversion to a prototype act, or if it is the conscious level of intention that is lost, the result may be to wonder what the purpose of the current actions is.

Feedback plays an essential role in complex behavior. With slips, it is of interest to discover under what conditions a slip can be discovered and when it cannot. The monitoring of actions is a basic component of a feedback control system, but the monitoring function requires that the comparison of intention and action be done at the same level of specification. Because complex acts have many differing levels of specification, each with their own relevant schemas and operations, the monitoring function must also be performed at many different levels. The performance of an action, from initial conceptualization through realization is then the process of decomposing the original intention into a sequence of physically performable acts, with multiple levels of feedback analysis accompanying the acts.

REFERENCES

Fitts, P. M., & Jones, R. E. (1947a, July). *Analysis of factors contributing to 460 "pilot error" experiences in operating aircraft controls* (Memorandum Report TSEAA-694-12). Aero Medical Laboratory, Air Materiel Command, Wright-Patterson Air Force Base, Dayton, OH.

Fitts, P. M., & Jones, R. E. (1947b, October). *Psychological aspects of instrument display. 1: Analysis of 270 "pilot error" experiences in reading and interpreting aircraft instruments* (Memorandum Report TSEAA-694-12A). Aero Medical Laboratory, Air Materiel Command, Wright-Patterson Air Force Base, Dayton, OH.

Freud, S. (1924). *A general introduction to psychoanalysis* (J. Riviere, Trans.). London: Alen & Unwin.

Fromkin, V. (Ed.). (1973). *Speech errors as linguistic evidence.* The Hague: Mouton.

Fromkin, V. (Ed.). (1979). *Errors of linguistic performance: Slips of the tongue, ear, pen, and hands.* New York: Academic Press.

James, W. (1890). *Principles of psychology.* New York: Holt.

Norman, D. A. (1973). Memory, knowledge, and the answering of questions. In R. Solso (Ed.), *Contemporary issues in cognitive psychology: The Loyola symposium* (pp. 135–165). Washington, DC: Winston.

Norman, D. A. (1979). *Slips of mind and an outline for a theory of action.* San Diego, CA: Center for Human Information Processing, University of California, San Diego.

Norman, D. A. (1981). Categorization of Action Slips. *Psychological Review, 88,* 1–15.

Norman, D. A. (1988). *The psychology of everyday things.* New York: Basic Books.

Norman, D. A., & Bobrow, D. G. (1979). Descriptions: An intermediate stage in memory retrieval. *Cognitive Psychology, 11,* 107–123.

Norman, D. A., & Draper, S. W. (Ed.). (1986). *User centered system design.* Hillsdale, NJ: Lawrence Erlbaum Associates.

Norman, D. A., Rumelhart, D. E., & The LNR Research Group. (1975). *Explorations in cognition.* New York: Freeman.

Norman, D. A., & Shallice, T. (1986). Attention to action: Willed and automatic control of behavior. In R. J. Davidson, G. E. Schwartz, & D. Shapiro (Ed.), *Consciousness and self regulation: Advances in research* (Vol. 4). New York: Plenum Press.

Reason, J. T. (1977). Skill and error in everyday life. In M. Howe (Ed.), *Adult learning*. London: Wiley.

Reason, J. T. (1979). Actions not as planned. In G. Underwood & R. Stevens (Ed.), *Aspects of consciousness*. London: Academic Press.

Rumelhart, D. E., Lindsay, P. H., & Norman, D. A. (1972). A process model for long-term memory. In E. Tulving & W. Donaldson (Ed.), *Organization of memory*. San Diego: Academic Press.

II
FROM ASSOCIATION
TO STRUCTURE

4 LEARNING BY ASSOCIATION: TWO TRIBUTES TO GEORGE MANDLER

Karalyn Patterson
MRC Applied Psychology Unit, Cambridge, United Kingdom

Many people taught me about psychology; but George Mandler taught me to be a psychologist. As may be the case with much procedural learning, this occurred more by a variety of indirect processes than by direct, declarative instruction. In other words, I (and his other doctoral students) learned by association with George. The extent to which we could hope to emulate him was of course limited; but as a role model, he was motivating, effective, and fun.

Personal tributes, even the most sincere (or perhaps especially those), pall quickly. Therefore, it is time to move on to the second meaning of my title. One of George Mandler's many significant contributions to psychology falls within the topic of associative learning. As a framework for appraising this contribution, I offer a discussion of a paper by George that appeared in the *Psychological Review* in 1962: "From Association to Structure" (hereinafter, for brevity, "Structure").

The central theme of "Structure" is that cognitive structures may emerge naturally out of associationist learning. This was a rather radical idea in 1962, when at least some psychologists still hoped to explain behavior without resort to cognitive processes. The intervening 30 years have of course seen a massive shift in favor of cognitive psychology. At least until recently, however, this shift of focus from one class (or view) of psychological processes to another entailed rather meager consideration of the relationship between them.

Mandler's paper is intriguing now partly because the recent connectionist (or parallel distributed processing) revolution has re-aroused interest in this relationship between learning down at the level of strengths of individual associations or connections, on the one hand, and cognitive structures like schemata, on the other. Mandler's proposal that the apparent discontinuity here might be more apparent than real finds major resonance in the connectionist literature (see, e.g., various chapters in McClelland & Rumelhart, 1986; Morris, 1989; Rumelhart & McClelland, 1986).

This is not meant to be the sort of archaeological expedition that concludes that there are no new ideas under the sun. The claim is neither that connectionism grew out of ideas in Mandler (1962) nor even that the essential seeds were lying dormant there. I merely suggest that some parallels with an approach of substantial current interest adds piquancy to a review of "Structure."

Mandler began with the question: "Do organisms learn generalizable, but discrete, responses in specific situations or are rules of behavior, maps or schemata laid down which connect various behaviors and environmental inputs?" (p. 415). Presumably the psychologists who argued for structural, schematized learning (Mandler's examples here were Piaget, Bartlett, Hebb, and the gestalt school plus its offspring) would not actually have denied the existence of specific associations. What they did deny was that such associations could be the foundation of the sort of organized behavior calling for schemata-like notions.

Mandler's own preferred definition of *structures* was as ". . . temporal and probabilistic linkages of inputs and behavior which are available in functional units" (p. 415). This definition of structure was deliberately much broader than the sometimes ultra-cognitive sense of schema. A structure in Mandler's terms might be a quite general and cognitive schema (like restaurant behavior—not, of course, one of his examples); but it might also be quite limited, as in a specific learned association or habit. The point of this breadth of definition was presumably to facilitate Mandler's argument for compatibility between associationist and cognitive views of behavior. Indeed, he wanted to claim even more than compatibility: ". . . it will be maintained here that . . . cognitive characteristics of the organism may be developed out of associationist processes" (p. 416).

The context, or contexts, in which Mandler developed this notion involved learning sets, warm-up effects, overlearning, and transfer of training, in both animal and human studies. In an effort to emphasize the aspects of "Structure" that seem most germane to current issues, I give unequal coverage to these various topics. Of special interest are the effects of high degrees of, or "over," learning.

Early in learning, Mandler suggested, responding is likely to consist of a series of discrete responses, partly because correct responses are still being interrupted by incorrect ones. As errors drop out, the sequence of behavior starts to become stable and integrated. "Integration refers to the fact that previously discrete parts of a sequence come to behave functionally as a unit; the whole sequence . . . behaves as a single component response has in the past; any part of it elicits the whole sequence" (p. 417). This response learning, as Mandler (1954) had already labeled it in a previous paper, was not the only important effect of continued practice: during overlearning, an integrated response sequence ". . . develops a structural representation, a "central" analogue of this new response unit which can function independently of the overt response sequence" (p. 417). Furthermore, he proposed that these "Analogic structures permit covert trial and error behavior, i.e., cognitive manipulation of previously established behavior. In this sense, the analogic representation of a prior behavior sequence is one possible 'hypothesis' to be applied to a particular situation" (p. 417).

All three of these ideas find ready parallels in the PDP framework. Mandler's response learning is clearly related to the process whereby connection strengths amongst units in a network are adjusted as a result of learning; and the idea that parts can elicit the whole is clearly related to pattern completion (McLaren, Kaye, & Mackintosh, 1989; Rumelhart, Hinton, & McClelland, 1986). PDP's version of a structure such as a schema is, according to Rumelhart, Smolensky, McClelland, and Hinton (1986), a coalition of tightly interconnected units, where the degree of structure corresponds to the tightness of the coupling. These authors also described the PDP version of a mental model in a way highly reminiscent of Mandler's "central analogue": if one network receives real-world input and relaxes to a state specifying an appropriate response, a second network that models the first one is a mental model. And just as Mandler's analogic structure corresponds to a hypothesis, enabling covert trial and error behavior, Rumelhart et al.'s "model" network settles to an interpretation not of a real-world state but of an intended action, allowing us to predict what would happen if we did that.

Another recent development in the connectionist approach includes some similar themes. Cohen, Dunbar, and McClelland (1990) have developed a PDP model to account for control of processing in the Stroop task. In this task, where the subject must respond to a stimulus (e.g., the word GREEN printed in red ink) with either word name or ink color, the phenomena to be accounted for are (a) how task instructions allow the subject (for the most part) to select the appropriate response, and (b) how one response (particularly the word name) interferes with computation or selection of the other. In Cohen et al.'s nonlinear, cascaded PDP model of this task, in addition to the two, partially overlapping, direct pathways (one for word, one for ink color) from stimulus to response, there is another module whose patterns of activation are determined by task instructions. Output from this extra module differentially adjusts activation levels in the two competing task-specific pathways, with the result that the pathway targeted by task instruction has greater impact on computation of the response. The idea of an instructional or contextual module that can modulate the control of behavior by more direct, stimulus–response connections seems to bear on Mandler's proposal of analogic structures that permit manipulation of learned associations.

Although various contributions to the PDP literature assert the compatibility of connectionist principles with cognitive structures, they tend to emphasize one significant difference between the two approaches. In cognitive or symbolic frameworks for learning, the acquisition of a new concept seems to entail a decision (by someone or something) to create a new schema. By contrast, in the subsymbolic or PDP approach, schemata emerge gradually (rather than abruptly) and naturally (rather than by fiat) (Rumelhart et al., 1986; Smolensky, 1986, 1988). It seems to me that Mandler's concept of schema construction had precisely this kind of natural and emergent character. He described how a variety of structures potentially relevant to a situational input might be assessed (an idea itself highly similar to Rumelhart et al.'s claim that schemata are recognition devices that evaluate their goodness-of-fit to the data being processed), and went on to suggest the following: If a structure that is selected and expressed behaviorally turns out to be incorrect,

> a new structure may occur, thus giving the appearance of an entirely discontinuous process, of shifting from hypothesis to hypothesis. We say "appearance" of discontinuity because a continuous process prior to the appearance of cognitive structures in fact gives rise to them. Structures are developed on the basis of associationist stimulus-response relationships but, once established, enable the organism to behave "cognitively." (pp. 417–418)

One major focus of "Structure" is the relationship between overlearning and transfer. Specifically, Mandler was interested in the impact of overlearned A–B associations on transfer in an A–B, A–C paradigm. He did not say, "look at these surprising data"; perhaps in 1962 the function relating degree of A–B learning to A–C performance was common currency. I must confess to having forgotten it, and was therefore very struck by its apparently counter-intuitive nature. In "Structure," Mandler plotted this function for seven studies, four with animal and three with human subjects. If the A–C performance of subjects with no prior training is taken to represent zero transfer and all other groups' degrees of transfer (positive or negative) are measured relative to this control, then the standard function relating amount of A–B training to A–C performance is U-shaped. The control group (zero transfer) forms the left-hand high point of the U. Subjects who had learned to, or a bit beyond, criterion showed very poor (typically the poorest) A–C performance. Moderate degrees of A–B overlearning still resulted in some negative transfer; but the arresting fact is that groups given still more post-criterion A–B trials showed either zero transfer or significant positive transfer, thus forming the right-hand high point of the U. Mandler did reassure the reader that A–B interference as evaluated by B responses during the very first few A–C trials is monotonically related to degree of A–B learning. "But, despite this increase in intrusion errors [as a function of prior A–B pairings], the overall efficiency in learning the transfer task is increased" (p. 423). What is one to make of this surprising outcome?

What Mandler made of it was structure from association (in fact, he made a number of other things of it, too, such as a consideration of proper controls for warm-up and learning-set effects; but I do not discuss these other points here).

". . . Overlearning experience with the old response and the formation of an analogic structure permits the subject to manipulate that response, to "think about" the problem without making overt errors" (p. 425). Well-trained B responses can be eliminated more easily because subjects have cognitive structures corresponding to these responses; but these cognitive structures emerged naturally from associative learning.

The naturally emergent aspect of this account is, as reiterated here, a cornerstone of PDP thinking. Is there anything in the PDP literature that relates specifically to overlearning and transfer of training? Perhaps not very specifically; but put more generally, the phenomenon that Mandler described in "Structure" is an instance of subjects' ability to discriminate between highly similar stimuli and to select appropriate responses to them. "Highly similar" seems the appropriate term because, even where each A stimulus paired with B is formally identical to the one paired with C, there are temporal, contextual or instructional cues that enable the subject to discriminate between the two sets of A stimuli. This broader conceptualization finds an echo in a PDP-based discussion of perceptual learning by McLaren, Kaye, and Mackintosh (1989). In animal learning studies, there are a number of demonstrations that simple exposure to two stimuli, say X and Y, can improve the rate of subsequent discrimination learning between them. McLaren et al. argued that repeated exposure to X and Y, even with no "consequences," results in an elaboration of the internal representations of these stimuli. Each exposure to X will tend to activate only a subset of its elements; elements common to various exposures will become connected and tend to activate one another. This unitization process for each of X and Y will facilitate subsequent discrimination learning, when one of the two stimuli becomes associated with reinforcement. Because X and Y are both encountered in the same environment, there will also be associations formed between some elements from the different stimuli; this generalization would have the effect of interfering with the subsequent requirement to discriminate between them. But because inhibitory connections between X and Y will also be established, the net impact of unrewarded exposure on subsequent learning will be beneficial.

Although McLaren et al do not specifically couch their discussion in terms of amount of pre-exposure to X and Y, one might hypothesize that the unitization process would increasingly dominate over generalization at higher exposure levels, perhaps even yielding something like a U-shaped function. Thus, although the parallel is not exact, this account of stimulus integration and the consequences of resulting structures for subsequent learning is reminiscent of Mandler's description of integration in response learning.

CONCLUSION

"Structure" is a paper that rewards re-reading in a number of ways. For one thing, it is good to be reminded that there was a time when cognitive psychologists were interested in learning. As Mandler (1985) has more recently noted, cognitive psychology has been largely concerned with steady-state processing, to the surprising exclusion of an interest in how the organism achieved its steady state. It is also intriguing and instructive to see behavior functions (such as the "U-shaped" ones discussed above) from human and animal studies put side by side. A major current worry about cognitive psychology is its narrow focus of theory and explanatory mechanism. We tend to be satisfied if we can give an account of our own data and delighted if we can also manage those of a close colleague using the same paradigm. Mandler's attempt to encompass some phenomena of rats learning mazes and human beings learning telegraph codes under the same explanatory principles is an excellent reminder that the goal of basic research in learning is to discover something about how organisms learn, not how they learn telegraph codes.

As for all of the parallels drawn here between "Structure" and the connectionist approach, there are of course dangers in reading too much into someone else's writing. "I beg the reader not to go in search of messages. It . . . forces on me clothes that are not mine (Levi, 1986, p. 3). In a sense, however, it does not matter whether the original thinking that lead to "Structure" bore much resemblance to the messages suggested here. What matters is that Mandler's thinking and writing was and is of a quality and depth to engage the reader and to call forth messages in the mind.

ACKNOWLEDGMENT

I am grateful to Leslie Henderson, Sheila Henderson, and Roy Patterson, who spent much of a rainy holiday in Portugal helping me to count, and select amongst, the ways to honor George Mandler.

REFERENCES

Cohen, J. D., Dunbar, K., & McClelland, J. L. (1990). On the control of automatic processes: A parallel distributed processing model of the Stroop effect. *Psychological Review, 97*, 332–361.

Levi, P. (1986). *The mirror maker*. London: Methuen.

McClelland, J. L., & Rumelhart, D. E. (1986). *Parallel distributed processing: Explorations in the microstructure of cognition* (Vol. 2). Cambridge, MA: MIT Press.

McLaren, I. P. L., Kaye, H., & Mackintosh, N. J. (1989). An associative theory of the representation of stimuli: Applications to perceptual learning and latent inhibition. In R. G. M. Morris (Ed.), *Parallel distributed processing: Implications for psychology and neurobiology* (pp. 102–130). Oxford: OUP.

Mandler, G. (1954). Response factors in human learning. *Psychological Review, 61*, 235–244.

Mandler, G. (1962). From association to structure. *Psychological Review, 69*, 415–427.

Mandler, G. (1985). *Cognitive psychology: An essay in cognitive science*. Hillsdale, NJ: Lawrence Erlbaum Associates.

Morris, R. G. M. (Ed.). (1989). *Parallel distributed processing: Implications for psychology and neurobiology*. Oxford: OUP.

Rumelhart, D. E., Hinton, G. E., & McClelland, J. L. (1986). A general framework for parallel distributed processing. In D. E. Rumelhart & J. L. McClelland (Eds.), *Parallel Distributed Processing: Explorations in the microstructure of cognition* (Vol. 1, pp. 45–76). Cambridge, MA: MIT Press.

Rumelhart, D. E., & McClelland, J. L. (Ed.). (1986). *Parallel distributed processing: Explorations in the microstructure of cognition* (Vol. 1). Cambridge, MA: MIT Press.

Rumelhart, D. E., Smolensky, P., McClelland, J. L., & Hinton, G. E. (1986). Schemata and sequential thought processes in PDP models. In J. L. McClelland & D. E. Rumelhart (Eds.), *Parallel distributed processing,* (Vol. 2, pp. 7–57). Cambridge, MA: MIT Press.

Smolensky, P. (1986). Information processing in dynamical systems: Foundations of harmony theory. In D. E. Rumelhart & J. L. McClelland (Eds.), *Parallel Distributed Processing: Explorations in the microstructure of cognition* (Vol. 1, pp. 194–281). Cambridge, MA: MIT Press.

Smolensky, P. (1988). On the proper treatment of connectionism. *Behavioral and Brain Sciences, 11,* 1–74.

PREFATORY REMARKS TO CHAPTER 5

James L. McClelland
Carnegie Mellon University

FROM ASSOCIATION TO STRUCTURE, REVISITED

In his article, "From Association to Structure," Mandler (1962) articulated a view of cognitive structure that disappeared during the heyday of classical cognitive psychology in the 1970s and early 1980s. This view certainly did not surface in Neisser (1967), the Bible of cognitive psychology when I was in graduate school. And yet the idea seems especially relevant to many of the ideas that are now growing out of connectionist models. To quote "From Association to Structure":

> it will be maintained here that there is now enough evidence available to suggest that, in some limited cases, cognitive characteristics of the organism may be developed out of associationist processes. (Mandler, 1962, p. 416)

To associate connectionist models with the specific varieties of associationism available in 1962 would, of course, be to miss several differences between contemporary connectionist theory and classical associationism. Nevertheless, there is something basically associationist about the connectionist networks that we work with today. They produce outputs in response to inputs. One of the key themes of work with these networks is the observation that they acquire structure—knowledge of regularities in the input and outputs and in the relations between them—through learning to produce particular outputs in response to particular inputs (Rumelhart & McClelland, 1986).

The paper reprinted here grows out of earlier work by Elman (1988) and then Servan-Schreiber, Cleeremans, and McClelland (1988) on a connectionist architecture that we call the *simple recurrent network*. In the simple recurrent network (Figure A), an input at Time *t*, together with a copy of the internal state (hidden

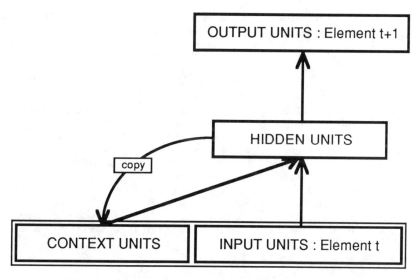

FIG A. The simple recurrent network of Elman (1988).

units in the figure) of the network from the previous time step, are treated as inputs for the purpose of predicting the element that will occur at time Step $t + 1$. Connectionist learning rules are learned to train the connections from context and input units to hidden units and from hidden units to output units: Basically, the network is learning to associate the next element with the prior element and its own prior internal representation. Gradually, the network learns to encode prediction-relevant information from the larger and larger spans of temporal context. Elman showed that this architecture could learn the structure of simple sentences, and Servan-Schreiber et al. followed up by showing that the architecture could in some cases learn to become, within *epsilon,* a replica of the finite state machine that generated the sequences on which the network was trained. That is, after training, the patterns on the hidden units—the representations learned by the network—came to correspond to the nodes of the grammar that was used to generate the sequences of elements. Each node could be reached by many different paths. What the paths leading to a node all had in common was the fact that the distribution of possible successors was identical. The network discovered this identity, and replicated the grammar. The representations that the network developed emerged as the result of the simple, associative learning process.

After the work just described, Cleeremans and I have continued to study simple recurrent networks, employing them as models of implicit human learning. The paper reprinted here (reprinted from the *Proceedings of the Cognitive Science Society, 1990*), describes the first stages of this investigation. More than the theoretical work that preceded it, this paper shares with all of Mandler's work a concern to relate theoretical ideas to behavior; to show that the idea that structure can emerge from association is actually consistent with the facts about how human beings learn structure from experience.

REFERENCES

Elman, J. L. (1988). *Finding structure in time* (CRL Technical Report 8801). San Diego, CA: Center for Research in Language, University of California, San Diego.

Mandler, G. (1962). From association to structure. *Psychological Review, 69,* 415–427.

Neisser, U. (1967). *Cognitive Psychology.* Englewood Cliffs, NJ: Prentice-Hall.

Rumelhart, D. E., & McClelland, J. L. (1986). On learning the past tenses of English verbs. In McClelland, J. L., Rumelhart, D. E., & the PDP Research Group (Eds.), *Parallel distributed processing: Explorations in the microstructure of cognition. Volume 2: Psychological and biological models* (pp. 216–271). Cambridge, MA: MIT Press.

Servan-Schreiber, D., Cleeremans, A., & McClelland, J. L. (1988). *Encoding sequential structure in simple recurrent networks* (Tech. Rep. CMU-CS-88-183). Department of Computer Science, Carnegie Mellon University, Pittsburgh, PA.

5 Learning the Structure of Event Sequences

Axel Cleeremans
James L. McClelland
Carnegie Mellon University

ABSTRACT

How is complex sequential material acquired, processed, and represented when there is no intention to learn? Recent research (Lewicki, Hill, & Bizot, 1988) has demonstrated that subjects placed in a choice reaction time task progressively become sensitive to the sequential structure of the stimulus material despite their unawareness of its existence. This paper aims to provide a detailed information-processing model of this phenomenon in an experimental situation involving complex and probabilistic temporal contingencies. We report on two experiments exploring a six-choice serial reaction time task. Unbeknownst to subjects, successive stimuli followed a sequence derived from "noisy" finite-state grammars. After considerable practice (60,000 exposures), subjects acquired a body of procedural knowledge about the sequential structure of the material, although they were unaware of the manipulation, and displayed little or no verbalizable knowledge about it. Experiment 2 attempted to identify limits on subjects' ability to encode the temporal context by using more distant contingencies that spanned irrelevant material. Taken together, the results indicate that subjects become progressively more sensitive to the temporal context set by previous elements of the sequence, up to three elements. Responses are also affected by carry-over effects from recent trials. A PDP model that incorporates sensitivity to the sequential structure and carry-over effects is shown to capture key aspects of both acquisition and processing of the material.

INTRODUCTION

In many situations, learning does not proceed in the explicit and goal-directed way characteristic of traditional models of cognition (Newell & Simon, 1972). Rather, it appears that a good deal of our knowledge and skills are acquired in an incidental and unintentional manner. The evidence supporting this claim is overwhelming: In his recent review article, Reber (1989) analyzed as many as about 40 detailed empirical studies that document the existence of implicit learning. At least three different paradigms have yielded robust results indicating that learning does not necessarily entail awareness of the resulting knowledge or of the learning experience itself: artificial language learning (Dulany, Carlson, & Dewey, 1984; Reber, 1967, 1989; Servan-Schreiber & Anderson, 1990), system control (Berry & Broadbent, 1984; Hayes & Broadbent, 1988), and sequential pattern acquisition (Cohen, Ivry, & Keele, 1990; Lewicki, Czyzewska, & Hoffman, 1987; Lewicki et al., 1988; Nissen & Bullemer, 1987; Willingham, Nissen, & Bullemer, 1989). The classic result in these experimental situations is that "subjects are able to acquire specific procedural knowledge (i.e., processing rules) not only without being able to articulate what they have learned, but even without being aware that they had learned anything" (Lewicki et al., 1987, p. 523). Related research with neurologically impaired patients (see Schacter, 1987, for a review) also provides strong evidence for the existence of a functional dissociation between *explicit memory* (conscious recollection) and *implicit memory* (a facilitation of performance without conscious recollection).

Despite this wealth of evidence documenting implicit learning phenomena, few models of the mechanisms involved have been proposed. This lack of formalization can doubtless be attributed to the difficulty of assessing subject's knowledge when it does not lend itself easily to verbalization. Indeed, whereas concept formation or traditional induction studies can benefit from experimental procedures that reveal the organization of subjects's knowledge and the strategies they use, such procedures often appear to disrupt or alter the very processes they are supposed to investigate in implicit learning situations (see Dulany, Carlson, & Dewey, 1984, 1985; Reber, Allen, & Regan, 1985, for a discussion of this point). Thus, research on implicit learning has typically focused more on providing existence demonstrations than on obtaining the fine-grained data needed to elaborate information-processing models.

Nevertheless, an understanding of such learning processes seems to be an essential preliminary step toward developing insights into central questions such as the relationship between task performance and verbalizable knowledge, the role that attention plays in learning, or the complex interactions between conscious thought and the many other functions of the cognitive system. In this paper, we report on a series of experiments inspired by Lewicki, et al.'s (1988) paradigm, and propose a detailed information-processing model of the task. These experiments placed subjects in a choice reaction time task, and manipulated the sequential contingencies of the material in a novel way that allows detailed data about subject's representations of the temporal structure to be obtained.

The main results of our experiments indicate that subjects unintentionally acquire a complex body of knowledge about the temporal structure of the material. We describe a PDP model that implements a simple mechanism to account for performance in this task. The model—trained in exactly the same conditions as subjects—captures key aspects of both acquisition and performance in this task. Its core mechanism implements the hypothesis that sequential structure gets induced as a direct result of an encoding of events *together* with an internal representation of the temporal context.

EXPERIMENT 1

Subjects were exposed to a six-choice reaction time task. The entire experiment was divided in 20 sessions. Each session consisted of 20 blocks of 150 trials. On any of the 60,000 trials, a stimulus could appear at one of six positions arranged in a horizontal line on a computer screen. The task consisted of pressing as fast and as accurately as possible on one of six corresponding keys. Unbeknownst to subjects, the sequential structure of the stimulus material was manipulated. Stimuli were generated using a small finite-state grammar that defined legal transitions between successive trials. Some of the stimuli, however, were not "grammatical." On each trial, there was a 15% chance of substituting a random stimulus to the one prescribed by the grammar. This "noise" served two purposes. First, it ensured that subjects could not simply memorize the sequence of stimuli, and hindered their ability of detecting regularities in an explicit way. Second, because each stimulus was possible on every trial (if only in a small proportion of the trials), we could obtain detailed information about what stimuli subjects did or did not expect at each step.

If subjects become increasingly sensitive to the sequential structure of the material over training, one would thus predict an increasingly large difference in the reaction times (RTs) elicited by predictable and unpredictable stimuli. Further, detailed analyses of the RTs to particular stimuli in different temporal contexts should reveal differences that reflect subjects' encoding of the sequential structure of the material.

Method

Subjects. Six subjects (CMU staff and students) aged 17–42 participated in the experiment. Each subject was paid $100 for his participation in the 20 sessions of the experiment, and received a bonus of up to $50 based on speed and accuracy.

Apparatus and Display. The experiment was run on a Macintosh II computer. The display consisted of six dots arranged in a horizontal line on the computer's screen. Each screen position was paired with a key on the computer's keyboard, also arranged in a line ('Z', 'X', 'C', 'B', 'N', 'M'). The stimulus was a small black circle that appeared immediately below one of the six dots. The timer was started at the onset of the stimulus and stopped by the subject's response. The RSI was 120 msec.

Procedure. Subjects received detailed instructions during the first meeting. They were told that the purpose of the experiment was to "learn more about the effect of practice on motor performance." Both speed and accuracy were stressed as being important. After receiving the instructions, subjects were given three practice blocks of 15 random trials each at the task. A schedule for the 20 experimental sessions was then elaborated. Most subjects followed a regular schedule of two sessions a day.

Stimulus Material. Stimuli were generated on the basis of the small finite-state grammar shown in Fig. 5.1. Finite-State grammars consist of nodes connected by labeled arcs. Expressions of the language are generated by starting at Node #0, choosing an arc, recording its label, and repeating this process with the next node. The vocabulary associated with the grammar we used consists of six letters ('T', 'S', 'X', 'V', 'P', and 'Q'), each represented twice on different arcs of the grammar (as denoted by the subscript of each letter). This results in highly context-dependent transitions, as identical letters can be followed by different sets of successors as a function of their position in the grammar (for instance, 'S1' can only be followed by 'Q', but 'S2' can be followed by either 'V' or 'P'). The grammar was constructed so as to avoid direct repetitions of a particular letter, because it is known (Bertelson, 1961; Hyman, 1953) that repeated stimuli elicit shorter reaction times independently of their probability of presentation. Finally, note that the grammar loops onto itself: the first and last nodes, both denoted by the digit 0, are actually the same.

Stimulus generation proceeded as follows. On each trial, three steps were executed in sequence. First, an arc was selected at random among the possible arcs coming out of the current node, and its corresponding letter recorded. The current node was set to be Node #0 on the very first trial of any block, and was updated on each trial to be the node pointed to by the selected arc. Second, in 15% of the cases, another letter was substituted to the letter recorded at Step 1 by choosing it at random among the five remaining letters in the grammar. Third, the selected letter was used to determine the screen position at which the stimulus

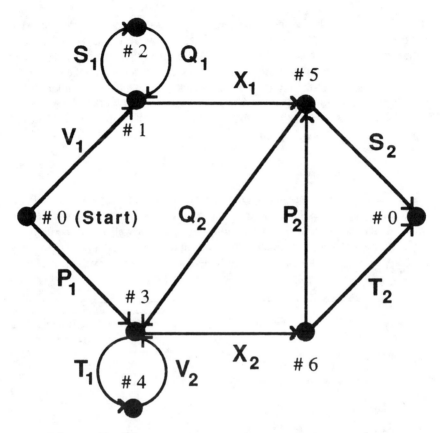

FIG. 5.1.   The finite-state grammar used to generate the stimulus sequence in Experiment 1.

would appear. A 6 × 6 Latin Square design was used, so that each letter corresponded to each screen position for exactly one of the six subjects.

Design.   The experiment consisted of 20 sessions of 20 blocks of 155 trials each. Each block was initiated by a "Get ready" message and a warning beep. After a short delay, 155 trials were presented to the subject. The first five trials of each block were entirely random so as to eliminate initial variability in the responses. These data points were not recorded. The next 150 trials were generated according to the procedure described earlier. After each block, the computer paused for approximately 30 seconds. The message "Rest Break" was displayed on the screen, along with information about subject's performance. This feedback consisted of the mean RT and accuracy values for the last block, and of information about how these values compared to those for the next-to-last block.

If the mean RT for the last block was within a 20-msec interval of the mean RT for the next-to-last block, the words "AS BEFORE" were displayed; otherwise, either "BETTER," or "WORSE" appeared. A 2% interval was used for accuracy. Finally, subjects were told about how much they had earned during the last block, and during the entire session up to the last block. Bonus money was allocated as follows: each reaction time under 600 msec was rewarded by 0.078 cents, each error entailed a penalty of 1.11 cents. These values were calculated so as to yield a maximum of $2.5 per session.

Results and Discussion

Figure 5.2 shows the average response latencies on correct responses for each of the 20 experimental sessions, plotted separately for predictable and unpredictable trials. A general practice effect is readily apparent, as well as an increasingly large difference between predictable and unpredictable trials. A two-way ANOVA with repeated measures on both factors [practice (20 levels) X trial type

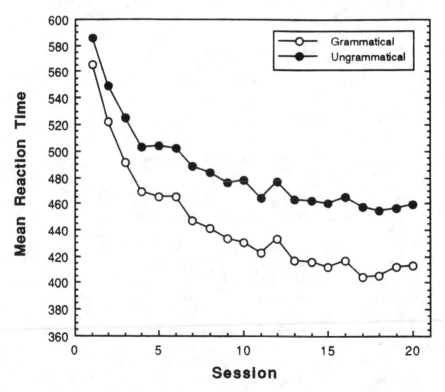

FIG. 5.2. Mean RTs for grammatical and ungrammatical trials for each of the 20 sessions of Experiment 1.

(grammatical vs. ungrammatical)] revealed significant main effects of practice [$F(19,95) = 9.491, p < .001, MSe = 17710.45$]; and of trial type [$F(1,5) = 105.293, p < .001, MSe = 104000.07$]; as well as a significant interaction [$F(19,95) = 3.022, p < .001, MSe = 183.172$]. It appears that subjects become increasingly sensitive to the sequential structure of the material. Yet, when interviewed after the task, all subjects reported feeling that the sequence was random, and failed to report noticing any pattern in the data but small alternations (e.g., the loops on Nodes #2 and #4).

Accuracy averaged 98.12% over all trials. The small difference between accuracy on predictable (98.35%) and unpredictable (96.68%) trials was not significant.

One mechanism that would account for the progressive differentiation between predictable and unpredictable trials consists of assuming that subjects, in attempting to optimize their reaction times, progressively come to anticipate successive events on the basis of an increasingly large temporal context set by previous elements of the sequence. In the grammar we used, most elements can be perfectly anticipated on the basis of two elements of temporal context, but some of them require three or even four elements of temporal context to be maximally disambiguated. For instance, the path 'SQ' (leading to Node #1) occurs only once in the grammar and can only be legally followed by 'S' or 'X'. In contrast, the path 'TVX' can lead to either Node #5 or Node #6, and is therefore not sufficient to perfectly distinguish between stimuli that occur only at Node #5 ('S' or 'Q') and stimuli that occur only at Node #6 ('T' or 'P'). One would assume that subjects initially respond to the predictions entailed by the shortest paths, and progressively become sensitive to the higher order contingencies as they encode more and more temporal context.

A simple analysis that would reveal whether or not subjects are indeed basing their performance on an encoding of an increasingly large temporal context was conducted. Its general principle consists of comparing the data with the probability of occurrence of the stimuli given different amounts of temporal context.

First, we estimated the conditional probabilities (CPs) of observing each letter as the successor of every grammatical path of Length 1, 2, 3, and 4 respectively. Next, the average RT for each successor to paths of Length 4 were computed, separately for successive blocks of four experimental sessions. Finally, 20 separate regression analyses were conducted, using each of the four sets of CPs as predictor, and each of the five sets of mean RTs as dependent variable. If subjects are encoding increasingly large amounts of temporal context, we would expect the variance in the distribution of their responses at successive points in training to be better explained by CPs of increasingly higher statistical orders.

Figure 5.3 illustrates the results of these analyses. Each point on the figure represents the r-squared coefficient of a specific regression analysis. Points corresponding to analyses conducted with the same amount of temporal context (1–4 elements) are linked together. Although the overall fit is rather low (note that

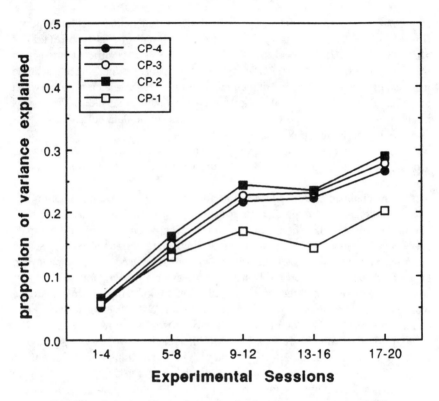

FIG. 5.3. Correspondence between the human responses and CPs after paths of Length 1–4 during successive blocks of four simulated sessions.

the vertical axis only extends to 0.5), the figure nevertheless reveals that subjects become increasingly sensitive to the temporal context set by previous elements of the sequence. One can see that the correspondence with the first-order CPs tends to level off below the fits for the second, third and fourth orders. The fits to the second, third, and fourth order paths are highly similar in part because their associated CPs are themselves highly similar.

In order to assess more directly whether subjects are able to encode three or four letters of temporal context, several analyses on specific successors of specific paths were conducted. One such analysis involved several paths of Length 3. These paths were the same in their last two elements, but differed in their first element as well as in their legal successors. For example, we compared 'XTV' versus 'PTV' and 'QTV', and examined RTs for the letters 'S' (legal only after 'XTV') and 'T' (legal only after 'PTV' or 'QTV'). If subjects are sensitive to three letters of context, their response to an 'S' should be relatively faster after 'XTV' than in the other cases, and their response to a 'T' should be relatively faster after 'PTV' or 'QTV' than after 'XTV'. Averaging over all candidate contexts of this type, we found that a slight advantage for the legal successors emerged in Sessions 8–12 and remained present over Sessions 13–16 and 17–20 ($p < .05$). Thus, there appears to be evidence of sensitivity to at least three elements of temporal context. However, no sensitivity to the first element of otherwise identical paths of Length 4 (e.g., 'XTVX' vs. 'PTVX and 'QTVX') was found, even during Sessions 17–20.

EXPERIMENT 2

Experiment 1 demonstrated that subjects progressively become sensitive to the sequential structure of the material and seem to be able to maintain information about the temporal context for up to three steps. The temporal contingencies characterizing this grammar were relatively simple, however, since in most cases, only two elements of temporal context are needed to disambiguate the next event perfectly.

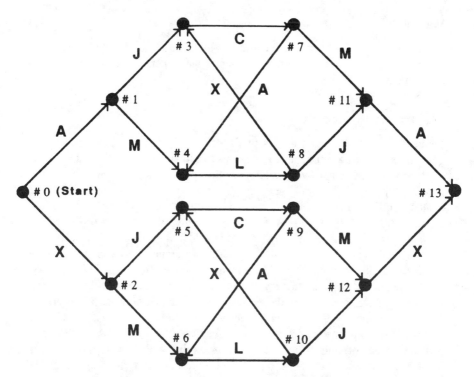

FIG. 5.4.   The finite-state grammar used to generate the stimulus sequence in Experiment 2.

Further, contrasting long-distance dependencies were not controlled for their overall frequency. In Experiment 2, a more complex grammar (Fig. 5.4) was used in an attempt to identify limits on subjects' ability to maintain information about more distant elements of the sequence. In this grammar, the last element ('A' or 'X') is contingent on the first one (also 'A' or 'X'). Information about the first element, however, has to be maintained across either of the two identical embeddings in the grammar, and is totally irrelevant for predicting the elements of the embeddings. Thus, in order to accurately predict the last element at Nodes #11 or #12, one needs to maintain information across a minimum of three intervening steps. Accurate expectations about the nature of the last element would be revealed by a difference in the RT elicited by the letters 'A' and 'X' at Nodes #11 and #12 ('A' should be faster than 'X' at Node #11, and vice-versa). Naturally, there was again a 15% chance of substituting another letter to the one prescribed by the grammar. Further, in order to avoid direct repetitions between the letters that precede and follow Node #13, a small loop was inserted at Node #13. One random letter was always presented at this point; after which there was a 40% chance of staying in the loop on subsequent steps.

Method

Six new subjects (CMU undergraduates and graduates, aged 19–35) participated in Experiment 2. The design of Experiment 2 was otherwise identical to that of Experiment 1.

Results and Discussion

Figure 5.5 shows the main results of Experiment 2. They closely replicate the general results of Experiment 1, although subjects were a little bit faster overall in Experiment 2. A two-way ANOVA with repeated measures on both factors [practice (20 levels) X trial type (grammatical vs. ungrammatical)] again revealed significant main effects of practice $(F(19,95) = 32.011, p < .001, MSe = 21182.79]$; and of trial type $[F(1,5) = 253.813, p < .001, MSe = 63277.53]$; as well as a significant interaction $[F(19,95) = 4.670, p < .001, MSe = 110.862]$.

Accuracy was 97% over all trials. The difference between grammatical (97.60%) and ungrammatical (95.40%) was significant $[t(5) = 2.294, p < .05]$.

Of greater interest are the results of analyses conducted on the responses elicited by the successors of the four shortest paths starting at Node #0 and leading to either Node #11 or Node #12 ('AJCM', 'AMLJ', 'XJCM' & 'XMLJ'). Among those paths, those beginning with 'A' predict 'A' as their only possible successor, and vice-versa for paths starting with 'X'. This only holds, however, if all four letters of each path are encoded. Indeed, the subpaths 'JCM' and 'MLJ' undifferentially predict 'A' or 'X' as their possible successors. The

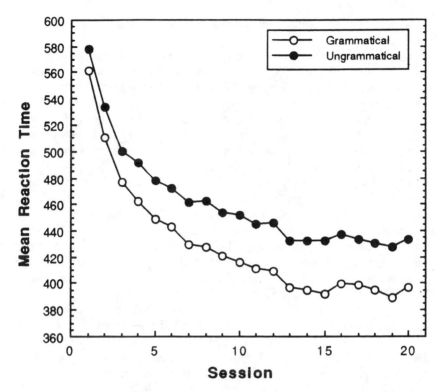

FIG. 5.5. Mean RTs for grammatical and ungrammatical trials for each of the 20 sessions of Experiment 2.

RTs on legal successors of each of these four paths (i.e., 'A' for 'AJCM' and 'AMLJ'; and 'X' for 'XJCM' and 'XMLJ') were averaged together and compared to the average RT on their illegal successors (i.e., 'X' for 'AJCM' and 'AMLJ'; and 'A' for 'XJCM' and 'XMLJ'), thus yielding two scores. Any significant difference between these two scores would mean that subjects are discriminating between legal and illegal successors of these four paths, thereby suggesting that they have been able to maintain information about the first letter of each path over three irrelevant steps. The mean RT on legal successors over the last four sessions of the experiment was 384.896, and the corresponding score for illegal successors was 387.847. A paired t test on this difference failed to reach significance [$t(5) = 0.571$, $p > 0.05$].

In summary, subjects do not appear to be able to encode long-distance dependencies when they span three items of embedded independent material; at least, they cannot do so in the amount of practice used here. However, there is clear evidence of sensitivity to at least the previous two elements of temporal context.

SIMPLE RECURRENT NETWORKS

Early models of sequence processing in CRT tasks (e.g., Laming, 1969) have typically assumed that subjects somehow compute the conditional probabilities for all relevant statistical orders, but failed to show how subjects might come to represent or compute them. In the following, we present a model of sequence processing that comes to elaborate its own internal representations of the temporal context despite very limited processing resources. The model consists of a Simple Recurrent back-propagation Network ('SRN'; see Cleeremans, Servan-Schreiber, & McClelland, 1989; Elman, 1988).

In the SRN (see Fig. A), the hidden unit layer is allowed to feed back on itself; so that the intermediate results of processing at Time $t - 1$ can influence the intermediate results of processing at Time t. In practice, the SRN is implemented by copying the pattern of activation on the hidden units onto a set of "context units" that feed into the hidden layer, along with the input units. All the forward-going connections in this architecture are modified by back-propagation. The recurrent connections from the hidden layer to the context layer implement a simple copy operation and are not subject to training.

As reported elsewhere (Cleeremans et al., 1989) an SRN trained to predict the successor of each element of a sequence presented one element at a time can learn to perform this "prediction task" perfectly on simple finite-state grammars like the one used in Experiment 1. Following training, the network produces the conditional probabilities of presentation of all possible successors of the sequence. Because all letters of the grammar were inherently ambiguous (i.e., predicting them requires more than the immediate predecessor to be encoded), the network must have developed representations of entire subsequences of events. Note that the network is never presented with more than one element of the sequence at a time. Thus, it has to elaborate its own internal representations of as much temporal context as is needed to achieve optimal predictions.

A complete analysis of the learning process is too long to be presented here (a full account is given in Servan-Schreiber, Cleeremans, & McClelland, 1988), but the key points are as follows: As the initial papers about back-propagation (e.g., Rumelhart, Hinton, & Williams, 1986) pointed out, the hidden unit patterns of activation represent an "encoding" of the features of the input patterns that are relevant to the task. In the SRN, the hidden layer is presented with information about the current letter, but also—on the context layer—with an encoding of the relevant features of the previous letter. Thus, a given hidden layer pattern can come to encode information about the relevant features of two consecutive letters. When this pattern is fed back on the context layer, the new pattern of activation over the hidden units can come to encode information about three consecutive letters, and so on. In this manner, the context layer patterns can allow the network to learn to maintain prediction-relevant features of an entire sequence.

To model our experimental situation, we used an SRN with 15 hidden units and local representations on both the input and output pools (i.e., each unit corresponded to one of the six stimuli). The network was trained to predict each element of a continuous sequence of stimuli generated in exactly the same conditions as for the human subjects. On each step, a letter was generated from the grammar as just described, and presented to the network by setting the activation of the corresponding input unit to 1.0. Activation was then allowed to spread to the other units of the network, and the error between its response and the actual successor of the current stimulus was then used to modify the weights.

During training, the activation of each output unit was recorded on every trial and transformed into Luce ratios to normalize the responses. For the purpose of comparing the model's and the subjects' responses, we assumed (a) that the normalized activations of the output units represent response tendencies, and (b) that there is a linear reduction in RT proportional to the relative strength of the unit corresponding to the correct response.[1]

This data was first analyzed in the same way as for Experiment 1 subjects, and compared to the CPs of increasingly higher statistical orders in 20 separate regression analyses. The results are illustrated in Fig. 5.6. In stark contrast with the human data (Fig. 5.3; note the scale difference), the variability in the model's responses appears to be very strongly determined by the probabilities of particular successor letters given the temporal context. The figure also reveals that the model's behavior is dominated by the first-order CPs for most of the training, but that it becomes progressively more sensitive to the second and higher order CPs. If training was to be continued beyond 60,000 exposures, the model's responses would come to approximate increasingly higher CPs.

Figure 5.7 illustrates a more direct comparison between the model's responses at successive points in training with the corresponding human data. First, we computed the average RT of each letter at each node of the grammar. This yields a set of 42 data points (due to noise, each of the six letters may occur at any of the seven different nodes). This analysis was conducted on RTs averaged over blocks of four successive experimental sessions, thus yielding five different sets of data. Next, a similar analysis was conducted on the model's responses. Finally, we conducted 25 separate regression analyses on these data. Each point in Fig. 5.7 represents the r-squared coefficient of a regression analysis using the model's responses at a particular point in training as predictor and the human data as dependent variable. One would expect the model's early performance to be a better predictor of the subjects's early behavior, and vice-versa for later points in training.

It is obvious that the model is not very good at capturing subjects's behavior: the overall fit is relatively low (note that the vertical axis only goes up to 0.5),

---

[1]Naturally, the second assumption is a simplification. We are currently in the process of exploring more realistic versions of this assumption.

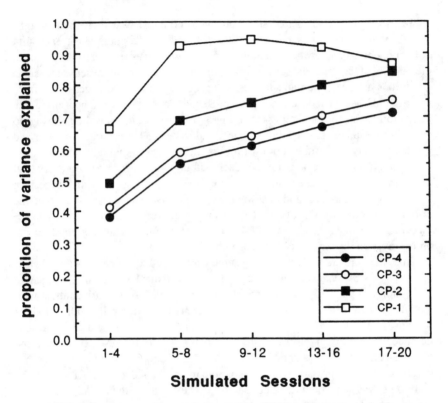

FIG. 5.6. Correspondence between the SRN's responses and CPs after paths of Length 1–4 during successive blocks of four simulated sessions.

and reflects only weakly the expected progressions. Basically, too much of the variance in the model's performance is accounted for by sensitivity to the temporal context.

However, exploratory examination of the data revealed that performance in this task depends on three other factors (in addition to the conditional probability of appearance of a stimulus):

First of all, it appears that a response that is actually executed remains primed for a number of subsequent trials (Remington, 1969). If it follows itself immediately, there is about 60 to 90 msec of facilitation, depending on other factors. If it follows after a single intervening response (e.g., as in 'VT-V'), there is about 25 msec of facilitation if the letter is grammatical at the second occurrence, and 45 msec if it is ungrammatical.

The second factor may be related: responses that are grammatical at Trial t but do not actually occur remain primed at Trial $t + 1$; the effect is somewhat weaker, averaging about 30 msec. The first two factors may be summarized by assuming that activations at Time t decay gradually over subsequent trials, and responses that are actually executed become fully activated, whereas those that are not executed are only partially primed.

The third factor is a priming, not of a particular response, but of a particular sequential pairing of responses. This can best be illustrated by a contrasting example, in which the response to the second 'X' is compared in 'QXQ-X' and 'VXQ-X'. The response to the second X tends to be about 10 msec faster in cases like 'QXQ-X', where the 'X' follows the same predecessor twice in a row, than it is in cases like 'VXQ-X', in which the first 'X' follows one letter and the second follows a different letter.

This third factor can perhaps be accounted for in several ways. We have explored the possibility that it results from a rapidly decaying component to the increment to the connection weights mediating the associative activation of a letter by its predecessor. Such "fast" weights have been proposed by a number of investigators (Hinton & Plaut, 1987; McClelland & Rumelhart, 1985). The idea

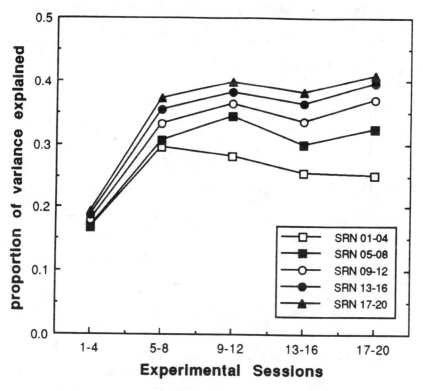

FIG. 5.7.   Correspondence between the SRN's responses and the corresponding human data during successive blocks of four sessions of training.

is that when 'X' follows 'Q', the connection weights underlying the prediction that 'X' will follow 'Q' receive an increment that has a short-term component in addition to the standard long-term component. This short-term increment is still present in sufficient force to influence the response to a subsequent 'X' that follows an immediately subsequent 'Q'.

In light of these analyses, one possibility for the relative failure of the original model to account for the data is that the SRN is partially correct, but that human responses are also affected by rapidly decaying activations and adjustments to connection weights from preceding trials. To test this idea, we incorporated both kinds of mechanisms into a second model.

This new simulation model was exactly the same as before, except for the following two changes:

First, it was assumed that pre-activation of a particular response was based, not only on activation coming from the network but also on a decaying trace of the previous activation:

$$respact[i](t) = act[i](t) + [1 - act[i](t)] * k * respact[i](t - 1)$$

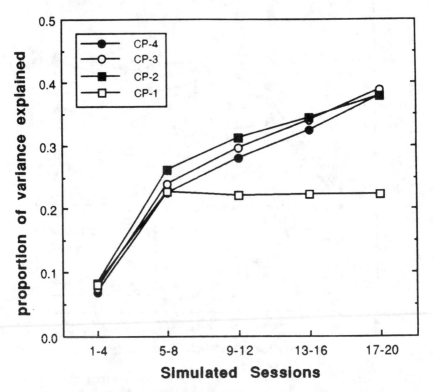

FIG. 5.8. Correspondence between the augmented SRN's responses and CPs after paths of Length 1–4 during successive blocks of four simulated sessions.

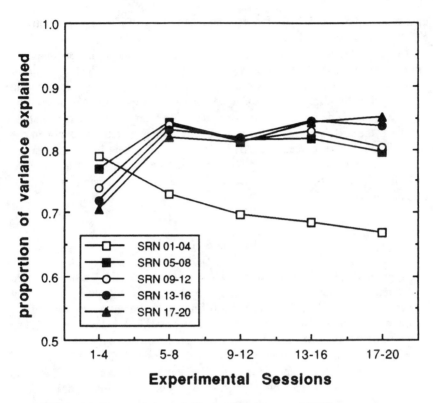

FIG. 5.9.   Correspondence between the augmented SRN's responses and the corresponding human data during successive blocks of four sessions of training.

where Act(t) is the activation of the unit based on the network at Time t, and Respact(t) is a kind of nonlinear running average that remains bounded between 0 and 1. When a particular response is executed, the corresponding respact is set to 1.0. The constant k is set to 0.5, so that the half-life of a response activation is one time step.

The second change is simply to assume that when weights are changed by the back-propagation learning procedure, there are two components, one of which is a small ($\varepsilon = 0.15$) but effectively permanent change (i.e., a decay rate slow enough to ignore for present purposes) and the other of which is a larger ($\varepsilon = 0.2$) change that has a half-life of a single time step.

With these changes in place, we observed that, of course, the proportion of the variance in the model accounted for by predictions based on one to four letters of temporal context is dramatically reduced (Fig. 5.8). More interestingly, the pattern of change in these measures, as well as the overall fit, is now quite similar to that seen in the data (Fig. 5.3).

Indeed, there is a similar progressive increase in the correspondence with the higher order CPs, with the curve for the first-order CPs leveling off relatively early, as in the human data.

A more direct indication of the good fit provided by the current version of the model is given by the fact that it now correlates extremely well with the performance of the subjects (Fig. 5.9; compare with the same analysis illustrated in Fig. 5.7). Late in training, the model explains about 86% of the variance of the corresponding human data. Close inspection of the figure also reveals, that, as expected, the SRN's early distribution of responses is a better predictor of the corresponding early human data. This correspondence gets inverted later on, thereby suggesting that the model now captures key aspects of acquisition as well. Indeed, at every point, the best prediction of the human data is the simulation of the corresponding point in training.

GENERAL DISCUSSION

In Experiment 1, subjects were exposed to a six-choice serial RT task for 60,000 trials. The sequential structure of the material was manipulated by generating successive stimuli on the basis of a small finite-state grammar. On some of the trials, random stimuli were substituted to those prescribed by the grammar. The results clearly support the idea that subjects become increasingly sensitive to the sequential structure of the material. Indeed, the smooth differentiation between predictable and unpredictable trials can only be explained by assuming that the temporal context set by previous elements of the sequence facilitates or interferes with the processing of the current event. Experiment 2 showed that subjects were relatively unable to maintain information about long-distance contingencies that span irrelevant material.

Taken together, these results suggest that in this task, subjects gradually acquire a complex body of procedural knowledge about the sequential structure of the material. They are clearly sensitive to more than just the immediate predecessor of the current stimulus; indeed, there is evidence of sensitivity to differential predictions based on two and even three elements of context. However, sensitivity to temporal context is clearly limited: Even after 60,000 trials of practice, there is no evidence of sensitivity to fourth-order temporal context. Of course, it remains possible that the subjects would eventually discover the fourth-order structure, just as the model can do.

The augmented SRN model provides a detailed, mechanistic, and fairly good account of the data. At this point it is difficult to be certain whether the model is capable of offering a complete account of all of the structure in the data. First, we have not explored the parameter space very extensively to discover whether it is possible to improve on the existing fit; and second, it is not clear just how much more systematic (as opposed to random) variance there is in the data to be accounted for.

It is often claimed that learning can proceed without explicit awareness (e.g. Reber, 1989; Willingham et al., 1989). In our case, it appears that subjects do become aware of the alternations that occur in the grammar (e.g., 'SQSQ' and 'VTVT' in Experiment 1), but have little reportable knowledge of any other contingencies. Given the fairly close correspondence of the augmented SRN with the subjects's performance, this class of model would appear to offer a viable framework for modeling this type of implicit learning.

ACKNOWLEDGMENT

This research was supported by a grant from the National Fund for Scientific Research (Belgium) to the first author and by an NIMH RSDA to the second author. This article is reprinted from the Proceedings of the Twelfth Annual Conference of the Cognitive Science Society (1990).

REFERENCES

Bertelson, P. (1961). Sequential redundancy and speed in a serial two-choice responding task. *Quarterly Journal of Experimental Psychology, 13*, 90–102.

Berry, D. C., & Broadbent, D. E. (1984). On the relationship between task performance and associated verbalizable knowledge. *Quarterly Journal of Experimental Psychology, 36A*, 209–231.

Cleeremans, A., Servan-Schreiber, D., & McClelland, J. L. (1989). Finite state automata and simple recurrent networks. *Neural Computation, 1*, 372–381.

Cohen, A., Ivry, R. I., & Keele, S. W. (1990). Attention and structure in sequence learning. *Journal of Experimental Psychology: Learning, Memory and Cognition, 16*, 17–30.

Dulany, D. E., Carlson, R. C., & Dewey, G. I. (1984). A case of syntactical learning and judgment: how conscious and how abstract? *Journal of Experimental Psychology: General, 113*, 541–555.

Dulany, D. E., Carlson, R. C., & Dewey, G. I. (1985). On consciousness in syntactical learning and judgment: A reply to Reber, Allen and Regan. *Journal of Experimental Psychology: General, 114*, 25–32.

Elman, J. L. (1988). *Finding structure in time.* (CRL Tech. Rep. No. 8801). San Diego, CA: Center for research in language, University of California, San Diego.

Hayes, N. A., & Broadbent, D. E. (1988). Two modes of learning for interactive tasks. *Cognition, 28*, 249–276.

Hinton, G. E., & Plaut, D. C. (1987). Using fast weights to deblur old memories. *Proceedings of the Ninth Annual Conference of the Cognitive Science Society.*

Hyman, R. (1953). Stimulus information as a determinant of reaction time. *Journal of Experimental Psychology, 45*, 188–196.

Laming, D. R. J. (1969). Subjective probability in Choice-Reaction experiments. *Journal of Mathematical Psychology, 6*, 81–120.

Lewicki, P., Czyzewska, M., & Hoffman, H. (1987). Unconscious acquisition of complex procedural knowledge. *Journal of Experimental Psychology: Learning, Memory, and Cognition, 13*, 523–530.

Lewicki, P., Hill, T., & Bizot, E. (1988). Acquisition of procedural knowledge about a pattern of stimuli that cannot be articulated. *Cognitive Psychology, 20*, 24–37.

McClelland, J. L., & Rumelhart, D. E. (1985). Distributed memory and the representation of general and specific information. *Journal of Experimental Psychology: General, 114,* 159–188

Newell, A., & Simon, H. A. (1972). *Human problem solving.* Englewood Cliffs, NJ: Prentice-Hall.

Nissen, M. J., & Bullemer, P. (1987). Attentional requirements of learning: Evidence from performance measures. *Cognitive Psychology, 19,* 1–32.

Reber, A. S. (1967). Implicit learning of artificial grammars. *Journal of Verbal Learning and Verbal Behavior, 6,* 855–863.

Reber, A. S. (1989). Implicit learning and tacit knowledge. *Journal of Experimental Psychology: General, 118,* 219–235.

Reber, A. S., Allen, R., & Regan, S. (1985). Syntactical learning and judgment, still unconscious and still abstract: Comment on Dulany, Carlson and Dewey. *Journal of Experimental Psychology: General, 114,* 17–24, 1985.

Remington, R. J. (1969). Analysis of sequential effects in choice reaction times. *Journal of Experimental Psychology, 82,* 250–257.

Rumelhart, D. E., Hinton, G., & Williams, R. J. (1986). Learning internal representations by error propagation. In D. E. Rumelhart & J. L. McClelland (Eds.), *Parallel distributed processing, I: Foundations* (pp. 318–362). Cambridge, MA: MIT Press.

Schacter, D. L. (1987). Implicit memory: History and current status. *Journal of Experimental Psychology: Learning, Memory and Cognition, 13,* 501–518.

Servan-Schreiber, D., Cleeremans, A., & McClelland, J. L. (1988). *Encoding sequential structure in simple recurrent networks* (Tech. Rep. CMU-CS-88-183). Department of Computer Science, Carnegie Mellon University, Pittsburgh, PA.

Servan-Schreiber, E., & Anderson, J. R. (1990). Learning artificial grammars with competitive chunking. *Journal of Experimental Psychology: Learning, Memory and Cognition, 16,* 592–608.

Willingham, D. B., Nissen, M. J., & Bullemer, P. (1989). On the development of procedural knowledge. *Journal of Experimental Psychology: Learning, Memory and Cognition, 15,* 1047–1060.

6

Subitizing: The Preverbal Counting Process

C. R. Gallistel and Rochel Gelman
University of California, Los Angeles

Many account for the capacity of infants, young children, and animals to discriminate small numerosities by an appeal to subitizing (Chi & Klahr, 1975; Davis & Pérusse, 1988; von Glasserfeld, 1982; Klahr & Wallace, 1973; Rumbaugh, Savage-Rumbaugh, & Hegel, 1987; Shipley & Shepperson, 1990). Despite the central role attributed to this process, there has never been an explicitly formulated model of it. Kaufman, Lord, Reese, and Volkman (1949) coined the term *subitizing* for the process used by adults to give rapid numerosity judgments for small arrays of simultaneously presented dots.

In the recent literature, the definitive experimental paper on subitizing is by Mandler and Shebo (1982). Their results, which confirm and extend results obtained in experimental investigations dating back to the turn of the century, are the starting point for the model we present here for the subitizing process. Additional sources of our model include the work of Meck and Church (1983), who have developed and experimentally tested a model of the counting mechanism in animals, and research showing that human adult numerical competence rests in part on conversions back and forth between verbal and written representations of numerosity (numerlogs or numergraphs) and a preverbal representation of numerosity in which numerosity is represented by statistically ill defined values on a mental number line (Dehaene, 1989; Dehaene, Dupoux, & Mehler, in press; Hinrichs, Yurko, & Hu, 1981; Holyoak, 1978; Holyoak & Mah, 1982).

Our hypothesis is that preverbal representatives of numerosity (preverbal numerons) are magnitudes generated by the counting mechanism proposed by Meck and Church (1983). The magnitude (point on the mental number line) of a numeron generated by this counting process is assumed to vary from one correct count of the same numerosity to the next. Thus, the values assigned to a given numerosity form a numeron probability density distribution on the mental number line. In accord with the animal counting model and the experimental findings on the representation of numerosity by animals, we assume that the variance of the numeron probability density function is a scalar function of the numerosity: the greater the numerosity, the greater the variance in the distribution of numerons representing that numerosity, hence, the greater the likelihood of confounding a numerosity with adjacent numerosities.

THE REACTION TIME FUNCTION

Mandler and Shebo's data, in common with all the previously published reaction time data, suggest that the process by which adults generate the numerlogs for arrays of one to six items involves a serially incrementing mechanism because there is a sizable and statistically significant increment in the reaction time for each additional item in the array whose numerosity is to be estimated (Figure 6.1). The reaction time data also suggest, however, that the process used in this range differs in some way from the process used with more numerous arrays. This is because the increments in mean reaction time, as array size increases from one to two (30 msec), two to three (80 msec), and three to four (200 msec), are smaller than the 300–325 msec/item increment seen in the *reaction-time method* with arrays greater than 6, where subvocal verbal counting is clearly being used. In the reaction-time method, the display of the array terminates with the subject's response, whereas with the *tachistoscopic method*, the presentation time of the array is fixed, usually at 200 msec. Another way to code the difference between these methods is to consider who controls the offset of the display; the subject (in the reaction-time method) or the experimenter (in the tachistoscopic method).

It has frequently been proposed that subitizing (Davis & Pérusse, 1988; Klahr & Wallace, 1973; Strauss & Curtis, 1984; Woodworth & Schlosberg, 1954) is a process analogous to those by which we perceptually categorize things like cows and trees. Mandler and Shebo did two control experiments that make this idea less plausible. First, they showed that the reaction time to name the arabic numerals "1, 2, 3, and 4" did not increase systematically. There is, of course, no

---

FIG 6.1.   The time to state the numerosity of an array of randomly arranged dots or circles as a function of the numerosity of the array in four different experiments. The panels on the left are from "reaction-time" experiments in which the array is displayed until the subject responds. These panels have the same horizontal and vertical scales. The panels on the right are from tachistoscopic experiments in which the array is only displayed for 200 msec (400 msec less than the time it takes to react to a one-item array). The upper two panels have the same horizontal and vertical scales. A. Data from Jensen, et al. (1950).

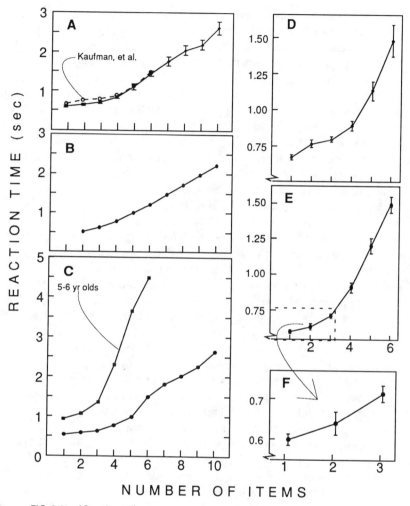

NUMBER OF ITEMS

FIG 6.1. (Continued)
Points are means of the median reaction times of the 5 subjects. Vertical bars show ±1 standard error of the mean. The superimposed open circles connected by a dashed line are the data from the tachistoscopic experiment in Panel D. The asymptotic slope of this function is sustained up to arrays of 30, the largest tested. B. Data from Saltzman and Garner (1948). They did not use arrays of only one. C. Data from Chi and Klahr (1975) for adults (lower curve) and 5–6-year-old children. D. Tachistoscopic data from Kaufman, et al. (1949), using same arrays as Jensen, et al. in their 'reaction-time' experiment. Vertical bars are ±1 standard error of the mean (n = 5). E. Data from Mandler and Shebo's (1982) tachistoscopic study. Vertical bars show 95% confidence interval. F. Larger scale display of Mandler and Shebo's data for the range 1–3. Vertical bars show 95% confidence levels.

reason why it should, because the recognition of these numerals is presumably mediated by a pattern-perception process. If the recognition of the oneness, twoness, threeness and fourness of random arrays were also mediated by a pattern perception process, then there would also be no reason to expect the systematic and very sizable increments in reaction time seen in the range from 1 to 4 (Figure 6.1, panels D and E). Sizable increments are seen over this range even in highly practiced subjects and even when the only arrays being shown are arrays in the range from one to three (see Mandler & Shebo, 1982, Figure 8). It has consistently been found that it takes practiced adult subjects about 300 msec longer to respond "four" to an array of four than to respond "one" to an array of one. This increment in reaction time within the subitizing range is equal to half the total latency to respond to a 1-item array (Jensen, Reese, & Reese, 1950; Kaufman et al., 1949; Mandler & Shebo, 1982).

Mandler and Shebo (1982) also showed that when they used 'canonical' arrays in which the arrangement of the dots composing a given numerosity was always the same, thereby making a strategy based on pattern recognition plausible, the reaction time function was flat over the range from one to five. Again, it is not surprising that the reaction time to recognize and numerically name distinctive spatial patterns does not increase systematically as a function of the numerosity of the dots composing the patterns, but this finding underscores the significance of the finding that when the spatial relations among the dots composing an array vary randomly from trial to trial, the reaction time function does increase systematically as a function of the number of dots.[1] It implies that the process whereby the subjects generate the numerlogs corresponding to these randomly arrayed sets is not a pattern-recognition process. The pattern recognition hypothesis for subitizing in infants has also been rejected by Cooper (1984) because the infants discriminate the numerosity of linear arrays of two and three.

It is often claimed that there is a discontinuity in the reaction-time data or in their slope somewhere in the range of numerosities between 3 and 8. Where in this range the discontinuity is imagined to be located has varied substantially from author to author. In the data from the tachistoscopic method (used by Kaufman, et al., 1949, and Mandler & Shebo, 1982, among others), the discontinuity in the slope of the reaction function is clear, as is its probable origin. In both of these tachistoscopic studies (where the display time is set at a constant

---

[1]The data plotted in Figures 10 & 11 of Mandler and Shebo (1982) come from the experiment where subjects were shown both random and canonical dot patterns. In this case the RT function for the random displays of 1, 2, and 3 is flat. Some might conclude that this result is inconsistent with the remaining data in Mandler and Shebo, their explanations, and our review of the literature. When we asked Mandler if this was the case, he noted that these data come from an experiment where subjects were told to look for canonical patterns and where a within subjects' design was used. He suggests that subjects took time to assimilate noncanonical displays in this range to their canonical representations of 2 and 3, a proposal, he noted, that explains why the RT function is elevated in this particular study. (Mandler, personal communication, April, 1990.)

value for varying set sizes), the reaction-time function accelerates steadily as the numerosity of the arrays increases from 1 to 6 (each successive unit increment in numerosity produces a greater increment in reaction time) and then it levels off abruptly to a reaction time of about 1.5 sec for all numerosities greater than 6 (even though, interestingly, the number reported increases systematically with numerosity up to numerosities at least as large as 200). When the display-offset time is controlled by the subject in the reaction-time method, there is the same acceleration over the range from one to six (Figure 6.1, panels A–C), but there is no leveling off. The leveling off of the reaction-time function in the tachisto-scopic paradigm is probably due to fading of the iconic image of the array, which puts an end to the operation of both verbal and preverbal serially incrementing (counting) processes. The use of fixed-time tachistoscopic presentations forces this leveling off. It is presumably of no significance for models of the process by which the mind generates verbal number judgments for arrays of six or less.

For the range 1–6, the reaction-time method and the tachistoscopic method yield superimposable reaction-time functions (Figure 6.1, panel A). This sug-gests that the processes that generate the appropriate numerlog are independent of the mode of presentation of the array over this range. There is an appreciable decline in absolute accuracy over this range. The Mandler and Shebo (1982) subjects gave the correct number 97.7% of the time on trials with an array of numerosity one but only 50.3% of the time on trials with numerosity six.

When the display of the array is sustained until the subject responds, there is no discontinuity in the slope of the reaction-time function (Figure 6.1, panels A–C). Chi and Klahr's (1975) efforts to discover a discontinuity by fitting straight lines to different subsets of the data has been trenchantly criticized by Allport (1975). Jensen et al. (1950) show more sensitivity to the problem of determining whether there is a discontinuity, and, if so, where it is. Although they claim to find a slope discontinuity between 6 and 7, what the data from all the studies show is a slope that steadily increases up to an asymptotic value somewhat greater than 300 msec/item (Figure 6.1, panels D and E). The steadiness of this acceleration is most apparent in the Mandler and Shebo data, which have the smallest uncertainty (Figure 6.1, panels E and F, vertical bars give 95% confi-dence intervals). The slope is within 10% of its asymptotic value when the numerosity exceeds 4.

THE ANIMAL COUNTING MECHANISM

The common laboratory animals (rats and pigeons) discriminate simultaneously and successively presented sets (of diverse composition) on the basis of their numerosity, for numerosities at least as high as 50 (Gallistel, 1990, Chapter 10). The upper limit on the animal capacity to discriminate numerosities has not been experimentally probed. Animals discriminate between the numerosities of simultaneously and sequentially presented stimuli or responses regardless of how widely separated the items are in time and space. Given the temporo-spatial range of stimulus presentations that support discriminations based on numerosity and the large numerosities that may be discriminated (e.g., 45 pecks versus 50 pecks—Rilling & McDiarmid, 1965; Rilling, 1967), it is difficult to envision any mechanism for deriving the mental representatives of numerosity (numerons) that underlie these discriminations other than a mechanism that sequentially passes through an ordered series of states, the last of which represents the cardinal numerosity of the set. Animals count sets of heterogeneous items as readily as sets of homogeneous items and they transfer the discrimination immediately to sets composed of stimuli that were not in the training set (Capaldi & Miller, 1988; Fernandes & Church, 1982). They also appear to perform addition and subtraction operations with representatives of numerosity (numerons), including numerals (Boysen & Berntson, 1989).

A finding from this literature that is important for our model of the subitizing process is the imprecision with which animals represent even small numerosities. Figure 6.2 gives data from a number-discrimination task in which the animal had to press a lever some fixed number of times in order silently to arm a food-dispenser. When the dispenser was armed and the rat's head interrupted a beam in front of the feeding cup, a pellet was dispensed. If, however, the rat interrupted the beam before the requisite number of presses had been made, it incurred a penalty whose severity was one of the experimental variables. Figure 6.2 plots the probability of the rat's interrupting a sequence of lever presses to try the feeder as a function of the number of presses it had made since the last interruption, when the penalty for premature interruptions was a 10-second time out. The between-curve variable is the number of presses required to arm the

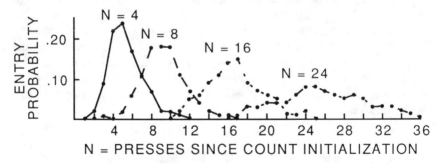

FIG 6.2.   The probability of breaking off to enter the food delivery area as a function of *n*, the number of presses made since the initialization of the response counter, for various values of *N*, the required number of presses, under conditions where a premature entry triggers a 10-second time-out but does not reset the response counter. (Redrawn from Platt & Johnson 1971, p. 401, by permission of author and publisher.)

feeder. Under these penalty conditions, the median number of presses before trying the feeder was equal to the required number for required numbers ranging from 4 to 24.

As striking as the systematic increase in the median number of presses given as a function of the number required is the variability in the number given even when the number required was as small as 4. It appears that the process by which the rat represents a number has approximately a scalar variance property—the variance in the estimate of a numerosity is proportionate to the magnitude of the estimate—and that the Weber fraction, the constant of proportionality, is high. The Weber fraction is high enough that 4 is often confused with 3 or 5 and, frequently, even with 2 or 6. Increasing the penalty for premature entry does not substantially reduce this variance. Rather, it causes the animal to adopt a more conservative criterion, only trying the feeder when its estimate of the number of presses given is on average a fixed amount greater than the number required.

Meck and Church (1983) proposed and tested a serially incrementing counting mechanism as a model of the process by which an animal estimates numerosity (generates numerons). Their counting mechanism is a minor modification of Gibbon's very successful model of the mechanism by which animals estimate temporal durations (Gibbon, 1977). In the model for estimating the duration of a temporal interval, a switch closes at the start of a to-be-timed interval, gating a stream of pulses from a clock into an accumulator. The switch opens at the end of the interval, at which point the value in the accumulator (the sum of the pulses in the stream), is multiplied by a constant approximately (but not usually exactly) equal to 1 and stored in memory for comparison to subsequent intervals. To make this model into a counter, Meck and Church (1983) proposed that the switches that gate the pulse stream from the clock to the accumulator can also operate in what they call an "Event mode." In this mode, each sequential event or each item in an array of simultaneously presented stimuli closes the switch for a fixed duration, so that the value in the accumulator at the end of a series of such 'one-shot' closures is proportional to the number of closures. Thus, in this model numbers are represented by magnitudes (the scaled contents of the accumulator), the very same magnitudes or at least the same kind of magnitudes that may be used to represent a continuous scalar variable like temporal duration.

The mechanism proposed by Meck and Church maps from to-be-counted events or stimuli to states of the integrator; thus states of the integrator constitute the numerons in this counting system. The mapping is one–one because each event gates one and only one (approximately equal) burst of pulses to the integrator; hence each successively counted entity is paired with a successively higher quantity in the integrator. The states of the integrator are run through in an order that is always the same because the ordering relation for quantity or magnitude (i.e., for the successive states of the integrator) is the same as the ordering relation for numerosity. The fact that adding successive increments to a quantity produces an ordered set of quantities just as adding successive ones produces an ordered set of numbers is part of the reason that quantity or magnitude can be represented numerically, and vice versa. Finally, the state of the integrator at the end of the series of events is taken to represent a property of the series (its numerosity), not a property of the final event itself. Thus the process envisioned by Meck and Church conforms to the principles that define a counting process (Gelman and Gallistel, 1978).

Meck and Church (1983) and Meck, Church, and Gibbon (1985) gave several lines of experimental evidence in support of their hypothesis that numerons in animals are magnitudes like the magnitudes that represent durations. The most persuasive evidence comes from an experiment in which they correctly predicted a transfer of a discrimination between two durations to a discrimination between two numerosities. If in both tasks the behavioral decision (which level to choose) depends on a comparison between two magnitudes, then one might expect to see immediate transfer from a judgment based on duration to one based on numerosity when the two counts yielded the same magnitudes as the two durations.

Meck and Church (1983) first taught the rat to press one lever when it heard a steady noise of 2 seconds' duration and the other lever when it heard a steady noise of 4 seconds' duration. Next they determined the duration discrimination function. They interspersed the training trials with test trials, on which the rat heard steady noise bursts of intermediate duration ($2 < d < 4$) and was not rewarded for either choice (there being no "correct" choice when the stimulus was intermediate between the trained values of 2 and 4). By means of these interspersed trials, they could measure the discrimination function, that is, the tendency to choose the "4-sec lever" as a function of the duration of the stimulus.

Finally, they interspersed counting trails. On these trials, the rats heard 1-second noise bursts alternating with 1-second silent segments. On any one trial, the discriminative test stimulus consisted of somewhere between 10 and 20 cycles of this stimulus. Both the total duration of the test stimuli (20–40 seconds) and the summed durations of their sound-on or sound-off segments (10–20 seconds) greatly exceeded both training durations (2 versus 4 seconds). Pilot work indicated that in the counting or "Event" mode, the switch gated pulses to the accumulator for about 200 milliseconds for each counted event. Thus, the accumulation from the counting of a sequence of 10 second bursts would match the accumulation from the timing of a single burst of 2 seconds' duration ($0.2 \times 10 = 2$) and the accumulation from the counting of 20 bursts would match the accumulation from the timing of a single 4-second burst ($0.2 \times 20 = 4$). The accumulations from timing these cyclical test stimuli would be very much greater than the accumulations that were rewarded during duration training, but the accumulations from counting the number of bursts would fall in the same range as the accumulations rewarded during duration training. Thus the rats might be expected to apply the decision rule learned for durations to the quantities generated by their counts of the number of bursts, which in fact they did (Figure 6.3).

The results in Figure 6.3, which were replicated and extended by Meck et al.

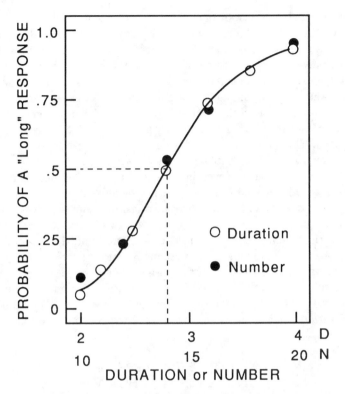

FIG 6.3. Probability of choosing the lever rewarded after the "long" (4-second) stimulus as a function of either the duration of a steady test stimulus or as a function of the number of cycles in a test stimulus consisting of alternating bursts of noise and silence. All the trials with durations other than the training durations (2 and 4 seconds) were interpolated unrewarded trials, as were all the trials with multiple bursts of noise (the number trials). The rats' generalization from the representation of a continuous variable (duration) to the numerosity of a discrete variable (noise bursts) suggests that both variables are represented by magnitudes. (Redrawn from Meck and Church 1983, p. 331, by permission of author and publisher.)

(1985), imply that the rat counts by making successive, roughly equal increments in the magnitude of some mental variable. In effect, the mind inverts the representational convention whereby numbers are used to represent linear magnitudes. Instead of using number to represent magnitude, the rat uses magnitude to represent number. Linear magnitude represents numerosity in the brain in the manner in which the lengths of the bars in a frequency histogram represent the underlying numbers of observations. The relevance of this model for the animal representation of number for our theory of subitizing is that it suggests that the primitive or preverbal mental representation of numerosity is by magnitudes, the same mental magnitudes or the same kinds of mental magnitudes that are used to represent continuous variables like durations. In our theory of subitizing, we assume that this is the preverbal representation of numerosity in human beings as well.

The high scalar variance in the rat's representatives of numerosity may have at least two sources: miscountings (failing to close the switch for every item or closing it more times than there are items) and an inherent imprecision in the magnitude of the values retained in memory as representatives of the experienced numerosities. This imprecision could arise from the characteristics of memory itself or it might arise from variability in the magnitudes resulting from a fixed number of switch closures, hence in the magnitudes corresponding to a fixed numerosity. The latter kind of scalar variance would arise if, for example, the stream of pulses obeyed Poisson statistics, so that the number of pulses gated to the accumulator varied from one 200 msec switch closure to the next. The data on the discrimination of temporal intervals—where omitted or supernumerary switch closures (miscountings) are presumably not a factor—reveal a similar high scalar variance. This suggests that a significant fraction of the variance in number estimates derives from the second source, a scalar variance inherent in the process by which a numerosity is mapped to the mental magnitude that represents it, a variance that cannot be reduced by reducing miscountings.

VERBAL AND NONVERBAL REPRESENTATIONS OF NUMEROSITY IN HUMANS

The verbal representation of numerosity by arbitrarily derived morphemes is profoundly different from a representation based on magnitudes. Magnitude manifests the same ordering as numerosity, whereas there is no ordering inherent in the morphemes. The magnitude representing 2 differs more from the magnitude representing 4 than from the magnitude representing 3. No such ordering of differences inheres in the numerlogs 'two,' 'three,' and 'four' nor in the numergraphs '1,' '2,' '3,' and '4.' Thus, estimates of numerosity based on verbal counts cannot exhibit the second of the two kinds of variance just specified. Imprecision in generating or recording the magnitude that represents *four* yields a magnitude more appropriate to represent *three* or *five* much more often than it yields a magnitude appropriate to *two* or *six,* but imprecision in writing '1' does not yield '2.' If anything, imprecision in writing '1' more often leads to confusion with '7' than with '2.' In short, the confusion matrices for numerlogs and numergraphs are not determined by the relative magnitudes of the numerosities they represent. Assuming one has learned some conventional verbal counting list, the only source of error in the verbal representation of number would appear to be miscounting, which may be reduced by a careful execution of the process that updates the partition between already-counted and not-yet-counted items in the course of a count.

The algorithms for addition and subtraction with verbal representatives of number also differ profoundly from the algorithms for performing these operations with magnitudes. The algorithm for combining two numerlogs to get a third numerlog that represents their sum requires knowledge of the base for the particular verbal/orthographic code that is being used (7 + 2 = 11 in a base 8 system) and the rules that govern carrying in place-value notation. None of this is required when two magnitudes are combined to yield a third magnitude, as, for example, when two line segments are laid end to end to generate the segment that is their sum.

In view of the profound differences between the verbal and nonverbal representations of numerosity one might suppose that human number processing relied on one or the other but not both at the same time. However, work on the reaction time in number comparison tasks (Dehaene, 1989; Dehaene, Dupoux & Mehler, in press; Hinrichs, Yurko & Hu, 1981; Holyoak, 1978; Holyoak & Mah, 1982) suggests that when human beings work with some kinds of verbally or symbolically presented number problems, they commonly map from the verbal representatives of numerosity to the more primitive nonverbal representation, compute solutions using the nonverbal representation, then map back from it to verbal answers. Evidence of this is the long established fact that the reaction time for a "greater than" or "less than" judgment between a remembered reference number and a newly presented comparison number is quicker the greater the interval between them, even for numbers that straddle decade boundaries. (One can judge 59 to be greater than 49 more quickly than one can judge 51 to be greater than 49.)

The most startling evidence for the hypothesis that human beings routinely map back and forth between their verbal and preverbal representations of numerosity comes from a profoundly acalculic neuropsychiatric patient (Dehaene, personal communication). When asked whether it was true that 2 + 2 = 4, the patient said "yes," but he also said "yes" when asked whether 2 + 2 = 3 and when asked whether 2 + 2 = 5, from which one is inclined to conclude that his answers were confabulations. However, when asked whether 2 + 2 = 9, he answered "no." It appears that he has lost access to the verbally created addition table that we learn in our early schooling but that he could still map from the numergraphs to their corresponding magnitudes (preverbal numerons), add the magnitudes to get an imprecisely specified third magnitude, and map from this third magnitude back to the numergraphs that correspond to approximately that magnitude. Because the specification of this third magnitude is imprecise, he cannot readily distinguish between numergraphic answers that correspond to closely adjacent magnitudes (nemrosities), but he can reject numergraphs that correspond to grossly different magnitudes.

These findings strengthen the hypothesis that the rudiments of the verbal system of number are learned by reference to a preverbal magnitude-based representation of number that is part of our animal heritage and that mappings back and forth between the preverbal representatives and the verbal representatives of number are a routine part of the mental manipulation of number. This hypothesis leads to our theory of subitizing.

A MODEL OF SUBITIZING

We suggest that in the subitizing range, human subjects use the preverbal counting process revealed in research on animals. We suggest that for small numerosities, the preverbal counter can run much faster than the verbal counting routine, so that the magnitude (the preverbal numeron) that represents the numerosity of an array is specified long before the verbal counting process has arrived at the correct numerlog. It is specified so much sooner that one can get the correct numerlog more quickly by using the preverbal counting mechanism (subitizing) to get the preverbal numeron and use the preverbal numeron to retrieve the numerlog. It is likely that this strategy would work even for numerosities much larger than 4 if it were not for the imprecision with which the preverbal numeron is specified. This imprecision leads to too many inaccurate responses. Because the variance (inaccuracy) in the specification of the magnitude of the numeron is scalar, the probability of giving a response that is erroneous by ±1 increases with the numerosity of the array. As the chance of making an error increases, the subject relies more frequently on the verbal count and less frequently on the answer generated by way of the subitizing process. When the size of the array exceeds four, the chance of an error in the answer generated by way of the subitizing process is so great that the subject always waits for the answer generated by verbal counting.

The verbal counting process and the preverbal counting process are both subject to error because of miscounting, that is, because of procedural failures that violate the one–one principle (Gelman & Gallistel, 1978). These miscounts are very common in children's counting, which is an important reason why the reaction-time function increases so much more steeply for kindergarten children than it does for adults (Figure 6.1 panel C). One of the skills that develops with extensive experience at counting is skill at choosing and applying the partitioning processes that segregate the already counted from the not yet counted in the course of enumeration (Gelman & Greeno, 1989). However, the preverbal counting process is subject to an additional source of variance. The values of the magnitudes yielded by this process on counts vary when there has been no miscounting. Hence the preverbal representative of a numerosity is a probability distribution defined over the equivalent of a mental number line. Thus, in the preverbal counting process, there is some likelihood of confounding the numeron for a given numerosity with the numerons for adjacent numerosities even when there has been no miscounting. We call this the *inherent variance*. The variance due to miscounts and the inherent variance both increase as a function of numerosity. But, the Weber fraction for the second source of variance is much higher than the Weber fraction for the first source, at least in skilled verbal counters. This is why skilled counters increasingly shift to reliance on the slower but more accurate verbal counting process as the numerosity increases from 1 to 4 or 5.

Further evidence that the preverbal counting mechanism is fast but inaccurate comes from an experiment by Rilling and McDiarmid (1965), who applied a signal-detection analysis to the pigeon's ability to discriminate the numerosities of its pecks. The pigeon had to choose between two illuminated side keys on the basis of the number of pecks it had just made on a center key. The experimental program controlled this number, that is, the side keys were illuminated after a preprogrammed number of pecks on the center key. Which side key was the correct (rewarded) key varied as a function of the preprogrammed number for the center key. The pigeons discriminated numerosities in the range 45–50 even though they pecked the center key at a rate of 6 pecks per second, which is twice as fast as humans can count (Figure 6.4). However, they were so inaccurate in their counts that they confounded 45 with 50 on 10–20% of the trials, and when

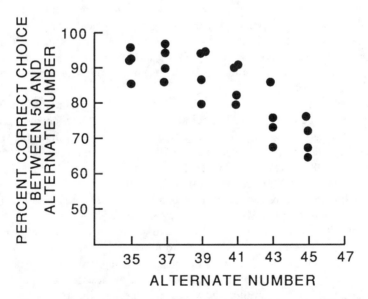

FIG 6.4.   Scatter plot from four determinations of a pigeon's ability to discriminate between a run of fifty key pecks and an alternative run whose number varied systematically in the range from thirty-five to forty-seven. (Redrawn from Rilling and McDiarmid (1965), p. 527, by permission of author and publisher.)

the difference to be discriminated was 48 versus 50, discrimination failed altogether. For the evidence that the pigeons based their discrimination on the numerosity of their pecks and not on the duration of their pecking, which covaried with numerosity, see Rilling (1967).

RELEVANCE OF THE PRESENT MODEL FOR STUDIES OF HUMAN INFANTS

The numerical abilities of infants have been studied by several research groups using one or both of two methods. In one of these, infants are first habituated to a display or set of displays with arrays of N items (usually ranging from 1 to 4). Their tendency to start responding again when they are then shown displays of a different value is taken as an index of their ability to discriminate between the two numerosities. In the second of these methods, infants encounter two displays with arrays of different values, for example 2 and 3, and their preference for one display over the other serves as evidence of their ability to discriminate between the two numerosities. A variant of the preference technique has been used to assess infants' abilities to respond intermodally to numerosity. For example, Starkey, Spelke, and Gelman (1990) showed infants a pair of side by side, heterogeneous displays that varied in numerosity (2 vs. 3) while two or three drum beats were heard through a hidden speaker placed midway between the displays. An infant's tendency to look systematically across trials at the display that contains either the same of a different number of items than the number of drumbeats serves as an index of their ability to link stimuli presented via different modalities on the basis of common numerosity.

Different groups of investigators, using one or another variant of the habituation or preference methods with either homogeneous or heterogeneous items in their displays, have converged on a common set of findings. Infants between 1 and 10 months of age discriminate reliably between two and three items (Antell & Keating, 1983; Starkey & Cooper, 1980; Strauss & Curtis, 1981; Starkey, Spelke & Gelman, 1983); they sometimes discriminate between three- and four-item displays (Strauss & Curtis, 1981); and they fail to discriminate between four and five items or four and six items (Starkey & Cooper, 1980; Strauss & Curtis, 1981). In addition, 4- to 6-month-old infants respond intermodally to numerosity. Starkey et al. (1990) have shown that 6- to 8-month-old infants have a reliable tendency to look at the display which matches in numerosity the number of drumbeats they hear on a given trial. Indeed, in one of these studies, infants even matched numerosity when then the visual and auditory inputs were presented sequentially. In a related study by Moore, Benenson, Reznick, Peerson, and Kagan (1987), infants looked at the numerosity that matched the number of sounds they heard during their first phase of testing. During the last phase of testing their behavior followed a common path in the infancy literature and responded to novelty, that is, they switched to pairing sounds and slides that differed in numerosity (See Starkey et al., 1990, for the pertinent analyses of the Phase 1 and 2 differences in Moore et al., 1987). In both phases, their responding was a systematic function of the relative numerosities of the auditory sequence and the array.

The above findings on infants' numerical abilities are typically taken as evidence that they do not count. For example, Strauss and Curtis (1984) write, "Finally, there is no evidence that infants can abstract numerosities larger than about three or four. Logically, there is no reason why a counting strategy should have such a limitation" (p. 144). We have here developed an account of preverbal counting for which there is a clear reason for such a limitation. Because the infant findings are much like those in studies of animals' abilities to count, both in terms of their different degrees of success as set sizes increase from 2 and 3 to 4 and 5, they are fully consistent with the hypothesis that infants do count and compare when given either sequential events or simultaneous arrays. More importantly, our preverbal counting model makes intelligible the basis of the numerical comparisons implied by the infants' patterns of responses across the different sizes used. If, as set size increases, the preverbal counting mechanism generates increasing variance in the resulting numerons, then discrimination between adjacent numerosities should start to break down at numerosities of 4 and 5. Similarly, discriminations between four and six items will be unreliable. For the variance in the estimate of a numerosity 4 is already high enough to produce confusion with 3 and 5 and the variance of the representations of 4 and 6 overlap enough to make discriminations difficult.

Given that we can readily incorporate the extant data base on human infants' abilities to represent numerosity into our preverbal counting model, it is premature to reject the hypothesis that infants count. Our account points to the kind of research that would provide suitable tests of this model. Studies are needed where one systematically varies the difference between pairs of set sizes so as to select stimuli that will generate varying degrees of discriminability in the numerons representing numerosity. Our prediction is that infants will fare better on those pairs where the resulting variances do not overlap appreciably than on those pairs where there is appreciable overlap in the probability density distributions. In absence of such data, it is premature to conclude that human infants do not use a nonverbal counting procedure, let alone that they use some undefined perceptual apprehension process (e.g., von Glaserfeld, 1982).

CONCLUSION

Verbal concepts and verbally mediated human behaviors must have a preverbal substrate, which evolved prior to the very recent evolution of the language ability, yet it is surprising how seldom cognitive psychology is able to link the verbal capacities to their preverbal antecedents. We believe that there is hope for establishing such a linkage in the number domain.

ACKNOWLEDGMENTS

Preparation of this chapter was supported in part by NSF grant #BNS 8961220 to Rochel Gelman.

REFERENCES

Allport, D. A. (1975). The state of cognitive psychology. *Quarterly Journal of Experimental Psychology, 27,* 141–152.

Antell, S. E., & Keating, D. P. (1983). Perception of numerical invariance in neonates. *Child Development, 54,* 695–701.

Boysen, S. T., & Berntson, G. G. (1989). Numerical competence in a chimpanzee (*Pan troglodytes*). *Journal of Comparative Psychology, 103,* 23–31.

Capaldi, E. J., & Miller, D. J. (1988). counting in rats: Its functional significance and the independent cognitive processes which comprise it. *Journal of Experimental Psychology: Animal Behavior Processes, 14,* 3–17.

Chi, M. T. H., & Klahr, D. (1975). Span and rate of apprehension in children and adults. *Journal of Experimental Child Psychology, 19,* 434–439.

Cooper, R. G., Jr. (1984). Early number development: Discovering number space with addition and subtraction. In C. Sophian (Ed.), *The origins of cognitive skills* (pp. 157–192). Hillsdale, NJ: Lawrence Erlbaum Associates.

Davis, H., & Pérusse, R. (1988). Numerical competence in animals. *Behavioral and Brain Sciences, 11,* 561–615.

Dehaene, S. (1989). The psychophysics of numerical comparison: A reexamination of apparently incompatible data. *Perception and Psychophysics, 45*(6), 557–566.

Dehaene, S., Dupoux, E., & Mehler, J. (in press). Is numerical comparison digital: Analogical and symbolic effects in two-digit number comparisons. *Journal of Experimental Psychology: Human Perception and Performance.*

Fernandes, D. M., & Church, R. M. (1982). Discrimination of the number of sequential events by rats. *Animal Learning and Behavior, 10,* 171–176.

Gallistel, C. R. (1990). *The organization of learning.* Cambridge, MA: Bradford Books/MIT Press.

Gelman, R., & Gallistel, C. R. (1978). *The child's understanding of number.* Cambridge, MA: Harvard University Press.

Gelman, R., & Greeno, J. G. (1989).On the nature of competence: Principles for understanding in a domain. In L. B. Resnick (Ed.), *Knowing and learning: Issues for a cognitive science of instruction.* Hillsdale, NJ: Lawrence Erlbaum Associates, pp. 125–186.

Gibbon, J. (1977). Scalar expectancy theory and Weber's Law in animal training. *Psychological Review, 84,* 279–335.

Hinrichs, J. V., Yurko, D. S., & Hu, J. M. (1981). Two-digit number comparison: Use of place information. *Journal of Experimental Psychology: Human Perception and Performance, 7,* 890–901.

Holyoak, K. J. (1978). Comparative judgments with numerical reference points. *Cognitive Psychology, 10,* 203–243.

Holyoak, K. J., & Mah, W. A. (1982). Cognitive reference points in judgments of symbolic magnitudes. *Cognitive Psychology, 14*, 328–352.

Jensen, E. M., Reese, E. P., & Reese, T. W. (1950). The subitizing and counting of visually presented fields of dots. *Journal of Psychology, 30*, 363–392.

Kaufman, E. L., Lord, M. W., Reese, T. W., & Volkman, J. (1949). The discrimination of visual number. *American Journal of Psychology, 62*, 498–525.

Klahr, D., & Wallace, J. G. (1973). The role of quantification operators in the development of conservation of quantity. *Cognitive Psychology, 4*, 301–327.

Mandler, G., & Shebo, B. J. (1982). Subitizing: An analysis of its component processes. *Journal of Experimental Psychology: General, 11*, 1–22.

Meck, W. H., & Church, R. M. (1983). A mode control model of counting and timing processes. *Journal of Experimental Psychology: Animal Behavior Processes, 9*, 320–334.

Meck, W. H., Church, R. M., & Gibbon, J. (1985). Temporal integration in duration and number discrimination. *Journal of Experimental Psychology: Animal Behavior Processes, 11*, 591–597.

Moore, D., Benenson, J., Reznick, S., Peerson, M., & Kagan, J. (1987). Effect of auditory numerical information on infants' looking behavior: Contradictory evidence. *Developmental Psychology, 23*, 665–670.

Platt, J. R., & Johnson, D. M. (1971). Localization of position within a homogeneous behavior chain: Effects of error contingencies. *Learning and Motivation, 2*, 386–414.

Rilling, M. (1967). Number of responses as a stimulus in fixed interval and fixed ratio schedules. *Journal of Comparative and Physiological Psychology, 63*, 60–65.

Rilling, M., & McDiarmid, C. (1965). Signal detection in fixed ratio schedules. *Science, 148*, 526–527.

Rumbaugh, D. M., Savage-Rumbaugh, S., & Hegel, M. T. (1987). Summation in the chimpanzee *(Pan troglodytes). Journal of Experimental Psychology: Animal Behavior Processes, 13*, 107–115.

Saltzman, I. J., & Garner, W. R. (1948). Reaction time as a measure of span of attention. *The Journal of Psychology, 25*, 227–241.

Shipley, E., & Shepperson, B. (1990). Countable entities: Developmental changes. *Cognition, 34*, 109–136.

Starkey, P., & Cooper, R. G. (1980). Perception of numbers by human infants. *Science, 210*, 1033–1035.

Starkey, P., Spelke, E. S., & Gelman, R. (1983). Detection of intermodal correspondences by human infants. *Science, 222*, 179–181.

Starkey, P., Spelke, E. S., & Gelman, R. (1990). Numerical abstraction in human infants. *Cognition*, 97–128.

Strauss, M. S., & Curtis, L. E. (1981). Infant perception of numerosity. *Child Development, 52*, 1146–1152.

Strauss, M. S., & Curtis, L. E. (1984). Development of numerical concepts in infancy. In C. Sophian (Ed.), *Origins of cognitive skills* (pp. 131–155). Hillsdale, NJ: Lawrence Erlbaum Associates.

von Glaserfeld, E. (1982). Subitizing: The role of figural patterns in the development of number concepts. *Archives de Psychologie, 50*, 191–218.

Wynn, K. (in press). Children's understanding of counting, *Cognition,*

Woodworth, R. S., & Schlosberg, H. (1954). *Experimental psychology: Revised edition.* New York: Holt, Rinehart & Winston.

PREFATORY REMARKS TO CHAPTERS 7 AND 8

Henry Gleitman
University of Pennsylvania

GEORGE MANDLER

I have been asked to preface chapters 7 and 8 with a few words about George Mandler—an odd task, considering that although George has been called many things, being a man of few words is surely not one of them. But I agreed anyway, in part, because it might be the only time in the 35 years that I have known him that I could say something to and about George without fear of being interrupted by someone whose voice is even louder and whose accent even more Central European than my own. And this despite the fact that I am his senior by easily 6 months, and that this age difference between us is apparently growing with every passing year.

How would I describe George? To begin with, he is intellectually very broad, one of the few remaining members of that endangered species, the "general psychologist." In some ways the chronology of his interests mirrors that of the field as a whole—from obscurely psychodynamics flirtations, through vaguely Hullian leanings, to musings about the philosophy of psychology, to the rediscovery of cognitive organization in memory and recognition, to an ever increasing interest in emotion and consciousness.

In each of these areas, the contributions he has made are important and lasting, some sufficiently so to be considered classic and misdescribed in elementary textbooks. But none of this captures what is really unique about George. One is a rock bottom Yankee no-nonsense "you show me" attitude, uttered in a loud Viennese accent. For wherever George has worked or thought, he cares about what is, the facts of the case, and tolerates no nonsense, fakery, or cant. When the little boy who said that the emperor had no clothes grew up, he became George Mandler. Now full-grown, he is perfectly willing to announce that A's clothes aren't there, that B's don't fit, that C's are ugly, and that D's, perhaps worst of all, are shamelessly borrowed. Put in more technical terms, George has an unfailingly accurate bullshit detector, and he doesn't hesitate to use his detector. Loudly.

Perhaps even more characteristic of George is that unlike so many of his contemporaries, he never takes himself seriously. At least as an academic. He is always ready to laugh at himself. Or at the outer trappings of the academic world: What's in and what's out, who's up and coming, and who is down and going, and all the rest. He'll just laugh his big, bellowing laugh, for to him such surface things don't really matter.

I esteem George for what he is. A man who knows what's worth caring about and what is not. A highly intelligent man. A literate man. A decent man. An old friend.

7

Some Trends in the Study of Cognition*

HENRY GLEITMAN
University of Pennsylvania

When I agreed to write a chapter on what we have learned about cognition since Wilhelm Wundt, I thought my only problem would be one of selection. For after all, how could we *not* have gone beyond Wilhelm Wundt, whom I—like so many of us—had been taught to regard as someone posterity can safely patronize: an indefatigable, erudite, but slightly pedantic champion of an outmoded elementarism, a man whom Stanley Hall called a "wonderful compiler and digester" (Hall, 1921); of whom William James said that "he wasn't a genius but a professor . . . an example of how much mere education can do for a man" (H. James, 1920, p. 263); whom Edna Heidbreder likened to "a careful housewife, industriously picking up after a growing science that . . . has not yet learned . . . to be neat. . . ." (Heidbreder, 1933, p. 96).

I soon discovered (greatly helped by several recent authors, e.g., Blumenthal, 1970, 1975) that this picture of our official founding father is simply false. It is a painting that is reminiscent of those purchased by Gilbert and Sullivan's Major

*Many of the ideas here presented come from a longtime collaborator who helped me with this paper, as with so many others, to the extent of being a de facto co-author—Lila R. Gleitman. I am also very grateful to several friends and colleagues who have been extremely generous in discussing this paper with me at various stages in its preparation: John Flavell, Julian Hochberg, John Jonides, Ulric Neisser, Elissa Newport, and Elizabeth Spelke.

83

General Stanley, who bought an ancestral home and then acquired a gallery of ancestor portraits to go along with it. Psychology is like General Stanley. It manufactures its ancestors to justify what it is doing now, creating a past that flatters its present.

Poor Wundt is a victim of this Stanley effect. For one thing, he never held the passive conception of mental life he is so often charged with. On the contrary, he might well be regarded as a forerunner of various constructive approaches to perception and memory. As he saw it, conscious experiences generally include elements of forward-looking anticipation which bind the future to the present.

Nor was Wundt the elementarist that later critics, such as the Gestalt psychologists, held him to be. (In this regard, they probably confused him with his American St. Paul, E. B. Titchener.) Consider some of his comments on language, which sound almost like a Wagnerian prelude to a work authored at M.I.T. Here is how he put it in the *Völkerpsychologie*:

> . . . A sentence does not consist of separate mental structures that emerge in consciousness, one by one, each existing as an individual word or an individual sound while all before and after sinks into oblivion. It rather remains in consciousness as a totality while it is being uttered. . . . As a result, all relevant components of a sentence are already mentally given in the brief moment when one first begins to utter it. . ." (Wundt, 1900, p. 235).

There is evidently more to Wundt than met the textbook writers' eyes. How much more I cannot say, for I do not have the stamina to go through the thousands of printed pages (according to some estimates, sixty thousand) that he bequeathed to posterity.

Under the circumstances, I had to change my approach to the question "What have we learned since Wilhelm Wundt?" I cannot very well assess how far we have come (especially given that I do not really know where we started from), for that would be too presumptuous. I do not want to chronicle the historical details of our intellectual pilgrimage, for that would be too tedious. Nor do I wish to relate our long wanderings through the behaviorist wilderness (during which cognition finally became respectable when it was found in rats), for that would be too depressing.

I will instead trace a few themes in the way several areas of cognition have been conceived. My focus will be on the *what* of cognition rather than on its *how*, on structure rather than on process: the way it is organized as we perceive objects, comprehend meanings, and make out another person's intentions, and the way these structures enter not just into what we know but also into what we know we know.

It is probably no coincidence that some of these themes have been foreshadowed by nineteenth-century psychologists, especially by Wilhelm Wundt.

A Parallel

A common theme runs through three different domains of cognitive life: visual perception, language, and the interpretation of behavior. Its basis is the distinction between two levels of psychological structure, one more peripheral and the other more central—the difference between what in language is called "surface" and "underlying structure."

In Language

In language, this distinction is by now a commonplace. There is a first-level organization of linguistic input that more or less corresponds to the sentences we actually hear—the surface form. This is somehow organized into a structure that is a closer approximation to the underlying sentence meaning—the underlying structure.

To recapitulate an oft-told tale, these two levels—surface and underlying structure—are very different. One demonstration is the fact that two or more different surface forms can go back to the same underlying structure. Thus:

The princess kissed the frog.

and its passive form,

The frog was kissed by the princess.

both refer to a common proposition and are to this extent paraphrases.

Another demonstration of the surface–underlying structure distinction comes from certain kinds of *ambiguities*. These show that one and the same surface form may go back to two or more different underlying structures. Examples include sentences such as

Kissing frogs can be amusing . . .

and

Smoking volcanoes can be dangerous . . .

In Visual Perception

As several psycholinguists have noted, the surface–underlying structure distinction drawn by linguists has an analogue in visual perception (e.g., Bever, 1970; Fodor, Bever, & Garrett, 1974). Here, surface structure corresponds to something close to the proximal stimulus on the retina, perhaps something which E. B. Titchener would have called the visual sensation (Titchener, 1896). The underlying structure, on the other hand, corresponds to the perception of the distal stimulus—the rock or the tree out there in the world rather than its projection on the retina. It is worth noting that the self-conscious demonstration of this distinction dates back to the Gestalt psychologists and their unceasing war against what they called the *constancy hypothesis*—the assumption that what we perceive corresponds directly to the proximal stimulus on our retina (Koffka, 1935). Their weapons in this war were analogous to those the linguists used to document the surface–underlying structure distinction: ambiguity and paraphrase. Thus they continually emphasized that the same proximal pattern can be perceived in two or more ways, as shown by an unending parade of ambiguous figures of which the Necker cube and the young woman/old woman picture are among the most familiar. The complementary side of their argument came from demonstrations that different proximal stimuli may all be perceived as equivalent in some important regard. Doors seen from different slants cast different trapezoidal images on the retina, but they are all perceived as rectangular; trees at different distances cast images of different size, but they are all perceived as having the same size. These various constancies—here, of shape and size—are the perceptual analogues of language paraphrase. Our perceptual system is somehow able to operate on all of the various trapezoidal images that the doorframe gives rise to and interpret them as a rectangle.

In Behavior

Something akin to the surface–underlying structure distinction may apply to yet another domain: our apprehension of behavior. As Tolman and other theorists taught us, we can look at behavior in both a *molecular* and a *molar* sense (Tolman, 1932). The molecular level corresponds to a surface organization: it is described as a series of particular movements. The molar level is closer to the center and thus more like the underlying structure: it is usually described as the goal or intention.

There is no doubt that any particular molar pattern can be expressed in a number of different molecular forms. This holds for rats who may traverse a path to the same goal in any number of ways—running, swimming, hobbling, or short-cutting, depending upon how Tolman and Lashley had rearranged their maze or brain (e.g., Woodworth, 1938, pp. 133–134). Much the same holds for people who may try to reach a goal by many different molecular means: thus slapping, jabbing, and punching may all be different behavior-surface forms that refer to a common underlying intentional structure. In effect, they are behavioral paraphrases. Their opposite is also found: two acts that are more or less alike on the surface but have two different underlying goal directions, thus representing the behavioral analogue of ambiguity. An example is violently shoving someone standing in the road. Is this a surface manifestation of intense dislike or an attempt to push the victim out of the path of a runaway truck? Another example was used in an episode of the late-lamented television series "Mary Hartman, Mary Hartman": mouth-to-mouth contact between man and woman, which may be kissing or artificial respiration.

Hierarchies of Levels

We should add a qualification. In both goal-directed behavior and in language (and perhaps in visual perception too), there are hierarchies of structure. As a result, the terms *surface* and *underlying form*—at least in an extended sense—are relative. In language, the levels of primary interest have been those that involve the sentence. But one can go below and consider morphological and phonological structures. Or one can go above and look at discourse. What serves as paraphrase or ambiguity will then depend upon the level under consideration. Given an appropriate discourse level, a sentence such as

The witch's curse was foiled

might then be an acceptable paraphrase for our initial sentence about the frog-kissing princess.

A similar multileveled hierarchical structure characterizes goal-directed behavior. There are not only goals but subgoals and subsubgoals and so on down the hierarchy until we finally reach the ultimate surface level of the muscle twitch. Which particular levels of the hierarchy shall we choose as the behavioral analogues of surface and underlying structure? In a way, the problem is quite analogous to that encountered in the analysis of language structures, but there is an important difference. The linguists have some agreed-upon conceptions about the various levels of the linguistic hierarchy. There is a phonological basement, a phonemic first story, and so on, all the way up to the levels of sentence meaning, with some interesting plans for the construction of several discourse penthouses. As far as I know, behavioral analysis has not yet reached this happy consensus (though there have been some attempts in this direction, e.g., Schank & Abelson, 1977). Suppose a smiling man lifts a baby to his head and plants his lips to the infant's. What is the appropriate description of the intention, the underlying behavioral structure? Is he kissing the baby? Pleasing its mother? Running for president? Thus far, there is no agreement. So, in the realm of behavioral description, one man's molecule is another's mole.

How Genuine Is the Analogy?

One may argue that the analogy sketched here is rather superficial. For there is little doubt that the mechanisms by which one moves from surface to underlying structures are quite different in the three domains. Perhaps so. But my point is not directed at the processes that underlie the traffic from cognitive periphery to center.

It merely notes that such a traffic occurs and that it is in some ways similar in the three cognitive realms. In all three, the would-be knower confronts a similar problem: how to apprehend an underlying sameness in a welter of changing surface forms. How this task is accomplished—by extraction of stimulus invariants, by various forms of inference, by the gradual development of internal rule systems whose forms may be in some sense pregiven—is another matter entirely.

A further argument for my cavalier disregard of mechanisms is provided by the perceptual constancies: of lightness, size, and shape. All three are phenomena within the same cognitive realm of visual perception. But we already know that the processes that underlie them are very different. Lightness constancy is ours largely by courtesy of evolution and lateral inhibition. Size and shape constancy may very well turn out to be based on early learning, at least in part. But this does not change the fact that all three belong to the same conceptual family and are so viewed by most perception psychologists. For in each case, the perceiver is posed with a similar problem and solves it successfully. Since this is so, all three are traditionally subsumed under the same general rubric. If this can be done within a given cognitive domain, why not across different ones?

I am arguing for an analogy based on structure rather than on process, but it is worth noting that there may be some similarities of process too. Consider the perception of size which clearly requires so-called "cues" for distance. By utilizing these cues (however this is done), the observer can see that he is dealing with an object of a given size and at a given distance. Psycholinguists point out that something like cues exist in language, whose role may be quite equivalent to those played by various cues to distance, orientation, and the like in visual perception. Thus passive forms such as

Noun verb *-ed by* Noun

provide cues in the form of *-ed by* which indicate that the conversational focus is on the object of the underlying sentence proposition rather than the subject. This allows us to extract the underlying proposition, a procedure that works even for nonsense words. Given the pseudosentence

The dax was riffed by the zup.

we immediately suppose that the *zup* was the *riffer*, the *dax* the *riffee*.

By and large this supposition will be correct, but sometimes it won't. If *dax* stands for *pig*, *rif* for *slaughter*, and *zup* for *gate*, the sentence becomes

The pig was slaughtered by the gate.

In this case the *zup* does not function as the *riffer*. Here, the *-ed by* provides a misleading cue to focus. But then the same sometimes happens in visual perception, where distance cues may also turn out to provide false information.

Collapsing Time

Suppose we grant that there is something valid about the notion of surface–underlying structure distinction that runs across a number of cognitive domains. What accounts for this dual structure? I believe that its essence has to do with the compression of time.

Consider the underlying structures which—crudely speaking—correspond to our mental representations of purpose, object, and meaning. These mental entities are themselves timeless, but I believe that they all refer to events that necessarily occur over time. They are reminiscent of T. S. Eliot's lines in "Burnt Norton":

> *Time present and time past*
> *Are both perhaps present in time future,*
> *And time future contained in time past.*

It seems to me that this describes a crucial facet of our mental structures. Purpose, object, and meaning are mental packagings of temporal unfoldings, but they themselves are outside of time. In this regard they are quite unlike the surface forms which do occur over time—almost by definition.

Collapsing Surface Behaviors—Purpose

Let us start with purpose. There is no one way in which we can divine another creature's purpose except by observing its behavior over time: its start, its progression, and its finish. Nor is one sequence of outward behavior patterns enough. As Tolman told us, one of the defining characteristics of purposive behavior is its docility: if one means does not attain the end, the organism will choose another (Tolman, 1932). At least in principle, our knowledge of another's purpose is similarly based on the observation of several different surface behaviors. We must know what happens when the starting point is altered, when obstacles are erected, and so on. Needless to say, we generally reach our cognitive decision on the basis of much less information, deciding that, say, Joe wants Mary without actually observing that he takes the appropriate detours when his normal path to Mary is blocked. But the point is that this cognitive decision about Joe's goal boils down to a prediction of his outward behavior on an infinite set of tests (all designed with appropriate qualifications about performance limitations). Will he climb over hurdles to reach his beloved (assuming that he can climb)? Will he swim across moats (assuming he can swim)? And so on and so on. The underlying mental structure we call *purpose* is a kind of mental shorthand which collapses all of these surface behavior forms which do take place in time, encapsulating them in a timeless mental structure in which temporal events exist only as a potentiality.

Collapsing Surface Perceptions—Object

One can argue that an analogous process of time packaging underlies the perception of objects. Consider a table. In the real world—of Newton, or of God—it doubtless exists as a genuine entity whose every parts (legs, tabletop) are simultaneously present in space. But psychologically speaking, our perception of the table is necessarily drawn out in time. Theorists of perception disagree about how this perception is achieved, but, however different their proposals, a reference to temporally extended events is a crucial component of virtually all (Gestalt psychology may be an exception). Thus John Stuart Mill regarded objects as "the permanent possibility of a sensation" (Mill, 1865). Helmholtz described the perception of a table as a compact mental expression of what would reach the eyes if the observer walked around it (Helmholtz, 1866/1962). Gibson emphasized stimulus invariants that necessarily extend over time, such as gradients of motion parallax (Gibson, 1950, 1966), while modern perceptual constructionists such as Hochberg and Neisser regard perceptual figures as a set of anticipations about the visual consequences of eye movements or other explorations (Hochberg, 1970, 1978; Neisser, 1976). In all these accounts, the underlying mental structure—the perception of the object—is a timeless expression of a potentially infinite set of sensory surface forms.

Surface and Deep Structure in Language

The analogy can probably be pursued into language as well. Language utterances are obviously sequential while their mental representation is not. Here again, we are faced with the phenomenon of temporal collapsing and the various issues it poses. As in the perception of objects and purpose, the mental representation of sentence meaning is—among other things—a timeless potentiality for a large number (in principle, an infinite number) of temporally extended utterances.

But in the case of language, several new problems crop up. For language is after all a device for communicating meaning between two sentient persons. To this extent, the transmission of meaning is necessarily different from, say, the perception of objects. Rocks and trees have no particular interest in letting us know of their existence; if we want to perceive them, we must willy-nilly rely on the kind intermediation of temporally extended proximal stimulus events. But why did evolution force us to use an analogous procedure when we try to communicate our meanings to other hearers? Why do we have to go through a cumbersome sequential apparatus in which our meaning is first stretched out in time (as we speak) and is then collapsed again (as our hearers understand)? The answer may be that there was no alternative. Given the limitations of our motor, sensory, and cerebral equipment, and the fact that human languages must convey an infinite set of possible messages with a finite set of means, the only way was to string the message units out in time. A further question arises when we consider the two syntactic organizations of a sentence: surface and underlying structure. Both represent hierarchical organizations that are superimposed upon a sequential arrangement. But why do we need two? Why can the speaker not simply articulate what is, so to speak, at the bottom level of the underlying structure, going from left to right? Would that not save an extra step for both speaker and listener?

There are many answers, some of which depend upon the particular version of modern grammatical theory one subscribes to. For our present purposes, I will adapt an approach (loosely patterned after Chomsky, 1971) which emphasizes the communicative function of the message, a function that is best served by having *both* a surface and an underlying structure. The underlying structure is a marvelously transparent rendering of the propositions that a sentence contains. Take our old standbys

The princess kissed the frog.

The frog was kissed by the princess.

What the princess did was to kiss the frog . . .

These and other amphibian tales all contain the same proposition about princess, kissing, and frog. But the surface structures tell us something else. Among other things, they specify which part of the proposition is in focus. This in turn is related to various presuppositions the speaker entertains about the listener's prior knowledge. If the hearer is already aware that the princess did something but does not know just what, one is likely to say

The princess kissed the frog . . .

If one presupposes that the hearer already knows that something happened to a frog, one is likely to inform him that

The frog was kissed by the princess . . .

To the extent that this is true, the active and passive forms (and many others) are not complete paraphrases. They contain the same underlying proposition, but they also include something else: the conversational focus, which typically indicates the speaker's beliefs about the listener's prior knowledge and conversational interests. Without these, we would prattle on endlessly and be even greater bores than we normally are. To avoid this, we must tell our conversational partners what we presuppose they already know, and this is one of the contributions of the surface form.

This function of language surface structure is again analogous to some phenomena of object perception. For there too, paraphrase is not complete. The size of a given object is perceived to be the same, whether it is far off or nearby. But this does not mean that we see no difference. Of course we do; the object looks further away in one case, and closer by in the other. The partial perceptual paraphrase that occurs (that is, size constancy) has obvious survival value. Our primitive ancestors would have been in considerable trouble if they mistook a saber-tooth tiger in the distance for a pussy-cat close at hand. But size constancy alone is clearly not enough. We have to know the properties of the object itself, but we must know more. We have to know our own relation to it: our distance from it, our orientation, and so on. And this is partially given by the perceptual equivalent of the surface structure—the particular pattern of sensory stimulation in the here-and-now. This too is relevant to survival. It pays to know just how far the saber-tooth tiger actually is so we can take the proper steps in preparation: run away if he is far away and pray if he is nearby.

Metacognition

These comments have been about ways in which we come to know. But we do not just know; we often also know that we know (and even more often, that we do not). This point predates official, scientific psychology by millennia. It is probably implicit in Aristotle's differentiation between memory and recollection; it appears in St. Augustine's contrast between memories that rush forth unbidden and others that have to be dragged out of hiding; it is found in John Locke's description of the two ways of gaining knowledge, empiricial experience and reflection. Our more immediate founding fathers, Wundt and James, were also sensitive to this distinction. Wundt contrasts the influence of past experiences of which one is not aware with those which are recognized as such, where there is an explicit awareness that one is dealing with memory (Wundt, 1918, p. 293). To James, the very term *memory* (or more precisely, secondary memory) is reserved for just those experiences that have this self-conscious, reflective property. As he put it: "[Memory proper] . . . *is the knowledge of an event or fact*, of which meantime we have *not been thinking, with the additional consciousness that we have thought or experienced before* . . ." (James, 1890, I, p. 648). To these fathers and great-great-grandfathers of our discipline, it was evidently clear that there is a psychology of knowing about knowing as well as a psychology of knowing.

That such subtle distinctions were ignored during much of the twentieth century, especially in America, is not surprising. A behaviorist-dominated era that had little patience with the study of knowledge was going to have none at all for the study of knowledge of knowledge. But by now this state of affairs exists no longer. A fair number of investigators have finally chosen to look where Aristotle and James looked before them, asking what people know about their own cognitive operations, what they know about the way they remember, solve problems, deal with language, and so on—a topic that generally goes under the somewhat portentous name of *metacognition*.

Method of Investigation

An explicit definition of metacognition is hard to come by, for it is not always clear where cognition ends and metacognition begins. But for the time being, I sidestep such boundary problems and deal with relatively clear cases. One such is meta-memory, as recently studied by a number of investigators whose primary focus is on developmental issues, Anne Brown, for example, and John Flavell (e.g., Brown, 1978; Flavell, 1978; Flavell & Wellman, 1977). One question concerns the extent to which the subjects know about their own memory. Do they know that a given item is in their memory store even though they cannot recall it at present? Can they assess how likely they are to recover it later on, or how much they would be helped by various prompts? Another question concerns the subject's knowledge (and command) of various strategies for memorizing and retrieving, such as rehearsing, organizing, and the like. To the extent that the subject does use a deliberate strategy (say, appropriate categorizing), we can be sure that there is metamemory as well as memory. The subject evidently anticipates that the present will soon become the past, and makes appropriate provisions to recover it in some future. By doing so, he shows that he knows something about his own mental operations.

A different topic of inquiry concerns metalinguistic abilities. Such abilities have provided the bulk of the data on which modern accounts of grammar rest. Chomsky's transformational accounts, and the variety of revisions and expansions that have followed, were ultimately based on the capacity of adult human speakers to reflect upon their language and give reports on whether sentences are well-formed, to judge and create paraphrases, and to note ambiguities. More recently, these metalinguistic abilities have been studied in their own right, often in a developmental context (e.g., H. Gleitman & L.R. Gleitman, 1979; L. R. Gleitman & H. Gleitman, 1970; L. R. Gleitman, H. Gleitman, & Shipley, 1972).

Some General Findings

What have such investigations taught us? To begin with, they have shown that cognitive and metacognitive achievements are, to some extent at least, separable. A number of examples come from language. Suppose a five- or six-year-old is presented with various sentences and asked "if they are good or if they are silly." Given the sentence

John and Bill is a brother.

one child responded:

Sure, they could be brothers. I know them. They are brothers.

The child's verbal *production* is fine. There is verbal concord in his own answer. But his metalinguistic judgment did not correspond to his linguistic act. His verbal production apparatus evidently knew about subject-verb agreement, but *he* did not (L. R. Gleitman, H. Gleitman, & Shipley, 1972).

Another finding is that metacognitive abilities increase with age and seem to show greater variability in the population than the cognitive capacities which underlie them. This point has been thoroughly documented in metamemory and in what might be called metaproblem-solving. Thus younger children are less able than older ones to predict their own memory span, do a poorer job at memory monitoring, use fewer and less sophisticated memorial strategies if they use any at all, are less competent in formulating problem-solving plans, and so on (e.g., Brown, 1978; Flavell & Wellman, 1977; Markman, 1977). Similar differences have been found in comparisons of normal with retarded populations.

The same general trend holds for metalinguistic skills. Differences between adults and between adults and, say, five-year-old children are relatively small and subtle with respect to their syntactic usage and their phonology. The pattern is very different when we turn to metalinguistic judgments where both populational variability and developmental differences are considerable.

Metacognition Is Easier for Underlying than for Surface Structures

Another finding brings us back to the surface–underlying form distinction with which we began. By and large, metacognition seems to be harder for surface than for underlying forms.

Let us begin with language. A number of investigators have shown that the lower the level of language feature, the harder it is to access metalinguistically. Consider meaning. When asked whether various sentences are "good" or "silly," kindergartners have much less trouble in commenting on matters of meaning and plausibility than in responding to syntactic issues. Take the sentence

The color green frightened George.

One five-year-old rejected this on the grounds that "Green can't stand up and go 'Boo.' " This contrasts with the seven-year-old who said, "Doesn't frighten me but it sounds OK" (L. R. Gleitman, H. Gleitman, & Shipley, 1972).

A similar pattern holds when we consider surface and underlying structure and the *detection of ambiguity*. To get at this relation, we studied children's explanations of jokes that are based on various kinds of language ambiguity. Children from six to twelve were read a number of jokes and were asked to rate each joke's "funniness" and also to explain just what it was that made it funny (Hirsh-Pasek, L. R. Gleitman, & H. Gleitman, 1978). Some jokes—such as they were—turned on ambiguities of surface structure, such as

Where would you go to see a man eating fish?

A sea-food restaurant.

Others hinged on underlying structure ambiguity. An example is

We're going to have my grandmother for Thanksgiving dinner.

You are? Well, we're going to have turkey.

The results showed that the underlying-structure jokes were easier to get and to explain than were those that depended on surface ambiguity.

The greater difficulty of metalinguistic access to surface as opposed to underlying forms is brought out most clearly when we turn to the most surfacey of all surface aspects of language: its sound pattern. Paul Rozin and Lila Gleitman have argued that metalinguistic awareness of this facet of language is enormously difficult to achieve; in their view, this is one of the important obstacles in learning to read an alphabetic script. While five-year-olds can be taught to distinguish between the concepts of sentence and word fairly easily, they find it much harder to distinguish between word, syllable, and sound. They have considerable trouble in segmenting words into syllables, and the greatest difficulty of all in segmenting words or syllables into phonemes (Rozin & Gleitman, 1977).

Related facts concern the difficulty of different reading systems. Logographies, which render meaningful words abstractly are easier to learn than the alphabetic system—a system that, not coincidentally, has been invented only once in human history (Gleitman & Rozin, 1977).

To sum up, there seems to be an orderly progression. The lower—the more surfacey—the level of linguistic representation, the harder it is to cope with metalinguistically.

This is not to say that these lower levels are not processed by the child as he hears or speaks. Of course they are. There is a well-known test of reading-readiness which evidently correlates well with later reading performance. Some children cannot correctly say "same" or "different" when confronted with pairs of words that differ in one phonological segment, such as *bat* versus *cat*. But there is evidence that the children who fail this test respond quite appropriately to sentences such as "Point to the bat" and "Point to the cat." They can hear and they can understand. What they *cannot* do is to make a metalinguistic judgment about a linguistic surface feature (Blank, 1968).

What about cognitive domains other than language? The immediate temptation is to see an analogue to memory, given the general run of the depth of process findings (e.g., Craik & Lockhart, 1972), better recall for underlying syntactic structure than for surface forms (e.g., Sachs, 1967), and similar effects. Even so, I am a bit worried. Do the memory results reflect a metamemory effect (in which case the analogy fits), an effect of memory proper (in which case it does not), or some interaction of the two? It is hard to say.

More directly relevant are metacognitive effects in the two realms which provided the initial parallel to the surface–underlying structure distinction—that is, visual perception and goal-directed behavior. There have been relatively few modern studies on metacognition in these areas (though some exciting beginnings are now being made by Flavell and his associates, e.g., Flavell, Shipstead, & Croft, 1978).

But I believe that we have a great deal of informal evidence that here too metacognitive awareness is easier for underlying than for surface forms. This is clearly so for visual perception. Most of us are conscious only of its end-product and content ourselves with reports of seeing the various objects of the visual world. Unless of course we are painters, especially Renaissance painters. In that case, we may well be masters of visual surface structure and be able to report—by brush, if not by mouth—on all manners of delicate, proximal-stimulus-related detail. Similarly for the perception of behavior. On watching a Monday-night football game, most of us are only aware that, say, the middle linebacker plunked himself on top of the opposing quarterback. We see the intention and its fulfillment, the behavioral underlying structure. The coaches—not to speak of Howard Cosell—can do more. They are exquisitely aware of many specific details of the linebacker's actual movements. They (and the player himself) note the surface as well as the underlying structure.

Further support for this general contention comes from the work of the men who provide the occasion for this centennial. For Wundt and his students may well be regarded as the first official students of metacognition. Consider Titchener. He and his students found that it was murderously difficult to focus on mental surface forms. It was too easy to fall into what Titchener called the *stimulus-error*. In studies of perception, this so-called "error" was to describe the stimulus (that is, the *object*) that produced the sensation rather than the sensation itself. In studies of thinking, it was to describe the *meaning* of the thought rather than such surface contents as images and feelings (Titchener, 1909).

An example is a Cornell study on touch blends in which subjects had to analyze the feeling of "clammy." They were blindfolded, required to touch a bunch of live oysters, and asked to describe their mental experience. After much urging and reinstructing, they finally came up with an acceptable catalogue of surface mental contents, such as "cold," "wet," "soft," "yielding to pressure," and "unpleasant imagery" (Zigler, 1923). It would have been much easier to give in to the stimulus error and describe the object as "a bunch of oysters," and one's own intention, "I'd like to get out of here."

Whether Titchener and Wundt were successful in their attempts to describe certain aspects of mental surface structures is debatable. But what is not debatable, and what they themselves would certainly have conceded, is that such surface metacognition (assuming it exists) is very much more difficult to describe than the metacognition of underlying structure forms.

What accounts for this pattern of relationships? What I have to say is probably just a restatement. Cognitive processes are generally directed toward some ends. If asked to reflect on one's cognitions, it is easier to describe these end-states (the perceived object or meaning or goal) than to describe the steps by which these ends are reached. This may be because we can only access our own mental operations through the time-collapsed mental packagings which these end-states represent. Or perhaps metacognition is a by-product of a set of internal monitoring systems (of a kind envisaged by, among others, Marshall & Morton, 1978) which somehow check on whether goals are reached, whether sentences make sense, and whether perceptual anticipations are met.

Given how little we know about cognition, it is hardly surprising that we know even less about metacognition. But at least we know that there is a distinction between the two. This distinction may very well help us to resolve some past debates, including some about consciousness. What Titchener called consciousness is a kind of metacognition of mental surface structures, which is hard if not impossible to attain. What Gestalt psychologists called consciousness might be regarded as metacognition of underlying structures. Perhaps we can take an even wilder step and suggest that what Freud called unconsciousness might be most usefully reinterpreted as a form of meta-noncognition, in which the patient ends up *not* knowing that he knows.

I have tried to sketch a few themes that characterize cognition as we have thought about it during the one hundred years since Wundt. I do not know whether we have progressed that much beyond him. Our techniques are more sophisticated, and there are many more of us, so we can inundate each other in a mass of facts. But much of what we now do and think was already implicit in Wundt, and in other nineteenth century figures. We could do worse than to go back for an occasional glance at our intellectual origins, if only to have a sense of what posterity will do for us one hundred years from now at Wundt's *bicentennial*, when some future Major General Stanley acquires *our* portraits.

REFERENCES

Bever, T. G. The cognitive basis for linguistic structures. In J. R. Hayes (Ed.), *Cognition and the development of language*. New York: Wiley, 1970.

Blank, M. Cognitive processes in auditory discrimination in normal and retarded readers. *Child Development*, 1968, 39, 1091–1101.

Blumenthal, A. L. *Language and psychology: Historical aspects of psycholinguistics*. New York: Wiley, 1970.

Blumenthal, A. L. A reappraisal of Wilhelm Wundt. *American Psychologist*, 1975, 30, 1081–1088.

Brown, A. L. Knowing when, where and how to remember: A problem of meta-cognition. In R. Glaser (Ed.), *Advances in instructional psychology*. New York: Halstead Press, 1978.

Chomsky, N. Deep structure, surface structure, and semantic interpretation. In D. Steinberg & L. A. Jabobovits (Eds.), *Semantics*. London: Cambridge University Press, 1971.

Craik, F. I. M., & Lockhart, R. S. Levels of processing: A framework for memory research. *Journal of Verbal Learning and Verbal Behavior*, 1972, 11, 671–684.

Flavell, J. H. Meta-cognitive development. In J. M. Scandura & C. J. Brainerd (Eds.), *Structural/process theories of complex human behavior*. Alphen a.d. Rijn, The Netherlands: Sijthoff and Nordhoff, 1978.

Flavell, J. H., Shipstead, S. G., & Croft, K. Young children's knowledge about visual perception: Hiding objects from others. *Child Development*, 1978, 49, 1208–1211.

Flavell, J. H., & Wellman, H. M. Meta-memory. In R. V. Kail & J. W. Hagen (Eds.), *Perspectives on the development of memory and cognition*. Hillsdale, N.J.: Erlbaum, 1977.

Fodor, J. A., Bever, T. G., & Garrett, M. F. *The psychology of language.* New York: McGraw-Hill, 1974.

Gibson, J. J. *The perception of the visual world.* New York: Houghton Mifflin, 1950.

Gibson, J. J. *The senses considered as perceptual systems.* New York: Houghton Mifflin, 1966.

Gleitman, H., & Gleitman, L. R. Language use and language judgement. In C. J. Fillmore, D. Kempler, & W. S-Y. Wang (Eds.), *Individual differences in language ability and language behavior.* New York: Academic Press, 1979.

Gleitman, L. R., & Gleitman, H. *Phrase and paraphrase.* New York: Norton, 1970.

Gleitman, L. R., Gleitman, H., & Shipley, E. The emergence of the child as a grammarian. *Cognition,* 1972, *1,* 137–164.

Gleitman, L. R., & Rozin, P. The structure and acquisition of reading I: Relations between orthographies and the structure of language. In A. S. Reber & D. Scarborough (Eds.), *Toward a psychology of reading.* Hillsdale, N.J.: Erlbaum, 1977.

Hall, G. S. In memory of Wilhelm Wundt: By his American students. *Psychological Review,* 1921, *28,* 154–155.

Heidbreder, E. *Seven psychologies.* New York: Appleton-Century-Crofts, 1933.

Helmholtz, H. von. *Treatise on physiological optics* (Vol. 2) (J. P. C. Southall, Ed. and trans. from 3d ed., 1909). New York: Dover Press, 1962. (Originally published, 1866.)

Hirsh-Pasek, K., Gleitman, L. R., & Gleitman, H. What did the brain say to the mind? In A. Sinclair, R. Jarvella, & W. J. M. Levelt (Eds.), *The child's conception of language.* New York: Springer-Verlag, 1978.

Hochberg, J. E. Attention, organization and consciousness. In D. I. Mostofsky (Ed.), *Attention: Contemporary theory and analysis.* New York: Appleton-Century-Crofts, 1970.

Hochberg, J. E. *Perception* (2d ed.). Englewood Cliffs, N.J.: Prentice-Hall, 1978.

James, H. (Ed.). *The letters of William James* (2 vols.). Boston: Atlantic Monthly Press, 1920.

James, W. *The principles of psychology* (2 vols.). New York: Holt, 1890.

Koffka, K. *Gestalt psychology.* New York: Harcourt, Brace, 1935.

Markman, E. M. Realizing that you don't understand: A preliminary investigation. *Child Development,* 1977, *48,* 986–992.

Marshall, J. C., & Morton, J. On the mechanics of Emma. In A. Sinclair, R. J. Jarvella, & W. J. M. Levelt (Eds.), *The child's conception of language.* New York: Springer-Verlag, 1978.

Mill, J. S. *An examination of Sir William Hamilton's philosophy.* London: Longman, Green, Longman, Roberts and Green, 1865.

Neisser, U. *Cognition and reality.* San Francisco: Freeman, 1976.

Rozin, P., & Gleitman, L. R. The structure and acquisition of reading II: The reading process and the acquisition of the alphabetic principle. In A. S. Reber & D. Scarborough (Eds.), *Toward a psychology of reading.* Hillsdale, N.J.: Erlbaum, 1977.

Sachs, J. S. Recognition memory for syntactic and semantic aspects of connected discourse. *Perception and Psychophysics,* 1967, *2,* 437–442.

Schank, R., & Abelson, R. *Scripts, plans, goals and understanding.* Hillsdale, N.J.: Erlbaum, 1977.

Titchener, E. B. *An outline of psychology.* New York: Macmillan, 1896.

Titchener, E. B. *Lectures on the experimental psychology of the thought processes.* New York: Macmillan, 1909.

Tolman, E. C. *Purposive behavior in animals and men.* New York: Century, 1932.

Woodworth, R. S. *Experimental psychology.* New York: Holt, 1938.

Wundt, W. *Völkerpsychologie* (Vol. 1). Leipzig: Verlag von Wilhelm Engelmann, 1900.

Wundt, W. *Grundriss der Psychologie* (13th ed.). Leipzig: Alfred Kröner Verlag, 1918.

Zigler, M. J. An experimental study of the perception of clamminess. *American Journal of Psychology,* 1923, *34,* 550–561.

8 Language Use and Language Judgment

Henry Gleitman
University of Pennsylvania

Lila Gleitman
University of Pennsylvania

During the past two decades, linguists in the tradition of generative grammar have made systematic use of their own "intuitions" as sources of data for understanding language organization. The term *intuition* refers to the basis for judgmental performances, in the terminology of these linguists. The judgments are usually restricted to a few topics: grammaticality, ambiguity, relatedness of sentences in form and meaning, and the like. The theories that are developed within generative grammar are, in the main, explanatory accounts of the structure of these judgments. This methodology is a familiar one in psychological studies, being in essence very little different from, say, judgments of brightness, hue, and saturation that are made in the color-vision laboratory. However, recently there have been a number of attacks on this method for studying language.

Sometimes the objections have come from within the cloisters of the grammarians themselves, and these are usually to the effect that the method lacks generality in one way or another, over the linguistic domain. After all, while it is plausible that all normally sighted men see alike and hence the visual judgments of one man are just like those of another, it is plain that all men do not speak alike. Thus some linguists have come face to face with the problem that their own judgmental performances do not accord too well with the judgments of the nonlinguist-in-the-street, even though he putatively speaks the "same" language. In fact, they sometimes even fail to dovetail with judgments from other linguists who are equally imbued with intuitive convictions (Ross, this volume; see also Gleitman and Gleitman, 1970). Another objection to the generality of theories based on intuition-derived judgments comes from the finding that these do not accord closely with data derived from naturalistic observation of speech; this result is sometimes said to show that the data source is biased and cannot be used to study human language *use* (Labov, this volume).

A different kind of attack on the intuitional approach has come mainly from psychologists studying nonjudgmental language tasks. Some objections center on the failure of derivational theories (such as that put forward by Brown and Hanlon, 1970) to organize tightly the naturalistic findings in language learning (Bever, 1970). Others concern the failure of these theories to account for the facts about language computations in real time, (for discussion, see Fodor and Garrett, 1966; Fodor, Bever, and Garrett, 1974).

In some quarters, the reaction to these complications has been to abandon all hope for learning about the mental organization of language by studying the structure of judgments. We have only to dig 30 or 40 years back into the history of language study to find that this scenario has been played out before. Surely the Bloomfieldian revolution was, in part, an attempt to get away from the enigmas of judgments and back to the "real" data of language: utterances said and heard by ordinary people (a group that clearly excludes academic linguists). Left to the social bigot were questions of "right" or "wrong" instances of language behavior. As E. A. Nida put it:

> If any judgments are to be passed upon the acceptability or so called correctness of some usage, these are left to the anthropologist and sociologist for an objective statement of the factors in the society which make certain persons more socially prominent and hence make their speech more acceptable, or to the man on the street, who is thoroughly accustomed to forming judgments upon the basis of his own egocentric attitudes and limited knowledge [Nida, 1949, p. 2].

In effect, many of the empiricists of a few decades ago evidently believed that no nonarbitrary formulation of notions of well-formedness, etc., were to be found, outside dialectology. Leonard Bloomfield more or less shared this view:

> The discrimination of elegant or "correct" speech is a byproduct of certain social conditions. The linguist has to observe it as he observes other linguistic phenomena, [but] this is only one of the problems of linguistics and, since it is not a fundamental one, it can be attacked only after many other things are known [Bloomfield, 1933, p. 22].

These voices from the past are reminiscent of recent comment to the effect that grammars constructed on judgmental bases are not psychologically "real"; are remote byways in the study of language; in short, are obscurantist and restrictive sources for a psychologically relevant study of language.

We do not agree that judgmental performances can be swept aside so easily in the search for an account of human language organization. The mental events that yield judgments are as relevant to the psychology of language, perhaps, as speech events themselves, even though the patterns of these two kinds of psychological response are demonstrably different. In any event, the burden of proof is on anyone who denies the psychological reality of linguistic judgments to explain their orderliness. In our view, the disparities between speech and comprehension on the one hand, and judgments on the other, require study and explication.

Accordingly, we have conducted a number of investigations into the ability of humans to give judgments about language, and compared these findings against individuals' abilities to use language in conversational exchange. Indeed, we too find differences in people's abilities to perform these two kinds of feat, differences that have to do with the ages and capacities of the subjects, and differences that have to do with the structure of the tasks that are put to them. But we do not consider such outcomes to be cause for dismay.

It always turns out that giving language judgments—retrieving and making use of one's intuitions—is relatively hard, compared to talking and understanding. Thus it is not surprising that we find extensive individual and population differences in performance on the harder judgmental tasks, compared to lesser differences in talking and understanding. We believe this is because judgmental performances require a higher order of self-consciousness than do speech performances. To give a language judgment, one must take a prior cognitive process (linguistic performance) as the object of a yet higher-order cognitive process (reflection about language performance or, as we have called it, *metalinguistic* performance) which may have properties of its own.

It is interesting that difficulties in forming judgments differ within the individual subject, depending on the level of language representation he must access for the task given to him. The *lower* the level of the language feature that must be attended to and focused on in any language-like task, the more difficult the task and the more variable the performance; also, the lower the level of the language feature that must be attended to, the later in development a child is able to perform the task. Meanings are easier to access for the sake of making judgments than syntactic forms, and syntax easier than phonology. Stated another way, it is hard to access language information in relatively raw, partly processed forms, and easier to access fully processed language (i.e., the information at the stage of processing when it has been meaningfully interpreted).

We believe these facts about people's performances in laboratory situations are relevant to a number of more interesting facts about their language use in everyday life; for example, their differing responsiveness to language embroidery in certain kinds of poetry and wit; and their differing likelihood of grasping the ideas behind phonographies (i.e., their ability to acquire alphabetic reading).

In the sections to follow, the structure of our findings on these topics is summarized. However, we do not believe we have unraveled, at anything like the required level of specificity, the sources of differential human behavior in the language domains we have looked at. We put forward this summary of interim outcomes for the purpose that they may invite further inquiry in related terms.

1. POPULATION DIFFERENCES IN METALINGUISTIC PERFORMANCE, IN THE PRESENCE OF RELATIVELY INVARIANT LINGUISTIC PERFORMANCE

It is obvious that there are large differences among normal adults, and between adults and children, with respect to the meaningful content of their speech. But differences among adults, and between adults and children, are smaller and more subtle with respect to their syntactic usage and their phonology. Even many retarded individuals and most 4-year-old normals achieve adequate syntactic form in their speech (Lenneberg, 1967) but they are not usually profound in what they say. These facts contrast with those for judgment-giving. At least for certain kinds of materials, we have found striking similarities across adults in the ability to think about and comment on semantic novelty in language, but enormous differences in the ability to think about and comment on surface syntactic novelty. In Section 1.1, we describe such outcomes in the context of paraphrasing tasks. The same principles describe the outcomes of classification tasks and ambiguity-detection tasks performed by younger and older children, described in Section 1.2. Finally, the same principles describe aspects of children's differing success in tasks related to the acquisition of alphabetic reading (Section 1.3).

1.1. Variation in Paraphrasing Skills among Adults

Gleitman and Gleitman (1970) and Geer, Gleitman, and Gleitman (1972) studied the abilities of adults to produce and recognize paraphrases of novel nominal sequences (compound nouns). The stimuli in the experiments generally consisted of sequences of three simple words. Two of the words were fixed nouns such as *bird* and *house*. The third word was another noun (such as *foot*) or a verb or adjective (such as *kill* or *black*); of course some of these words had alternate categorial status (e.g., *kill* can be used nominally). The three-word sequences were taped and presented orally, with either of two stress patterns (132 or 213 stress) that are common for compound nouns. As the words were combined in various orders, this procedure yielded some simple nominal phrases such as *black bird-house* and *black-bird house*, but it also yielded some sequences that are harder to interpret, such as *bird house-black* and *bird-black house*. After suitable instructions, subjects were asked to produce or recognize phrasal paraphrases of these sequences. That is, the subject is being asked to realize that a *black-bird house* is a *house for black-birds* or a *house where birds who are black live*.[1]

The task is, we believe, a relatively natural and transparent one with which to inquire whether people can think about the relatedness among sentences. Everybody has been asked, from time to time, to say something "in his own words." Thus it seems an easy matter, when asked for another phrase meaning the same as *black bird-house*, to respond "That's a bird-house painted black." Surely this is easy enough to do in the context of real conversation. Upon seeing a black bird-house, even for the first time, presumably an adult can say "Look: there's a black bird-house." No normal English-speaking adult would, we presume, say instead "Look! there's a bird-house black!"

Yet we found massive differences between two educational groups (clerical workers and Ph.D. candidates) in the ability to perform a variety of tasks related to paraphrasing compounds of this kind. On many occasions, the clerical workers *would* maintain that *bird-house black* was

---

[1] A question immediately arises whether subjects can discriminate among the stress patterns of contextless compounds. It is well known that the stress effects are subtle, and are often ignored depending on the context in which the phrase is used (Bolinger and Gerstman, 1957). The question here is what the subject will do if there is no biasing context to guide him: Can he retrieve a meaning for these sequences guided solely by the meanings of the words and the rule-governed clues of stress and serial order? In this series of experiments, a number of precautions were taken so as to make the results interpretable. First, the stimuli were submitted to judges who had to determine the stress patterns, until a completely reliable tape of the stimuli was achieved. Second, subjects' responses were submitted to internal analysis to see whether, in general, they responded to "easy" instances in terms of the stress and order patterns. That is, if the subject responded identically to *black bird-house* and *black-bird house*, he was thrown out of the subject pool, because if he did this it was possible he simply did not understand the instruction in the experiment. Finally, in some versions of the experiment, the subject was asked to repeat the stimulus item after paraphrasing it. If the subject misrepeated the stimulus with any frequency he was removed from the subject pool (or, in one analysis his data were analyzed in terms of this problem, for it may have reflected a relevant memorial difficulty that could account for some of the population differences we found; see Geer, Gleitman, and Gleitman, 1972).

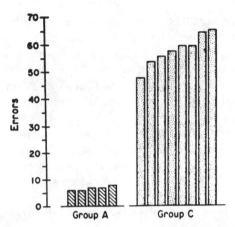

Figure 6.1.   Forced-choice performance on a paraphrasing task by Ph.D. candidates (Group A) and clerical workers (Group C).

There were 144 stimulus items. As the Figure shows, the eight clerical workers in this version of the task came close to being wrong on half of them. That is, superficially, the performance of this group seems to be at chance levels. However, internal analyses of these results and those from a variety of other paraphrase tests reveals that both groups of subjects were highly systematic in their response styles, only they were different. Since scoring of "right" or "wrong" was in terms of syntactic, rather than semantic, analysis of the stimuli, the clerical group makes more of what we called "errors," but their performance was orderly nevertheless. Scoring in terms of plausibility or meaningfulness would approximately reverse the number of errors between the groups; that is, the *differences* between the groups in paraphrasing performance would be maintained. [From Gleitman, L. R., and Gleitman, H., *Phrase and paraphrase*, © 1970, W. W. Norton, New York, p. 133.]

another way of saying *black bird-house*, contrary to what we believe their speech performance would be like. In fact, on a variety of paraphrasing tasks (even with simpler two-word compounds) there was no overlap at all in performance scores for members of the clerical and Ph.D. candidate groups. Figure 6.1 shows these population effects for a forced-choice task which required subjects to identify the correct paraphrases, from two choices, for three-word compound nouns.[2]

A closer look at the findings reveals that the group differences were larger or smaller depending on the particular oddity in the stimulus

---

[2]It is of some interest that we could find no simple means to teach the clerical group to perform as the Ph.D. group performed. For instance, clerical workers listened to the stimuli over and over again, with feed-back as to correct choices and a financial reward for each correct choice made. Finally, their performance for a list of 72 stimuli came close to that of the uninstructed Ph.D. group. Then both groups were given a new, but closely equivalent, list of stimulus phrases from which to choose. Now the disparities in performance for the two groups appeared again, and in the same measure. Thus there is no easy way around the fact that these populations differed in their approach to paraphrasing.

phrase: The group differences were largely attributable to syntactic, not semantic, problems posed by the novel compound nouns. Thus the two groups paraphrased more or less equivalently such semantic oddities as *house foot-bird* ("a bird with large feet who lives in houses," or "a live-in livery-bird"). On the contrary, only the most educated group handled perceived syntactic oddity by changing the categorial assignments of words (e.g., *bird house-black* was paraphrased by an educated subject as "a blackener of houses who is a bird" and *eat house-bird* as "a house-bird who is very eat"). The response style of the clerical group was quite different. These subjects approached syntactic oddities by ignoring, rather than manipulating, their syntactic properties. *Bird house-black* was typically paraphrased by this group as "a black bird who lives in the house"; *eat house-bird* was paraphrased as "everybody is eating up their pet birds." In short, when taxed, the average group focused on meaning and plausibility, while the highly educated group focused on the syntax even when meaningfulness was thereby obscured (as in the response "a house-bird who is very eat").

Notice that the syntactic oddities in these materials posed greater problems than the semantic oddities for both groups; but also that the between-group differences were much greater for the syntactic oddities than for the semantic oddities. Manipulation and puzzle solving with low-level syntactic features seem to be attributes of linguistically talented people. This difference is apparent even in so far as one can show that the syntactic structures in question are handled adequately, in the context of normal speech and comprehension, by both populations.

Consider as an example Table 6.1 which lists the free paraphrases of both educational groups for the item *house-bird glass*. We can assume that every speaker of English, approximately, knows how to use *glass* both adjectivally (*a glass house*) and nominally (*a piece of glass; a glass to drink from*). Yet the less-educated subjects often interpreted *house-bird glass* as *glass house-bird*, a *house-bird made of glass*, or even as *glass bird-house*. Why not *glass used to make a house-bird* or *the glass used by the house-bird*, solutions which simultaneously resolve the semantic and syntactic properties of the stimulus item? (Notice particularly that there are no clear differences of semantic oddity for the two response types: Anyone who can conceive of and believe in a glass house-bird ought to be able to conceive of and believe in the glass which is used to manufacture such house-birds). But even in a forced-choice situation, when both options were displayed, the clerical group preferred the inversion still. The structure of these findings suggests that only the most-educated group will consider least-common categorial assignments for the component words of the stimuli (i.e., *glass* as noun rather than adjective) in this situation.

In short, the clearest difference between these populations is in *focusing*

TABLE 6.1

Responses of Two Populations to the Task of Paraphrasing the Orally Presented Novel Compound, *house-bird glass*[a,b,c]

Responses of Seven Ph.D. Candidates .
1. glass for making house-birds
2. a very small drinking cup used by a canary
3. glass for house-birds
4. glass for house-birds
5. *a way of describing thickness of glass—glass as thick as (or in the shape of) glass of a bird-house
6. glass that protects house-birds
7. the glass that is produced by birds around the house

Responses of Seven Clerical Workers
1. *a glass house-bird
2. *house-bird that's in a glass
3. a drinking glass or a cup made out of glass of a bird in a house
4. *a bird that is made of glass
5. *a special glass to use in a bird's house
6. *a house-bird made from glass
7. *a glass house-bird

" From Gleitman and Gleitman (1970).

[b] Hyphenation in the cited form represents the internal subcompound (i.e., the stress on this whole compound noun is 132).

[c] An asterisk marks the responses that fail to take into account the fact that the last word in such compounds is the head noun and thus must be the first (leftmost) noun in a paraphrase (a relative clause or prepositional phrase) that mirrors its syntactic and semantic properties. Thus the head noun of this compound is *glass*. For the internal sub-compound (*house-bird*), the same principle should apply: The rightmost noun (*bird*) in the compound is its head, and thus should appear in the leftmost position of a relative clause or prepositional phrase paraphrase of it. One Ph.D. candidate, but six clerical workers, err in applying this principle consistently, for this example. Similar performance disparities were observed for 144 similar stimuli, as well as in simplified (two-word) versions of them, and under a variety of task conditions.

on the syntactic issues, accessing and manipulating language knowledge in a noncommunicative setting. Clearly this does not imply that adults are all equal in their ability to analyze complicated meanings in everyday life. But across a range broad enough to be of considerable psychological interest, all normal individuals can realize consciously that some expressions within their semantic compass (however limited this may be) are meaningless or odd in meaning. Everyone realizes that there is something peculiar about the sentence *George frightened the color green* and can "fix it up" via some semantic change. But not everyone can focus on a syntactic anomaly and perform an appropriate syntactic manipulation to repair it, even if they are in productive control of the construction during ongoing conversational exchange. In this sense, meaning can be brought to conscious attention more readily than can syntactic form. Apparently, descending to phonological levels, the facts are similar. Jotto, Scrabble, anagrams, and cryptograms—all in part phonological puzzles—require skills that are probably unequally distributed in the population. One might conclude that puns are not the lowest form of humor after all.

The findings just presented seem to fit naturally with many experimental demonstrations that it is easier to remember and report on global semantic properties of heard or seen language than on its lower-level features. For example, Sachs (1967) and Fillenbaum (1966) demonstrated that subjects store the gist of connected discourse over indefinite periods of time but quickly lose hold of its exact syntactic form; Bransford and Franks (1971) in a quite different experimental setting showed essentially the same thing: When matters get complicated or time passes, linguistic stimuli are unavailable for verbatim report but the semantic facts remain. Reason dictates that phonological and syntactic analysis are implicated in the recovery of meaning from speech, but apparently these relatively early or "raw" stages of linguistic processing decay fairly quickly; perhaps this is why they are comparatively unavailable to reflection. Such familiar reading phenomena as the "eye–voice span" (Levin and Kaplan, 1970) and the word-superiority effect (e.g., Baron, in press) are probably subject to similar interpretation (for discussion, see Rozin and Gleitman, 1977).

1.2 Variations in Metalinguistic Performance as a Function of Developmental Level

The difficulty and variability of adult judgments about syntactic and phonological properties of their language are reflected in some aspects of development. Shatz (1972) and Gleitman, Gleitman, and Shipley (1972) asked children to detect and comment about anomalous sentences. The instructions were deliberately vague: "Tell me if these sentences are good or if they are silly." They found that children of 5 years typically were able to recognize and comment on matters of meaning and plausibility of the stimulus sentences. For example *The men wait for the bus* was rejected by some 5-year-old suburbanites on grounds that only children wait for busses. *The color green frightens George* was rejected on grounds that "green can't stand up and go 'Boo!'" But violations of syntax that scarcely affected meaningfulness went unnoticed by these kindergartners (examples are *Claire and Eleanor is a sister; Morning makes the sun to shine*), even though these children did not make such errors in their own spontaneous speech.

On the contrary, 7-year-olds usually accepted semantically odd or implausible sentences as "good" and "not silly." For example, a subject responded to *The color green frightens George* by saying "Doesn't frighten me, but it sounds OK." But these same subjects rejected meaningful but syntactically anomalous sentences. For example, in response to *Claire and Eleanor is a sister*, a 7-year-old commented "You can't use *is* there: Claire and Eleanor *are* sisters." Sometimes these verbally talented 7-year-olds, like the highly educated adults described earlier, manipulated the categorial content of anomalous sentences in considering their acceptability. As an example, in response to *Boy is at the door*, a subject said "If his name is *Boy*. You should—the kid is named *John*, see? *John* is at the door or *A* boy is at the door or *The* boy is at the door or *He's* knocking at the door." Table 6.2 shows how these subjects' judgments accorded with adults' judgments, for all the stimulus sentences in the investigation.

Overall, these findings suggest that the surface structure anomaly is harder for the kindergartner to spot than the meaning anomaly, while the syntactic anomaly becomes more salient to the 7-year-old in response to vague instructions about "good" and "silly" sentences.

We achieved essentially the same result in a task that requires the detection and report of ambiguity. Forty-eight children, ranging from 6 to 11 years, were asked to explicate verbal jokes, presented orally. Ambiguities that turned on word-meaning (e.g., the two interpretations of *bank*) or underlying structure (e.g., *Would you join me in a bowl of soup?*) were easiest for all age groups, and accessible even to the youngest subjects. But phonological deformations and segmentation ambiguities (e.g., *You ate 10 pancakes? How waffle!*) and surface-structure ambiguities (e.g., *Where would you go to see a man eating fish?*) were hardest for all age-groups, and almost uniformly inaccessible to the younger subjects (Hirsh-Pasek, Gleitman, and Gleitman, 1978). Similar findings have been reported by others (Fowles and Glanz, 1977; Kessel, 1970), though some investigators of similar issues (e.g., Shultz and Pilon, 1973) have classified the linguistic stimuli somewhat differently, and consequently interpret the developmental sequence differently also.

Summarizing, differences in the levels of linguistic analysis accessible to reflection at various ages contrast with the facts of speech acquisition: Children learn to *speak* with adequate syntactic form well before they express very complex thoughts, but they come to *notice* oddities of thought (that are within their compass) before oddities of syntax and phonology, even for instances where they have productive control. Many findings in the literature dovetail with our own on this topic. Children of age 5 can be taught the difference between the concepts "word" and "sentence" with little difficulty, but it is hard for them to distinguish among such concepts as "word," "syllable," and "sound" (Downing and Oliver, 1973). Children of ages 5 and 6 have some mild difficulty segmenting speech into words (Holden and MacGinitie, 1972) often failing to isolate connectives and

TABLE 6.2
Conformance of Children's Judgments of Grammaticality to Those of Adults[a,b]

Example sentences	Adult judgment	Subjects' ages in years						
		5	5	6	7	7	7	8
1. *John and Mary went home.*	wf	+	+	+	+	+	+	+
2. *John went home and Mary went home.*	wf	+	+	+	+	+	+	+
3. *Two and two are four.*	wf	+	+	+	+	+	+	+
4. *Claire and Eleanor is a sister.*	d	−	−	+	+	+	+	+
5. *My sister plays golf.*	wf	+	+	+	+	+	+	+
6. *Golf plays my sister.*	d	+	+	+	+	+	+	+
7. *Boy is at the door.*	d	+	+	+	+	+	+	+
8. *I saw the queen and you saw one.*	d	−	−	−	−	+	+	+
9. *I saw Mrs. Jones and you saw one.*	d	+	+	+	+	+	+	+
10. *Be good!*	wf	+	+	+	+	+	−	+
11. *Know the answer!*	d	−	−	−	+	−	+	+
12. *I am eating dinner.*	wf	+	−	+	+	+	+	+
13. *I am knowing your sister.*	d	−	−	−	+	+	+	+
14. *I doubt that any snow will fall today.*	wf	+	−	+	+	+	−	+
15. *I think that any snow will fall today.*	d	−	−	+	+	+	+	+
16. *Claire loves Claire.*	wf/d							
17. *I do too.*	wf	+	−	+	−	+	+	+
18. *The color green frightens George.*	wf	−	+	+	−	−	+	−
19. *George frightens the color green.*	d	+	+	+	+	+	+	+
Total "+" judgments for all sentences		12	10	15	15	16	17	17

[a] Adapted from Gleitman, L. R., Gleitman, H., and Shipley, E. The emergence of the child as grammarian, *Cognition*, 1972, 1(2/3), 137–152.

[b] Children were asked to judge a list of orally presented sentences as "good" or "silly," and these judgments were compared to those of adults. The adult judgments were provided by three independent judges who indicated whether each sentence was well-formed (wf) or deviant (d). The children's judgments are marked "+" if they agree with those of the adult and "−" if they do not, regardless of their explanations. Sentence 16 cannot be scored in this manner; whether or not it is deviant depends upon whether the same referent is assumed for both nouns. The names in Sentences 4 and 9 were chosen to be familiar; in Sentence 16 the child's own name was used.

determiners as separate words. They have greater difficulty in segmenting words into syllables (Rosner, 1974; Liberman *et al.*, 1974). And they have the greatest difficulty of all in segmenting words or syllables into phonemes (Elkonen, 1973; Rosner and Simon, 1971; Gleitman and Rozin, 1973a). In sum, the lower the level of linguistic representation called for, the more difficult it is for young children to respond to noncommunicative linguistic activities in these terms. We have claimed (Rozin and Gleitman, 1977) that a major cognitive problem in reading can be viewed as a subpart of this more general problem of "metalinguistic" awareness, where large individual differences coexist with identical tacit linguistic knowledge. Some evidence for this claim follows.

1.3 Learning to Read Is Harder Than Learning to Talk

One of the most striking examples of individual difference in language-like behavior is the acquisition of alphabetic reading. While a few individuals learn to read almost overnight and without instruction (Read, 1971), most require a substantial period of training, and a significant number fail to attain literacy even after years in school. The success and scope of reading acquisition varies as a function of intelligence (Singer, 1974; Thorndike, 1971), motivational and cultural factors (Downing, 1973), and internal differences in the nature of the writing system that is to be acquired (Gleitman and Rozin, 1973a; Rozin and Gleitman, 1977). This individual variation exceeds by orders of magnitude the differences that are observed in the acquisition of speech and comprehension of a first language.

Adequate speech is acquired over broad ranges of general intelligence; for example, spoken language of a character similar to that of normals emerges even among retardates, although progress is slower (Lenneberg, 1967; Lackner, 1976; Morehead and Ingram, 1976). Furthermore, despite many differences in cultural ambiance and differences in the languages that are being learned, normal children seem to pass through similar sequences of developmental accomplishments within the same narrow time-frame (Brown, 1973; Lenneberg, 1967; Slobin, 1973; 1975). Moreover, spoken language seems to emerge more or less equivalently under a variety of input content and presentation conditions; in both character and rate, language learning is remarkably insensitive to differences in the speech styles of caretakers (Newport, Gleitman, and Gleitman, 1977). Successful language-like communicative means are achieved even by children radically deprived of linguistic input (Herodotus, 460 B.C.; Feldman, Goldin-Meadow, and Gleitman, 1978). Finally, the spoken-language skills are resilient in early life, often surviving damage to the speech centers of the brain and to the speech apparatus (Lenneberg, 1967).

Summarizing, there are substantial differences among individuals both in acquisitional rate and in eventual level of attainment for written language, even though formal and specific training is usually available to the learner. In contrast, the similarities in rate and character of spoken language acquisition are striking, even though the conditions for acquisition are here variable and diffuse.

What account can be given for the fact that what appears to be the more general and complex task (learning to speak and understand) is less difficult and less variable than what appears to be a trivial derivative of this (learning to write and read a script based on a known spoken language by a learner who is certainly older and possibly wiser)? Clearly, the difference has only indirectly to do with the visual modality itself. Manual–visual languages seem to be acquired in much the same way as spoken languages, by deaf children reared by signing parents (Newport and Ashbrook, 1977).

We believe that the major problem in learning to read has to do with the cognitive prerequisites to understanding alphabetic systems in particular: Properties of these orthographies require their users to become aware of and to focus attention on language in relatively raw or superficial representations, approximately at the level where *tap*, *apt*, and *pat* have the same components, only rearranged. Failure to achieve this fundamental insight about the nature of alphabets characterizes an overwhelming majority of individuals who do not achieve literacy (Firth, 1972; Liberman *et al.*, 1977; Calfee, Lindamood, and Lindamood, 1973). Thus the same approach that characterized our approach to the paraphrasing, ambiguity, and classification tasks seems useful in understanding the task of reading acquisition as well.

The aspiring reader is asked to reflect about language, and so to acquiesce in a number of judgments that make sense of alphabetic notation. The teacher asks him to realize that *pit* and *pat* start with "the same sound," that *pit* starts with what *tip* ends with, and that *pit* is decomposable into "p," "i," and "t." Such units are analyzed for spoken language acquisition without awareness, in terms of an evolutionarily old and highly evolved mental circuitry (for discussion in this evolutionary context, see Rozin, 1976); no conscious awareness or judgments are required. Prior evidence has been given that tasks that require judgments will pose greater difficulty than tasks that do not require judgments. Furthermore, we also have presented evidence that conscious recognition and awareness are especially hard to come by when the focus must be on molecular, rather than more molar, language representations. Taken together, these positions predict that learning to read should be harder and more variable than learning to talk, a fact we have just documented; furthermore, they predict that learning to read a script organized around word-meanings (a logography) should be easier than learning to read a script organized around phonology (a syllabary or alphabet), a claim which we document below (based on Gleitman and Rozin, 1977; Rozin and Gleitman, 1977).

1.3.1 Writing Systems, and the Acquisition of Reading

The natural history of writing reveals a conceptually orderly progression. Orthographic convention proceeds, almost uninterruptedly over time, in a single direction: At every advance, the number of symbols in the script decreases; concurrently, and as a direct consequence, the abstractness of the relations between the written symbols and the meanings increases. Pictographic scripts (which render "whole ideas") appeared earliest and were invented most frequently in separate cultural developments; abstract logographies (which render meaningful words) tend to be later, but still are frequent; syllabic scripts are yet later and rarer; the alphabet (phonemic writing) seems to have been invented but once, and latest (Gelb, 1952; Jefferey, 1961; and for a review see Gleitman and Rozin, 1977).

This succession of historical insights seems noncoincidental to us: The more analytic the unit, the harder it is to bring to conscious attention; and surely the invention of a script has to count as a prime case of self-conscious language manipulation. It was evidently easier to see that language consists of a sequence of words than that it consists of a sequence of sounds. It is of some interest here that many syntactic as well as phonological facts were ignored in the early writing systems: The Aegean logographies and syllabaries did not represent grammatical function words and morphemes very systematically, but only the "meaningful" substantives, verbs, etc. Given that these analytic insights were ultimately achieved, however, it does not seem surprising that each primitive script gave way in time to its more analytic successor. Obviously, if the number of symbols in the script is reduced, learning is broader and the problem of memorization is diminished during the course of attaining full literacy.

However, in the view of Rozin and Gleitman, decreasing the number of symbols in a script came at a cost. If the writing system abstracts away from the meanings it conveys, the decipherer will have to recover the meanings from the now encoded form in which they have been rendered. Learners of an alphabet are required to recognize, quite consciously, the phonological and syntactic substrata of language. On the suppositions sketched above, this ought to produce wide variability in the success of reading acquisition, and success ought to be correlated with the ability to give phonological judgments. There is much evidence in favor of this position.

Eimas et al., (1971) have shown that even 4-week-old infants can and will discriminate phonological properties of speech sounds relevant to language; they can discriminate, for example, between ba and pa. While humans are not the sole possessors of such discrimination skills (Kuhl and Miller, 1975) and although humans can also discriminate categorically among acoustic stimuli not relevant to speech (Cutting and Rosner, 1974), the findings of Eimas et al. clearly speak to the fact that the acoustic discriminative apparatus on which language learning is ultimately based are in place approximately from birth. But a well-known "reading-readiness test" (mis)named the Auditory Discrimination Test (Wepman, 1958) is based on the fact that some kindergartners cannot correctly say "different" or "same" in response to pairs of words that differ in one phonological segment (e.g., *pat* and *bat*) or are identical (e.g., *pat* and *pat*). From the demonstration of Eimas *et al.*, we know that these 5-year-olds can *hear* the differences in such stimuli. They can even correctly repeat the stimulus items which they could not judge on the Wepman Test (Blank, 1968). Furthermore, the failing 5-year-olds do have the capacity to give judgments: they can correctly say "same" and "different" in response to written stimuli (e.g., they can discriminate between the visual displays BAT and PAT, and judge them to be "different," even though they cannot read them; Smith, 1974). Evidently the child who fails the Wepman test is very circumscribed in his deficits. His weakness appears only when he is asked to give a *judgment* about the sound properties of linguistic stimuli. Yet the Wepman test is a fairly useful predictor of early reading success, suggesting that the judgment faculty is implicated in learning to read.

In a similar vein, Firth (1972) has shown that groups of third graders matched for IQ, but differing in reading skills according to the estimates of their teachers, perform identically on such semantic tasks as guessing plausible completions of incomplete orally presented sentences; but the ability to provide consensual pronunciations for written nonsense words (such as *nide* or *prit*) appropriately classified these children in 98% of instances. It is of particular importance that the ability to perform word-segmentation and construction tasks continues to distinguish successful from unsuccessful readers all the way through twelfth grade (Calfee, Lindamood, and Lindamood, 1973; Rosner, 1972).

1.3.2. The Conceptual Demands of Orthographies

We have just argued that even at advanced stages and over a broad IQ range, the ability to think about phonology is a trait characteristic of good readers of alphabets. Rozin and Gleitman investigated this issue directly, by attempting to teach failing readers, and children with poor prognosis for reading acquisition, to read scripts of varying kinds. Their approach stemmed from the view that written language, for which there presumably exist no specific evolutionary adaptations, must be learned under the control of self-conscious, metalinguistic apparatus (whatever that may turn out to be). If so, the meaning-based scripts ought to pose less of a learning problem than the sound-based scripts, because of the relative difficulties of making judgments at these levels. Using a variety of notations, they attempted to teach logographies, syllabaries, and alphabets to Philadelphia-area school children.

Even those children with the poorest prognosis for reading success (inner-city children from schools whose reading achievement norms were catastrophically below national norms) acquired logographies with little difficulty. A logographic script taught by Gleitman and Rozin (1973a) was based on pictorial representations; more impressive, a script taught by Rozin, Poritsky, and Sotsky (1971) used Chinese characters with English translations; three examples of their sentences are shown in Figure 6.2. Children who had failed to acquire reading skills in first and second grades learned to recognize 30 characters in this script and read the materials with fair to adequate comprehension in from 5 to 8 hours of instruction.

The picture-based logography of Gleitman and Rozin was next expanded into a syllabary. See Figure 6.3 for samples of this script. Each item in the script represented a single syllable. Some of these were based on the logography; for example, an element such as *can* now represented the noun *can*, the auxiliary *can*, and the first syllable in *candy*. Some syllables had no word basis, such as the *dy* syllable which appears in *candy*. The children were taught both the syllabic elements and a convention for combining them. After 5–7 hours of instruction with 22 syllables and 16

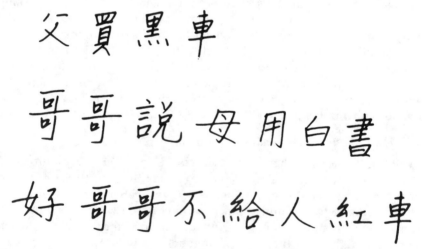

Figure 6.2. A few sentences in modern Chinese, with English interpretations.
Failing learners of an alphabet were taught to read Chinese characters, but with English interpretation. Samples are shown above. Reading across from left to right, these sentences can be translated as: *top*—father buys (a) black car; *middle*—older-brother says mother uses (the) white book; *bottom*—good older-brother (would) not give (the) man (a) red car. Note the approximately one-to-one mapping of English words to unitary Chinese characters (words in the translation that are not directly represented in the Chinese characters are included in parentheses). (From Rozin, P., Poritsky, S., and Sotsky, R., American children with reading problems can easily learn to read English represented by Chinese characters, *Science*, 1971, **171**, 1264–1267, Fig. 2. Copyright 1971 by the American Association for the Advancement of Science.)

Figure 6.3. Samples of writing from a syllabary script used by Gleitman and Rozin for initial reading instruction.

Pictorial clues were used, as shown above, to help the children identify the syllable units. Boxes, lines, or dots were used to supply syllable segment boundaries. In some versions of this curriculum, boundary and picture clues were dropped out later in the instruction period. After 5–7 hours of instruction with 22 syllables and 16 polysyllabic words containing these, 5 inner-city kindergartners were able adequately to identify *new* polysyllabic words (that they had not been taught, but were in their oral vocabularies) in the syllabic notations. [From Gleitman, L., and Rozin, P., Teaching reading by use of a syllabary, *Reading Research Quarterly*, 1973, **8**(No. 4), p. 471, Fig. 4.]

polysyllabic words containing these, 5 inner-city kindergartners were able to identify *new* polysyllabic words (that they had not been taught, but which were in their oral vocabularies) in the syllabic notation (Gleitman and Rozin, 1973a).

A much more extensive syllabic script was acquired during the first year of schooling by inner-city 6-year-olds taught in a normal classroom setting by their own teachers. Figure 6.4 shows a page from an intermediate-level reader used in this project. Adequate fluency was achieved in this notation; but during this same time, neither these children nor a matched group of control children. learning to read by traditional means, adequately acquired the phonemic concepts of an alphabet (Rozin and Gleitman, 1977).

Summarizing, the logography was easier to acquire than the syllabary, which is based on the phonological properties of words. But the syllabary is a gross, molar representation of phonology. It was easier to acquire than the more analytic phonemic (alphabetic) script. Thus the population with poor reading prognosis differed from successful readers most in acquiring the phonemic concepts of an alphabet, and least in acquiring the ideas

"Sill•y   Mon•go,   a   key   will

not   o•pen   the   sand,   and   no

litt•le   sea•le   is   in•side."

Figure 6.4.   A page from an intermediate-level reader in the syllabary curriculum for reading acquisition.

This kind of writing was used by classroom teachers as a preliminary instructional device, in a number of Philadelphia-area kindergartens and first grades. Adequate fluency was achieved with this notation in from one to nine months, depending on the population of learners. About 70 syllabic elements are used in this version of the *Syllabary* reading curriculum. In the example here, some pictorial clues have been dropped out of the notation: the word *sand* was initially introduced with a pictorial hint (a sand bucket), but by this point in instruction is recognized from the letter array alone. From Rozin, P. and Gleitman, L. R. The structure and acquisition of reading II: The reading process and the acquisition of the alphabetic principle. In A. S. Reber and D. Scarborough (Eds.), *Toward a psychology of reading*. © 1977, L. Erlbaum Associates, Fig. 6, p. 120.] Hillsdale, N.J.

behind a logography: Phonology, not meaning, is at the crux of the early reading problem. The essential difficulty for poor readers seems to be in accessing their own phonological machinery. They have the requisite phonological organization in their heads; their problem is how to get to it.

Our supposition, then, is that unsuccessful beginning readers are generally characterizable as those who fail to acquire the alphabetic insight and thus read logographically. It is striking that failing readers are not people who literally can read nothing. They can read many hundreds of words but (as this is often put) they stop learning at about the "fourth grade level" of reading achievement. This level involves reading with comprehension a couple of thousand (at most) simple words, in context. It is of some interest that normal readers of logographic scripts (Chinese readers) acquire a recognition vocabulary of only a few thousand items (Leong, 1973), this number apparently representing a limit on rote acquisition of arbitrary visual displays. Similarly, most deaf readers of English script (who are clearly denied the phonological route to reading acquisition) learn to read very slowly and generally do not attain as high a level of skill as hearing individuals (Furth, 1966; Gibson, Shurcliff, and Yonas, 1970). Gleitman and Rozin concluded that the failing American reader has learned a logography, not an alphabet.

2. ARE THE METALINGUISTIC FUNCTIONS RELATED TO LANGUAGE USE AND LEARNING?

We have speculated elsewhere (Gleitman, Gleitman, and Shipley, 1972) that the metalinguistic function may be a single example of a more general metacognitive organization in humans. That is, a variety of cognitive processes seem themselves to be the objects of higher-order cognitive processes in the same domain—as if the homunculus perceived the operation of a lower-order system. Examples of metacognition in memory would be recollection (when we know that we remember) and intentional learning (when we know we must store the material for longer retrieval). On this view, there need be no formal resemblance between metacognition and the cognitive processes it sometimes guides and organizes. Rather, one might expect to find resemblances among the higher-order processes themselves, a general executive function which may take on aspects of what is sometimes called "the self." Thus language-judgment functions, in particular, could be orthogonal to language functions. One need have no disposition to think about language in order to use it appropriately.

The recent literature in psycholinguistics largely supports this interpretation. A wide variety of experiments effectively demonstrate that the structural relationships among sentences described in generative grammars (derived from the data of *judgments*) are not the same relationships required to describe language information-handling in real time (for which the data are *speech* and *comprehension* measures; for discussion see Bever, 1970; Fodor, Bever, and Garrett, 1974). As we mentioned in introductory comments, some have concluded from such facts that grammatical descriptions lack psychological reality. But it seems more realistic to conclude only that their relevance is not to speech and comprehension directly. Rather, grammars reflect the judgmental ("metalinguistic") aspects of language knowledge more directly than they do knowledge of language itself. Whatever resemblance exists between language processing strategies and grammars may derive from the fact that the human builds his grammar out of his observation of regularities in his own speech and comprehension. Whatever differences exist between these organizations may derive from the fact that the "executive" thinking capacities have properties of their own, which enter into the form of the grammars they construct.

Although we have argued that the metafunctions, if they exist, need not enter into the deployment of the cognitive processes they subserve, sometimes they may. Though one often remembers without awareness that one is remembering, more self-conscious activities are possible, and seem to be implicated in the structure of findings in memory experiments. For example, it is apparently possible to report what is in one's memory store ("yes, I'll recognize it if you mention it") without being able to retrieve the information (Hart, 1967). Furthermore, adults perform better on intentional memory tasks than on incidental memory tasks, presumably because they can willfully institute such strategies as rehearsal in aid of the memory functions when the task demands this. Analogously, metalinguistic functions may enter into speech and comprehension on those occasions when one wishes to pun or orate, or to read or write poetry; that is, when language manipulations are part of the definition of the task.

Could the metalinguistic functions enter into the process of learning a first language? The studies we have cited would argue not, for the language functions seem developmentally to precede the metalanguage functions, with only some rare exceptions. The children we studied judged sentences for syntactic form only some years after they used these forms correctly; they organized speech-sounds phonologically years before they could bring this organization (or a related one) to bear on the problem of understanding alphabets. There are some similar findings for other putative metafunctions. For example, unless specially instructed to rehearse, young children do no better in intentional learning tasks than they do in incidental learning tasks (Yendovitskaya, 1971). Perhaps this is because they have no functioning "metamemory" that spontaneously institutes the appropriate strategies available to memory.

Summarizing, we take the evidence to suggest that judgmental functions in language are separate from the language functions both on descriptive grounds (the data of linguistic judgments do not organize the findings for speech and comprehension in real time) and on developmental grounds (the presumed metafunctions are developmentally late to appear).

Some arguments can be made in favor of a more intimate connection between language and metalanguage, although these are perhaps not logically compelling. Some parallels exist between the development and use of restricted language-specific syntactic devices and the development and deployment of metalinguistic skills, as we have defined these. That is, certain elaborate inflectional devices appear only under special linguistic–cultural circumstances (present in creoles but not in pidgins, Sankoff and Laberge, 1973; present in speech but not in early writing systems, Gelb, 1952), are late to develop in the history of the individual (Slobin, 1973), and show extensive individual variation in rate of development, owing to environmental effects (Newport, Gleitman, and Gleitman, 1977) and, possibly, capacity differences (Lenneberg, 1967). The same is true for the metalinguistic functions which show extensive variability (Gleitman and Gleitman, 1970) and environmental sensitivity (reading disabilities of the sort we have described are largely isolated within restricted socioeconomic groups). Approximately these same aspects of language are those which seem to make trouble for the judgment-giver (he has more difficulty making syntactic judgments than semantic judgments; etc.).

3. SUMMARY AND DISCLAIMERS

We suppose that individual differences in language behavior occur more severely at the judgmental level than at the speech and comprehension level. We have invoked such ill-defined notions as "metalinguistic awareness" and "accessibility" to describe such findings. That is, we claim the differences in tacit knowledge are small in comparison to differences in the ability to make such knowledge explicit. We have some evidence that suggests greatest judgmental difficulty with least processed linguistic representations. However, our descriptions of these matters are at present merely metaphorical and not a little fuzzy. But the facts of individual language difference suggest that we will have to look seriously at the problem of "conscious knowledge."

ACKNOWLEDGMENTS

We wish to express our great intellectual debt to two colleagues whose collaboration with us is directly responsible for many of the ideas expressed in this paper. Many of the positions taken were developed in a collaboration with Paul Rozin, in the context of studies on the acquisition of reading (Gleitman and Rozin, 1973a, 1973b, 1977; and Rozin and Gleitman, 1974, 1977; see Section 1.3 of the present paper for summary discussion). A rather different physiological approach to the questions of *accessibility* and *metacognition* appeared in Rozin (1976) where many of our findings on reading are also discussed. Other contributions to the ideas discussed here come out of our collaboration with Elizabeth Shipley on topics in child language learning (Shipley, Smith, and Gleitman, 1969; Gleitman, Gleitman, and Shipley, 1972). The work described in this chapter was funded by Grant #5 R01 MH 23505 from the National Institutes of Health and The William T. Carter Foundation, whose support we gratefully acknowledge.

REFERENCES

Baron, J. The word-superiority effect. In W. K. Estes (Ed.) *Handbook of learning and cognitive processes.* Hillsdale, New Jersey: Erlbaum. In press.

Bever, T. G. The cognitive basis for linguistic structures. In J. R. Hayes (Ed.), *Cognition and the development of language.* New York: Wiley, 1970.

Blank, M. Cognitive processes in auditory discrimination in normal and retarded readers. *Child Development,* 1968, **39,** 1091–1101.

Bloomfield, L. *Language.* New York: Henry Holt, 1933.

Bolinger, D. L. and Gerstman, L. J. Disjuncture as a cue to constructs. *Journal of the Acoustical Society of America,* 1957, **29,** 778.

Bransford, J. D. and Franks, J. J. The abstraction of linguistic ideas. *Cognitive Psychology,* 1971, **2,** 331–350.

Brown, R. *A first language: The early stages.* Cambridge, Massachusetts: Harvard University Press, 1973.

Brown, R. and Hanlon, C. Derivational complexity and order of acquisition in child speech. In J. R. Hayes (Ed.), *Cognition and the development of language.* New York: Wiley, 1970.

Calfee, R. C., Lindamood, P., and Lindamood, C. Acoustic–phonetic skills and reading—kindergarten through twelfth grade. *Journal of Educational Psychology,* 1973, **64,** 293–298.

Cutting, J. E. and Rosner, B. S. Categories and boundaries in speech and music. *Perception and Psychophysics,* 1974, **16,** 564–570.

Downing, J. (Ed.), *Comparative reading: Cross-national studies of behavior and processes in reading and writing.* New York: Macmillan, 1973.

Downing, J. and Oliver, P. The child's conception of "a word." *Reading Research Quarterly,* 1973–74, **9,** 568–582.

Eimas, P. D., Siqueland, E. R., Jusczyk, P., and Vigorito, J. Speech perception in infants. *Science,* 1971, **171,** 303–306.

Elkonin, D. B. USSR. Trans. by R. Raeder and J. Downing. In J. Downing (Ed.), *Comparative reading: Cross-national studies of behavior and processes in reading and writing.* New York: Macmillan, 1973.

Feldman, H., Goldin-Meadow, S. and Gleitman, L. Beyond Herodotus: The creation of language by linguistically deprived deaf children. In A. Lock (Ed.), *Action, gesture and symbol: The emergence of language.* New York: Academic Press, 1978.

Fillenbaum, S. Memory for gist: Some relevant variables. *Language and Speech,* 1966, **9,** 217–227.

Firth, U. *Components of reading disability.* Unpublished Doctoral dissertation, University of New South Wales, Kensington, N.S.W., Australia, 1972.

Fodor, J. A., Bever, T. G. and Garrett, M. F. *The psychology of language: An introduction to psycholinguistics and generative grammar.* New York: McGraw Hill, 1974.

Fodor, J. A. and Garrett, M. F. Some reflections on competence and performance. In Lyons, J. and Wales, R. S. (Eds.), *Psycholinguistic papers.* Edinburgh: Edinburgh Univ. Press, 1966.

Fowles, B. and Glanz, E. Competence and talent in verbal riddle comprehension. *Journal of Child Language,* 1977, **4,** 433–452.

Furth, H. G. *Thinking without language: Psychological implications of deafness.* New York: Free Press, 1966.

Geer, S. E., Gleitman, H., and Gleitman, L. Paraphrasing and remembering compound words. *Journal of Verbal Learning and Verbal Behavior,* 1972, **11,** 348–355.

Gelb, I. J. *A study of writing: The foundations of grammatology.* Chicago: University of Chicago Press, 1952.

Gibson, E. J., Shurcliff, A., and Yonas, A. Utilization of spelling patterns by deaf and hearing subjects. In H. Levin and J. P. Williams (Eds.), *Basic studies on reading.* New York: Basic Books, 1970.

Gleitman, L. R. and Gleitman, H. *Phrase and paraphrase.* New York: W. W. Norton and Co., 1970.

Gleitman, L. R., Gleitman, H., and Shipley, E. The emergence of the child as grammarian. *Cognition*, 1972, **1**, 137–164.

Gleitman, L. R. and Rozin, P. Teaching reading by use of a syllabary. *Reading Research Quarterly*, 1973a, **8**, 447–483.

Gleitman, L. R., and Rozin, P. Phoenician go home? (A response to Goodman). *Reading Research Quarterly*, 1973b, **8**, 494–501.

Gleitman, L. R. and Rozin, P. The structure and acquisition of reading I: Relations between orthographies and the structure of language. In A. S. Reber and D. Scarborough (Eds.), *Toward a psychology of reading.* Hillsdale, New Jersey, Erlbaum, 1977.

Hart, J. T. Memory and the memory-monitoring process. *Journal of Verbal Learning and Verbal Behavior*, 1967, **6**, 385–391.

Herodotus. *The Persian Wars,* c. 460 B.C., Rawlinson, G. (Tr.) New York: Random House, 1942.

Hirsh-Pasek, K., Gleitman, L. R., and Gleitman, H. What did the brain say to the mind? In A. Sinclair, R. Jarvella, and W. J. M. Levelt (Eds.), *The Child's Conception of Language.* Berlin, Heidelberg, New York: Springer-Verlag, 1978.

Holden, M. H., and MacGinitie, W. H. Children's conceptions of word boundaries in speech and print. *Journal of Educational Psychology*, 1972, **63**, 551–557.

Jeffery, L. H. *The local scripts of archaic Greece.* Oxford: Clarendon Press, 1961.

Kessel, F. S. The role of syntax in the child's comprehension from ages six to twelve. *Monographs of the Society for Research in Child Development*, 1970, **35**(6).

Kuhl, P. K. and Miller, J. D. Speech perception by the chinchilla: Voiced–voiceless distinction in alveolar plosive consonants. *Science*, 1975, **190**, 69–72.

Labov, W. Locating the frontier between social and psychological factors in linguistic variation. This volume.

Lackner, J. R. A developmental study of language behavior in retarded children. In D. M. Morehead and A. E. Morehead (Eds.), *Normal and deficient child language.* Baltimore: University Park Press, 1976.

Lenneberg, E. H. *Biological foundations of language.* New York: Wiley, 1967.

Leong, C. K. Hong Kong. In J. Downing (Ed.), *Comparative reading: Cross-national studies of behavior and processes in reading and writing.* New York: Macmillan, 1973.

Levin, H., and Kaplan, E. L. Grammatical structure and reading. In H. Levin and J. P. Williams (Eds.), *Basic studies on reading.* New York: Basic Books, 1970.

Liberman, I. Y., Shankweiler, D., Fischer, F. W. and Carter, B. Explicit syllable and phoneme segmentation in the young child. *Journal of Experimental Child Psychology*, 1974, **18**, 201–212.

Liberman, I. Y., Shankweiler, D., Liberman, A. M., Fowler, C., and Fischer, F. W. Phonetic segmentation and recoding in the beginning reader. In A. S. Reber and D. Scarborough, (Eds.), *Toward a psychology of reading.* Hillsdale, New Jersey: Lawrence Erlbaum Associates, 1977.

Morehead, D. M. and Ingram, D. The development of base syntax in normal and linguistically deviant children. In D. M. Morehead and A. E. Morehead (Eds.), *Normal and deficient child language.* Baltimore: University Park Press, 1976.

Newport, E. L. and Ashbrook, E. Development of semantic–syntactic relations in the acquisition of American Sign Language. Manuscript, University of California at San Diego, 1977.

Newport, E., Gleitman, H. and Gleitman, L. R. Mother, I'd rather do it myself: Some effects and non-effects of maternal speech style. In C. E. Snow and C. A. Ferguson (Eds.),

Talking to children: Language input and acquisition. Cambridge, England: Cambridge University Press, 1977.

Nida, E. A. *Morphology: The descriptive analysis of words.* Second ed. Ann Arbor, Michigan: University of Michigan Press, 1949.

Read, C. Pre-school children's knowledge of English phonology. *Harvard Educational Review,* 1971, **41,** 1–34.

Rosner, J. *The development and validation of an individualized perceptual skills curriculum.* Learning Research and Development Center, University of Pittsburgh. Publication 1972/7. 1972.

Rosner, J. Auditory analysis training with prereaders. *The Reading Teacher,* 1974, **27,** 379–384.

Rosner, J., and Simon, D. P. *The auditory analysis test: An initial report.* Learning Research and Development Center, University of Pittsburgh, Publication 1971/3, 1971.

Ross, J. R. Where's English? This volume.

Rozin, P. The evolution of intelligence and access to the cognitive unconscious. In J. Sprague and A. N. Epstein (Eds.), *Progress in psychobiology and physiological psychology,* Vol. 6. New York: Academic Press, 1976.

Rozin, P. and Gleitman, L. R. The structure and acquisition of reading II: The reading process and the acquisition of the alphabetic principle. In A. S. Reber and D. Scarborough (Eds.), *Toward a psychology of reading.* Hillsdale, New Jersey: L. Erlbaum Associates, 1977.

Rozin, P., Poritsky, S., and Sotsky, R. American children with reading problems can easily learn to read English represented by Chinese characters, *Science,* 1971, **171,** 1264–1267.

Sachs, J. S. Recognition memory for syntactic and semantic aspects of connected discourse. *Perception and Psychophysics,* 1967, **2,** 437–442.

Sankoff, G. and Laberge, S. On the acquisition of native speakers by a language. *Kivung,* 1973, **6**(1), 32–47.

Shatz, M. Semantic and syntactic factors in children's judgment of sentences. Unpublished manuscript, University of Pennsylvania, 1972.

Shipley, E. F., Smith, C. S. and Gleitman, L. R. A study in the acquisition of language: Free responses to commands. *Language,* 1969, **45,** 322–343.

Shultz, T. and Pilon, R. Development of the ability to detect linguistic ambiguity. *Child Development,* 1973, **44,** 728–733.

Singer, H. IQ is and is not related to reading. In S. Wanat (Ed.), *Intelligence and reading.* Newark, Delaware: International Reading Association, 1974.

Slobin, D. Cognitive prerequisites for the development of grammar. In C. A. Ferguson and D. I. Slobin (Eds.), *Studies of Child Language Development.* New York: Holt, Rinehart and Winston, 1973.

Slobin, D. I. The more it changes . . . on understanding language by watching it move through time. In *Papers and Reports on Child Language Development,* No. 10. Department of Linguistics, Stanford University, Sept. 1975.

Smith, J. A. The relationship between phonemic sensitivity and the effectiveness of phonemic retrieval cues in preliterate children. Unpublished Doctoral dissertation. University of Pennsylvania, 1974.

Thorndike, W. E. Reading as reasoning: A study of mistakes in paragraph reading. *Journal of Educational Psychology,* 1971, **8,** 323–332. (Also in *Reading Research Quarterly,* 1970–1971, **6,** 425–434.)

Wepman, J. M. *Wepman auditory discrimination test.* Chicago: Language Research Associates, 1958.

Yendovitskaya, T. V. Development of memory. In A. V. Zaporozhets and D. B. Elkonin (Eds.), *The psychology of preschool children.* Cambridge, Massachusetts: M.I.T. Press, 1971.

 MEMORY

9 Recall, Recognition, and Implicit Knowledge

Donald Broadbent
University of Oxford, England

In recent years, a great deal of experiment, publication, and debate has been engendered by the question of implicit knowledge (e.g., Berry & Broadbent, 1984, 1987a, 1988; Broadbent, Fitzgerald, & Broadbent, 1986; Dulany, Carlson, & Dewey, 1984; Lewicki, 1986; Lewicki, Hill, & Bizot, 1988; Mathews et al., 1989; Perruchet, Gallego, & Savy, in press; Perruchet & Pacteau, in press; Reber, 1967; Reber, Kassin, Lewis, & Cantor, 1980; Sanderson, 1989; Stanley, Mathews, Buss, & Kotler-Cope, 1988). Some experiments seem to show that people can learn to perform actions without being able to give verbal accounts of them. However, many investigators question this, and argue that the testing of verbal knowledge has been inadequate. When I listen to these discussions, they remind me of an interchange that George Mandler and I had in the 1970s, about recall and recognition. My guess is that the newer disagreements are about the same psychological issue. In any case, however, they certainly illustrate the same problems of misunderstanding and communication. People involved now should take heed to what George was saying then.

AN OLD DEBATE

George has been, throughout his career, skeptical about the merits of an associative stimulus–response approach. People who believe in such an approach could use it to explain the differences between recall and recognition. In recall, there are few stimuli attached to the response of naming the desired past experience; in recognition, many more. A straight associationist could well therefore expect that recognition will usually be easier than recall.

125

On such a view, recognition depends on the surface stimuli and their associations, not on any internal cognitive operation. It should make little difference whether the material being remembered is organized internally by the person, into categories and structures. Such organization could be allowed to play a part in recall, as a desperate stratagem of an associative system trying to acquire some stimuli to elicit responses. It should not work in recognition. But George had shown (Mandler, Pearlstone, & Koopmans, 1969) that material organizable into categories can be recognized better as well as recalled better. So, he contended that retrieval mechanisms were operative in recognition also, even though in a sense the material to be "retrieved" was already present as a stimulus (Mandler, 1972, 1980). The notion was that some items in a test would be recognized immediately, by a mechanism of perceptual type; but for others, the person would try to retrieve the item and check success against the material present.

To George, this point was moderately crucial, because of the impact on associationism. Any other approach must therefore be resisted, if it looked as if it questioned the resemblance of recall and recognition. Into this potential bear pit I wandered innocently in pursuit of another problem: What is the status of unrecalled material? Is it forgotten primarily because the original experience left a trace of insufficient "strength"? Or, are the retrieval mechanisms so important that many unrecalled items are perfectly accessible by other routes?

I thought the latter; in other words, my cosmic position was the same as George's. The detailed paradigm we used was however quite different. We presented lists of words, asked for recall, and then gave a recognition test only for those items that had not been recalled. (Not very subtle? Try doing it with a memory drum; this was one of the first computer-controlled memory experiments in Britain.) One could then compare such a test with a conventional recognition test for all items; in the conditions of interest to us, the scores on the two tests were equal and therefore the forgotten items were being recognized as well as the recalled ones. In other words, there was no way that failure of recall could be due solely to low "strength" of associations (Broadbent & Broadbent, 1975).

Of course getting such an effect would depend on some items being easier to retrieve in one test condition, and other items in the other test condition. By counting introspections, we found that people who expected a recall test used strategies of linking items into sequences; which would not be much help in a recognition test. Conversely, those who expected a recognition test tended to associate each item with some distinctive other image; which would scarcely help with recall. Repeating the procedure, so that subjects knew they were likely to get both kinds of test, abolished the effect.

So, we saw ourselves as battling for the importance of retrieval routes, and as being true cognitivists. George, however, saw it as vital that the same items were easier to recognize and also to recall, because otherwise one would be supposing that the two processes were separate; no retrieval in recognition. Hence, he felt we had to be wrong, and launched a fresh series of arguments and experiments to disagree (Rabinowitz, Mandler, & Patterson, 1977a). Conversely, we were horrified that somebody should think that retrieval routes were less important than properties of the individual item; he or she must be a wicked associationist. Battle was joined and raged in the JEP: General (Broadbent & Broadbent, 1977; Rabinowitz, Mandler, & Patterson, 1977b).

As one might expect from this "bombing one's own troops" situation, the argument was not, at the explicit level, very profitable. The bucket is certainly half full; there are certainly experimental conditions in which the same items are easier to remember by any testing method. But it is also half empty; there are also conditions in which the two methods are independent. Gradually it dawned on both sides that the things we shared were more fundamental than the things on which we dissented. So we left off.

As a result, I myself tend to forget some of the points that arose, that now look quite interesting. For instance, George thought our result might be due to poor organization of the material in short-term memory with inexperienced subjects. But when we looked deliberately at the effect of number of categories, we found it was present; so George's emphasis on retrieval and organization was valid even in a single short exposure, without subtle and devious training of the subjects.

Again, he was worried by our experimental design; we had deliberately avoided testing of recognition for recalled and forgotten items from the same list on the same person. Our reason was that one test might contaminate the other. But this is obviously insensitive, and George could produce some past papers that found no overall improvement in a recall test if it was preceded by a recognition test. So he used that procedure, and demonstrated that recognition followed by recall found the same items to be best by both methods.

We did not like that either, so we returned to our computer, and this time we gave a recognition test for *half* the items in the list. A subsequent recall test showed that those items did better than the remainder of the list did, as common sense might suggest. If so, however, why had George found those earlier papers showing that recall was unaffected on average by earlier recognition testing? The reason was that the beneficial effect was entirely confined to the items that were recognized in the first test. If you had seen an item in a recognition test, and confidently rejected it, your chance of later recalling it was worse than that of an untested item. Exactly what would happen to the average score depended on the number of recognized and unrecognized items, and we on our side could find other studies that showed a beneficial effect of earlier recognition on later recall. Negative experiences have an effect on memory just as positive ones do.

THE LESSONS OF THE PAST

There were therefore four kinds of conclusion from this episode. Fist, there were the underlying agreements. It is not enough to look at the overt conditions, and the earlier experience with those conditions, to predict the action that will follow. One must also consider the structure of the material, and the task that is being attempted. People who think recall is totally different from recognition are therefore wrong.

Second, there were a certain number of raw facts; organization helps memory right down to single exposures and short-term retention, and experience of an item can "unlearn" it as well as learn it, and above all, organization really does help recognition as well as recall.

Third, there was probably something that did not become explicit, because we stopped too soon, but that was a truth that George had seen and I had not. Although there is no dividing line between recall and recognition, there is nevertheless a mixture of processes within recognition. I was hoping that one could regard all memory function as the tapping of a single (organized) structure, the differences between tests of memory being reducible to differences in the point of entry to the structure, or in the number of points. Thus, recognition could be seen as the retrieval of a context given an event, and recall as the retrieval of an event given a context. The same set of rules would govern both. This would have been parsimonious, but it did not take enough account of the difference between feeling that a face is familiar, and knowing the identity of the person. George did accept that difference, and he was quite right; the effect of an earlier presentation on tachistoscopic threshold is different from the effect of "level of processing" on a forced-choice test of memory (Jacoby & Dallas, 1981; Tulving, Schacter, & Stark, 1982).

Fourth, there is a lesson about looking for the core of the debate rather than the periphery. We spent most of our time debating correction factors in scoring, or the danger of drawing conclusions from absences of significant differences. We each assumed we knew why the other wanted to make certain claims; "obviously" George had a strength model, and "obviously" I was reintroducing S–R theory. The irony in this case is that we were both ultimately after the same thing; more usually, but just as unprofitably, one person may be after a goal at right angles to that of the antagonist, rather than incompatible with it.

IMPLICIT AND EXPLICIT

If we turn now to the discussion of control through implicit knowledge, there are close parallels to the discussion of recall and recognition. The paradigm experiment is one in which the person is able to choose the correct reaction while in a task, but is unable later to recall the key characteristics that controlled the behavior. Clearly, this phenomenon occurs (Berry & Broadbent, 1984; Lewicki, 1986; Reber, 1967). From generations of work on recall and recognition we should find nothing surprizing about it. We should also expect that, under special circumstances, recall may sometimes be better than recognition (Watkins & Tulving, 1975). Indeed that is so; one can give a verbal instruction, which the person can later show evidence of remembering, and yet in the task context the instruction is not applied. (Berry & Broadbent, 1984, 1987b). In the traditional situation of verbal learning, the explanation given would be that the changed external conditions did not allow the crucial information to be retrieved, although it was present in the person; and in some tasks showing a lack of effect of instruction, one can improve performance by associating the key information with the exact situation rather than with a pre-training episode (Berry & Broadbent, 1984, 1987b).

Why then is there debate and concern about the phenomenon? It is rarely related to these familiar data, and is rather seen as important for some view of "conscious" or "explicit" knowledge. Authors do not often spell out what they mean by these terms; they have to take something for granted, and can perhaps hope that people will attach meaning to these particular words because they are common in everyday life. The words are also especially close to human experience. This may be a dangerous assumption however; Tulving distinguished unanswerably eight quite different senses in which the relatively simple word "retrieval" has been used in the literature (Tulving, 1983, p. 177).

If the participants in any argument about "consciousness" can be persuaded to stop briefly for a moment and explain themselves, it is usually easy to reveal 10 or 12 different issues interweaving and confusing each other. There is the issue of verbal report; but people may say they experience something that is inexpressible. There is the question of memory versus perception; can a person who has lost all ability to recall even meeting their spouse 5 minutes ago, be said to be conscious during the meeting? There is the issue of awareness of oneself as an experiencer; there is the issue of control processes versus representations; and there is the issue of social versus individual processes. Although intimately connected, these issues are logically quite different; and one of the negative effects of the cognitive revolution, in which George has played so honorable a part, is to have rendered respectable again a degree of conceptual confusion that behaviorism was beginning to clear up.

In the particular area of control through implicit knowledge, nobody seriously doubts the experimental findings. For example, people who have experienced strings of letters obeying a grammatical constraint will be able to judge whether entirely new strings conform to that constraint; but will not be able to respond to an open-ended request to state the rules. A lot of people find this interesting. They differ, however, in the reasons that underlie their interest. Some think that it is an attempt to show that processes go on unconsciously that are similar to those we can report; some think that the result is an attempt to show that individual exemplars in experience are unimportant, and that learning takes place through abstraction of general rules. Some think these experiments are aimed at questions of the relation between declarative and procedural knowledge, or more generally of knowledge and action. Some think that affirmative results imply the existence of separate stores of the same functional nature; others think rather that they argue for different informational operations.

Whichever of these is seen as the debate, the author may then be an ardent supporter or else be outraged by the suggestion. The vigor of the discussions suggests that stances on these issues are very crucial to the individual's basic view of psychology, as well they might be. Sometimes, however, the bystander may suspect that the basic view is the same even though the debaters think they are different, as happened to George and me.

Take as an example the question of tests of explicit knowledge. In the grammar-learning situation, it is clear that people who can judge strings as grammatical can also display knowledge in other ways; their learning is not confined to the concrete situation. Dulany et al. (1984) showed that these subjects could underline better than chance the portion of the string that is relevant to the decision; even though they cannot respond well to an open-ended request for rules. Correspondingly, Dienes (1990) found that the subjects can perform above chance on a decision about the legitimacy of single letters, when given a string that is known to be grammatical and asked whether the single letter can follow it. Particularly striking, Perruchet and Pacteau (1990) showed that the subjects can perform well on tests of bigram probability of letters out of context; and that training on bigrams will transfer to grammaticality judgments.

Similar results appear in the control tasks of Berry and Broadbent (1984, 1988). Although people do badly on verbal questionnaires about the tasks, they can reveal knowledge by being placed back in a sample situation drawn from the original task (Berry & Broadbent, 1987a). The successful performance of trained operators appears on such tests only on trials identical to those they have seen and on which they have been rewarded for successful performance (Marescaux, Luc, & Karnas, 1989).

If some associationists from the 1950s were revived without knowledge of intervening events, they would regard these results as confirming familiar findings. They knew that people who can perform a recognition judgment on one set of stimuli, can also perform it on a fresh set that is not identical, as long as it is similar. This clearly has no prediction to make for the case of recall, where the eliciting stimuli are widely different from the original situation; so our associationists would be unsurprised. Yet Dulany et al., and Perruchet and Pacteau, obviously regard the result as in some way contrary to the original claim of Reber (1967). Perhaps they feel this because they know that Reber is not a dust-bowl associationist, being one of those who find the language of "consciousness" useful. So they feel that his belief in unconscious learning of rules would lead him to expect a different result from these alternative tests of knowledge. The concealed assumption seems to be that data can only be called "unconscious" if it can never reveal itself by any event that the person can report. People certainly know what they have judged the legitimacy of a bigram to be; so at that point the knowledge must be "conscious."

Yet Reber himself did not accept that the technique of Dulany et al. (1984) is an adequate test of "explicit" knowledge; he rather regarded it as another test of implicit knowledge (Reber, Allen, & Regan, 1985). On his interpretation of "consciousness" it is not surprising that unconscious knowledge shown by grammatical judgments will also reveal itself through underlining, or no doubt by bigram judgments. The temptation for him must be to regard the newer experimenters in their turn as simple associationists, who regard any knowledge as explicit if it is revealed in overt behavior. But this cannot be the correct characterization, for Dulany equally used the terminology of conscious experience. (Dulany, 1984; Dulany, Carlson, & Dewey, 1985). Rather the difference between the two views must lie in the unstated meanings of that terminology. My guess is that, without realizing it, each group shares important beliefs and yet differs in some of the details. A conjecture, which neither might recognize, is that each thinks of the experiences we report to each other as being drawn from some location or set of "conscious" events; whereas any supposed "unconscious" events must resemble digestion or the immune response by belonging to a separate and non-overlapping set. However, one group assumes that any event whose effect can be detected in "consciousness" must belong totally to that set. Thus, if people can correctly underline key letters, an act of which they are certainly conscious, that knowledge cannot be unconscious. The other group assumes that events in one set may influence events in the other, without being identical to them. Thus a recognition-type test is not a fair test of unconscious knowledge. On that view, it is not then clear how one knows to which set an event belongs.

An alternative view might be that this debate illustrates the ambiguities and problems of the language of "conscious and unconscious." Rather, one could with profit look at the lessons George Mandler taught me 15 years ago.

LESSONS FOR IMPLICIT KNOWLEDGE
FROM CLASSIC RECOGNITION

George's point was that the important difference is not between recall and recognition, but between two kinds of recognition. The existence of these two kinds can be shown by, for example, separating recognition responses into fast and slow, and examining the effects of list organization on the two categories separately; or by comparing the effects of organizational variables after short and after long retention intervals (see Mandler, 1980, for a review). Fast responses made soon after the event has been experienced show little effect of organization, and are apparently reflecting rather different processes from those involved in slow responses or those made after long retention intervals. There was in fact good evidence for two kinds of recognition even before the contributions of Jacoby and Dallas (1981) or of Tulving et al. (1982).

In terms of everyday experience, there is certainly a kind of recognition in which the presentation of an event retrieves the whole complex of representations associated with its previous experience. Seeing the face of an old friend may call up not merely the name, but memories of that person's political beliefs, favorite beer, and likely reaction to this or that social gambit. It allows in fact manipulation of stored past information so as to "look-ahead" and compare possible future actions. From that point of view some investigators can understandably take recognition as associated with "consciousness." But intelligent machines operate not only in a "look-ahead" mode, but in a "look-up table" mode that shows rather different information-processing characteristics (Broadbent, FitzGerald, & Broadbent, 1986). In that mode, the stored effects of the past have their impact only by producing outputs that have been successful in similar previous situations, and there is no internal model of the world. Each mode has its own merits, and good chess-playing programs will usually include both.

If we use such an analysis, avoiding the debatable term *consciousness*, then recognition may be performed by a look-up table as well as by a look-ahead system. The feeling of familiarity on which fast recognition responses are based shows some of the characteristics of the former rather than the latter; in terms of the earlier example, it does not necessarily give rise to any awareness of the previous conditions under which the person was seen, of the name, or any internal symbol that can be manipulated to try out possible future states of the world. It remains tied to the input event. The use of a recognition test of knowledge, by Dulany, or by Perruchet and Pacteau, provides useful information, but cannot by itself distinguish transportable knowledge from that which is tied to the original context.

Two questions immediately arise. First, are those authors who use recognition tests "wrong" in treating them as tests of consciousness? No, but they are not "right" either. It all depends on the definition you wish to attach to that threadbare word. If you prefer to regard success at any recognition test as a criterion of consciousness, fine; only then we need a word to draw the distinction between two kinds of recognition.

Second, and finally, how can we find satisfactory tests of the presence of look-ahead processing? Perhaps in some of the ways that George Mandler has used so trenchantly to distinguish two kinds of recognition; by finding the experimental variables that allow recall as well as recognition, or prevent recall while allowing (some?) kinds of recognition (Berry & Broadbent, 1988).

REFERENCES

Berry, D. C., & Broadbent, D. E. (1984). On the relationship between task performance and associated verbalizable knowledge. *Quarterly Journal of Experimental Psychology, 36A*, 209–231.

Berry, D., & Broadbent, D. E. (1987a). The combination of explicit and implicit learning processes in task control. *Psychological Research, 49,* 7–15.

Berry, D. C., & Broadbent, D. E. (1987b). Explanation & verbalization in a computer-assisted search task. *Quarterly Journal of Experimental Psychology, 39A,* 585–609.

Berry, D., & Broadbent, D. E. (1988). Interactive tasks and the implicit-explicit distinction. *Quarterly Journal of Experimental Psychology, 36A,* 209–231.

Broadbent, D. E., & Broadbent, M. H. P. (1975). The recognition of words that cannot be recalled. In P. M. A. Rabbitt & S. Dornic (Eds.), *Attention & performance* (Vol. V, pp. 575–590). New York: Academic.

Broadbent, D. E., & Broadbent, M. H. P. (1977). Effects of recognition on subsequent recall. *Journal of Experimental Psychology: General, 106,* 330–335.

Broadbent, D. E., FitzGerald, P., & Broadbent, M. H. P. (1986). Implicit and explicit knowledge in the control of complex systems. *British Journal of Psychology, 77,* 33–50.

Dienes, Z. (1990). *Implicit concept formation.* Unpublished doctorate thesis, University of Oxford, Oxford, England.

Dulany, D. E. (1984, November). *A strategy for investigating consciousness.* Paper presented at meetings of the Psychonomic Society, San Antonio, TX.

Dulany, D. E., Carlson, R. A., & Dewey, G. I. (1984). A case of syntactical learning and judgment: How conscious and how abstract? *Journal of Experimental Psychology: General, 113,* 541–555.

Dulany, D. E., Carlson, R. A., & Dewey, G. I. (1985). On consciousness in syntactic learning and judgment: A reply to Reber, Allen, and Regan. *Journal of Experimental Psychology: General, 114,* 25–32.

Jacoby, L. L., & Dallas, M. (1981). On the relationship between autobiographical memory and perceptual learning. *Journal of Experimental Psychology: General, 110,* 306–340.

Lewicki, P. (1986). *Nonconscious social information processing.* Orlando: Academic Press.

Lewicki, P., Hill, T., Bizot, E. (1988). Acquisition of procedural knowledge about a pattern of stimuli that cannot be articulated. *Cognitive Psychology, 20,* 24–37.

Mandler, G. (1972). Organization and recognition. In E. Tulving & W. Donaldson (Eds.), *Organization of memory* (pp. 139–166). New York: Academic Press.

Mandler, G. (1980). Recognizing: The judgment of previous occurrence. *Psychological Review, 87,* 252–271.

Mandler, G., Pearlstone, Z., & Koopmans, H. S. (1969). Effects of organization and semantic similarity on recall and recognition. *Journal of Verbal Learning & Verbal Behavior, 8,* 410–423.

Marescaux, P-J., Luc, F., & Karnas, G. (1989). Modes d'apprentissage selectif et non-selectif et connaissances acquises au controle d'un processus: Evaluation d'un modele simule. *Cahiers de Psychologie Cognitive, 9,* 239–264.

Mathews, R. C., Buss, R. R., Stanley, W. B., Blanchard-Fields, F., Cho, J., & Druhan, B. (1989). Role of implicit and explicit processing in learning from examples: A synergistic effect. *Journal of Experimental Psychology: Learning, Memory, & Cognition, 15,* 1083–1100.

Perruchet, P,. Gallego, J., & Savy, I. (in press). A critical reappraisal of the evidence for unconscious abstraction of deterministic rules in complex experimental situations. *Cognitive Psychology.*

Perruchet, P., & Pacteau, C. (in press). Synthetic grammar learning: Implicit rule abstraction or explicit fragmentary knowledge? *Journal of Experimental Psychology: General.*

Rabinowitz, J. C., Mandler, G., & Patterson, K. E. (1977a). Determinants of recognition and recall: Accessibility and generation. *Journal of Experimental Psychology: General, 106,* 302–329.

Rabinowitz, J. C., Mandler, G., & Patterson, K. E. (1977b). Clarifications, refutations, and resolutions. *Journal of Experimental Psychology: General, 106,* 336–340.

Reber, A. S. (1967). Implicit learning of artificial grammars. *Journal of Verbal Learning and Verbal Behavior, 5,* 855–863.

Reber, A. S., Allen, R., & Regan, S. (1985). Syntactical learning and judgment, still conscious and still abstract: Comment on Dulany, Carlson, & Dewey. *Journal of Experimental Psychology: General, 114,* 17–24.

Reber, A. S., Kassin, S. M., Lewis, S., & Cantor, G. (1980). On the relationship between implicit and explicit modes of learning a complex rule structure. *Journal of Experimental Psychology: Human Learning & Memory, 6,* 492–502.

Sanderson, P. M. (1989). Verbalizable knowledge and skilled task performance: Association, dissociation, and mental modes. *Journal of Experimental Psychology: Learning, Memory, & Cognition, 15,* 729–747.

Stanley, W. B., Mathews, R. C., Buss, R. R., & Kotler-Cope, S. (1988). Insight without awareness: On the interaction of verbalization, instruction and practice in a simulated process control task. *Quarterly Journal of Experimental Psychology, 40A,* 135–165.

Tulving, E. (1983). *Elements of episodic memory.* Oxford: Oxford University Press.

Tulving, E., Schacter, D. L., & Stark, H. A. (1982). Priming effects in word-fragment completion are independent of recognition memory. *Journal of Experimental Psychology: Learning, Memory, & Cognition, 8,* 336–342.

Watkins, M. J., & Tulving, E. (1975). Episodic memory: When recognition fails. *Journal of Experimental Psychology: General, 104,* 5–29.

10 Implicit and Explicit Memory: An Old Model for New Findings

Peter Graf
University of British Columbia

> *A teacher affects eternity: he can never tell where his influence stops.*
> —H. B. Adams (1838–1918)

On a recent visit to a local art gallery, the chance meeting with a young woman and her warm and cheerful greeting started me on a frenzied search of memory. She looked so familiar, yet I did not recognize her. Who do I know with long brown hair? Who likes silk-screens and watercolors? The mystery was solved when the woman explained she was glad to have passed her statistics exam.

A feeling of *familiarity in the absence of recognition* occurs most frequently when we meet someone in an unexpected place, but it is also triggered by a range of other out-of-context stimuli, such as a book or movie title, an uncommon scent, or the sound of a voice. What causes this phenomenon? What are the mental processes that mediate it? What is the relationship between familiarity without recognition and true recognition (of a previous encounter with an item)? In the 1970s, George Mandler raised and addressed these important questions in a series of papers that culminated in an influential theoretical model (Mandler, 1980). In addition to familiarity without recognition and true recognition, this model explained other major memory phenomena, including the word frequency paradox and recognition failure of recallable words. The fact that this model continues to shape and direct contemporary investigations is a tribute to George's profound and inspiring understanding of human memory.

Mandler postulated two bases for recognition—familiarity and retrieval—and he argued that these components make independent contributions to recognition test performance. He defended this claim, in part by pointing to Warrington and Weiskrantz's (1970) observations that in amnesic patients some aspects of memory can function normally even when others are severely impaired. A direct test of this prediction about the memory functions of amnesic patients (Graf, Squire, & Mandler, 1984) stimulated parallel investigations of test performance dissocia-

135

tions in healthy individuals (e.g., Graf & Mandler, 1984; Graf, Mandler, & Haden, 1982; Jacoby & Dallas, 1981; Tulving, Schacter, & Stark, 1982). And the combined findings from these studies served as a major impetus for recent research on what is now widely known as implicit and explicit memory (cf. Graf & Schacter, 1985).

Implicit and explicit describe the mental set that guides subjects' performance on different memory tests. Performance of standard memory tests, such as recall and recognition, is called *explicit* because subjects attempt to recollect information from a specific prior study episode in a conscious and deliberate manner. In contrast, performance of priming tests, such as word completion and word identification, is called *implicit* because it taps the influence of prior study episodes in the absence of subjects' conscious attempts to recollect them. Research on implicit and explicit memory has mushroomed in recent years. It has yielded a range of new methods for assessing implicit memory, and revealed important similarities and differences between implicit and explicit memory test performance. However, theoretical understanding of these findings has developed more slowly, and as yet no account of the perceptual and cognitive processes that underlie implicit and explicit memory test performance has gained widespread acceptance.

To remedy this situation, I invite you to consider Mandler's recognition model as an account for the findings from implicit and explicit memory tests. Several previous papers have established the applicability of this model to some results in this domain (Graf & Mandler, 1984; Graf et al., 1982; Mandler, Graf, & Kraft, 1986); this chapter demonstrates that it can accommodate all major findings. Toward this goal, the following section briefly reviews prominent findings from research on implicit and explicit memory, and the final section explains these with the help of Mandler's model.

PROMINENT FINDINGS

Current interest in implicit and explicit memory was ignited by studies of patients with anterograde amnesia (e.g., Cohen & Squire, 1980; Graf et al., 1984; Warrington & Weiskrantz, 1970; for reviews see Shimamura, 1989; Tulving & Schacter, 1990). They showed that even though amnesics' explicit memory test performance is severely impaired, their performance of implicit memory tests can be entirely normal. This puzzling finding inspired investigators whose efforts had previously focused more narrowly (exclusively) on explicit memory test performance. It raised questions about memory functions that are selectively spared versus impaired in organic amnesia. It motivated experiments on how memory functions change over the course of life—from early childhood through to late adulthood (for a review see Graf, 1990; Light, 1988). And most important to cognitive psychology, this finding initiated widespread research into the nature of the mental processes or the systems that underlie implicit and explicit memory performance.

Most of the extant research on implicit and explicit memory can be arranged into two basic groups: One is composed of experiments that manipulated study tasks, that is, how To-Be-Remembered (TBR) materials were processed during the study trial, and the other includes those that manipulated the type of TBR materials that were presented for study. The first two parts of this section review the major findings from each group. The focus is on experiments with healthy young adults because they have been extensively studied and thus provide the most comprehensive data base. The third part gives a brief description of a recent experiment that addressed questions about the functions of implicit and explicit memory—how they transfer information within and across study/test settings.

Task Effects. Memory test performance reflects the type of encoding engaged by different study tasks. This widely accepted idea is supported by a myriad of experiments that manipulated study trial activities by, for example, requiring subjects to answer questions about the meaning of TBR words (e.g., Does the word belong to the category fruit?) or about their appearance (e.g., Is the word written in capital letters?) (for a review see Cermak & Craik, 1979). The well-known results from recall and recognition tests—higher performance after semantic than nonsemantic study tasks—highlight the importance of semantic/elaborative processing for explicit remembering.

More recent experiments that assessed both implicit and explicit memory point to a more complex relationship between study trial activities and test performance, however. Concretely, the findings show three patterns of implicit/explicit test effects. The first comes from experiments that presented TBR words in conditions that focused processing either on the meaning of words or on their physical appearance (e.g., Graf & Mandler, 1984; Jacoby & Dallas, 1981). The result showed the familiar levels of processing effect—higher performance after the semantic than nonsemantic task—on explicit memory tests. More importantly, there was no effect due to the different study tasks on implicit memory (word completion and word identification test) performance.

A different pattern of effects was revealed by experiments that examined retention of TBR words that subjects either read or generated with the help of cues (e.g., Jacoby, 1983; Roediger & Blaxton, 1987). To illustrate, Jacoby had subjects study antonym pairs, such as UNDER–OVER, either by reading them or by generating the second word from each pair when given the first as a cue (e.g., UNDER—???). Retention of the right-hand word from each pair was assessed with a recognition test and a word identification test. The recognition results showed higher performance in the generate (78%) than read condition (72%), whereas identification performance showed more priming in the read (15%) than generate (7%) condition.

A third pattern of results was revealed by experiments that focused on memory for newly acquired associations between unrelated words (e.g., Graf & Schacter, 1987, 1989; Schacter & Graf, 1986). In these experiments, subjects were shown a list of unrelated cue-target pairs (e.g., COFFEE—WALLET) and then were given a word completion test in which some word stems appeared in the same context as in the study list (COFFEE—WAL_____) and others appeared in a different context (TABLE—WAL_____). The instructions were to complete the stems with the first words that came to mind. Under these conditions, a tendency to write more studied words as completions in the same- versus different-context condition shows implicit memory for associations that were newly acquired during the study trial. The experiments showed such evidence, but only when the study tasks required subjects to relate paired words in a meaningful manner (i.e., with semantic/elaborative processing); tasks that did not require this type of processing showed no evidence of associative priming (Graf & Schacter, 1985). The same finding was also observed with explicit memory tests. Interestingly, however, the results showed that the amount of associative priming was comparable across a range of elaborative study tasks that produced substantially different levels of explicit memory (free and cued recall) test performance (Graf & Schacter, 1989; Schacter & Graf, 1986).

In combination, these findings highlight the complex relationship between study trial processing and retention performance; study tasks that increase performance of explicit memory tests can have no effect, similar effects, or opposite effects on implicit memory test performance. To understand this relationship, the final section of this chapter focuses on the nature of processing that is induced by each study trial activity, as well as by each memory test. My overall goal is to show how study trial processing relates to that engaged by implicit and explicit memory tests.

Materials Effects.   An equally complex pattern of effects has emerged from experiments that manipulated materials between study and testing. The best known finding in this area is that priming effects are generally larger for TBR words that were studied and tested in the same sensory modality (e.g., visual), than for words that were presented in different sensory modalities (e.g., auditory at study and visual at testing; e.g., Clarke, & Morton, 1983; Kirsner, Milech, & Standon, 1983; Roediger & Blaxton, 1987; Schacter & Graf, 1989). In contrast, recall and recognition performance typically show minimal effects or no effects due to study/test modality manipulations.

Other material manipulations influence both implicit and explicit memory performance, with the pattern of effects being either the same or different across test types. Both similar and different effects across tests were observed in experiments that varied the language (Spanish, English) (e.g., Watkins & Peynircioglu, 1983) or the symbolic form (words, pictures) (e.g., Weldon & Roediger, 1987) in which TBR items were presented for study and testing. To illustrate, in a recent experiment Graf and Miki (1990) presented subjects with three types of items: simple objects (e.g., BRUSH, PENCIL), black-and-white photos of the same objects, and written names of the objects. Explicit memory was assessed with a word (i.e., object–name) recognition test and a free recall test, whereas implicit memory was assessed with a word (i.e., object–name) identification test and with a picture (i.e., black-and-white photos of the objects) identification test.

The results, listed in Table 10.1, highlight three points. First, explicit memory test performance was as expected—higher on photos and objects than on written words. Second, the pattern of effects produced by study-list words, photos, and objects was similar across the two explicit memory tests. Third, the two implicit memory tests revealed a different pattern of effects; word identification showed a large priming effect for written words and a smaller effect for photos, whereas picture identification showed a large priming effect for photos and no effect for words. Objects produced intermediate priming effects on both tests. The effects for words and pictures indicate that priming increases when the study materials match the format of the cues provided for testing. The combined findings in Table 10.1 illustrate that whether material manipulations have the same or different effects on implicit and explicit memory depends on the specific tests that are used.

More subtle influences of materials on retention performance were revealed by experiments that varied only the appearance of TBR targets (e.g., written words) between study and testing. The results are ambiguous, however. Some experiments have shown significantly larger priming effects for words presented in the same visual format at study and testing than for words displayed in different formats. Jacoby and Hayman (1987), for example, found higher identification test performance on words tested in a normal lower-case type font after subjects studied the words in the same lower-case font than after studying them in a large (10 times larger than normal) unusual type font. In contrast, a large

TABLE 10.1
Average (%) Explicit and Implicit Memory Test
Performance Following Study of Three Item Types*

	Study-List Items		
	Words	Photos	Objects
Explicit Tests			
Word recognition	63	95	96
Free recall	21	50	58
Implicit Tests			
Word identification	18	5	12
Picture identification	3	34	18

*Tabled values show priming on the implicit memory tests.

number of experiments have shown little or no effect on the magnitude of priming even when the appearance of printed words or sentences changed substantially between study and testing (e.g., Carr, Brown, & Charalambous, 1989; Clarke & Morton, 1983; Levy & Kirsner, 1989). Clarke and Morton (1983), for example, presented words for study either in typed or handwritten form and found comparable facilitation effects on subsequent identification of words that were tested in typed form, and Scarborough, Cortese, and Scarborough (1977) found no effect on lexical decision task performance when they changed the case (upper to lower) of words between study and testing.

These conflicting findings were illuminated by a recent experiment (Graf & Ryan, 1990) in which TBR words were presented for study and testing either in the same or in a different unusual type font (Applesoft *pudgy* or *shadow*). A word identification test and a word recognition test were used to assess implicit and explicit memory, respectively. The results showed format specific priming effects but only when subjects were given a study task that focused processing on the visual appearance of the target words (i.e., when required to rate the words for readability) and not when the study task directed processing to semantic attributes (i.e., when required to rate the words for pleasantness). Equally important, recognition test performance showed the same pattern of effects. We used these and related findings to argue that format specific effects occur only when subjects focus processing on the sensory and perceptual features of TBR targets, and we suggested that this type of processing can be engaged either directly by means of study task instructions or indirectly by presenting materials in a highly unusual format.

To summarize this section, it is clear that some material manipulations influence implicit but not explicit memory performance, whereas others influence both and produce either a similar or different pattern of effects across test types. And still other more subtle manipulations have no effect on either form of memory unless they are combined with study tasks that focus processing on sensory and perceptual features of the TBR items.

Setting Effects.   Effects due to the setting or environment in which an experiment is carried out are interesting for two reasons. First, the setting presents stimuli or materials that may influence performance even though subjects do not deliberately attend to them during study. Second, interest comes from previous work which demonstrated that a change in the environment between study and testing can reduce explicit memory test performance (e.g., Godden & Baddeley, 1975); yet to my knowledge, no one has examined whether setting manipulations influence implicit memory. The findings (from the last section) that material manipulations can have large effects on implicit memory raise the possibility that priming is also highly sensitive to setting manipulations.

To examine this possibility, TBR items (words or word pairs) were studied in one of two settings: the gallery of the University of British Columbia's (UBC) main swimming pool or a games arcade at the UBC undergraduate student center. These two settings, which are located in adjacent buildings on the UBC campus, differ in several respects, including visual and spatial cues, smell, temperature, noise, and crowd levels. Testing occurred either in the same setting as study or in the other setting. Implicit memory was assessed with a category production test and a word completion test, whereas explicit memory was assessed with a category cued recall test and a letter-cued recall test (for more details see Graf, 1988).

The results are shown in Table 10.2. They underline two findings: first, priming effects were larger when study and testing were in the same versus different settings, and second, this manipulation had no effect on either explicit memory test. The latter finding conflicts with the results from Godden and Baddeley (1975), but it is consistent with a report by Smith (1979) who showed that setting effects disappear when test instructions direct subjects to think themselves back into the original learning environment. All explicit memory tests involve thinking back; the appropriate mental set is induced by the instruction to recollect information from a specific prior episode. In contrast, in the absence of a prior-episode-directed mental set, implicit memory performance is guided only by cues from the test form, by the instructions and the setting, and thus is highly likely to be influenced by a change in setting between study and testing. This reasoning and the overall pattern of results in Table 10.2 are relevant to understanding the different functions of implicit and explicit memory: Explicit memory is suited for the export/import of information across study/test settings, whereas implicit memory is specialized for making information available in the context in which it was acquired.

TABLE 10.2
Average (%) Explicit and Implicit Memory Test
Performance When Study and Testing Occurred
in the Same Setting or in Different Settings*

	Study-Test Setting	
	Same	Different
Explicit Tests		
Category-cued recall	62	62
Letter-cued recall	46	43
Implicit Tests		
Category production	33	22
Word-stem completion	24	14

*The settings used were the gallery of a large swimming pool and a games arcade in an undergraduate student center. The tabled values show priming on the implicit memory tests.

Summary. This brief review of research is far from being comprehensive; the goal was to focus on important similarities and differences between implicit and explicit memory test performance. What is highlighted by these findings is, first, that both study task and material manipulations can influence performance of implicit and explicit memory tests; second, that performance effects on one test type can occur in the absence of effects on the other test type; and, third, that the pattern of effects across test types can be either similar or different. To understand this combination of findings, the next section of the chapter examines the nature of processing that is recruited (by tasks and/or materials) during the study trial and by each memory test, and it emphasizes how study processing maps onto test trial processing. This exercise is facilitated by Mandler's model that identifies the processes that mediate implicit and explicit memory test performance.

ORGANIZING PROCESSES FOR IMPLICIT AND EXPLICIT MEMORY

To understand Mandler's account of these findings, we must consider it in the context of a general framework that derives from the work of Kolers and his colleagues (e.g., Kolers, 1975; Kolers & Ostry, 1974). This framework holds that retention is best understood in terms of the cognitive operations that are engaged by different study and test activities. Kolers proposed that a task like reading a word or sentence, for example, requires a particular set of sensory-perceptual and conceptual analyzing operations, and that engaging these operations has the same effect as practicing a skill—it increases the fluency and efficiency with which they can be carried out subsequently. By this reasoning, performance of a memory test is facilitated to the extent that it engages the same set or a similar set of mental operations as a preceding study task; more generally, remembering is determined by the degree of overlap between study and test processing. This view of memory is generally known as Transfer Appropriate Processing (TAP) (cf. Morris, Bransford, & Franks, 1977).

The concept of TAP—that performance is determined by the degree of overlap between study and test processing—does not itself explain similarities and differences between implicit and explicit memory effects; it is a framework for thinking about memory test performance. Within this framework, any meaningful explanation of implicit/explicit effects must specify the processes that underlie each form of memory. Cognitive psychology provides several dimensions for classifying processing, including shallow versus deep (Craik & Lockhart, 1972), automatic versus controlled (Hasher & Zacks, 1979), and data- versus resource-limited (Norman & Bobrow, 1975). Mandler's extensive empirical and theoretical work has underscored the advantages of defining processes in terms of two memory organizing consequences—integration and elaboration (Mandler, 1980, 1988), and in several previous papers we have used this distinction to explain similarities and differences between implicit and explicit memory (e.g., Graf & Mandler, 1984; Graf et al., 1982; Graf & Schacter, 1987, 1989; Mandler, 1988).

Integration results from processing that bonds the features of a target into a coordinated whole or unitized representation; it occurs when we either perceive coherence among separate stimulus components (e.g., under the guidance of pre-existing representations or Gestalt laws like proximity and good continuation) or conceive a structure for processing target features concurrently (cf. Graf & Schacter, 1989; Mandler, 1980, 1988). Elaboration results from processing that associates a target with other mental contents; it occurs when a target is encoded in relation to the experimental situation (e.g., other targets, situational cues, relevant prior knowledge), thereby embedding its unitized representation in a network of other representations. We have made two assumptions: first, that each study task engages a combination of integrative and elaborative processing, and that tasks differ by emphasizing one or the other type of processing. The second assumption is that implicit memory tests engage primarily integrative processing whereas explicit memory tests engage primarily elaborative processing. Thus, consistent with TAP, implicit memory test performance is assumed to reflect primarily study/test overlaps in integrative processing, whereas explicit memory test performance is assumed to reflect primarily study/test overlaps in elaborative processing.

An intuitive analysis of the processing requirements of different memory tests serves to validate these assumptions. Implicit memory tests require subjects to name items in response to category labels, to complete words in response to word fragments (e.g., GRA_____; V _ _ L _ N), or to identify briefly presented words. In all cases, performance requires perceiving or conceiving a structure that organizes (integrates) the cueing information and thereby specifies a target or target set. Study trial integration facilitates this type of processing because once unitized, a representation has the tendency to become completely re-integrated even when only some of its components are subsequently reprocessed (e.g., Horowitz & Prytulak, 1969; Mandler, 1980, 1988). Priming effects are thus an index of the increased integration produced by study trial processing. Explicit memory tests require subjects either to recollect previously studied items in response to cues (cued recall test), in the absence of cues (free recall test), or to decide what targets had appeared in a previously studied list (recognition test). In all cases, performance requires retrieval of information that associates a target with a specific prior episode. Therefore, elaboration during the study trial facilitates explicit remembering because it involves encoding targets in relation to the experimental situation, thereby establishing the associations that link each target with a specific learning episode.

To explain the wide range of priming effects summarized in the preceding sections, Mandler's model focuses on the nature of processing engaged at testing, and on how this processing overlaps with the integrated representations encoded during the study trial. When implicit memory is assessed with a visual word identification test, for example, processing is focused primarily on sensory and perceptual features of written words. The size of priming effects reflects the extent to which test processing overlaps with study trial processing and thereby triggers the reintegration of encoded representations. This overlap (and thus priming) is greatest when the same written words were presented for study, and is smaller for study-list spoken words, for study-list words in a different language, for subject generated words, and for items in a different symbolic form (i.e., pictures).

The failure to find different priming effects with some material manipulations also fits this interpretation. It occurs because with an average of almost two decades of practice reading printed and handwritten words, the typical college student subject has accumulated a large repertoire of well-practiced word identification procedures. Thus, only extreme manipulations (like that used by Jacoby & Hayman, 1987) are likely to invoke a detailed feature analysis of TBR words. Ordinary manipulations (e.g., upper/lower case, handwriting) are unlikely to engage an extensive analysis of TBR words—especially of details about their appearance—because subjects have spent a life-time ignoring these aspects of words by focusing instead on their semantic and other attributes.

The lack of effects due to some material manipulations emphasizes that priming reflects the overlap in processing—not materials—between study and testing. This idea is underlined by the results from Graf and Ryan (1990). They showed that the same material manipulation produced format specific effects when study trial processing focused on the sensory/perceptual features of TBR words but not when it focused on their semantic attributes. But not all study-task-induced processing influences priming. Graf and Ryan found an effect when words were displayed in unusual type fonts (Applesoft *pudgy* and *shadow*); others showed words in familiar fonts and found no difference in priming effects with semantic and nonsemantic study tasks (e.g., Graf et al., 1982; Jacoby & Dallas, 1981). We assume that the latter occurred because common words are processed primarily in terms of pre-existing analyzing procedures, and these are executed automatically and independently of the requirements of different study tasks.

In addition to materials and study trial activities, two other sources affect the study/test processing overlap. The first—processing induced by different tests—depends on the type of test cues (e.g., written vs. spoken words, words vs. pictures) and test instructions. Roediger and his colleagues have emphasized effects due to different tests in several recent papers (e.g., Roediger & Blaxton, 1987; Weldon & Roediger, 1987). A second factor is the setting in which TBR items are studied and tested. The cues provided by each setting induce processing that becomes part of the representations established during the study trial, and a change in these cues reduces the probability that test processing overlaps with study trial processing.

CONCLUSION

This chapter features Mandler's model as an account for the major findings from research on implicit and explicit memory. Because Mandler's work has already covered the domain of explicit memory, I focused on implicit memory. Even though I did not discuss other available explanations, my motivation was not to portray Mandler's model as the only account for the extant findings. Instead, the goal was to argue that this model deserves more serious consideration. The foremost reason is its ability to accommodate the wide range of extant findings. A second reason comes from the fact that it shows the ways in which the new research on implicit and explicit memory is connected with previous research, thereby lending some continuity to our enterprise. A third and final reason is that Mandler has provided a quantitative version of his model that enables us to make strong predictions and thus conduct better research.

ACKNOWLEDGMENTS

Preparation of this chapter was supported by a grant from the Natural Sciences and Engineering Research Council of Canada. I thank Karen Gallie, Laureen Miki, and Lee Ryan for helpful comments on earlier drafts.

REFERENCES

Carr, T. H., Brown, J. S., & Charalambous, A. (1989). Repetition and reading: Perceptual encoding mechanisms are very abstract but not very interactive. *Journal of Experimental Psychology: Learning, Memory, and Cognition, 15*, 763–778.

Cermak, L. S., & Craik, F. I. M. (1979). *Levels of processing in human memory.* Hillsdale, NJ: Lawrence Erlbaum Associates.

Clarke, R., & Morton, J. (1983). Cross modality facilitation in tachistoscopic word recognition. *Quarterly Journal of Experimental Psychology, 35A*, 79–96.

Cohen, N. J., & Squire, L. R. (1980). Preserved learning and retention of pattern-analyzing skill in amnesia: Dissociation of knowing how and knowing that. *Science, 210*, 207–210.

Craik, F. I. M., & Lockhart, R. S. (1972). Levels of processing: A framework for memory research. *Journal of Verbal Learning and Verbal Behavior, 11*, 671–684.

Godden, D. R., & Baddeley, A. D. (1975). Context-dependent memory in two natural environments: On land and under water. *British Journal of Psychology, 66*, 325–331.

Graf, P. (1988). *Implicit and explicit memory in same and different environments.* Paper presented at the annual Psychonomic Society Meeting, Chicago, IL.

Graf, P. (1990). Life-span changes in implicit and explicit memory. *Bulletin of the Psychonomic Society, 28*, 353–358.

Graf, P., & Mandler, G. (1984). Activation makes words more accessible but not necessarily more retrievable. *Journal of Verbal Learning and Verbal Behavior, 23*, 553–568.

Graf, P., Mandler, G., & Haden, M. (1982). Simulating amnesic symptoms in normal subjects. *Science, 218*, 1243–1244.

Graf, P., & Miki, L. (1990). Implicit and explicit memory in advertising. Paper presented at the annual meeting of the Canadian Psychological Association, Ottawa, ON.

Graf, P., & Ryan, L. (1990). Transfer appropriate processing for implicit and explicit memory. *Journal Experimental Psychology: Learning, Memory & Cognition, 16,* 978–992.

Graf, P., & Schacter, D. L. (1985). Implicit and explicit memory for new associations in normal and amnesic subjects. *Journal of Experimental Psychology: Learning, Memory, and Cognition, 11,* 501–518.

Graf, P., & Schacter, D. L. (1987). Selective effects of interference on implicit and explicit memory for new associations. *Journal of Experimental Psychology: Learning, Memory, and Cognition, 13,* 45–53.

Graf, P., & Schacter, D. L. (1989). Unitization and grouping mediate dissociations in memory for new associations. *Journal of Experimental Psychology: Learning, Memory, and Cognition, 15,* 930–940.

Graf, P., Squire, L. R., & Mandler, G. (1984). The information that amnesic patients do not forget. *Journal of Experimental Psychology: Learning, Memory, and Cognition, 10,* 164–178.

Hasher, L., & Zacks, R. T. (1979). Automatic and effortful processes in memory. *Journal of Experimental Psychology: General, 108,* 356–388.

Horowitz, L. M., & Prytulak, L. S. (1969). Redintegrative memory. *Psychological Review, 84,* 519–531.

Jacoby, L. L. (1983). Remembering the data: Analyzing interactive processes in reading. *Journal of Verbal Learning and Verbal Behavior, 22,* 485–508.

Jacoby, L. L., & Dallas, M. (1981). On the relationship between autobiographical memory and perceptual learning. *Journal of Experimental Psychology: General, 110,* 306–340.

Jacoby, L. L., & Hayman, C. A. G. (1987). Specific visual transfer in word identification. *Journal of Experimental Psychology: Learning, Memory, and Cognition, 13,* 456–463.

Krisner, K., Milech, D., & Standon, D. (1983). Common and modality-specific processes in the mental lexicon. *Memory and Cognition, 11,* 621–630.

Kolers, P. A. (1975). Memorial consequences of automatized encoding. *Journal of Experimental Psychology: Human Learning and Memory, 1,* 689–701.

Kolers, P. A., & Ostry, D. J. (1974). Time course of loss of information regarding pattern analyzing operations. *Journal of Verbal Learning and Verbal Behavior, 13,* 599–612.

Levy, B. A., & Kirsner, K. (1989). Reprocessing text: Indirect measures of word and message level processes. *Journal of Experimental Psychology: Learning, Memory, and Cognition, 15,* 407–417.

Light, L. L. (1988). Preserved implicit memory in old age. In M. M. Gruenberg, P. E. Morris, & R. N. Sykes (Eds.), *Practical Aspects of Memory: Current Research and Issues, 2,* 90–95. Chichester, England: Wiley.

Mandler, G. (1980). Recognizing: The judgment of previous occurrence. *Psychological Review, 87,* 252–271.

Mandler, G. (1988). Memory: Conscious and unconscious. In P. R. Solomon, G. R. Goethals, C. M. Kelley, & B. R. Stephens (Eds.), *Memory: Interdisciplinary approaches* (pp. 84–106). Springer-Verlag: New York.

Mandler, G., Graf, P. & Kraft, D. (1986). Activation and elaboration effects in recognition and word priming. *Quarterly Journal of Experimental Psychology, 38a,* 645–662.

Morris, C. D., Bransford, J. D., & Franks, J. J. (1977). Levels of processing versus transfer appropriate processing. *Journal of Verbal Learning and Verbal Behavior, 16,* 519–533.

Norman, D. A., & Bobrow, D. G. (1975). On data-limited and resource-limited processes. *Cognitive Psychology, 7*(4), 44–64.

Roediger, H. L., & Blaxton, T. A. (1987). Effects of varying modality, surface features, and retention interval on priming in word-fragment completion. *Memory and Cognition, 15,* 379–388.

Scarborough, D. L., Cortese, C., & Scarborough, H. S. (1977). Frequency and repetition effects in lexical memory. *Journal of Experimental Psychology: Human Perception and Performance, 3,* 1–17.

Schacter, D. L., & Graf, P. (1986). Effects of elaborative processing on implicit and explicit memory for new associations. *Journal of Experimental Psychology: Learning, Memory, and Cognition, 12,* 432–444.

Schacter, D. L., & Graf, P. (1989). Modality specificity of implicit memory for new associations. *Journal of Experimental Psychology: Learning, Memory, and Cognition, 15,* 3–12.

Shimamura, A. P. (1989). Disorders of memory: The cognitive science perspective. In F. Boller & J. Grafman (Eds.), *Handbook of neuropsychology* (Vol. 3, pp. 35–73). New York: Elsevier.

Smith, S. M. (1979). Remembering in and out of context. *Journal of Experimental Psychology: Human Learning and Memory, 5,* 460–471.

Tulving, E., & Schacter, D. L. (1990). Priming and human memory systems. *Science, 247,* 301–306.

Tulving, E., Schacter, D. L., & Stark, H. A. (1982). Priming effects in word-fragment completion are independent of recognition memory. *Journal of Experimental Psychology: Learning, Memory, and Cognition, 8,* 336–342.

Warrington, E. K., & Weiskrantz, L. (1970). Amnesic syndrome: Consolidation or retrieval? *Nature, 228,* 628–630.

Watkins, M. J., & Peynircioglu, Z. (1983). On the nature of word recall: Evidence for linguistic specificity. *Journal of Verbal Learning and Verbal Behavior, 22,* 385–394.

Weldon, M. S., & Roediger, H. L. (1987). Altering retrieval demands reverses the picture superiority effect. *Memory and Cognition, 15,* 269–280.

11 On Relating the Organizational Theory of Memory to Levels of Processing

Gordon H. Bower
Stanford University

David J. Bryant
Stanford University

It is fitting in this festschrift to focus on some of the themes that guided George Mandler's memory research, and relate those themes to contemporary developments in memory theory. For these purposes, we would like to briefly review the salient themes of one of Mandler's most influential papers, "Organization and Memory." It was published in the initial volume of the new serial *The Psychology of Learning and Motivation* edited by Kenneth and Janet Spence (1967). By chance, Bower also had an article in this same volume, and soon assumed editorship of that series.

TO ORGANIZE IS TO MEMORIZE

Mandler's thesis in that seminal article was that memory was strongly influenced by the way learners attempt to organize the to-be-remembered materials. After reviewing some earlier Gestalt ideas about memory, Mandler stated his theoretical program in a series of three propositions, as follows:

> First, memory and organization are not only correlated, but organization is a necessary condition for memory. Second, the organization of, and hence memory for, verbal material is hierarchical, with words organized in successively higher-order categories. Third, the storage capacity within any one category or within any level of categories is limited. (Mandler, 1967, p. 328)

Mandler also spelled out more specifically what he meant by organization:

> A set of objects or events are said to be organized when a consistent relation among the members of the set can be specified and, specifically, when membership of the

objects or events in subsets (groups, concepts, categories, chunks) is stable and identifiable. (Mandler, 1967, p. 330)

Other ideas central in memory theory at the time Mandler was writing were George Miller's notions of *chunking* and that memory capacity was limited in terms of chunks (Miller, 1956). As applied to the memory task of interest to him, Mandler had a ready identification for what should count as the "chunks" for subjects learning to recall lists of words: Chunks should be the meaningful groups, clusters, and categories of list-words that subjects might notice and use to relate the words to one another. Evidence for such chunking in free recall had already been reported by Bousfield (1953), who described how subjects clustered in free recall taxonomically related words that had been presented to them in random order. In collaboration with Endel Tulving, his then-colleague at the University of Toronto, Mandler extended the underlying idea, believing that subjects would find their own organization and subjective chunks even when the list-words did not fall into simple taxonomic categories.

SUBJECTIVE ORGANIZATION

To study the formation and utilization of such subjective groupings, Mandler and Zena Pearlstone (1966) invented the experimental paradigm of unconstrained sorting of list-words followed by free recall. In that procedure, subjects sort the list words (on cards) into whatever meaningful categories or subjective groupings they may notice, going through the deck of word-cards repeatedly until they attained consistent groupings for two trials. Typically, subjects used two to seven categories (mean of 4.3) for a list of 52 unrelated words, reaching criterion of consistent sorting in about six trials. When asked unexpectedly for free recall of the list words, subjects recalled about 40% of the words; those who had settled upon a larger number of subjective groupings during the sorting task produced greater recall. In fact, free recall increased as a linear function of the number of subjective categories people discovered in the collection of words, with a positive slope of between 2 and 6 words per added category depending on conditions (see Figure 11.1). Thus, the more subjects divided and classified the list-words, the more they organized the material, the better was their memory for it.

In order to show that what was important for memory was organization rather than study trials, Mandler ran yoked control subjects. Each free-sorting subject was yoked to a control subject who was constrained to sort the words into the same number of categories as the first subject had freely selected. These yoked subjects took nearly twice as long to arrive at a consistent sorting; despite these extra trials, however, the yoked subjects recalled about the same number of words from the list. In further control experiments, Mandler found that recall was affected in the same positive manner by number of sorting categories whether (a)

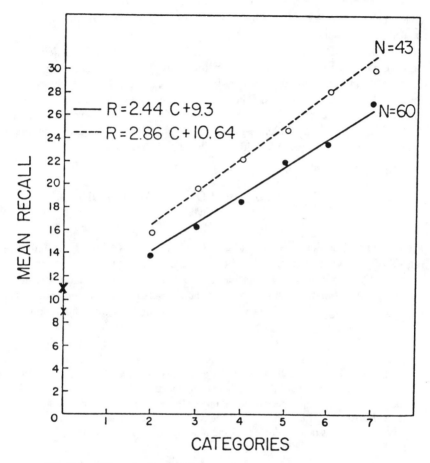

FIG 11.1.   Mean recall as a function of the number of categories subjects were instructed to use in sorting 52 words. Filled circles are for all
60 subjects; open circles are for only those 43 subjects who used
categories based on word meanings. Reproduced from Mandler (1967)
"Organization and Memory" by permission of the author and the publishers, Academic Press.

the subjects did or did not expect a recall test after the sorting task (i.e., intentional versus incidental learning), and (b) the number of categories was self-
selected by the free-sorting subject or was pre-specified by the experimenter, as
in the yoking experiment mentioned above.

Such results supported Mandler's general thesis. Memory was seen as a
natural consequence or by-product of organizational (or item relating) processes
carried out on the materials. Note that sorting items into meaningful groups
requires comparing, relating, and contrasting their semantic features to one an-

other. The critical variable for recall was the extent of organization the subject was able to impose upon (or find in) the material, not the number of trials required to do so or the intention to memorize or the ability to select one's preferred number of categories. The results provided considerable support for Mandler's first and third themes mentioned above. The support for his second theme, of hierarchical retrieval schemes, was indirect and relied more on arguments about how subjects were ever able to recall more than seven chunks or categories. More direct evidence for hierarchical retrieval schemes came along later (e.g., Bower, Clark, Lesgold, & Winzenz, 1969).

BOWER'S RESEARCH ON ORGANIZATION
AND MEMORY

Stimulated by Mandler's papers and those on his Toronto colleague, Endel Tulving (1962, 1964), Bower began his own research on organizational factors in memory. Organizational theory in memory began as a revolt against stimulus-response association psychology, much as the Gestalt approach to perception also began in revolt against elementary associationism. In describing this revolt, the first author wrote:

> A modest revolution is afoot today within the field of human learning, and the rebels are marching under the banner of 'cognitive organization.' Although there is little altogether new under this psychological sun, the newer organizational man does have a different perspective and slant of attack on memory problems than do his S–R associationistic progenitors. The result has been a changing emphasis in what research gets done by the rebels and how they talk about it. (Bower, 1970, p. 18–19)

The research program carried out by Bower during that period had several related theoretical themes, summarized in two review chapters (Bower, 1970, 1972): (a) that people stored materials in terms of how they organized them into subjective groups or units; (b) that these groups came to act almost as all-or-none units in recall and in causing interference; (c) that groupings were determined by numerous Gestalt perceptual factors surrounding the presentation of the materials; (d) that repeated material is not recognized if it is regrouped into novel perceptual units upon its repetition, with the consequence that reorganization caused by regrouping of materials into different chunks seriously disrupted the normal benefits of repetition on memory. Evidence was also obtained for how memory benefited whenever the learning materials could be organized into hierarchies of categories, so that recall of a top-level chunk could iteratively cue retrieval of subordinate chunks contained in it.

In addition, Bower was interested in how the overall organization of a list of material affected the encoding and memory for single items embedded in the list. This topic was pursued most thoroughly in the context of people learning paired-associate lists, in which the nominal stimulus and response terms of the entire list did or did not follow some simple rule. Example rules were that the stimulus and response words of all pairs in the list were rhymes, or members of the same category, or related by simple inversion of letters, and so on. The point of the demonstration experiments was that learners were searching for rules characterizing entire sets of learning materials (S–R pairs), and that the difficulty of learning a single item or pair could not be assessed without considering whether it fit into a general rule covering the whole list. Such research was the verbal-learning equivalent of the Gestalt dictum that "the whole determines the parts" of a psychological field; the rule characterizing a set of S–R pairs would be an "emergent" property of the whole set, not an especially salient feature of any pair in the set when it was considered in isolation.

THE SUCCESS, THEN WANING
OF ORGANIZATION THEORY

All of these findings were compatible with the "Mandler Manifesto" set forth in his 1967 article. By the early to mid-1970s, the organizational steamroller had taken over memory research, become the dominant theoretical stance, and "won the day." And then a curious thing happened: As organizational theory became the accepted doctrine, it lost its enthusiastic thrust, it lost its dedicated adherents, and several counter-revolutionary movements began to crop up. Moreover, several totally new areas of memory research developed attractively, areas to which organizational theory had relatively little to contribute. Some of the newer research topics were those pertaining to the semantic-episode memory distinction, the knowledge-base underlying semantic question-answering, memory-search strategies, and the relation between recall and recognition. Although Mandler contributed to these research areas (e.g., Mandler, 1980), it was not to make special pleadings for organizational theory.

Part of the counter-revolution was conducted by John Anderson in league with the first author (Anderson, 1972; Anderson & Bower, 1973). In fact, the Trojan horse of that counter-revolution was sneaked into the last section of Bower's (1972) paper at the "Organization of Memory" conference. To set the stage for that development, readers should be apprised that one of the organizational theorist's criticisms of association theory had been that the latter seemed unable to account for free recall: What were the "stimuli" and the "responses" that were being associated? A second objection was that associationism could not account for Old/New item recognition, for example, in the continuous recognition memory task introduced by Shepard and Teghtsoonian (1961). Clearly, subjects were not associating the response they made ("New") upon initial presentation of each stimulus; otherwise, they would not call it "Old" upon its later presentation.

Anderson effectively solved both these problems with his Free Recall from an Associative Network (FRAN) model. Anderson showed how association theory could be slightly modified to handle both recognition memory and so-called organizational effects in free recall. First, Old/New recognition was assumed to be based on the subject learning an association between a presented item and a list-context marker; upon later testing with the item, the person presumably would assess the strength of this association to the list marker, judging it to be Old (or from the presented list) if its strength was above a criterion set to reject most nonlist distractors (for details see Anderson & Bower, 1972, 1974). Second, free recall was supposedly simulated by a search process that followed list-tagged associative pathways connecting different words from the studied list. During study of each word, two processes were assumed to occur: (a) tagging that word node in memory as having occurred on the list, and (b) following associative pathways from that word node (in semantic memory), searching for other list-words, and tagging any such connections to use later as retrieval routes during recall. FRAN also established a special ENTRYSET of list items that was connected to the list tag, which were the most central, highly-connected items on the list, and from which the model (subject) began its free recall.

With these assumptions, FRAN was able to simulate nearly all the classic results on free recall—the serial position curve, the effects of list length, study time, lengthened retrieval times, inter-item associations, category clustering, and so on. Importantly, FRAN showed the strong correlation between recall levels and degree of subjective clustering (sequential stereotypy in output) that formerly had been proposed as crucial evidence for the organizational view of free recall. And FRAN was a patently associationist model, albeit with a few novel wrinkles.

At that point, Bower became convinced that many of the memory phenomena ascribed to organizational processes could be recast as well in terms of an enriched model of associative processes, after incorporating perceptual processes (e.g., to deal with Asch's (1969) many demonstrations of mnemonic consequences of perceptual unity). Assuredly, organizing was relating, but what was relating of verbal items other than finding semantic, phonetic, or other kinds of pre-existing relations between these items in semantic memory, then tagging those relations as useful for recalling one item given the other? After FRAN, Anderson and Bower developed HAM (1973), a more general associative model of relational learning based on a presumed semantic network, and tried to show how that theory might deal with memory for sentences, facts, and inter-related clusters of facts. At the same time, Collins & Quillian (1969, 1972) were proposing their network model of hierarchical semantic memory and retrieval of facts by the spreading of activation through the network; Rumelhart, Lindsay, and Norman (1972; also Norman & Rumelhart, 1975) were elaborating their ELINOR model of episodic and semantic memory; and Kintsch (1974) was elaborating his model of propositional encoding and retrieval to deal with people's memory for coherent text and stories. These developments regarding memory for facts and texts became prominent foci of research and theoretical activity over the ensuing decade.

THE LEVELS OF PROCESSING THEORY OF MEMORY

Alongside those developments, however, the interest of verbal-learning researchers in organizational factors in memory continued unabated. Some of the revolutionary fervor of organizational theory was picked up by a newcomer on the theoretical scene, namely the levels of processing (LOP) framework, also originated by luminaries of the "Ebbinghaus Empire" at the University of Toronto (Craik & Lockhart, 1972; Craik & Tulving, 1975). The main point of LOP theory was that memory for a verbal item depended greatly on the kind of cognitive processing the subject carried out on that item. The processing could be controlled by orienting questions referring to the item's meaning, sound, or visual appearance. The idea was that each level of processing set up a separate memory trace which persisted for more time the deeper the processing.

As originally formulated, the LOP framework assigned little role to organizational processes in determining memory performance. Rather, it emphasized the processing of individual items and minimized the involvement of overall list organizational factors in memory. In a typical LOP experiment, for example, the list as a whole may have no obvious categorical structure, and subjects are instructed merely to answer whatever study question is asked of each item. Although the LOP framework is sometimes blamed for the waning interest in organization theory (e.g., Battig & Bellezza, 1979), it seems to us that, on the contrary, the organizational viewpoint has been kept alive by work within the LOP framework. The two approaches are not incompatible, despite their having generally focused on different aspects of the encoding process. As the LOP framework has been revised and developed (e.g., Craik & Tulving, 1975; Lockhart, Craik, & Jacoby, 1976), it has moved toward a synthesis of its ideas with those of organization theory. In the remainder of this chapter we examine how the LOP framework has been expanded and now includes organizational ideas.

In the paradigmatic LOP experiment, subjects are presented with a list of to-be-remembered (TBR) words. They encode these words according to study questions intended to induce semantic, phonetic, or structural encoding—one question for each list word. For a TBR word such as *DOG*, an example of a semantic question would be, "Is it a MAMMAL?"; of a phonetic question, "Does it rhyme with FOG?"; of a structural question, "Is it printed in upper case letters?" Of interest are differences in free recall or recognition of words processed according to these different questions. Unlike an organization experiment, the TBR words in an LOP experiment are not to be inter-related, and the subject is not instructed (or even encouraged) to produce a hierarchical or associative grouping of the items in the list. Nonetheless, we believe that the study questions in a LOP experiment imply certain kinds of organizations. The question "Is it a MAMMAL?" asks subjects to relate the TBR word to that category. Similarly, the question, "Does it rhyme with FOG?" refers to the subject's knowledge of rhyming relationships among words, and suggests a group of words that rhyme with FOG. Even the structural question causes words to be grouped according to how they are printed, thus organizing them, at least on a superficial level. These study questions relate items to the subject's pre-existing knowledge of categories, rhymes, and orthographic styles.

COMPARING ORGANIZATION TO LEVELS
OF PROCESSING

Organization has traditionally been a somewhat fuzzy concept, and our way of thinking about it may not agree with some operational definitions that have been suggested (e.g., Tulving, 1968, p. 15). However, our perspective on organization does coincide with Mandler's (1967) more theoretical definition quoted earlier in this chapter. What Mandler believed to be important for memory was that the material to be learned should be grouped according to some relation at the time of encoding. In our view, a study question in an LOP experiment specifies just such a relation between the TBR item and some property or concept. Moreover, the LOP framework has demonstrated that grouping or associating items with their semantic categories is especially important for good retention.

To illustrate the close relation of organization to semantic processing, we will consider several findings in the LOP tradition from an organizational perspective. A frequent result in LOP experiments is that semantic encoding produces better free recall and recognition memory than does phonetic and other forms of nonsemantic encoding (e.g., Craik & Tulving, 1975; Hyde & Jenkins, 1969). This finding has been interpreted as indicating that semantic encoding causes memory traces that are either more resistant to interference (Craik & Lockhart, 1972), or more elaborate (Anderson & Reder, 1979), or more distinctive (Moscovitch & Craik, 1976). However, this finding can also be viewed as evidence that classifying the word-lists semantically provides stronger retrieval cues for later recall than does classifying the words by phonetic or print groupings. Thus, the categories provide meaningful cues with strong associations to facilitate recall of the TBR words related to them. Grouping by rhyme relationships causes poorer memory because rhyming leads to less distinctive memory traces.

Another common finding in LOP experiments, first reported by Craik and Tulving (1975), is that "Yes" items which fit the category of their study question (e.g., Is is a MAMMAL?–DOG) are later better recognized and recalled than "No" items which do not fit their category question (e.g., Is it a MAMMAL?–

APPLE). This Yes–No difference in recall is typically explained in terms of elaboration (Anderson & Reder, 1979; Craik & Tulving, 1975); that is, a positive relation between a study question and its TBR word offers a greater number of informative links between the item and the category of the study question that can be stored and later used in retrieval. This connecting of TBR words to permanent memory structures, which can later serve as retrieval cues, is seen as a primary determinant of memory performance (Hunt & Mitchell, 1978; 1982). This idea is similar to a basic thesis of organization theory that memory depends on whether items can be grouped under or associated to some higher order cue (Mandler, 1967; 1972).

When people answer a category question in the LOP paradigm, or when they group together items in one of Mandler's sorting experiments, they are not *creating* an organization or an association. These relationships between items exist in the subject's permanent memory. What LOP or organizational study instructions do is direct the subject to *attend to,* encode, or reactivate a particular pre-existing association between the list items and semantic or phonetic categories. The LOP question leads the subject to consider, among the many possible associations and relations, a specific association to represent the "episode" of having studied a particular item in the list. Thus, whether relating an item to a question (as in LOP experiments) or grouping it with other list items (as in a sorting experiment), subjects are led to attend to various relations between items in their pre-existing memory structures, with the consequence that they recall these subjective groupings together. A difference between the two is that organization theory has concerned itself primarily with relations between TBR items in a list, whereas LOP theory has dealt with relations between TBR items and extralist categories or words.

DIFFERENTIATING WITHIN THE SEMANTIC LEVEL OF PROCESSING

An incompleteness of the initial LOP framework was that it failed to differentiate further within the various levels of processing. Surely, many types of semantic and phonetic questions can be asked about any given TBR word, and all the many variants of semantic and phonetic processing cannot be expected to yield equivalent memory performances. One can also ask how memory for an item would vary if it were presented and processed two or more times during study, each time perhaps in a different manner. Craik and Lockhart (1972) originally hypothesized that continued processing of an item at the "same level" or in the same manner upon its repetition would yield no improvement in memory. Although initially supported by the weak enhancement of recall produced by massed phonetic rehearsal of a word, their hypothesis was soon disputed and modified by later results showing memory enhancements due to well-spaced repetitions of words processed in the same manner (e.g., see the review in Zechmeister & Nyberg, 1982). Much of the follow-up research investigated how memory varied with the type and number of semantic questions asked of a TBR word during its presentation.

An early example of such research was a study by Klein & Saltz (1976). They selected four semantic dimensions (happy-sad, pleasant-unpleasant, fast-slow, big-little) along which their subjects were to rate a set of TBR words. Pilot subjects rated the happy-sad dimension as highly correlated with the fast-slow and pleasant-unpleasant dimensions, but there were low correlations among the size and speed dimensions. Subjects in the memory experiment rated a list of words according either to only one of the dimensions, or to two uncorrelated dimensions (e.g., pleasantness and size), or to two correlated dimensions (e.g., pleasantness and happiness). In a later free recall test, subjects showed greater recall for words that had been rated on two correlated dimensions as opposed to just one dimension, but greatest recall of all for words rated on two uncorrelated dimensions. Klein and Saltz concluded that specifying a word on several meaning dimensions improved its memory, and more so when the dimensions offered nonredundant information about the word. An alternative interpretation is that these uncorrelated attributes can serve as independent, nonredundant retrieval cues to guide recall of the items satisfying both groupings.

A related study by Johnson-Laird, Gibbs and deMowbray (1978) extended Klein and Saltz's findings to rating tasks involving conceptual categories. In the Johnson-Laird et al. study, subjects categorized words according to whether or not they were "natural consumable solids." Recall was higher as the number of categories that a word satisfied increased, going from all three (e.g., apple), to two (e.g., coal), to only one (e.g., coca cola), to zero (e.g., perfume). This study clarified the parallel between semantic encoding and categorical organization: Study tasks that relate an item to more categories result in much better retention and memory performance.

Working in Bower's lab, Brian Ross (1981) found that elaboration for memory was best conceived in terms of the number of categorical/organizational relations subjects noticed about a word. He demonstrated that memory for a word was related to the number of such decisions a subject had to make about it earlier. Ross replicated the Johnson-Laird et al. study, but with subjects making Yes-No decisions about list words according to one of three criteria: the ALL group responded "Yes" only if a TBR word matched all three properties of the category (natural, consumable, solid); the ANY group responded "Yes" if a TBR word matched any one or more of the three properties; and the EACH group made a separate "Yes/No" decision for each of the three properties for each word. Assuming a serial self-terminating search through the properties for making the encoding decisions, Ross calculated the expected number of decisions subjects would make in each condition according to the number of properties a TBR word actually possessed (see Table 11.1). Subjects in the ALL condition needed to

TABLE 11.1
Expected Number of Decisions for the Three
Orienting Tasks of Ross's (1981) Experiment 2

| Task | Number of Target Properties | | | |
	0	1	2	3
ALL	1.00	1.33	2.00	3.00
ANY	3.00	2.00	1.33	1.00
EACH	3.00	3.00	3.00	3.00

Note. From "The more the better?: Number of decisions as a determinant of memorability" by B. H. Ross,
1981, *Memory & Cognition, 9,* p. 27. Copyright 1981 by
Psychonomic Publications. Reprinted by permission.

check every property of a word before saying "Yes," and could say "No" only
after encountering a property missing in the TBR item. Thus, the expected number
of decisions these subjects had to make increased with the number of properties of
the TBR item. Subjects in the ANY condition needed to find only one property that
the TBR item possessed in order to say "Yes," and could terminate their search
upon finding a first such property. Consequently, the number of decisions they
needed to make *decreased* as the number of properties the TBR item possessed
increased. Finally, in the EACH condition, subjects were forced to make three
explicit "Yes/No" decisions regardless of how many properties the TBR item
possessed. Note that in this case, the properties corresponded to complementary
categories whatever the answer to them: something not "natural" is "man-made";
something not "solid" is liquid, gaseous, or abstract. Thus, even a "No" decision
about a specific property implied a "Yes" connection of the word to an alternative
category; this may be why Ross observed no recall differences in his EACH
condition depending on the number of "Yes" decisions.

Ross's data are shown in Table 11.2. It was not possible to find lists of words
that could be used in all four conditions. Consequently, Ross used one set of
words for the 0 and 3 decision conditions, and different words for the 1 and 2
decisions condition. Therefore, the only comparisons counterbalanced for word
type are 0 versus 3, and 1 versus 2; these mean recall percentages are shown in
Table 2. Those means show that recall conformed closely to the predictions
derived from the number of decisions. For words with increasing number of
properties (0 vs. 3; 1 vs. 2), their recall increased in the ALL group, but decreased in the ANY group. Recall was relatively constant and high in the EACH
group where subjects made the same number of decisions for all items (0 = 3; 1
= 2). Apparently we may conclude that the greater the number of properties or
categories to which subjects are forced to relate a given item, the greater will be
their later recall of that item.

A simple account for the preceding findings can be provided based on stan-

TABLE 11.2
Proportion Recalled in Ross's (1981) Experiment 2

Task	Number of Target Properties			
	0	3	1	2
ALL	.227	.377	.178	.252
ANY	.367	.218	.233	.182
EACH	.404	.409	.209	.267

Note. From "The more the better?: Number of decisions as a determinant of memorability" by B. H. Ross, 1981, *Memory & Cognition, 9,* p. 27. Copyright 1981 by Psychonomic Publications. Adapted by permission. The only counterbalanced comparisons are those between 0 and 3 properties, and between 1 and 2 properties.

dard ideas within association theory (see Figure 11.2 as an aid to this discussion). Imagine that subjects learn the categories or properties in the questions that they are repeatedly asked regarding list-words in LOP experiments, learning them by associating these categories (like "metal" and "mammal") to a List node in memory. Imagine further that subjects implicitly recall these properties or categories to use as retrieval cues when they are later asked to recall the list-words. Suppose too, that each pre-existing association between a list-word and a property or category (such as "silver" to "metal") that subjects are forced to attend to as they study the word thereby becomes strengthened. These strengthened associations will be used to facilitate later recall of that word when it is implicitly cued with that property. In addition, the more implicit cues (properties or categories) the subject can generate from the List-node, and the greater their associative connections to a given list-word, then the greater the probability of recall of that list-word.

These principles account for Ross's findings. The greater number of properties or relations noticed for a given list-word, the more property-to-word associations that are strengthened, so that the list-word's recall is boosted. The retrieval process proceeds by the spreading of activation along associative pathways, starting from the List-node in memory, thence to the category questions (like "natural," "consumable," and "solid"), and thence to the intersection of the activation spreading to the list words that satisfy these properties (see Figure 11.2). The Johnson-Laird et al. (1978) findings have the same explanation as do Ross's. The Klein and Saltz (1976) findings are also accommodated in that (a) two independent property cues serve as better retrieval cues than does one property, and (b) two redundant, overlapping properties do not provide separate retrieval routes (or associations) to facilitate recall of a list-word, and so are hardly better than a single cue. The connection between this associative theory and Mandler's position is that both emphasize the subjects' active attention to the categorical associations of the list-words as they are studied, and hypothesize that subjects use these noticed categories as retrieval cues to aid later recall.

ORGANIZATIONAL FACTORS IN LOP EXPERIMENTS

Several researchers have recognized that free recall in standard LOP experiments is strongly related to the overall organization of the word-list in addition to the processing performed on each word (e.g., Bellezza, Cheesman, & Reddy, 1977; Einstein & Hunt, 1980). Much of this research, however, has been aimed primarily at comparing memory performance produced by whole-list organizational strategies in contrast to semantic processing of single items in the LOP format. For example, Bellezza et al. (1977) contrasted free recall of subjects instructed to link TBR words into a story (or to place large groups of items into mental images) versus others instructed simply to process each word semantically but separately, such as defining it or using it in a sentence. They found not only that story linking and interactive imagery produced better recall than separate semantic elaboration, but that variation in the quality of the organizational strategy had far greater influence on free recall than did variation in semantic tasks focused on single items. Perhaps the basic message of such experiments is that free recall of a list of words requires study methods that interrelate and organize the items, and that "deep processing" of individual items without regard to their relationships to other list items does little to promote free recall (although it may promote recognition). Mandler's Manifesto of organization still held true, indeed with an impact on free recall sometimes greater than the influence of different levels of processing.

Bryant (1990) has investigated the influence on free recall of a subtle organizational factor embedded in the standard LOP experiment. As noted, traditional LOP experiments focus exclusively on how the orienting question presented along with a TBR word affected its later recall. Relations between TBR items were ignored, as were relations between items and other questions asked within the study contest. But the associative analysis developed above, as well as Mandler's organizational approach, suggests that these inter-item and other category-to-item relations may be important determinants of free recall. Bryant's research illustrates a substantial impact of these whole-list organizational variables in an LOP experiment, specifically noting the influence on an item's free recall of the questions asked about other items in the list.

In one of Bryant's experiments, subjects studied a list of words either by answering taxonomic or rhyming questions. Twelve questions were used in each list, with each question paired with four words for a list length of 48. Examples of the study questions and TBR words are shown in Table 11.3. Each question was paired with two positive or "Yes" items. Examples of "Yes" items in Table 11.3 are "Iron—METAL?" and "Blue—COLOR?". Each question was also

TABLE 11.3
Examples of Taxonomic and Rhyming List Structures Employed
in Bryant's (1990) Experiment 1

| | | TAXONOMIC LISTS | | |
Category Type	Example	Response Type	Example	Related to:
Unrelated	A RELATIVE	Yes	Father	RELATIVE
	A RELATIVE	No	Echo	—
Related	A METAL	Yes	Iron	METAL
	A METAL	No	Music	—
Experimental	A COLOR	Yes	Blue	COLOR
	A COLOR	Yes/No	Steel	METAL

| | | RHYMING LISTS | | |
Rhyme Type	Example	Response Type	Example	Rhymes with:
Unrelated	LANE	Yes	Pain	LANE
	LANE	No	Salad	—
Related	FLOUR	Yes	Sour	FLOUR
	FLOUR	No	Paint	—
Experimental	GLOVE	Yes	Shove	GLOVE
	GLOVE	Yes/No	Hour	FLOUR

Note. From "Implicit associative responses influence encoding in memory" by D. J. Bryant, 1990, Memory & Cognition, 18, p. 350. Copyright 1990 by Psychonomics Publications. Reprinted by permission.

paired with two negative items, of which there were two different types. Some of the negative items were unrelated to any category question in the list, such as "Music—METAL?" in Table 11.3; these were dubbed the pure "No" items. The other negative items were unrelated to the question asked of them, but were, in fact, related to a question presented earlier in the list; these were dubbed "Yes/No" items. An example in Table 11.3 is "Steel—COLOR?" which yields a negative answer, but is related to another, earlier category, namely metals. The type of negative item was the major manipulation in the study. Subjects completed a free recall test immediately after studying each list.

As noted before, the standard result we expected was for the "Yes" items to be recalled much better than the pure "No" items. The crucial question was whether the "Yes/No" items related to a question in the list would be recalled any better than the pure "No" items that were not related to any question in the list. The results of Bryant's Experiment 1 are shown in Table 11.4. Recall of "Yes/No" items in the taxonomic condition was intermediate between that of "Yes" and pure "No" items. In the rhyming condition, however, recall of "Yes/No" items was no better than that of "No" items. Thus, subjects were able to use the implicit semantic relationships between "Yes/No" words and category questions to improve their recall of those items, but apparently could not use the implicit rhyming relationships to aid recall.

TABLE 11.4
Proportion Free Recalled in Taxonomic
and Rhyming Lists of Bryant's (1990)
Experiment 1

List Type	Item Type		
	Yes	*Yes/No*	*No*
Taxonomic	0.52	0.29	0.08
Rhyming	0.20	0.08	0.09

Note. From "Implicit associative responses influence encoding in memory" by D. J. Bryant, 1990, *Memory & Cognition, 18,* p. 350. Copyright 1990 by Psychonomics Publications. Reprinted by permission.

The *Yes/No* effect for semantic categories was the primary result of interest in this experiment. The associative model depicted in fragmentary form in Figure 11.2 can be used to explain these results as well as those of Ross and earlier LOP experiments. The circled words in Figure 2 denote nodes in semantic memory; the List node is set up to record the episodes in the study list. The categories Metal, Conducts Electricity, and Mammal refer to the questions asked of items in the list. The lines denote associative connections either set up or utilized during the list-presentation trial; illustrated are the prior associations for "Yes" items (such as "Silver to Metal") and for "Yes/No" items (such as "Iron to Metal"), and the weaker episodic associations encoding the temporal contiguity of the category question to "No" items (such as "Iron to Mammal" and "Apple to Metal"). The associations for "Yes" items are stronger than for pure "No" items because the former basically prime and reactivate a familiar, strong relation, whereas the latter association is only momentarily strengthened by temporal contiguity of the question category and the item yielding a "No" response. The connection for the "Yes/No" item (Iron to Metal) is a dashed line to indicate that its strength depends upon this connection being recognized and reactivated within the time the "Iron—Mammal?" episode is occurring.

Free recall is presumed to proceed, as noted before, by the spreading of activation from the List node to the categories and thence to the associated words in an amount increasing with their degree of association. Using the arguments about encoding outlined earlier, this retrieval model leads to the expectation that free recall would be best for a "Yes/Yes" item (such as copper), next best for "Yes" items, next for "Yes/No" items, and worst for pure "No" items. This was exactly the ordering of free recall Bryant found for his semantic conditions. The same analysis, for reasons difficult to summarize briefly, does not apply to the rhyming condition. Roughly speaking, the Yes/No effect may fail to appear with rhyming questions because rhymes are not as strongly represented or as salient in

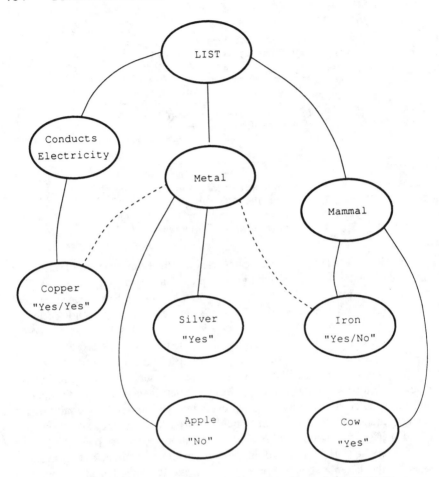

FIG 11.2. Hypothetical diagram of a fragment of associative memory showing various types of word nodes and their associative connections (lines between nodes). See text for explanation. Reproduced from Bryant (1990) by permission of the author and the publisher, Psychonomic Publications.

long-term memory, cause little elaborative activity during encoding, and so are less likely to enhance encoding of "Yes/No" items.

Subsequent follow up experiments by Bryant clarified the semantic Yes/No effect and supported the associative model illustrated in Figure 11.2. One control experiment found the semantic "Yes/No" advantage over "No" items even when the pure "No" items themselves could have been grouped into categories (of two or four). What was important was that the relevant category was primed (or associated to the List context) by its having appeared in the list being learned.

Another experiment showed that the less often a given semantic category question was presented during study, the weaker was the semantic Yes/No effect for items related to that category. Thus, if each category were presented only twice instead of four times, giving subjects less opportunity to notice its relationship to "Yes/No" items, the category provided less enhancement of recall of those "Yes/No" items. This can be understood in the model of Figure 11.2, since more trials of associating the question category to the List should enhance its accessibility to cue retrieval of the list words.

In addition, the theory predicts, and Bryant found, that inclusion of an additional category question related to a "Yes" item (e.g., Copper conducts electricity and is also a metal) boosted its recall. That is, the item on its single presentation was related to its question and to an earlier question category as well. This boosting of recall is reminiscent of Ross's (1981) results, except that Bryant's subjects were relating the items implicitly to an earlier category as well as encoding them with respect to their category question.

A final experiment by Bryant demonstrated that the Yes/No effect depended on subjects' consciously noticing the relation of a "Yes/No" item to an earlier category in the list. In this experiment, subjects were asked to make two decisions about each item: whether or not the word belonged to the category question presented with it, and whether or not it belonged to any other category question presented earlier in the list. Of interest was how well subjects later recalled "Yes/No" items they had earlier failed to recognize as being related to a category question in the list. In fact, subjects recalled these "Yes/No" items no better than pure "No" items. On the other hand, if subjects did recognize that there had been a category related to a "Yes/No" item presented earlier, they recalled the "Yes/No" item roughly as well as "Yes" items. Thus, when subjects could think back and make the connection between the current TBR word and a previous study question, they were able to use that category to encode the item. These results support the theory depicted in Figure 11.2. If the link of the "Yes/No" item to its category is not noticed so that it is not activated and strengthened during the word's presentation, then the connection (dashed line in Figure 2) will be weak and inoperative during recall.

CONCLUDING COMMENT

Beginning with a review of one of George Mandler's seminal papers, we have traced some of the developments surrounding his thesis, that memory is a product of organization, especially when memory is measured by the free recall of large bodies of materials. Starting as a revolutionary doctrine in th mid-1960s, Mandler's thesis gradually gained adherents and empirical support. Moreover, the basic thesis is still alive and well in verbal memory theory, where it appears as a complementary factor to the levels of processing framework that seemed for a while to have pushed organizational ideas off center stage. In our review of this literature, we have recast some of the organizational ideas in terms of a network of reactivated semantic associations which are used in encoding list items and in cuing their retrieval in inter-related clusters. Our review concluded by showing how a subtle organizational influence, the Yes/No effect in free recall of semantic associates, could be found as predicted by our associative analysis of the standard LOP experiment.

The thematic path of research we have traced is just one of many our field will associate with George Mandler. He has been a powerful, influential force for the past 35 years in determining the direction of research on human memory. The body of his memory research work, alongside his many other provocative writings on philosophy of mind, emotion, and value, stands as eloquent testimony to the generative originality of this brilliant scientist. We are much in his debt for having stimulated and guided our collective research enterprise.

ACKNOWLEDGMENTS

The first author's research is supported by an NIMH grant MH-13950 and grant AFOSR 87-0282 from the Air Force Office of Scientific Research. David Bryant is a graduate student at Stanford University. It is fitting that his undergraduate training was at the University of Toronto, an institution where George Mandler worked in the 1960s. During that time, Bryant worked with Endel Tulving, an important collaborator with Mandler on the organizational approach to memory.

REFERENCES

Anderson, J. R. (1972). A simulation model of free recall. In G. H. Bower (Ed.), *The psychology of learning and motivation* (pp. 315–378). New York: Academic Press.

Anderson, J. R., & Bower, G. H. (1972). Recognition and retrieval processes in free recall. *Psychological Review, 79*, 97–123.

Anderson, J. R., & Bower, G. H. (1973). *Human associative memory*. New York: Wiley.

Anderson, J. R., & Bower, G. H. (1974). A propositional theory of recognition memory. *Memory & Cognition, 2*, 406–412.

Anderson, J. R., & Reder, L. M. (1979). An elaborative processing explanation of depth of processing. In F. I. M. Craik & L. S. Cermak (Eds.), *Levels of processing in human memory* (pp. 385–403). Hillsdale, NJ: Lawrence Erlbaum Associates.

Asch, S. E. (1969). Reformulation of the problem of association. *American Psychologist, 24*, 92–102.

Battig, W. F., & Bellezza, F. S. (1979). Organization and levels of processing. In C. R. Puff (Ed.), *Memory organization and structure* (pp. 321–346). New York: Academic Press.

Bellezza, F. S., Cheesman, F. L., & Reddy, B. G. (1977). Organization and semantic elaboration in free recall. *Journal of Experimental Psychology: Human Learning and Memory, 3*, 539–550.

Bousfield, W. A. (1953). The occurrence of clustering in the recall of randomly arranged associates. *Journal of General Psychology, 49*, 229–240.

Bower, G. H. (1970). Organizational factors in memory. *Cognitive Psychology, 1,* 18–46.

Bower, G. H. (1972). A selective review of organizational factors in memory. In E. Tulving & W. Donaldson (Eds.), *Organization of memory* (pp. 93–137). New York: Academic Press.

Bower, G. H., Clark, M. C., Lesgold, A. M., & Winzenz, D. (1969). Hierarchical retrieval schemes in recall of categorized word lists. *Journal of Verbal Learning and Verbal Behavior, 8,* 323–343.

Bryant, D. J. (1990). Implicit associative responses influence encoding in memory. *Memory & Cognition, 18,* 348–358.

Collins, A. M., & Quillian, M. R. (1969). Retrieval time from semantic memory. *Journal of Verbal Learning and Verbal Memory, 8,* 240–247.

Collins, A. M., & Quillian, M. R. (1972). Experiments on semantic memory and language comprehension. In L. W. Gregg (Ed.), *Cognition in learning and memory* (pp. 117–137). New York: Wiley.

Craik, F. I. M., & Lockhart, R. S. (1972). Levels of processing: A framework for memory research. *Journal of Verbal Learning and Verbal Behavior, 11,* 671–684.

Craik, F. I. M., & Tulving, E. (1975). Depth of processing and the retention of words in episodic memory. *Journal of Experimental Psychology: General, 104,* 268–294.

Einstein, G. O., & Hunt, R. R. (1980). Levels of processing and organization: Additive effects of individual item and relational processing. *Journal of Experimental Psychology: Human Learning and Memory, 6,* 588–598.

Hunt, R. R., & Mitchell, D. B. (1978). Specificity in nonsemantic orienting tasks and distinctive memory traces. *Journal of Experimental Psychology: Human Learning and Memory, 4,* 121–135.

Hunt, R. R., & Mitchell, D. B. (1982). Independent effects of semantic and nonsemantic distinctiveness. *Journal of Experimental Psychology: Learning, Memory and Cognition, 8,* 81–87.

Hyde, T. S., & Jenkins, J. J. (1969). Differential effects of incidental tasks on the organization of recall of a list of highly associated words. *Journal of Experimental Psychology, 82,* 472–480.

Johnson-Laird, P. N., Gibbs, G., & deMowbray, J. (1978). Meaning, amount of processing, and memory for words. *Memory & Cognition, 6,* 372–375.

Kintsch, W. (1974). *The representation of meaning in memory.* Potomac, MD: Lawrence Erlbaum Associates.

Klein, K., & Saltz, E. (1976). Specifying the mechanism in a levels-of-processing approach to memory. *Journal of Experimental Psychology: Human Learning and Memory, 2,* 671–679.

Lockhart, R. S., Craik, F. I. M., & Jacoby, L. (1976). Depth of processing, recognition and recall. In J. Brown (Ed.), *Recall and recognition* (pp. 75–102). London: Wiley.

Mandler, G. (1967). Organization and memory. In K. W. Spence & J. T. Spence (Eds.), *The psychology of learning and motivation: Advances in research and theory, vol. 1* (pp. 327–372). New York: Academic Press.

Mandler, G. (1972). Organization and recognition. In E. Tulving & W. Donaldson (Eds.), *Organization of memory* (pp. 139–166). New York: Academic Press.

Mandler, G. (1980). Recognizing: The judgment of previous occurrence. *Psychological Review, 87,* 252–271.

Mandler, G., & Pearlstone, Z. (1966). Free and constrained concept learning and subsequent recall. *Journal of Verbal Learning and Verbal Behavior, 5,* 126–131.

Miller, G. A. (1956). The magical number seven, plus or minus two: Some limits on our capacity for processing information. *Psychological Review, 63,* 81–97.

Moscovitch, M., & Craik, F. I. M. (1976). Depth of processing, retrieval cues, and uniqueness of encoding as factors in recall. *Journal of Verbal Learning and Verbal Behavior, 15,* 447–458.

Norman, D. A., & Rumelhart, D. E. (1975). *Explorations in cognition.* San Francisco: Freeman.

Ross, B. H. (1981). The more, the better?: Number of decisions as a determinant of memorability. *Memory & Cognition, 9,* 23–33.

Rumelhart, D. E., Lindsay, P. H., & Norman, D. A. (1972). A process model of long-term memory. In E. Tulving & W. Donaldson (Eds.), *Organization and memory* (pp. 197–246). New York: Academic Press.

Shepard, R. N., & Teghtsoonian, M. (1961). Retention of information under conditions approaching a steady state. *Journal of Experimental Psychology, 62,* 302–309.

Tulving, E. (1962). Subjective organization in free recall of "unrelated" words. *Psychological Review, 69,* 344–354.

Tulving, E. (1964). Intratrial and intertrial retention: Notes towards a theory of free-recall verbal learning. *Psychological Review, 71,* 219–237.

Tulving, E. (1968). Theoretical issues in free recall. In T. R. Dixon & D. L. Horton (Eds.), *Verbal behavior and general behavior theory* (pp. 2–36). Englewood Cliffs, NJ: Prentice-Hall.

Zechmeister, E. B., & Nyberg, S. E. (1982). *Human memory: An introduction to research and theory.* Monterey, CA: Brooks/Cole.

12

Memory for Representations of Visual Objects

Lynn A. Cooper
Columbia University

Of the many topics in the field of cognitive psychology that the work of George Mandler has illuminated, his contributions to our understanding of the nature of memory and of consciousness are perhaps the most central. Mandler's insightful analyses of mental life—in particular, his 1985 "Cognitive psychology: An essay in cognitive science"—have never failed to inform, inspire, charm, and challenge. However, until recently, I have viewed his work from the vantage point of an interested outsider. My own longstanding research committment to problems of perceptual representation, in particular the representation of visual objects and transformations on objects, seemed somewhat removed from the issues to which Mandler's most concentrated efforts were directed.

I find it most fitting that the opportunity to prepare a paper for a volume honoring George Mandler's contributions to psychology has come at a time when my own direction of research and thinking is making clear contact with issues in memory representation that George has addressed repeatedly. More specifically, Mandler's (1980, 1982, 1985) distinction between *integrative* and *elaborative* aspects of memory representations and processes lies at the heart of a line of work that I am currently pursuing in collaboration with Daniel Schacter. Accordingly, in this chapter I will outline the logic and central thesis of this work, as well as summarize some initial experimental findings. The relevance of George Mandler's observations to interpretations of the findings will become clear as the discussion and the arguments unfold. The chapter is divided into three sections. In the first, the general logic, some selected literature motivating the problem, and the overall research approach are laid out. Next, results from some initial experiments demonstrating dissociations in memory for aspects of representations of visual objects are described. Finally, the use of such dissociations as tools for investigating the structure of object representations is discussed.

EXPLORATIONS OF MEMORY FOR REPRESEN-
TATIONS OF VISUAL OBJECTS: AN OVERVIEW

It is clear that much of our visually guided behavior relies on the ongoing construction of a mental representation of the objects and relationships among objects in the environment. Such behavior generally proceeds in a relatively uninterrupted fashion; rarely do we collide with the concealed surfaces of three-dimensional objects or register surprise when previously hidden aspects of object structure are revealed as a result of patterns of eye fixation or of observer movement. Moreover, we generally accomplish feats such as locomotion through the environment in the absence of any conscious identification, recognition, or familiarity with the objects in our surroundings. There are, however, other sorts of occasions and perceptually driven tasks for which recognition of an object or recollection of its identity are crucial (e.g., spotting an acquaintance in a crowd, behaving in conformity with traffic signs, finding one's way back to a previously visited location).

Observations like these suggest that questions about the representation and recognition of objects could fruitfully be united with more general questions concerning the nature of human memory. In particular, the distinctions between activation and elaboration in memory (e.g., Mandler, 1985), between automatic and nonautomatic memory access (e.g., Hasher & Zacks, 1979), between indirect and direct tests of memory (e.g., Allen & Jacoby, 1990), and between implicit and explicit forms of remembering (e.g., Graf & Schacter, 1985; Schacter, 1987; Tulving & Schacter, 1990) provide a framework in which to view memory for perceptual representations of objects and events.

A set of empirical phenomena of central importance for the present discussion involves dissociations between the conscious remembering of previously presented material, expressed on standard tests of recognition and recall, and the unintentional retrieval of such information, measured in terms of performance facilitation on tests that do not make reference to conscious recollection of the material. This latter form of memory, sometimes referred to as *implicit memory* (see, e.g., Schacter, 1987), has most frequently been assessed via *priming effects,* in which facilitation of performance attributable to previous study of or exposure to a set of target items is observed, often in the absence of conscious remembering of the items or the study episode. Priming effects and attendant dissociations between implicit and explicit expressions of memory have been reported for both normal and amnesic subjects, and can be obtained with a variety of different experimental manipulations (see Richardson-Klavehn & Bjork, 1988; Schacter, 1987, for recent reviews).

Considerable research on priming has emphasized the use of verbal materials with tests of implicit memory including word fragment completion and lexical decision. And, the use of verbal responses, for example, naming or identifying pictures of familiar objects, has characterized much of the work on priming with nonverbal materials as study/test items (see, e.g., Durso & Johnson, 1979; Kirsner, Milech, & Stumpfel, 1986; Warrington & Weiskrantz, 1968; Weldon & Roediger, 1987; for a review, see Schacter, Delaney, & Merikle, in press). Of particular relevance to the present discussion are the few reports of priming of nonverbal materials that are not pictures of nameable items. Mandler, Nakamura, and Van Zandt (1987) have shown that brief exposures to geometric shapes can influence later judgments of the brightness of the shapes, as well as judgments of preference (cf., Kunst-Wilson & Zajonc, 1980); Musen and Treisman (1990) have recently reported priming in the copying of briefly presented dot patterns.

Research on amnesic patients has also demonstrated priming effects with nonverbal materials. Warrington and Weiskrantz (1968) reported substantial savings when amnesic patients identified familiar objects from a graded series of fragmented pictures, with the procedure repeated on subsequent trials and days of testing. Using a similar experimental task, Milner, Corkin, and Teuber (1968) obtained reductions in identification errors from initial presentation to a delayed test for the severely amnesic patient H.M. Again using this patient as a subject, Gabrieli, Milberg, Keane, and Corkin (in press) have shown that H.M. was as likely as normal controls to reproduce a previously presented pattern when asked to draw any figure in an unconnected arrangement of dots from a matrix. Importantly, a dissociation between priming of the dot completion task and recognition was obtained. H.M., while showing intact pattern priming, was impaired on an explicit test of recognition of the previously presented patterns.

The selected group of studies cited earlier demonstrates that priming can be observed when nonverbal materials are used as study/test items, and, in some cases, that priming and recognition of such materials can be experimentally dissociated. These findings comprise one of the empirical underpinnings of the research to be described later. A second comes from neuropsychological studies of patients with specific visual processing deficits (see, e.g., Sartori & Job, 1988; Warrington, 1982; Warrington & Taylor, 1978). Riddoch and Humphreys (1987a, 1987b), for example, have described a patient who was severely impaired in the ability to name common objects or display other forms of semantic and functional knowledge of objects, but who nonetheless appeared able to access knowledge about object structure. Despite the impairments, the patient performed normally on a task that required discrimination between common objects and structurally anomolous nonobjects.

These results have an intriguing correspondence with the observations about forms of perceptual representation of objects and events at the beginning of this section, and they invite the following speculation: *Information about the relationships among components of an object, or its global three-dimensional struc-*

ture, might be represented in a form accessible to automatic processes and, hence, implicit tests of memory. Other information about objects, including their meaning and function, might be represented in a form accessible primarily by conscious, elaborative processes, and, hence, be revealed by explicit tests of memory. Phrased in the language of Mandler (1985), the suggestion is that representation of structural information about an object requires only the activation or integration of its schema in memory, whereas the representation of information about object identity and meaning requires elaborative processing. The further suggestion is that these different aspects of the representation of an object can be experimentally dissociated by assessing the nature of the information available to automatic or implicit tests of memory versus that accessible by conscious or explicit tests.

DISSOCIATIONS BETWEEN STRUCTURAL AND NONSTRUCTURAL ASPECTS OF OBJECT REPRESENTATIONS: INITIAL EXPERIMENTAL FINDINGS

How might the previously discussed speculation be evaluated, in the absence of a clinical syndrome suggesting a representational dissociation? Schacter, Cooper, and Delaney (1990a, 1990b) have recently developed an appropriate experimental technique, and certain features of the procedure and results are summarized below. The task devised to assess implicit memory for information about structure was an *object decision task* requiring that a line drawing of an object be classified as to whether or not it depicted a structure that could exist in the three-dimensional world. That is, subjects studied drawings of unfamiliar three-dimensional constructions, adapted from Cooper (1988, 1990), some of which are shown in Figure 12.1. Half of the drawings depicted *possible objects*—objects whose surfaces and edges are connected in such a way that, while unfamiliar, they could potentially exist in the world. Other drawings displayed *impossible objects*—objects whose surfaces and edges contain violations that would make it impossible for them to exist as actual three-dimensional structures (cf., Penrose & Penrose, 1958).

To assess implicit memory for these unfamiliar objects, subjects were given 100-ms. exposures to drawings of either previously studied or nonstudied possible or impossible structures. They then had to determine whether each object was or was not possible. This object decision task can be regarded as an implicit test of remembering in that it does not make reference to or require conscious recollection of any previous encounter with a presented object. If object decision performance can be facilitated by prior study of the test objects, then evidence of implicit memory for three-dimensional objects with no pre-experimental representation in memory would be obtained.

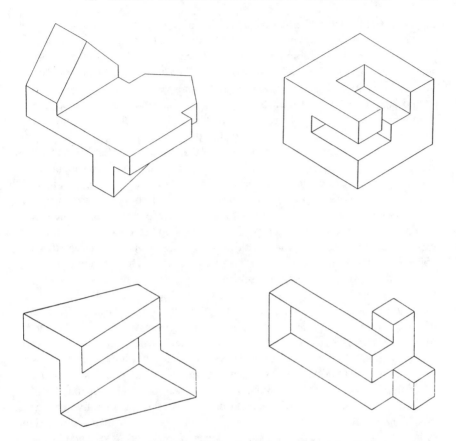

FIG. 12.1. Representative objects from the set used by Schacter, Cooper, and Delaney (1990a). Possible objects are displayed at the top of the figure, and impossible objects at the bottom.

Manipulation of the conditions under which the objects are initially studied or encoded is a crucial part of the logic of this experimental procedure. Briefly, we reasoned that to perform the object decision task, information must be extracted about the global, three-dimensional structure of the presented object. That is, an object can only be judged "possible" following an analysis of the structural relations among its various components. We reasoned further that facilitation of object decision performance should only be obtained following study tasks that lead to the encoding of information about three-dimensional object structure. In contrast, encoding tasks that do not promote the acquisition of structural information should not facilitate subsequent object decision performance.

To evaluate the specificity of this hypothesized implicit or automatic memory for unfamiliar objects, in all our experiments we have compared potential priming or object-decision facilitation effects with explicit remembering of target objects, assessed by "yes/no" recognition. Our initial expectation was that considerable levels of recognition memory should be obtained following a variety of study tasks, as long as those tasks enabled the acquisition of distinctive information about each studied object. Although elaborative processes like recognition should be able to make use of different types of information, we expected that priming should only be observed following the acquisition of information specifically about the three-dimensional structure of an object.

Consider the basic experimental situation that we used to demonstrate a dissociation between retrieval of structural versus semantic information about representations of visual objects. Subjects studied sets of objects containing both possible and impossible items under one of two conditions. The *structural encoding condition* was designed to draw attention to information about the global structure and relations among parts of each object. In this condition, each object was viewed for 5 seconds, and subjects were asked to determine whether the object appeared to be facing to the left or to the right. This encoding task was compared with a study condition requiring the *generation of elaborative encodings* of the objects. Subjects examined each object and were asked to think of and say aloud something familiar that the object reminded them of most. This task, which requires relating the unfamiliar objects to pre-existing knowledge structures, was expected to produce the sort of semantically rich and distinctive encodings that are known to enhance explicit or conscious memory performance.

If the idea motivating this experiment has merit—namely, that structural and semantically-based knowledge about objects can be functionally separated—then the following pattern of results should be observed: The elaborative encoding task should yield substantially higher levels of recognition than the left/right task, because of the known relation between distinctiveness of encoding and level of explicit memory performance. However, these elaborative encodings, though useful for recognition, should not be expected to facilitate object decision judgments relative to the left/right encoding task. This is because, by hypothesis, the left/right task promotes encoding of a structural representation of an unfamiliar three-dimensional object, and such a structural representation should support performance on the object decision task.

The results of this experiment, shown in Figures 2 and 3, clearly support this set of predictions and demonstrate the desired dissociation in performance attributable to conditions of encoding. Consider, first, performance on the object decision task, displayed in Figure 12.2 as percent correct on the "possible/impossible" judgment as a function of encoding condition (left/right vs. elaborative), type of test object (possible vs. impossible), and whether or not a tested object was previously displayed during the study phase of the experiment. A priming effect, that is, facilitation of the object decision judgment as a result of prior study, shows up in these data as an advantage of decisions made to studied over nonstudied objects.

OBJECT DECISION

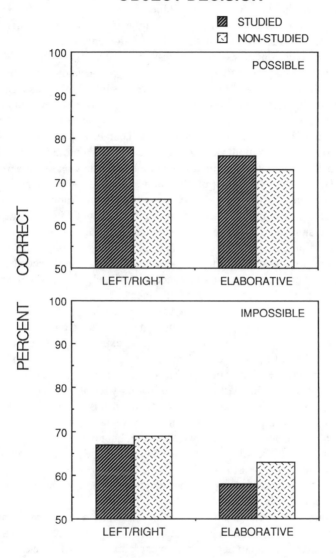

FIG. 12.2.   Percent correct on the object decision task, as a function of object type (possible vs. impossible), encoding condition (left/right vs. elaborative), and presence or absence of previous study. Data are adapted from Schacter, Cooper, and Delaney (1990a).

For possible objects, the results accord well with our expectations. In the left/right encoding condition, studied objects were classified significantly more accurately than nonstudied objects, thus demonstrating a priming effect. In contrast, no significant priming of "possible" judgments was found under elaborative encoding conditions. For impossible objects, there is no evidence that study in either encoding condition facilitated object decision performance. This failure to obtain priming of judgments of "impossibility" is a persistent result, a complete discussion of which is outside the scope of this chapter. Suffice it to say that we have investigated the conditions contributing to this finding extensively (see Schacter, Cooper, Delaney, Peterson, & Tharan, in press, for details). Our current conjecture is that impossible objects cannot be represented in memory by a system that computes structural descriptions of relations among parts of an object. Because of constraints on the nature of structural relations that can be represented, internal models of such physically incongruous relations cannot support or facilitate judgments based on information about the structure of visual objects. In summary, the pattern of results shown in Figure 12.2 demonstrates, first, that priming (as an index of automatic activation or of implicit memory) can be obtained for unfamiliar, three-dimensional objects, and, second, that such facilitation of object decision performance depends selectively on access to structural aspects of the representation of an object.

Another key finding of this experiment emerges when performance on explicit recognition is considered in conjunction with performance on the object decision task. Figure 12.3 displays recognition results, expressed as percentage of hits (studied) and false alarms (nonstudied) as a function of the same study and test variables in Figure 12.2. For possible objects, a clear crossover interaction between type of encoding task and type of memory test is apparent. On the object decision task, considerable priming was obtained following left/right encoding but not following elaborative study; in contrast, recognition performance was significantly enhanced by elaborative encoding, but not by left/right study. These data, then, clearly demonstrate a dissociation between memory for structural aspects of unfamiliar objects—accessed by implicit or indirect tests—and memory for semantic aspects of object representations—accessed by explicit or direct tests of recognition.

Subsequent research has established this dissociation more firmly and delineated additional characteristics of the underlying memory representations. Further evidence for the dissociation comes from experiments in which temporal properties of the encoding situation (e.g., whether the study task was presented one versus four times, whether one or two different encoding tasks were required) have been shown to influence levels of recognition memory, but not the magnitude of priming effects (Schacter, Cooper, Delaney, Peterson, & Tharan, in press). In addition, Schacter, Cooper, and Delaney (1990a) have shown that priming on the object decision test is confined to situations in which information specifically about global structural relations, rather than simply any perceptual

RECOGNITION

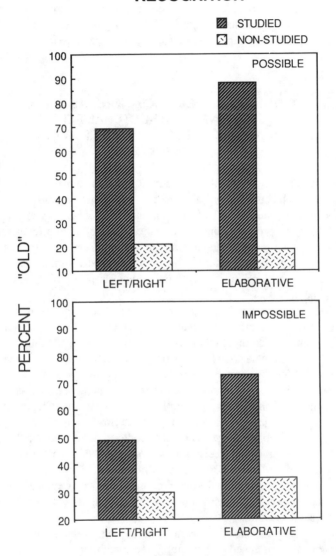

FIG. 12.3.   Percent "old" responses on the recognition task, as a function of object type (possible vs. impossible), encoding condition (left/right vs. elaborative), and presence or absence of previous study. Data are adapted from Schacter, Cooper, and Delaney (1990a).

attribute of an object, is encoded and subsequently tested. A study task requiring subjects to determine whether an object contained more horizontal or vertical line segments failed to produce priming on the object decision task and yielded recognition at a level comparable to that obtained under conditions of left/right encoding.

USING MEMORY DISSOCIATIONS AS A TOOL FOR INVESTIGATING STRUCTURAL REPRESEN- TATIONS OF OBJECTS: SOME PRELIMINARY RESULTS

Of the various directions that this program of research on memory for representations of visual objects is taking, the one that I find most promising has implications not only for the analysis of implicit and explicit memory effects, but also for models of the processes underlying object perception and recognition. This line of work uses the experimental situation that we have developed as a tool for exploring the nature of the information embodied in structural representations of unfamiliar three-dimensional objects that supports the priming obtained in the object decision task.

The logic of the research approach can be sketched in the following way: One possible view of the nature of structural representations of objects might hold that only information concerning relationships among component units (regardless of how such units are conceptualized) is preserved in the underlying mental representations. Under this account, aspects of visual information irrelevant to the coding of relations should not be represented in and, hence, accessible from structural descriptions of objects. Furthermore, if structural representations of this sort mediate object decision priming, then information concerning attributes like object size, color, reflectance, and contour definition should not affect performance on the object decision task. Variations in other forms of information, for example, depicted orientation, direction of illumination, occlusion of intersections, and dimensional structure, might serve to enhance or to reveal certain relations while obscuring others and, thus, might be expected to influence object decision priming.

In short, this program of research is examining, empirically, what forms of information are contained in structural representations of objects by asking whether study-to-test changes in particular types of information affect object decision performance, compared with explicit recognition. To the extent that such changes reduce or modify the magnitude of priming or recognition effects, we can conclude that the system accessed by the memory task *does represent* the form of information in question. If, however, priming or recognition effects persist in the face of study-to-test changes in certain forms of information about objects, then we have reason to believe that the representational system being tapped by the relevant memory test *is not sensitive* to the type of information undergoing the change.

We have recently completed an experiment asking whether information about object *size* is encoded in the mental representations accessed by implicit and explicit memory tasks (Cooper, Schacter, & Ballesteros, 1990). The experiment consisted of an initial phase in which possible and impossible objects were encoded under structural (left/right) study conditions. For half of the subjects, the studied objects were defined as "small," and for the other half the objects were 2.5 times as large (the "large" study group). Half of the subjects encoding small objects were tested with objects of the same size (half studied, half non-studied), and the other half of the subjects were tested with the larger object set. Similarly, half of the subjects studying the large objects were tested with large objects, and the other "large" study group was tested with the smaller objects. As usual, different groups were used to assess object decision and recognition performance.

The results of this experiment can be summarized as follows: For possible objects, facilitation of object decision judgments to studied over nonstudied items is obtained when encoded and tested objects are the same in size. This is the usual priming effect for structural encoding described above. The novel finding of the present experiment is that substantial priming is exhibited when the size of the tested object is different (either larger or smaller) from the size shown during study. The magnitude of this priming effect—around 16% facilitation of "possible" responses to studied over nonstudied objects—is equal to or greater than the amount of priming obtained under conditions of equivalent study/test object sizes. In contrast, explicit memory under these same encoding and test conditions shows a very different pattern. Recognition of size-changed objects is significantly impaired, relative to the same-size condition. This finding of a decrease in level of recognition with study-to-test change in stimulus size is consistent with results obtained by Jolicoeur (1987), and it provides evidence once again of a dissociation between representations underlying performance on implicit and explicit tests of memory.

The experiment described above serves as an example of how memory dissociations in general and, more specifically, persistence and change in patterns of priming and levels of recognition can be used to investigate the nature of the information preserved in structural representations of visual objects. Following the logic outlined earlier, we can conclude from the present results that information about object size is not preserved in the representational system accessed by object decision judgments and hypothesized to encode specifically relational, structural information about the global organization of the surfaces of an object. The system accessed by explicit recognition, however, does appear to be sensitive to object size as a characteristic of an object's distinctive encoding. Hence, performance on recognition, but not on object decision, is impaired by changes in object size from study to test. Ongoing research should help to clarify the nature of the types of visual information that are and are not preserved in structural representations of objects.

CONCLUDING REMARKS

The program of research sketched in this chapter is motivated by questions concerning the nature of perceptual representations underlying our knowledge about objects in the world and by some fundamental issues in the study of human memory. From the point of view of work on object perception, the line of inquiry offers a paradigm for investigating the nature of the information contained in object representations that are accessed by particular sorts of tasks. From the point of view of studies of human memory, the experiments provide evidence for a dissociation between the information accessed by different tests of memory and possibly between underlying representational systems as well. That is, the experimental results can be seen as demonstrating that there is a system for representing information about the global structure of three-dimensional objects that is dissociable from a system that represents information about object meaning and associations, as well as certain visual properties like object size.

The interpretation of experiments showing dissociations of performance on different tests of memory, in both normal subjects and various amnesic populations, is currently an issue surrounded by considerable controversy. One set of researchers favors an interpretation of such dissociations as evidence for multiple memory systems (e.g., Schacter, in press; Tulving & Schacter, 1990). Others have argued that accounts more parsimonious than the multiple-systems view can offer equally successful explanations of dissociation phenomena (cf., Jacoby, 1983; Masson, 1989; Roediger, Weldon, & Challis, 1989). Mandler (1985) seems clearly to advocate this latter position, preferring to describe dissociation phenomena in terms of *processes* (activation versus elaboration, unconscious versus conscious retrievals) as opposed to memory systems.

Regardless of the theoretical perspective from which the results of the present experiments are viewed (and, I have tried to remain neutral in this exposition, although I fear that the language I have used smacks of a multiple-systems orientation), it is the phenomena themselves and the dissociation effects reported by other investigators as well that intrigue and challenge. What are the implications of these and related findings for the nature of human thinking, memory, and consciousness? This is the sort of question that has guided George Mandler's continuing contributions to the study of the human mind, and that I have tried to touch on here with specific reference to the representation of visual objects.

ACKNOWLEDGMENTS

I would like to express my appreciation to George Mandler for his many contributions to our understanding of the nature of human mental processes. I would also like to thank him for his longstanding and continued interest in and support of my research and professional career.

The experimental work reported in this paper was supported by Air Force Office of Scientific Research Grant 90-0187 to Daniel L. Schacter and Lynn A. Cooper.

REFERENCES

Allen, S. W., & Jacoby, L. L. (1990). Reinstating study context produces unconscious influences of memory. *Memory & Cognition, 18,* 270–278.

Cooper, L. A. (1988). The role of spatial representations in complex problem solving. In S. Steele & S. Schiffer (Eds.), *Cognition and representation* (pp. 53–86). Boulder, CO: Westview.

Cooper, L. A. (1990). Mental representation of three-dimensional objects in visual problem solving and recognition. *Journal of Experimental Psychology: Learning, Memory, and Cognition, 16.*

Cooper, L. A., Schacter, D. L., & Ballesteros, S. (in preparation). *Priming and structural representations of objects: Effects of object size.* Manuscript in preparation.

Durso, F. T., & Johnson, M. K. (1979). Facilitation in naming and categorizing repeated pictures and words. *Journal of Experimental Psychology: Human Learning and Memory, 5,* 449–459.

Gabrieli, J. D. E., Milberg, W., Keane, M. M., & Corkin, S. (in press). Intact priming of patterns despite impaired memory. *Neuropsychologia.*

Graf, P. M., & Schacter, D. L. (1985). Implicit and explicit memory for new associations in normal and amnesic patients. *Journal of Experimental Psychology: Learning, Memory, and Cognition, 11,* 501–518.

Jacoby, L. L. (1983). Perceptual enhancement: Persistent effects of an experience. *Journal of Experimental Psychology: Learning, Memory, and Cognition, 9,* 21–38.

Jolicoeur, P. (1987). A size-congruency effect in memory for visual shape. *Memory & Cognition, 15,* 531–543.

Kirsner, K., Milech, D., & Stumpfel, V. (1986). Word and picture identification: Is representational parsimony possible? *Memory & Cognition, 14,* 398–408.

Kunst-Wilson, W. R., & Zajonc, R. B. (1980). Affective discrimination of stimuli that cannot be recognized. *Science, 120,* 557–558.

Mandler, G. (1980). Recognizing: The judgment of previous occurrence. *Psychological Review, 87,* 252–271.

Mandler, G. (1982). The integration and elaboration of memory structures. In F. Klix, J. Hoffmann, & E. van der Meer (Eds.), *Cognitive research in psychology* (pp. 33–40). Amsterdam: North Holland.

Mandler, G. (1985). *Cognitive psychology: An essay in cognitive science.* Hillsdale, NJ: Lawrence Erlbaum Associates.

Mandler, G., Nakamura, H. K., & Van Zandt, B. J. S. (1987). Nonspecific effects of exposure on stimuli that cannot be recognized. *Journal of Experimental Psychology: Learning, Memory, and Cognition, 13,* 646–649.

Masson, M. E. J. (1989). Fluent reprocessing as an implicit expression of memory for experience. In S. Lewandowsky, J. Dunn, & K. Kirsner (Eds.), *Implicit memory: Theoretical issues* (pp. 123–138). Hillsdale, NJ: Lawrence Erlbaum Associates.

Milner, B., Corkin, S., & Teuber, H. L. (1968). Further analysis of the hippocampal amnesic syndrome: 14 year follow-up study of H. M. *Neuropsychologia, 6,* 519–533.

Musen, G., & Treisman, A. (1990). Implicit and explicit memory for visual patterns. *Journal of Experimental Psychology: Learning, Memory, and Cognition, 15,* 127–137.

Penrose, L. S., & Penrose, R. (1958). Impossible objects: A special type of visual illusion. *British Journal of Psychology, 49,* 31–33.

Richardson-Klavehn, A., & Bjork, R. A. (1988). Measures of memory. *Annual Review of Psychology, 36,* 475–543.

Riddoch, M. J., & Humphreys, G. W. (1987a). Picture naming. In G. W. Humphreys & M. J. Riddoch (Eds.), *Visual object processing: A cognitive neuropsychological approach* (pp. 107–143). London: Lawrence Erlbaum Associates.

Riddoch, M. J., & Humphreys, G. W. (1987b). Visual object processing in optic aphasia: A case of semantic access agnosia. *Cognitive Neuropsychology, 4,* 131–186.

Roediger, H. L. III, Weldon, S., & Challis, B. H. (1989). Explaining dissociations between implicit and explicit measures of retention: A processing account. In H. L. Roediger III & F. I. M. Craik (Eds.), *Varieties of memory and consciousness Essays in honor of Endel Tulving* (pp. 3–41). Hillsdale, NJ: Lawrence Erlbaum Associates.

Sartori, G., & Job, R. (1988). The oyster with four legs: A neuropsychological study on the interaction of visual and semantic information. *Cognitive Neuropsychology, 5,* 105–132.

Schacter, D. L. (1987). Implicit memory: History and current status. *Journal of Experimental Psychology: Learning, Memory, and Cognition, 13,* 501–518.

Schacter, D. L. (in press). Perceptual representation systems and implicit memory: Toward a resolution of the multiple memory systems debate. In A. Diamond (Ed.), *Development and neural bases of higher cognition. Annals of the New York Academy of Sciences.*

Schacter, D. L., Cooper, L. A., & Delaney, S. M. (1990a). Implicit memory for unfamiliar objects depends on access to structural descriptions. *Journal of Experimental Psychology: General, 119,* 5–24.

Schacter, D. L., Cooper, L. A., & Delaney, S. M. (1990b). Implicit memory for visual objects and the structural description system. *Bulletin of the Psychonomic Society, 28(4),* 367–372.

Schacter, D. L., Cooper, L. A., Delaney, S. M., Peterson, M. A., & Tharan, M. (in press). Implicit memory for possible and impossible objects: Constraints on the construction of structural descriptions. *Journal of Experimental Psychology: Learning, Memory, and Cognition.*

Schacter, D. L., Delaney, S. M., & Merikle, E. P. (in press). Priming of nonverbal information and the nature of implicit memory. In G. H. Bower (Ed.), *The psychology of learning and motivation.* New York: Academic Press.

Tulving, E., & Schacter, D. L. (1990). Priming and human memory systems. *Science, 247,* 301–396.

Warrington, E. K. (1982). Neuropsychological studies of object recognition. *Philosophical Transactions of the Royal Society, London, B298,* 15–33.

Warrington, E. K., & Taylor, A. M. (1978). Two categorical stages of object recognition. *Perception, 7,* 695–705.

Warrington, E. K., & Weiskrantz, L. (1968). New method of testing long-term retention with special reference to amnesic patients. *Nature, 217,* 972–974.

Weldon, M. S., & Roediger, H. L. III (1987). Altering retrieval demands reverses the picture superiority effect. *Memory & Cognition, 15,* 269–280.

13 On the Specificity of Procedural Memory

Fergus I. M. Craik
University of Toronto

I became a fully paid-up member of the George Mandler fan club shortly after I heard him introduce a paper he was giving at an international conference some years ago with the statement: "The experiments I will present today stem from the brilliant work of two previous researchers—Gus Craik and George Mandler." It seemed typical of the man that he was prepared to share his moment of glory in the spotlight with a humble member of the audience. The ensuing chapter (Mandler, 1979) remains one of my favorite Mandler pieces, although I was disappointed to note that the introduction of the written version had been trimmed somewhat—a space limitation, no doubt.

George's work and my own have probably come closest in the experiments and ideas that have sought to amalgamate his notions of memory organization (e.g., Mandler, 1967, 1972) with the concepts and results coming from the work on levels of processing (Craik & Lockhart, 1972; Craik & Tulving, 1975). In fact the proposal that free recall performance depended both on the type of processing carried out on the item itself, and on the organizational links among items was one made in the Mandler (1979) chapter just cited. These notions have also been developed and extended by Reed Hunt, Gilles Einstein, and their colleagues (e.g., Einstein & Hunt, 1980; Hunt & Einstein, 1981).

The central proposal made by Mandler (1979) was that two processes—integration and elaboration—operate on the mental representation of an event during the encoding or learning phase. Mental representations are seen as schemas, consisting of perceptual and semantic components, and the relations among them (Graf & Mandler, 1984). When an event is presented, its schema is activated and one effect of this activation is to strengthen the internal organization of the schema's components. In the case of a novel event, presumably a new schema is created, but again the processing operations will act to strengthen internal organizational links among the relevant components. This enhancement of internal organization is referred to as *integration*, and Mandler's suggestion is that this type of processing makes the event more accessible in the sense that re-presentation of one or more components has a greater likelihood of bringing the whole representation into conscious awareness. The processes of elaboration, on the other hand, strengthen the links among different schemas, and create new links between schemas. This type of processing is held to make representations more retrievable, in that more retrieval paths are formed and existing paths strengthened (Graf & Mandler, 1984).

Mandler has utilized these concepts to give accounts of rote learning, free and cued recall, paired-associate learning, and recognition (Mandler, 1979, 1980, 1982). A more recent application has been to the phenomena referred to variously as priming, implicit memory, procedural memory, and memory without awareness. The essential demonstration in these cases is that the previous presentation of an item facilitates present performance on a task involving the item, although the item may not be "remembered" in the usual sense. Thus, previous presentation can facilitate word completion from partial cues (Tulving, Schacter, & Stark, 1982; Warrington & Weiskrantz, 1970), perceptual identification of words (Jacoby & Dallas, 1981; Winnick & Daniel, 1970) and pictures (Warren & Morton, 1982), and the fluent reading of text passages (Kolers, 1975, 1976). Such implicit memory effects (to use Schacter's, 1987, terminology) differ from explicit measures like recall and recognition in that they appear to depend more heavily on surface information than on deep, semantic information, they require very precise reinstatement of the initial conditions of presentation, they are very long lasting, and appear to be unimpaired in various groups of subjects (e.g., young children, older adults, and amnesic patients) whose explicit memory performance *is* impaired relative to that of young adults (see Richardson-Klavehn & Bjork, 1988, for an extensive review).

The contribution of Peter Graf, George Mandler, and their colleagues (e.g., Graf & Mandler, 1984; Graf, Mandler, & Haden, 1982; Graf, Squire, & Mandler, 1984) has been to show first that word completion given the first three letters (ONI--; JUI--) is facilitated by the previous presentation of the complete word (onion, juice), but that a level of processing manipulation at presentation has no effect on subsequent completion (see also Jacoby & Dallas, 1981). However, if the same three initial letters are presented as an explicit cue to recall a previously presented word, semantic processing is now superior to nonsemantic processing (Graf & Mandler, 1984) and controls perform better than amnesics (Graf et al., 1984). That is, even although word presentation and the "retrieval cues" remain the same, the types of retrieval processing invoked by instructions are affected by different types of information. The suggestion is that word stem completion relies heavily on activation and on surface information (which is induced equally by shallow and deep orienting tasks, and is available equally to controls and amnesics), whereas explicit cued recall depends on elaboration and semantic processing (which is induced by "deeper" orienting tasks, and is more available in controls than in amnesics). The demonstrations are convincing and they are accompanied by a plausible and elegant theoretical account.

EXPERIMENTS ON READING TRANSFORMED TEXT

The experiments I describe were designed to cast further light on the types of information that facilitate a particular implicit memory task—the re-reading of text passages printed in transformed typography. This work stems from the ideas and findings of Paul Kolers, but the results are relevant also to our understanding of the concepts of integration and activation.

The paradigm is one in which subjects are presented with short text passages printed in difficult to read transformed typographies; for the purposes of exposition these typographies may be thought of as mirror-image printing or as inverted text, although a variety of different geometrical transformations were used. In all cases the print itself was one in common use (i.e., no ornate fonts were used) but the letters or words were rotated or inverted. The task was to read the text passage as quickly and accurately as possible, and the measure was average reading time per word. More particularly, subjects re-read the same passages a week after their first reading; the interest here lies in the savings in reading time shown by subjects on the second reading, and whether such savings scores are affected by changes in the typography from first to second reading. If, for example, a subject acquires skill in reading two different transformed typographies (A and B), and can read them equally well; and if that subject reads a passage in typography A on the first reading, it is of interest to discover whether he or she shows more savings when he or she re-reads the passage in typography A than if the subject re-reads the passage in typography B. If that result is found, it suggests that the subject is retaining not only some information about the gist of the passage and the general skill of reading passages in A and B, but is also retaining highly specific information relating to that passage presented in that orthography.

This claim was made by Kolers (1976) with respect to subjects re-reading pages of transformed text after intervals up to 15 months. He had subjects read 160 pages of text in transformed typography over the course of several days; about 1 year later, six of the subjects came back and read 98 pages of text in the same typography. In this second phase, half of the pages had been read before in Phase 1, and half were new pages from the same books as the other pages. The results showed that subjects retained the general skill of reading the transformed typography from Phase 1 to Phase 2. More dramatically, pages read for the second time were read slightly faster than new pages, and this second result provided the basis for Kolers' claim that subjects were retaining highly specific pattern-analyzing operations (that is, specific to that page of text in that orthography) for at least 1 year.

However, there is a simpler and perhaps more plausible account of Kolers' results. If subjects remembered even a little about the content of previously read pages, this retained knowledge may have given them the slight advantage (5%–6%) over new pages. Kolers considered this possibility but rejected it, although not on very compelling grounds. The issue is clearly an important one to resolve one way or another; if subjects are really able to "retain" (in some sense) complex perceptual patterns that can facilitate performance a year later, it casts a rather different light on the capabilities and specificity of procedural memory in human subjects.

Tardif and Craik Experiment

Tardif and Craik (1989) reported an experiment that addresses the issue of the types of information retained after reading text passages in transformed typographies. In outline, subjects read passages in each of two transformed typographies (A and B) in the first phase of the experiment. One week later, they returned and re-read the passages, either in the identical typography, in the other practiced typography, or in a completely new typography (C). Subjects also read new text passages in each of the three typographies. This design should provide an answer to several relevant questions. For example, comparing old passages with new passages, are subjects' reading times faster for old passages? If so, reading performance may be said to benefit from the retention of conceptual or gist information. Also, are reading times faster for passages presented in the previously practiced typographies (A & B) as opposed to passages presented in typography C? If so, presumably subjects have retained the general skill of reading these original typographies. Finally, is there an additional advantage to re-reading an old passage in its original typography, as opposed to re-reading it in the other practiced typography? In this case, both the passages and the orthographies are familiar, so any further advantage must be associated with the specific combination of that passage in that orthography. A positive finding here would sustain Kolers' claim. The design is shown in Table 13.1.

In greater detail, 18 undergraduate subjects participated in the experiment. The passages were approximately 180 words in length; they were taken from popular science magazines, and each passage was presented on a separate sheet of paper. Four typographies were used: Normal type; Inverted; Mirror-Image; and Reversed-Spelling (the letters were presented normally, but words were read from right to left). On Week 1, each subject read 12 passages—four each in Normal typography and in two of the three transformed typographies; however, the first passage in each typography was regarded as practice and did not appear in the second session. Thus, nine passages were re-read 7 days later in Session 2 (see Table 13.1) along with three new passages. The different transformed ty-

TABLE 13.1
Design of the Experiment by Tardif and Craik (1989)

Week 1		Week 2
Three passages in A	—	re-read in A re-read in B re-read in C
Three passages in B	—	re-read in A re-read in B re-read in C
Three passages in Normal	—	re-read in A re-read in B re-read in C
(Not presented)	—	read in A read in B read in C

A, B, and C are three different transformed typographies. The actual typographies used were counterbalanced, but C was always the new typography encountered only in Week 2.

pographies were counterbalanced over subjects so that each typography (Inverted, etc.) appeared equally often as A, B, and C in the overall experiment.

Subjects were tested individually; they read each passage aloud. If a subject could not read a given word after 10 sec, he or she moved on to read the rest of the sentence, but then returned to the missing word for a further 10 sec. If the subject still failed to produce the word, the experimenter read it out. Errors were corrected in the same way. The measure taken was the average reading time per word, including the time taken to correct errors.

The results of the study (expressed as average reading times in seconds per word for passages read in the second session) are shown in Fig. 13.1. With respect to the passages, the figure shows that new passages took longer to read than passages presented on Week 1 (N, B, and A)—that is, subjects retained information about the passages that facilitated reading 1 week later. Within the old passages, those read originally in a transformed typography (A & B) were re-read somewhat faster than those read originally in Normal typography, although this effect was not statistically reliable.

With respect to Week 2 typography, Fig. 13.1 shows that passages read in Typography C (the new typography) took longer to read than those presented in A or B. That is, subjects retained the skills of reading in both A and B, and this enabled them to read both old (N, B, A) and new passages more rapidly. However, the experiment yielded no evidence in favor of a further advantage associated with re-reading a passage in its original typography. Graphically, there is a very slight advantage when passages were re-read in the identical typography

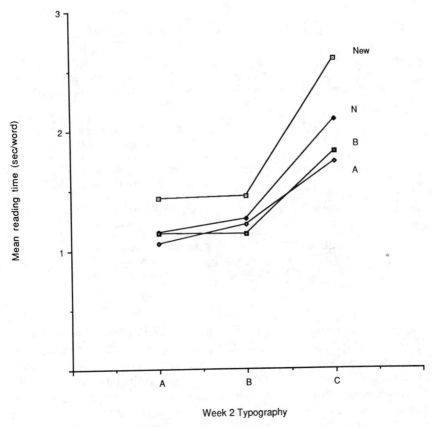

FIG. 13.1   Reading times in the second session as a function of experimental condition; "new" items were not read in Session 1; N = Normal orthography, B = Orthography B, and A = Orthography A in Session 1. Data from Tardif and Craik (1989) Experiment 1.

(AA and BB as opposed to AB and BA) but a t test of this comparison yielded $t(17) = 0.79$, a value far short of statistical significance.

Overall then, the experiment provided good evidence for the retention of both information about the passages themselves (presumably some memory for the contents of each passage) and information about the typographies (presumably the general skill of reading these particular transformations). But there was no support for the more interesting claim that highly specific pattern-analyzing operations were retained to facilitate re-reading a passage in its original typography. This last result thus fails to confirm Kolers' (1976) findings, although it is in line with results reported by Horton (1985).

However, it was a little unsettling that a small advantage was found in the present results, when same-typography repetitions were compared with different-typography repetitions. The mean reading time for "same" passages was 1.09 sec/word, compared with 1.15 sec/word for "different" passages. The difference in mean reading times was therefore about 5%—a value close to that reported by Kolers. Accordingly, I decided to repeat a simplified version of the experiment, focussing on re-reading passages in either the same or the alternate typography. This follow-up experiment involved more subjects; it also used rather easier passages, and utilized two transformed typographies that were as different from each other as possible. The main purpose of the study was to adjudicate between Horton (1985) and Tardif and Craik (1989) on the one hand, and Kolers (1976) and Masson (1986) on the other. Is there reliable evidence for the retention of highly specific pattern-analyzing operations when the materials and conditions are favorable?

Craik and Gemar Study

The experiment was conducted in collaboration with Michael Gemar, and was carried out by Lori Johnson. The design was straightforward; 24 undergraduate subjects read 20 paragraphs in the first session, 10 in one transformed typography, and 10 in a second transformed typography. They returned 1 week later, and read 30 paragraphs in the same two typographies; of these 30, 10 Week 1 paragraphs were re-read in their original typographies, 10 Week 1 paragraphs were re-read in the alternate typography, and 10 new paragraphs were read for the first time. The principal question at issue was whether familiar (Week 1) paragraphs re-read in the identical typography were read faster than familiar paragraphs re-read in the other (but equally practiced) typography.

In greater detail, the paragraphs were shorter than those used in the Tardif and Craik experiments; on average they were 73 words in length. They dealt with a variety of everyday matters and were drawn from textbooks, magazines, and newspapers.

A typical example follows:

> Hunting and gathering societies tended to move within well-defined territories. When the food supply in one area was depleted, they moved to another, frequently settling in or near some former camp site. Groups sometimes used the same regular circuit of sites every year. Moves were frequently stimulated by seasonal changes that reduced the supply of food in one section of a territory while increasing it in another.

The two transformed typographies used in the experiment were chosen from the set described by Kolers and Perkins (1975). We looked for two transformations that yielded relatively low levels of transfer from one to the other and were of approximately equal difficulty. On the basis of Kolers and Perkins' results we chose what they describe as "I" and "rM" script. Figure 13.2 shows further paragraphs in these two typographies. Kolers and Perkins had shown that practice on one specific script can transfer to a greater or lesser extent to performance on a second script; in their terminology 0% transfer means that practice on Script A has no beneficial effects on Script B, whereas 100% transfer means that practice on A is as beneficial as is practice on B to later performance on B. They found that transfer from rM to I was 44% and from I to rM was 52%. Kolers and Perkins also reported that, after practice, subjects read a page of I text in 3.23 minutes and a page of rM text in 3.57 minutes.

In the initial session, subjects first read three practice paragraphs in one of the two scripts, and then read 10 test paragraphs in that script. Following this block, they were given 3 practice and 10 test paragraphs in the other script. They read

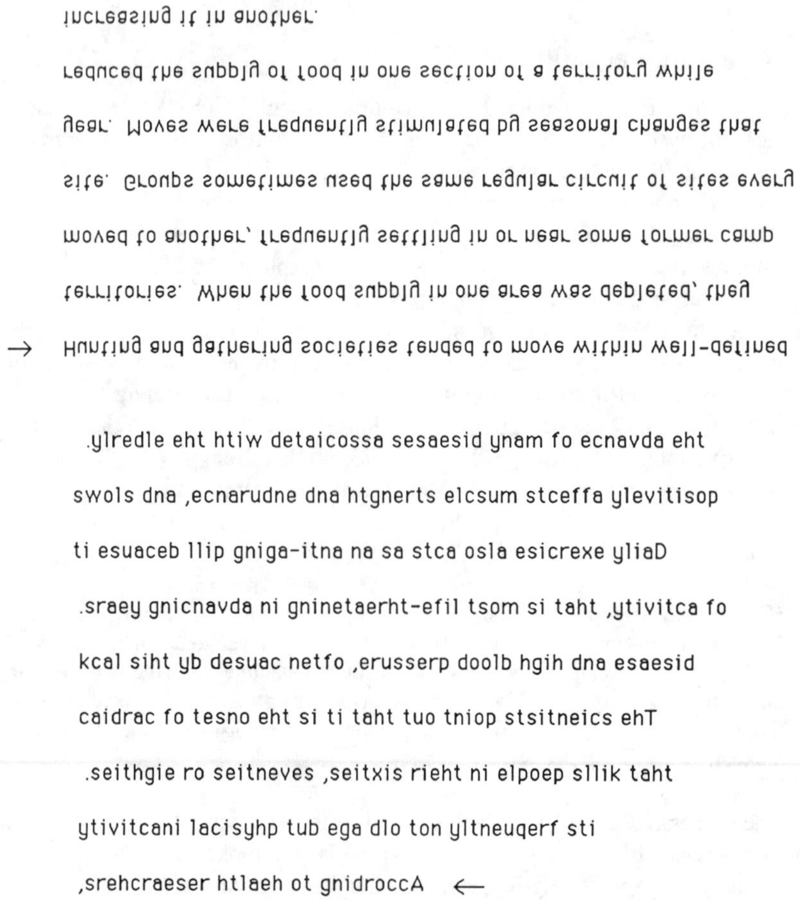

juclɹɐꙅʇuϱ ʇʇ ʇu ɐuoʇɥǝɹ·

Leqnɔǝq ʇɥǝ ꙅnbbjʎ oʇ ʇooq ʇu ouǝ ꙅǝɔʇʇou oʇ ɐ ʇǝʅʅʇʇoɹʎ ʍɥʇʅǝ

ʌǝɐɹ· Hoʌǝꙅ ʍǝɹǝ ʇɹǝqnǝuʇʃʎ ꙅʇʇwnʃɐʇǝq pʎ ꙅǝɐꙅouɐʃ ɔɥɐuqǝꙅ ʇɥɐʇ

ꙅʇʇǝ· Ɓɹonbꙅ ꙅowǝʇʇwǝꙅ nꙅǝq ʇɥǝ ꙅɐwǝ ɹǝqnɐɹ ɔʇɹɔnʇʇ oʇ ꙅʇʇǝꙅ ǝʌǝɹʎ

woʌǝq ʇo ɐuoʇɥǝɹ· ʇɹǝqnǝuʇʃʎ ꙅǝʇʇʃʇuϱ ʇu oɹ uǝɐɹ ꙅowǝ ʇoɹwǝɹ ɔɐwb

ʇǝʅʅʇʇoɹʇǝꙅ· ʍɥǝu ʇɥǝ ʇooq ꙅnbbjʎ ʇu ouǝ ɐɹǝɐ ʍɐꙅ qǝbjǝʇǝq' ʇɥǝʎ

→ Hnuʇʇuϱ ɐuq ϱɐʇɥǝɹʇuϱ ꙅoɔʇǝʇʇǝꙅ ʇǝuqǝq ʇo woʌǝ ʍʇʇɥʇu ʍǝʅʅ-qǝʇʇuǝq

.ylredle eht htiw detaicossa sesaesid ynam fo ecnavda eht

swols dna ,ecnarudne dna htgnerts elcsum stceffa ylevitisop

ti esuaceb llip gniga-itna na sa stca osla esicrexe yliaD

.sraey gnicnavda ni gninetaerht-efil tsom si taht ,ytivitca fo

kcal siht yb desuac netfo ,erusserp doolb hgih dna esaesid

caidrac fo tesno eht si ti taht tuo tniop stsitneics ehT

.seithgie ro seitneves ,seitxis rieht ni elpoep sllik taht

ytivitcani lacisyhp tub ega dlo ton yltneuqerf sti

,srehcraeser htlaeh ot gnidroccA ←

FIG. 13.2.   Examples of passages in I and rM typographies.

aloud, and their reading was tape-recorded. If subjects could not determine a word after 20 sec, the word was provided; similarly, if an error was made, the experimenter indicated the error and had the subject try again. The second session followed after 1 week. In this session, subjects first read two new paragraphs in each of the two scripts, and then read 30 paragraphs of which 20 were old (Week 1) and 10 were new. Of the 10 presented initially in Script I, 5 were re-presented in I and 5 were switched to rM; similarly 5 were retained in rM and 5 were switched from rM to I. Of the 10 new paragraphs, 5 were read in I, and 5 in rM. The order of the 30 paragraphs was randomly determined. The order of scripts and paragraphs, and the combination of a particular script with a particular paragraph was counterbalanced over subjects.

The major results are shown in Table 13.2. Not surprisingly the old paragraphs were read faster than the new paragraphs; but more interestingly, paragraphs re-read in their original scripts were read more rapidly (0.83 sec/word) than paragraphs switched to the other script (0.87 sec/word). The effect is a small one—about 5%—but it is comparable to the size of effect reported by Kolers (1976) and also found by Tardif and Craik (1989). However, in the present case the effect is a reliable one; a 2 × 2 analysis of variance on the old paragraphs yielded a significant interaction [$F(1,23) = 7.37, p < .05$]. Also, a t test on the combined Same-script conditions versus the combined Different-script conditions yielded $t(23) = 2.45, p < .05$.

The present experiment thus reverses the conclusion drawn from the Tardif and Craik study, although the size and direction of the effects are comparable between the two experiments. From the present study, it appears that Kolers was correct in his claim that highly specific pattern-analyzing operations persist over lengthy time periods, and can facilitate subsequent processing of the same material. Kolers' point of view has also been supported by Masson (1986).

However, before this revised conclusion is finally accepted, one other factor should be considered. The initial reading times varied enormously over different words in a passage, and it seemed possible that the overall effect shown in Table 13.2 might not be attributable to a general increase in reading fluency for passages re-read in the same typography but, rather, to substantial re-reading sav-

TABLE 13.2
Reading Times (Sec/Word) on Week 2
of the Craik and Gemar Study

Week 1 Orthography	Week 2 Orthography	
	I	rM
I	0.84	0.88
rM	0.87	0.83
(New)	1.03	0.97

ings for only a few words in each passage. That is, if a particular word takes a very long time to decipher on Week 1, it is likely that the same word will show the greatest savings on Week 2. Moreover, it seems possible that if the passage in question is re-read in the same typography, savings will be even greater. The subject may recognize the pattern that produced such difficulty on the previous occasion, and therefore read the word relatively quickly in the second session.

In order to get further information on this question, reading times were obtained for each individual word. This laborious feat was accomplished by heroic undergraduate assistants who listened to the tape-recorded subjects' readings, and entered each word "on-line" into a computer. This procedure was carried out both for the initial reading and the re-reading of each passage on Week 2. The computer then calculated both the initial reading times for each word read by a particular subject, and the savings on that word when re-read in the second session. Further, the computer sorted each subject's initial reading times into quintiles—the fastest fifth through to the slowest fifth—and the savings were calculated separately for passages re-read in the same orthography and for those switched to the different orthography. The results are shown in Fig. 13.3.

If it was the case that the overall benefit to passages re-read in the same orthography came essentially from a few words that took a long time to read in the first session, then the greater savings associated with Same re-reading should be restricted to Quintile 5. In fact, Fig. 13.3 shows the opposite pattern of results. The greatest overall savings are of course associated with Quintile 5 (because words read quickly on Session 1 cannot be read much faster on Session 2) but the Same condition is associated with greater savings on all quintiles *except* the fifth. That is, the overall effect shown in Table 13.2 appears to hold for all words except those that took a long time to decipher in Session 1.

The data shown in Fig. 13.3 were analyzed by a 2 × 5 analysis of variance (after log transformation to smooth the large differences in variance among the quintiles). The analysis showed large effects of Quintile [$F(4,92) = 462.4, p < .001$] and of Same versus Different [$F(1, 23) = 28.8, p < .001$]; the interaction between Quintile and Same/Different was also reliable [$F(4,92) = 7.67, p < .01$]. Subsequent post hoc Tukey tests ($\alpha = .05$) revealed that Same was associated with significantly greater savings for Quintiles 1, 2, and 3 only. The apparent benefit to Same in Quintile 4 was not reliable, and neither was the reversal in Quintile 5.

So, surprisingly, the benefit associated with re-reading transformed passages in the identical orthography is apparently restricted to those words read relatively fluently on the first occasion. Before commenting on this result, two other features of the data shown in Fig. 13.3 may be mentioned. First, the negative "savings" shown by words in Quintiles 1 and 2 simply means that words read very rapidly in Session 1 were read somewhat slower in Session 2—a slight regression to the mean. Second, it seemed likely that many words in the first few quintiles would be common function words such as "and, the, this, of, but," and

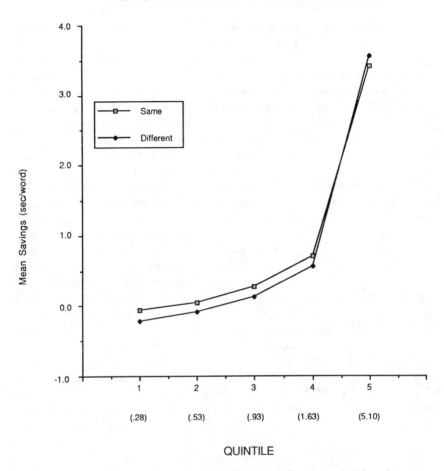

FIG. 13.3.   Savings scores (sec/word) between first and second readings as a function of absolute reading times on the first session.

so on. If this is so, then such words would likely appear in both the Same and Different conditions. If there is substantial overlap in the actual words making up the Same and Different groups, it would present something of a puzzle: Why are words in the identical orthography condition read faster than words in the changed orthography condition if the words themselves are substantially the same? Our heroic undergraduates were pressed into service yet again, and this time their labors revealed that there were indeed overlaps between Same and Different conditions; for Quintiles 1–5 the proportions of words that were common to the two conditions were .39, .42, .31, .21, and .07 respectively. This finding is discussed later.

Some interesting conclusions may be drawn from the results of the Craik and Gemar study. First, it provides support for Kolers' claim that highly specific pattern-analyzing operations are retained over long retention intervals. It is true that the present experiment examined retention over 1 week as opposed to over 1 year in Kolers' case, but nonetheless the retention of such highly specific procedures seems remarkable. Second, the additional benefit to Same over Different orthography repetition appears to be restricted to those words read most fluently on the first occasion. Although this was not the expected result, it may be tentatively suggested that perhaps this result illustrates the same kind of dissociation within the re-reading paradigm as that previously observed by Graf, Mandler, and others in memory paradigms. That is, perceptual aspects of stimuli are most relevant to the retention of truly procedural operations. If the information used to read a transformed word is substantially perceptual on both occasions (as it may be when relatively fluent "reading procedures" are used) then retention of the same surface form will be beneficial. If, however, difficult words are deciphered by more semantic, problem-solving means, then retention of the same *surface* form will be irrelevant to performance on the second reading.

A third point follows from the finding that there is a substantial overlap of common words between the Same and Different conditions for the first three quintiles. Because the words are substantially the same words, yet Same orthography shows more savings than Different orthography, it may be suggested that the re-reading benefit is associated essentially with *words in their context* (i.e., with linguistic patterns rather than with individual words). This argument is an extension of the more obvious point that the same *letters* are necessarily repeated in the Same and Different conditions; the effect is not connected with the repetition of letters, however, but the repetition of words. The present finding suggests that in some cases the crucial patterns are phrases rather than words in isolation.

CONCLUSION

Further work, as the saying goes, is required to corroborate the findings described here, and also to document more clearly the conditions under which these re-reading benefits are (Kolers, 1976; Masson, 1986) and are not (Horton, 1985; Tardif & Craik, 1989) observed. However, it does seem an exciting possibility that perceptual information is somehow preserved, and that this information persists to facilitate performance in subsequent tasks (e.g., re-reading of transformed text, word and picture completion, word identification) that *require* perceptual information for their successful and speedy completion.

I agree with Graf and Mandler (1984) and with Jacoby (1983) that such effects can be viewed as showing that different memory and perceptual tasks require different types of information for their effective completion, although other investigators have accounted for the same patterns of results in terms of different memory systems (Tulving & Schacter, 1990). To turn again to Mandler's distinction between integration and elaboration, I assume that the perceptual or surface form effects illustrated in the Craik and Gemar study are examples of integration (i.e., the initial reading serves to activate specific word patterns, and to meld specific surface forms to the pre-existing word schema).

A slightly different way of describing the effects is to suggest that they represent a type of perceptual learning; that highly specific pattern-analyzing operations are brought into play to perceive and comprehend the text on the first reading, and that the execution of these operations modifies the perceptual system in a subtle, yet specific and possibly *permanent* way. One implication of this modification of the system is that carrying out the same sequence of operations on a subsequent occasion will be facilitated. It is not that "activation" persists over time (as the "priming" metaphor suggests) but simply that the underlying structures have been modified so that when the relevant processing operations are again required, they can be run off more fluently (Jacoby, 1982).

As a further suggestion, the beneficial effects of such possibly permanent modifications may require extensive contextual support to be detected. That is, the operations in question may not reflect the simple processing of the particular word or other pattern on which the experimenter is focusing, but may reflect, rather, a broadly integrated processing configuration. If this is so, the perceptual learning effects under discussion may show their greatest facilitative effects on subsequent occasions when the whole original configuration of processing is re-established, either by reinstatement of the original environmental context, or by reinstatement of the same mental context. Embedding subtle perceptual learning operations in a rich matrix of semantic or schematic knowledge may thus be one way in which future perceptual benefits are boosted, given that the well-learned and well-integrated schematic knowledge can be re-invoked with relative ease. This suggestion may provide an explanation for Graf and Schacter's (1985) finding that word stem completion effects for new word pairings benefit from semantic processing of the word pair.

It may also provide an explanation of why color after-effects (the McCollough effect) are found for meaningful words, but not for nonwords (Allan, Siegel, Collins, & MacQueen, 1989). That is, the apparently surface form or "data-driven" effects associated with stem completion and color after-effects may depend on (or be enhanced by) supportive semantic processing.

So much for speculation. To recapitulate my opening anecdote, the present set of ideas does stem inevitably from the previous contributions of the many friends and colleagues whose work has been cited in the previous pages. But George Mandler's theoretical and empirical contributions have been especially helpful to me, as they have been a central part of our field for the past 40 years or so. It is a pleasure to pay tribute to George, to thank him for help in the past, and to look forward to discussing his future ideas over a glass or two of my native country's best known product!

ACKNOWLEDGMENTS

This chapter was prepared with the help of a grant from the Natural Sciences and Engineering Research Council of Canada. I am also grateful to Lori Johnson, Ian Frijters, Gina Grimshaw, Rita Simek-Nelmes, and Jennifer Smith for help in running and analyzing the second experiment reported.

REFERENCES

Allan, L. G., Siegel, S., Collins, J. C., & MacQueen, G. (1989). Color aftereffect contingent on text. *Perception and Psychophysics, 46,* 105–113.

Craik, F. I. M., & Lockhart, R. S. (1972). Levels of processing: A framework for memory research. *Journal of Verbal Learning and Verbal Behavior, 11,* 671–684.

Craik, F. I. M., & Tulving, E. (1975). Depth of processing and the retention of words in episodic memory. *Journal of Experimental Psychology: General, 104,* 268–294.

Einstein, G. O., & Hunt, R. R. (1980). Levels of processing and organization: Additive effects of individual-items and relational processing. *Journal of Experimental Psychology: Human Learning and Memory, 6,* 588–598.

Graf, P., & Mandler, G. (1984). Activation makes words accessible, but not necessarily more retrievable. *Journal of Verbal Learning and Verbal Behavior, 23,* 533–568.

Graf, P., Mandler, G., & Haden, P. (1982). Simulating amnesic symptoms in normal subjects. *Science, 218,* 1243–1244.

Graf, P., & Schacter, D. L. (1985). Implicit and explicit memory for new associations in normal and amnesic subjects. *Journal of Experimental Psychology: Learning, Memory, and Cognition, 11,* 501–518.

Graf, P., Squire, L. R., & Mandler, G. (1984). The information that amnesic patients do not forget. *Journal of Experimental Psychology: Learning, Memory, and Cognition, 9,* 164–178.

Horton, K. D. (1985). The role of semantic information in reading spatially transformed text. *Cognitive Psychology, 17,* 66–88.

Hunt, R. R., & Einstein, G. O. (1981). Relational and item-specific information in memory. *Journal of Verbal Learning and Verbal Behavior, 20,* 497–514.

Jacoby, L. L. (1982). Knowing and remembering: Some parallels in the behavior of Korsakoff patients and normals. In L. S. Cermak (Ed.), *Human memory and amnesia* (pp. 97–122). Hillsdale, NJ: Lawrence Erlbaum Associates.

Jacoby, L. L. (1983). Remembering the data: analyzing interactive processes in reading. *Journal of Verbal Learning and Verbal Behavior, 22,* 485–508.

Jacoby, L. L., & Dallas, M. (1981). On the relationship between autobiographical memory and perceptual learning. *Journal of Experimental Psychology: General, 110,* 306–340.

Kolers, P. A. (1975). Memorial consequences of automatized encoding. *Journal of Experimental Psychology: Human Learning and Memory, 1,* 689–701.

Kolers, P. A. (1976). Reading a year later. *Journal of Experimental Psychology: Human Learning and Memory, 2,* 554–565.

Kolers, P. A., & Perkins, D. N. (1975). Spatial and ordinal components of form perception and literacy. *Cognitive Psychology, 7,* 228–267.

Mandler, G. (1967). Organization and memory. In K. W. Spence & J. T. Spence (Eds.), *The psychology of learning and motivation* (Vol. 1 pp. 327–372). New York: Academic Press.

Mandler, G. (1972). Organization and recognition. In E. Tulving & W. Donaldson (Eds.), *Organization of memory* (pp. 139–166). New York: Academic Press.

Mandler, G. (1979). Organization and repetition: Organizational principles with special reference to rote learning. In L.-G. Nilsson (Ed.), *Perspectives on memory research* (pp. 293–327). Hillsdale, NJ: Lawrence Erlbaum Associates.

Mandler, G. (1980). Recognizing: The judgment of previous occurrence. *Psychological Review, 87,* 252–271.

Mandler, G. (1982). The integration and elaboration of memory structures. In F. Klix, J. Hoffman & E. van der Meer (Eds.), *Cognitive research in psychology* (pp. 33–40). Amsterdam: North-Holland.

Masson, M. E. J. (1986). Identification of typographically-transformed words: Instance-based skill acquisition. *Journal of Experimental Psychology: Learning, Memory, and Cognition, 12,* 479–488.

Richardson-Klavehn, A., & Bjork, R. A. (1988). Measures of memory. *Annual Review of Psychology, 39,* 479–543.

Schacter, D. L. (1987). Implicit memory: history and current status. *Journal of Experimental Psychology: Learning, Memory, and Cognition, 13,* 501–518.

Tardif, T., & Craik, F. I. M. (1989). Reading a week later: Perceptual and conceptual factors. *Journal of Memory and Language, 28,* 107–125.

Tulving, E., & Schacter, D. L. (1990). Priming and human memory systems. *Science, 247,* 301–306.

Tulving, E., Schacter, D. L., & Stark, H. (1982). Priming effects in word-fragment completion are independent of recognition memory. *Journal of Experimental Psychology: Human Learning and Memory, 8,* 336–342.

Warren, C., & Morton, J. (1982). The effects of priming on picture recognition. *British Journal of Psychology, 73,* 117–129.

Warrington, E. K., & Weiskrantz, L. (1970). Amnesic syndrome: consolidation or retrieval? *Nature, 228,* 628–630.

Winnick, W. A., & Daniel, S. A. (1970). Two kinds of response priming in tachistoscopic word recognition. *Journal of Experimental Psychology, 84,* 74–81.

14 Cognitive Pathologies of Memory: A Headed Records Analysis[1]

John Morton

M.R.C. Cognitive Development Unit, London

The Headed Records model of memory (Morton, 1990; Morton & Bekerian, 1986; Morton, Hammersley, & Bekerian, 1985) gives an account of a variety of experimental findings as well as a means of talking about our experience of our own memory. In this chapter, I explore some pathological phenomena of memory in terms of the model. The advantage of this approach is that it enables the various conditions to be seen in a particular relation to each other and the normal function of memory.

THE HEADED RECORDS MODEL

The basis of the Headed Records (HR) model is that our memory is divided up into discrete *records*. Either all of a record is accessed or none of it. Each record is linked to a *Heading*. The *headed record* is the basic structural unit in memory. HRs are structurally unrelated to one another. Behavior or subjective experience that might lead one to believe in the existence of associations between records are due to the unconscious, automatic operation of the accompanying processes.

In common with many other theorists, I regard the memory system as having the primary functions of interpreting the perceptual world and guiding actions. In the course of serving these functions, memory will have to be interrogated. This will normally happen without our conscious intervention. Memory can also be

---

[1]George has always understood Headed Records but never believed it. I have reciprocated by believing a number of George's ideas without really understanding them. I hope this offering will bring us closer together.

consciously interrogated, and this is the form of memory search with which we are more familiar. Within the model, the first thing that happens when memory is interrogated is that a *description* is formed. This is the information used in the search, the term being taken from Norman and Bobrow (1979). Search is carried out of headings only. Headings are searched in parallel. The objective of the search is to find a heading that matches the description according to some criteria. If such a match is found, then the linked record is made available for further processing and will be examined to see if it fulfills the current *task demands*. If the record that has been retrieved does not fulfill these task demands, then a new description is formed and the search cycle is repeated (see Williams & Hollan, 1981).

This modest beginning has far reaching implications for the way in which memory operates. The model contrasts with most other models of memory in that it is explicitly *not* freely content addressable.[2] In terms of the model, information that is in the record need not be duplicated in the heading in any form. But only headings are searched. Thus it is that information that is central to an event memory does not necessarily serve as a cue for the recall of that memory. The converse of this is that information in the heading need not be present in the linked record. Thus, something that would be a reliable cue for a set of knowledge might be unretrievable if that set of knowledge was accessed by other means. The most common example of such a principle operating in practice is with people's names. We all have the experience of being aware of everything we know about an individual, other than their name. Yet their name would, surely, serve as a guaranteed cue to this information.

The account of this phenomenon in HR terms is that the name forms a part of the heading for the record containing the information in question. As we see here, the headings have a number of components, and it is not necessary for the match between heading and description to be complete. It would be possible, then, for the record to be accessed by some other cue, such as the place where the subject of the record had last been encountered. Given that the record had been retrieved, all the information contained within it would potentially be available. However, there is no way (by definition) of retrieving the contents of the headings, and the name would not be retrievable. For another individual, of course, the name could be in the record and the situation would not arise. Such variability in memory organization is as much a burden to the theorist as it is to the owner of the memory.

A further class of memory experience that appears to be ubiquitous is the experience of a memory being triggered spontaneously by something that was just a part of the background for an event and irrelevant to the content of the memory. Common triggers of such experiences are specific locales in town or

---

[2]I also assert this as a fact about all human memory other than those owned by theorists to the contrary.

country, scents, and certain pieces of music. Here is an example taken verbatim from an informant:

> A couple of years ago I changed my perfume. The perfume I wore before that I had worn during a very unhappy time in my life. A few months ago, I found this large bottle of perfume and thought "I can't let this go to waste" and sprayed some on. Almost immediately I was back in hospital coming around after having my stomach pumped.

Thinking of the incident did not remind this woman of that particular perfume. The associated smells were those more typical of hospitals. However, the processes of memory formation had operated in such a way as to put the smell of the favorite perfume in the heading—perhaps because it was the last sensory experience before unconsciousness. Speculation apart, the principle exists in the HR model of the possibility of information acting as a retrieval cue that is incidental to the content of the memory record that is retrieved.

The Structure and Content of the Records

There are no constraints on the structure of records, which can take whatever form happens to have been computed by the current processing. Collections, lists, hierarchies, schemas are examples of the possible data structures. The content of records also depends on the nature of the current processing. There are two broad classes of record, which can be classified as primary and secondary. Primary records are those that result from the normal activity of interpretation of the perceptual world. Secondary records are those that result from the retrieval of primary records in the course of reminiscence or the retrieval of a primary record that is being used as the basis of a narrative. In the case of the narrative, the form of code will have been changed into a verbal one.

The Components of the Heading

Headings have a number of components. Roughly speaking, anything that contributes to the retrieval of a record will be in the heading. I say "roughly speaking" because the system is not that simple. To start with, the ostensive cue may have been transformed by the processes involved in forming the description. Second, the effect of a cue may be indirect—that is, the cue may serve to help retrieve one record that may contain information that can serve as a cue for the target information.

An experimental way of determining the components of headings is through a comparison of the relative effectiveness of variables on recognition memory compared with recall. The reason for this lies in the difference between the way these two tasks map onto the HR framework. Recognition memory involves the subjects' judging whether or not the presented material had previously been experienced. This requires that the material should form a description that matches a heading and that the record that is retrieved contains information that enables the evaluation system to decide whether or not the task demands have been satisfied. In recall, the subject is given only some notion of the topic and the circumstances of the previous encounter. The material itself has to be found in a record. The data indicate that the literal form of the stimulus serves as a cue in recognition memory. In recognition memory for text, high- and low-level propositions are equally well recognized (Yekovitch & Thorndyke, 1981). In free recall, the higher level propositions are better reported in spite of instructions for literal recall (Kintsch, 1974). The natural interpretation of this would be that the literal form of each sentence is directly addressable (i.e., constitutes a heading) whereas the results of cognitive processing is that only what is evaluated as most important finds its way into the record. Equally, the sensitivity of recall to state and context variables contrasted with the relative insensitivity of recognition memory also indicates that such variables are to be found in headings (Bower, 1981; Eich, 1980; Godden & Baddeley, 1975, 1980).

Headings and Descriptions

Retrieval depends on a match between the description and the heading. I have remarked on how the relationship between the given cue and the description is open. Unless one is concerned with recognition memory, it is clear that there needs to be a process of description formation that will pick out the most likely descriptors from the given cue. If you are asked "Could you tell me the address of your best friend, please?", the control processes will guarantee that the variable ⟨best friend⟩ will be filled in before a search for the address is instituted. The reason for this is that ⟨best friend⟩ is not a plausible heading for a record. Clearly, for the search process to be rational the set of descriptors and the set of headings should overlap. Indeed, the only reasonable state of affairs would be that the creation of headings and descriptions is the responsibility of the same mechanism. Elsewhere I show how this principle, allied with developmental factors, gives us a cognitive account of infantile amnesia (Morton, 1990).

The second aspect of the heading-description match follows from our interpretation of the recognition-recall differences. I claimed earlier that there was a need for the representation of internal states and environmental features both in the headings of recalled records and in the descriptions used for that recall. The simplest conception for our purposes is to imagine a set of registers in which these states are noted. These will be updated automatically. In addition to indices of mood and physiological state, I would imagine there to be registers of time, place and purpose. Thus, we are usually aware of the day and the time. By being "aware," I mean to say that there is no need for reflection. The contrast is the archetypal American tourist in Europe: "If this is Amsterdam, it must be Tuesday." Some people seem to be aware of the season, the month, and even the date. And we know who we are talking to even in silence with our eyes closed.

The Notion of Self

As we have seen, our memory includes records of a number of kinds. Some of these reflect our experience and, in effect, contain plans for action that are appropriate for us to use. In this respect, my records are (at least, in principle) appropriate for me to use. They reflect my age, size, weight, strength, degree of expertness, acceptable level of risk, experience, abilities, and a host of other personal factors. These records contrast not only with the records for the equivalent situation in someone else's memory—which would reflect their own particular characteristics, but also with the records in my own memory system of other people's experience. Such records could arise through my witnessing events in which others were the main characters, through witnessing events in which I was the recipient of a particular behavior or through hearing or reading about real or imaginary events. Although on occasions one might try to incorporate someone else's behavior into one's own routines, this is normally done with circumspection. To take an extreme view, faced with a crisis involving a crocodile infested river I would be very unlikely to dive boldly in no matter how many times I had seen Tarzan pull off the trick. At a more mundane level, while knowing about the possibility of sending a bottle of wine back in a restaurant, the first time I felt the wine deserved it I could not run the routine. Following the resulting humiliation in the form of an unforgiving companion I rehearsed the routine mentally until it was no longer something belonging to others. Then I could run it.

What is true about behavioral schema is also true about other kinds of records. My opinions of other people—and so the way I would react toward them—is not to be confused with the opinions of a third party, which I may be very familiar with. To be more precise, our behavior toward a friend, or even a close acquaintance, will be guided by a schema-like record or set of records.

To translate this into HR terms there are two possibilities. The first is that in the given situation a record is retrieved and then evaluated for its validity for oneself. There would be two ways of doing this, one by reference to some list of one's relevant characteristics and the other by noting whether there was a reference to self in the record. The second possibility is that one component of the Description indexes ⟨self⟩ and that this is matched by a component of the headings of appropriate records. Now, although the evaluation of a record is not to be strictly equated with consciousness, there is a relation between the two, and I am rarely aware of courses of action that I reject as being inappropriate for me. Consider, also, what happens when you are asked if you have ever been to Acapulco or Milan. The fact of knowing other people who have been to these places and who have told you about them in great detail, not to mention the films you have seen that have been located there, does not lead to error in report, so far as I can see. It does not even seem to give rise to memories of the reports of others—at least, not before one has arrived at an answer for oneself. This is not, of course, evidence; it merely indicates why I choose the option of having a notion of self as a part of description and headings, used in the same way that the instantaneous present is used.

A further elaboration of the notion of self in the headings can be seen if one habitually spends time in distinct environments where there are gross differences in normative behavior. This is most striking with language, where habitual swearing may be the norm in one environment, but not in the other. The switch of language register is effortless for most people.

I am going to use the idea of ⟨self⟩, both in records and as a heading to provide the basis of an account of one case of functional amnesia and, then, the phenomenon of multiple personality.

"LUMBERJACK": A CASE OF MISLAID IDENTITY

The advantage of functional amnesia is that a subject can act as his or her own control. P.N. was a patient who was studied by Schacter, Wang, Tulving, and Freedman (1982). He was 21 at the time of the investigation, having left school 5 years earlier. He had approached a policeman in downtown Toronto complaining of excruciating back pains. When questioned at the hospital, P.N. could not remember his name, address, or scarcely anything else personal apart from a nickname, "Lumberjack," and that he had worked for a courier service in town a year earlier. The courier service later confirmed that the patient had worked for them and had been given the nickname "Lumberjack" by his fellow workers.

P.N. knew the city he was in and could name many downtown streets as well as the names of the local baseball and ice hockey teams. He knew the name of the prime minister of Canada and "possessed some information about recent political events." A cousin saw P.N.'s picture in the paper and reported that his grandfather, to whom he had been extremely close, had died the previous week. P.N. did not recognize his cousin, nor could he recall the funeral or anything about his grandfather.

The amnesia cleared shortly afterward while P.N. was watching an elaborate cremation and funeral in the final episode of "Shogun." P.N. reported that as he watched the scene, an image of his grandfather gradually appeared in his mind. He then remembered his grandfather's death as well as the funeral that followed.

A number of experimental tests were given during the amnesic episode and subsequently. One of these was the Famous Faces test, where the subject is asked to provide names to faces from the present and the past. In this test there was no difference in P.N.'s performance during the amnesic episode and after it.

A more revealing test was that of Episode Cuing. In this task, the subject is given a word and requested to retrieve a specific personal memory associated with it. Retrieval was either constrained or not. In the constrained conditions the instructions were to recall something from before the onset of amnesia. In the unconstrained condition there were no restrictions. In the constrained condition P.N. failed to retrieve anything to 7 of the 24 cues. In addition, the median response time was 40 secs, more than twice the unconstrained mean. Most of these memories were drawn from the relatively intact "island" of episodic memories. Median unconstrained age was 1.5 days for P.N. compared with 5 months for a control. After recovery the figure increased to 60 months. In the unconstrained condition there was a massive change in the two sessions. During the amnesic episode only 14% of P.N.'s memories dated from before the onset of the amnesia, whereas in the second session the figure was 92%.

The period of his life that P.N. managed to recall during the amnesic episode was characterized by the nickname "Lumberjack" that was specific to that period, and by his reports, both during and after the amnesia, that this period was a very happy one. The Headed Records account is rather similar to Schacter et al.'s speculations on the matter. These authors picked up Estes' (1972) notion of hierarchically organized "control elements" that can activate or inhibit specific kinds of information that are nested under them. They speculate that the name is "the ultimate control element" that gave P.N. access to his "Lumberjack" days. They also suggest that the affective component might be an organizing principle.

In Headed Records terms, P.N. can be characterized as lacking one element of his set of possible Descriptions. This is the Descriptor ⟨self⟩. The mechanism of how this came about might be better described in psychodynamic terms. The result, however, is that the only personal records that could be retrieved were those with "Lumberjack" in the Headings. In addition, nonpersonal records, which contain general knowledge, would be unaffected because, for the retrieval of such information, usually in secondary records, there would be no task requirement to specify the ⟨self⟩ component.

MULTIPLE PERSONALITY—MULTIPLE ⟨SELF⟩

According to DSM-III (American Psychiatric Association, 1980), the Multiple Personality Disorder (MPD) is characterized by the existence within an individual of two or more distinct personalities, each of which is dominant at a particular time. The dominant personality determines the individual's behavior. In a survey of 100 MPD cases (Putnam, Guroff, Silberman, Barkan, & Post, 1986), episodes of amnesia were reported in 98% of the patients. Indeed, 72% of patients had one or more personalities who denied the existence of other personalities.

One such case that was studied experimentally was reported by Ludwig, Brandsma, Wilber, Bendfeldt, and Jameson (1972; Brandsma & Ludwig, 1974). The patient was a 27-year-old man called Jonah. When he was first admitted to hospital Jonah had had a long history of episodes in which he had lost his memory. During one such incident he had attacked his wife with a butcher's knife, running both her and their daughter out of the house. At such times, his wife had informed him, he referred to himself as Usoffa Abdulla, Son of Omega.

While in the hospital he experienced variable periods of memory lapse during which he would undergo a personality change. In fact, three personalities were identified, each with separate identities and different names. Communication with these personalities was facilitated by means of hypnosis, although they all emerged spontaneously for varying periods.

Jonah: Jonah was regarded as the primary personality by the other ones. He claimed to be unaware of the existence of any of the other personalities. He described himself as shy, sensitive, passive, and highly conventional. He also tended to appear frightened and confused while being interviewed.

Sammy: Unlike the other personalities, Sammy could coexist in consciousness with Jonah, in addition to taking over completely. He claimed awareness of the existence of the other personalities but knew most about Jonah. He claimed to be always ready to appear when Jonah needed legal advice or needed to get out of trouble. Indeed, when Jonah landed in jail, Sammy took over for a whole week. Sammy described himself as purely intellectual and rational. He is reported as displaying no emotion.

King Young: Apparently, whenever Jonah cannot find the right words to say when chatting to women he has a sexual interest in, King Young takes over. He claims to know about the other personalities only "indirectly" but knows Jonah "mildly." He views himself as pleasure oriented and as a ladies' man.

Usoffa Abdulla: Whenever Jonah is in any physical danger, Usoffa takes over completely and leaves as soon as the danger is over. He claims to know Jonah very well but the other personalities only "indirectly." His sworn duty is to watch over and to protect Jonah. Usoffa is described as a cold, belligerent, and angry person. "He is generally sullen, silent, occasionally sarcastic, and primed to respond aggressively to any threat or challenge. He views himself as physically powerful and immune to pain and from the vantage point of the authors can present himself as quite a formidable and scary person to interview." (p. 300)

A variety of tests were administered to the four alter personalities. On three intelligence scales all four came within the low normal range. Apparently the four gave exactly the same answers to content questions (equivalent to a context free "semantic" memory). Results on personality and diagnostic scales were in accordance with the clinical observations of the personalities.

Transfer of learning behaved as though what Jonah had learned was known to the other three, but no other knowledge was shared. The experiment involved paired associate learning. One of the personalities was presented with a list of 10 words, each paired with a response word. The list was presented until learned to the criterion of three successive perfect trials. The other three personalities were called in turn and were required to respond to each stimulus word with "the one word that goes *best*" with it. Then the personality originally trained was retested. This procedure was repeated for all four personalities. The error data are given in the table with the scores for the personality originally tested on each list under-lined. It can be seen in Table 14.1 that the other personalities appear to know something about Jonah's list. Apart from that there is no transfer.

In another experiment, a list of 10 paired associates was presented to Jonah. He was then tested with the stimulus words, making four errors. On the next presentation he was error free. The same list was then presented in the same way to King Young who made two errors on the first trial and one on the next. Usoffa and Sammy were then error free. With another list Usoffa had the list first and made four, two, and one error on three trials. King Young, Sammy, and Jonah were then all error free on their trials in spite of each personality claiming not to remember engaging in the task previously. We have then what looks like very good savings in a learning task to contrast with very poor transfer in a memory task. To account for these data I assume that, as with Lumberjack, Jonah's event records are headed differently for the four personalities. These headings will differentiate the selfs. In addition, I follow Mandler, Rabinowitz, and Simon (1981) in believing that word pairs are generally stored as units. The pairs would be represented in the headings in their stimulus form and in the records in a processed form. A typical HR for an S–R pair could be partially represented as:

$$A, \ S\text{-}R \rightarrow s\text{-}r, \ a$$

where A is the heading appropriate for the personality doing the current learning and s-r is the cognitive product of processing the pair that has a trace of the personality. The cued recall trials amount to creating a description of $B, \ S$ for the change of personality. This will not match any element of the heading. Note that if there were variation in the form of the S–R representation and a record were retrieved, the contents would not pass the task specification and would thus be

TABLE 14.1
Errors/10 on PA Lists Learned by One Alter

	Responder			
Learner	Jonah	K. Young	Sammy	Usoffa
Jonah	*4*	3	4	5
K. Young	9	*1*	10	9
Sammy	9	10	*1*	7
Usoffa	10	10	10	*0*

rejected. In the learning task, on the other hand, the stimulus, and thus the description, consisted of the S–R pair. Records, then, would be retrieved automatically. Further, because the task specification did not demand ⟨self⟩ verification (as it does with the cued recall), the contents of the records from personality A could be transferred to another record labeled as B. Transfer was also found on the blocks subtest of the WAIS and with the Logical Memory task from the Weschler—stories of paragraph length.

These cases of transfer contrast with situations in which there is no transfer. We saw this with the cued recall task. Transfer was also missing from a GSR test for emotionally laden words. For each personality a couple of words were obtained that had strong personal significance. These words were combined together into a list with a number of neutral words. The list was then read out to each of the personalities. An appreciable GSR was found from each personality for the words that they had provided. Jonah's words provoked a response in the other three, but there were no other cross responses. The form of this transfer corresponds to that found in the paired associate task (Table 14.1).

Another case from whom relevant data have been obtained was studied by Nissen, Ross, Willingham, Mackenzie, and Schacter (1988). This was a 45-year-old woman with a number of mutually amnesic personalities. This patient showed no transfer in recognition memory for words or in interpretation of ambiguous texts. On the other hand she did show repetition priming of perceptual identification of words. These would have been expected from the position I have been putting forward or from Mandler's position (1980; Mandler, Pearlstone, & Koopmans, 1969, 1986). Recognition memory would be attributed to processes responsible for relational code, whereas perceptual identification is a function of integrative, perceptual processes, which are context independent. The latter would also be responsible for the perceptual familiarity effect that mediates transfer in a four-alternative forced-choice task involving faces. However, this patient also showed no priming with a stem completion task—where the subject is given a string of three letters and is required to produce a word. This task is not responsive to the level of processing in the priming task, unlike recognition memory (Graf & Mandler, 1984), and normally shows priming effects with amnesics (Graf, Squire, & Mandler, 1983; Warrington & Weizkrantz, 1970). Responsibility for this task, then, would be assigned to perceptual processes and one should find transfer across personalities. This result poses problems for everyone.

A NOTE ON AMNESIA

My assumption is that the breakdown in amnesia is multifaceted and variable, much as is breakdown in dyslexia (Coltheart, Patterson, & Marshall, 1980; Patterson et al., 1985). I only mention here some general principles of how amnesia might be treated in the HR framework. The distinction is clear between perceptual processes and the HR system itself. As with Mandler, I take it that the former are intact, and that some of the tasks performed by amnesics rely on perceptual processes (see Graf et al., 1983). For example, it has been shown that amnesics suffer on a task requiring them to distinguish between recency and situational frequency (Huppert & Piercy, 1976). Items that have occurred more often seem to be more recent. But this is exactly the error made by normal subjects with an experimental design that prevents them from using records or span information (Morton, 1968).

Within an HR model there are a number of ways that apparent forgetting can take place. The material may not be laid down in either headings or in records. These problems would affect recognition and recall respectively. Particular kinds of information may not be represented in new records. This could have the effect of the record being rejected by the evaluation process on the basis of particular task specifications. This is the principle used to account for the failure of cued recall and the successful transfer of learning in the case of Jonah, described earlier. This could also account for the massive increase in proactive interference in list learning with amnesics except where the contexts are exaggeratedly distinct (Winocur & Kinsbourne, 1978).

Another possible feature is that heading or description formation might be altered. If both are altered then there would be no anterograde amnesia but there would be retrograde amnesia. This is the principle I have used to account for infantile amnesia (Morton, 1990). If heading formation alone is changed then there could be no retrograde amnesia but there would be anterograde amnesia. Then, of course, these factors, together with others, could co-occur in ways that are unique, and, again, as with acquired dyslexia, we will find the need to define a number of subtypes.

REFERENCES

Bower, G. H. (1981). Mood and memory. *American Psychologist, 36,* 129–148.

Brandsma, J. M., & Ludwig, A. M. (1974). A case of multiple personality: diagnosis and therapy. *International Journal of Clinical and Experimental Hypnosis, 22,* 216–233.

Coltheart, M., Patterson, K. A., & Marshall, J. C. (Eds.). (1980). *Deep dyslexia.* London: Routledge & Kegan Paul.

Eich, J. E. (1980). The cue-dependent nature of state-dependent retrieval. *Memory & Cognition, 8,* 157–173.

Estes, W. K. (1972). An associative basis for coding and organisation. In A. W. Melton & E. Martin (Eds.), *Coding processes in human memory* (pp. 161–190). Washington, DC: Winston.

Godden, D. R., & Baddeley, A. D. (1975). Context-dependent memory in two natural environments: On land and underwater. *British Journal of Psychology, 66,* 325–331.

Godden, D. R., & Baddeley, A. D. (1980). When does context influence recognition memory? *British Journal of Psychology, 71,* 99–104.

Graf, P., & Mandler, G. (1984). Activation makes words more accessible, but not necessarily more retrievable. *Journal of Verbal Learning and Verbal Behavior, 23,* 553–568.

Graf, P., Squire, L. R., & Mandler, G. (1983). The information that amnesic patients do not forget. *Journal of Experimental Psychology: Learning, Memory & Cognition, 10,* 164–178.

Huppert, F., & Piercy, M. (1976). Recognition memory in amnesic patients: Effects of temporal context and familiarity of material. *Cortex, 12,* 3–20.

Kintsch, W. (1974). *The representation of meaning in memory.* Hillsdale, NJ: Lawrence Erlbaum Associates.

Ludwig, A. M., Brandsma, J. M., Wilber, C. B., Bendfeldt, F., & Jameson, D. H. (1972). The objective study of a multiple personality. *Archives of General Psychiatry, 26,* 298–310.

Mandler, G. (1980). Recognizing: The judgment of previous occurrence. *Psychological Review, 87,* 252–271.

Mandler, G., Pearlstone, Z., & Koopmans, H. J. (1969). Effects of organization and semantic similarity on recall and recognition. *Journal of Verbal Learning and Verbal Behavior, 8,* 410–423.

Mandler, G., Rabinowitz, J. C., & Simon, R. A. (1981). Coordinate organisation: The wholistic representation of word pairs. *American Journal of Psychology, 94,* 209–222.

Morton, J. (1968). Repeated items and decay in memory. *Psychonomic Science, 10,* 219–220.

Morton, J. (1990). A Commentary. *The Psychologist: Bulletin of the British Psychological Society, 3,* 3–10.

Morton, J., & Bekerian, D. A. (1986). Three ways of looking at memory. In N. E. Sharkey (Ed.), *Advances in cognitive science* (Vol. 1, pp. 43–71). Chichester: Ellis Horwood.

Morton, J., Hammersley, R. H., & Bekerian, D. A. (1985). Headed records: A model for memory and its failures. *Cognition, 20,* 1–23.

Nissen, M. J., Ross, J. L., Willingham, D. B., Mackenzie, T. B., & Schacter, D. L. (1988). Memory and awareness in a patient with multiple personality disorder. *Brain and Cognition, 8,* 21–38.

Norman, D. A., & Bobrow, D. G. (1979). Descriptions: an intermediate stage in memory retrieval. *Cognitive Psychology, 11,* 107–123.

Putnam, F. W., Guroff, J. J., Silberman, E. K., Barban, L., & Post, R. M. (1986). The clinical phenomenology of multiple personality disorder: review of 100 recent cases. *Journal of Clinical Psychiatry, 47,* 285–293.

Schacter, D. L., Wang, P. L., Tulving, E., & Freedman, M. (1982). Functional retrograde amnesia: a quantitative case study. *Neuropsychologia, 20,* 523–532.

Warrington, E. K., & Weizkrantz, L. (1970). Amnesia: Consolidation or retrieval? *Nature, 228,* 628–630.

Williams, M. D., & Hollan, J. D. (1981). The process of retrieval from very long memory. *Cognitive Science, 5,* 87–119.

Winocur, G., & Kinsbourne, M. (1978). Contextual cuing as an aid to Korsakoff amnesics. *Neuropsychologia, 16,* 671–682.

Yekovitch, F. R., & Thorndyke, P. (1981). An evaluation of alternative functional models of narrative schemata. *Journal of Verbal Learning and Verbal Behavior, 20,* 454–469.

IV

CONSCIOUSNESS

15

The Revival of Consciousness in Cognitive Science

Tim Shallice
University College, London

For the first third of this century two very different, indeed antithetical, cultures—the American and the German—were the main source of new developments in psychology. The rise to power of the Nazi party in Germany in 1933 and the loss by emigration or death of many creative German psychologists left psychology dominated by one national cultural tradition—the American—which at that epoch was itself dominated by behaviorism.

Of course, as we all know, a central plank of behaviorism was the view that "the time seems to have come when psychology must abandon all reference to consciousness" (Watson, 1914). Why should psychology have been dominated for so many years by this essentially counterintuitive position? It is worth contrasting the way by which Watson rejected preceding scientific frameworks that used, among other approaches, the introspective method with the arguments of the polemicists of 40 years later who attacked behaviorism itself. Watson devoted only a single unscholarly paragraph to the problems of the introspective method as applied in the imageless thought controversy. He then argues that because the body–mind problem is intractable, it should be eliminated from science and that "there is no reason why appeal to consciousness should ever be made in any of the truly scientific fields [of psychology such as] experimental pedagogy, psychology of drugs, psychology of advertising" (Watson, 1914, p. 13). That was the end of his argument, what little there was of it. By contrast, when behaviorism itself was confronted in the 1950s and 1960s the rejection was based on detailed critiques both of Hullian grand theory (Koch, 1954, MacCorquodale & Meehl, 1954) and of Skinnerian theory by Chomsky (1959) (see also Taylor, 1964). Because an intellectual assessment of the empirical disputes of the imageless thought controversy and of the introspectionist method is entirely possible, although it leads to rather different conclusions from Watson's (see e.g., Humphrey, 1951; Ericsson & Simon, 1985), Watson's failure to confront his predecessors intellectually suggests that the behaviorist position on consciousness should be viewed as ideology rather than science. Indeed this would also fit with behaviorism's having very considerable popularity outside psychology as well as within it, as it did particularly in the 1920s (Burnham, 1968) (see also Schwartz, 1986).

The depth of the ideological tarring that reference to consciousness received under behaviorism is shown by the slowness with which it returned to favor within psychology even after behaviorism had been shown to be intellectually moribund. There was a 20-year gap between the intellectual death of behaviorism and the revival of consciousness as a proper subject of scientific enquiry. In the 1960s even such a staunch cognitivist as George Miller (1962) could begin a discussion of consciousness by suggesting that we "ban the word (consciousness) for a decade or two until we can develop more precise terms for the several uses which 'consciousness' now obscures." (p. 25) Neisser, who in a fascinating early article (1963) had theorized on the relation between the conscious/unconscious and Freudian secondary/primary process was "strangely circumspect about the problem of consciousness" (Mandler, 1975, p. 43) in his much higher profile book (1967). Indeed Bisiach (1988) points out that the subject index of the Kling and Riggs (1971) edition of *Woodworth & Schlosberg's Experimental Psychology* contains no reference to consciousness.

It was not until the 1970s that attempts were made to link consciousness with mainstream information-processing psychology. Moreover, the first three groups of theorists—Atkinson & Shiffrin, 1971; Shallice, 1972; Posner & Klein, 1973—lost much of the potentially liberating aspects of the use of the concept in the limited types of information-processing concepts that they employed. It was not until 1975 with Mandler's chapter "Consciousness: Respectable, useful and probably necessary" that the concept was adequately resurrected, the behaviorist slurs were properly answered, and a possible approach to the concept compatible with its general liberating philosophical function was sketched out. It is not surprising that its author was one of the few individuals who combined a modern cognitive psychologist's technical expertize with a deep understanding of prewar German psychology.

INFORMATION-PROCESSING APPROACHES TO CONSCIOUSNESS

When in the early 1970s information-processing psychologists began to confront the problem of consciousness directly they adopted two main assumptions:

1. Philosophically they implicitly or explicitly adopted the position that became known as functionalism (Putnam, 1960; Dennett, 1978) although,

when it was considered, the complete reduction of phenomenology to a system-level concept was rejected (Shallice, 1972).

2. Within this philosophical approach they mapped consciousness within a phenomenological conceptual framework onto the operation, input to, or output from one component within the system viewed from an information-processing perspective.

Four different positions were put forward. The first, that of Atkinson & Shiffrin (1971), emphasized the content aspects of consciousness by identifying it with the contents of an all-purpose short-term store, that was required, for instance, for the laying down of traces in long-term storage. Basically the same position had been suggested by Waugh & Norman (1965), but in 1960s fashion their position on awareness was an unstressed aspect of their paper. In two other theoretical positions it was the control aspect of consciousness that was stressed, and both papers emphasized its role in the inhibition of potentially competing activity, which could, however, be carried out if it required sufficiently low levels of resource. In this respect the accounts developed ideas put forward by Neisser (1963) that there are two modes of processing—one generally serial, secondary-process (in Freudian terms), and conscious and the other generally parallel, primary-process, and nonconscious. The position of Posner & Klein (1973) was that consciousness corresponded to the operation of a general-purpose, limited-capacity system, a view extended by Posner & Snyder (1975) to account for experimental results on the facilitation and inhibition produced by primes. My account, instead, took consciousness to be the input that selected which of many parallel-acting action-systems—analogous to productions with an activation function or action- (or thought-) schemas—would dominate its competitors through mutually inhibitory competition. Only the selector input of the dominant action-schema could be certain to control action, would enter a long-term memory system—episodic memory (see Shallice, 1978)—and be an input to the language system.

The culmination of these early 1970s theoretical analyses of consciousness was Mandler's (1975) panoramic article. Where the other theorists in attempting to break the behaviorist straitjacket had remained within a rather narrow information-processing conceptual framework, Mandler's approach was much broader. His approach went beyond his contemporaries in three separate ways. First he situated his more technical arguments within a more detailed defence of why it is important to consider consciousness in psychology. He answered directly Watson's famous dismissive remarks. His most powerful argument is as relevant now as then. "In general, American psychologists particularly have shied away from looking at the functional significance of consciousness. This is at least surprising, since we are faced with a characteristic of the human species that is without exception. Given the rather weak evidence that psychologists have accepted as indicating the evolutionary significance of such vague concepts as aggression and intelligence, why avoid a phenomenon as indisputedly characteristic of the human species as consciousness?" (Mandler, 1975, p. 55)

Secondly his discussion of what needed to be explained was much more subtle than that of the other theorists. Instead of just considering one or two of the properties of consciousness as requiring explanation, he presented a wide range of functions that a system corresponding to consciousness must have. These were basically derived from a phenomenological analysis of the range of mental processes in which consciousness was in some way involved. They included (a) "choice and selection of action systems," (b) modification and interrogation of long-term plans, (c) the initiation of retrieval from long-term memory, (d) commentary on the organism's current activity, (e) the construction of storable representations of the current activity, (f) the accessing of cognitive processes to language, and (g) "trouble-shooting" about the inappropriate operation of structures not normally represented in consciousness. From 1975 on, these represented an absolute minimum set of properties that any theory of consciousness would need to explain in order to have any plausibility.

On the theoretical level, Mandler took a position that was a development of Posner & Klein's in that he considered consciousness to be the property of one particular and special cognitive system. Although like Posner & Klein he saw consciousness as a product of a limited-capacity system, he paid far more attention to the complexity of the nonconscious systems. Unlike Posner & Klein's perspective where the limited-capacity system corresponding to consciousness was a processor, he saw it more as the coordinator or conductor of many unconscious systems. In this respect his theoretical position foreshadows that of a number of theorists of the 1980s.

CONSCIOUSNESS SINCE MANDLER (1975)

The late 1970s and the 1980s have produced one clear victory for the early theorists. The status of consciousness in cognitive science has changed from the abandoned prescientific term of the 1950s, through the still repressed but occasionally visible concept of the 1960s and the province of highly speculative theorizing of the 1970s, to the empirical and theoretical commonplace of the 1980s. The change has been built on certain solid scientific foundations. These have, however, been almost entirely empirical. At the same time the concept has been used much less critically than would have been possible 10 years before even though theoretical progress has been far less obvious.

Empirically many phenomena have been described where an account of the subject's experience is a central part of the discovery. A situation is discovered in which the phenomenological reports given by the subject differ from what would be expected *a priori* given the subject's behavior. In cognitive psychology, attention to whether the experimental paradigm gives rise to experience that would *a priori* be appropriate for it—or, more interestingly, gives rise to qualitatively different or absent experience—has led to major new developments in both perception (Marcel, 1983a; Cheesman & Merikle, 1985; Tipper & Driver, 1988) and in memory (e.g., Jacoby, Woloshyn & Kelley, 1989: Gardiner & Java, in press). Explanations of the dissociations have become an accepted part of the theorizing in at least the second of the two fields (e.g., Tulving, 1985; Mandler, 1989). An intellectually powerful attempt has been made at least in the first of two areas to produce a quasi-behaviorist critique (Holender, 1986), but it has not fitted with the Zeitgeist.

In neuropsychology, too, many phenomena with a similar type of phenomenological structure have been described where a dissociation exists between the behavior and experience of a patient. They include blindsight, completion phenomena in amnesia, and aspects of prosopagnosia, dyslexia, and aphasia (see for review Shallice, 1988a; Weiskrantz, 1988; Schacter, in press). In addition phenomena have been described where it appears to be the patient's experienced certainty in the correctness of the response, when it is in fact an error, that leads to its not being corrected—as in optic aphasia (Beauvois & Saillant, 1985) and confabulatory frontal amnesia (Delbecq-Derouesne, Beauvois, & Shallice, in press). Again the use of phenomenological accounts has been criticized, in the case of blindsight from a more explicitly behaviorist perspective (Campion, Latto, & Smith, 1983), but these criticisms have not been generally accepted (see Weiskrantz, 1987 for response; Shallice 1988a for review).

These empirical discoveries were based on accepting accounts of experience as scientific evidence. They have not been matched by any major theoretical advances. Indeed the position that phenomenal reports are valuable but "consciousness" is not a useful scientific concept is probably still tenable (see Allport, 1988; Wilkes, 1988 for relevant discussions). This position is made slightly more attractive by the looseness with which the concept is used. Thus in neuropsychology one sees explanations of dissociations between experience and behavior in terms of a disconnection between a particular processing system and a "consciousness system." What this system might be doing in processing terms is left completely vague as is how it achieved this extraordinary phenomenological status.

RECENT THEORIZING ON CONSCIOUSNESS

On the level of theorizing about consciousness, Marcel (1983b), Baars (1983) and Mandler (1984) have stressed that the content of consciousness is constructed; it is not merely the reactivating of an existing structure, as certain of the 1970s theories (e.g., Atkinson & Shiffrin, 1971; Shallice, 1972) would suggest. However as Mandler (1984) points out, "there are certain stimuli and situations that demand immediate conscious constructions, regardless of the current set, intention, or context. The most obvious are intense stimuli—of sound, sight, pain, heat, or cold . . . . . they are also instances of single schemas (and even features) determining conscious content". Complementarily, there are examples where construction is clearly occurring without consciousness—aspects of perceptual processing that Helmholtz characterized by "unconscious inference" and habituation phenomena, for instance. More critically, Rumelhart & McClelland (1986) have characterized "relaxation" as being the dominant mode of computation in the brain. Yet if the output of the relaxation process is the activation of multiple output units then the output can be considered to be a construction. Yet there is no reason to assume that the multiple outputs of a single relaxation process have anything to do with consciousness. Being constructed therefore seems a more basic property of cognition than is consciousness and its being constructed may not help one to understand what is special about conscious content.

Mandler's (1975) theory that the cognitive system contains a large number of subsystems with operations that are essentially nonconscious and a special system with states or outputs related to consciousness has implicitly or explicitly been a popular position in the 1980s. Many new metaphors have been put forward to characterize the special system. Most can be seen as elaborations of one of Mandler's functions of consciousness. For Marshall & Morton (1978) it was a monitoring system. Baars (1983) has seen it as an AI global data-base/general broadcasting system. Johnson-Laird (1983) has viewed it as analogous to the operating system of a computer, and Umilta (1988), even closer to Mandler, as a high-level control system. Schacter (1989), too, has a related position. He sees it as a system that takes the output of processing modules and transmits it to the executive systems; it is not clear though what, if any, processing it does. Gazzaniga (1985) sees Mandler's commentary function as critical, arguing that it is a left-hemisphere system that interprets the output of other modules, but O'Keefe (1985) makes the different neurophysiological suggestion that consciousness corresponds to the output of the hippocampus.

In my view there is a tension between most such positions and another aspect of Mandler's (1975) argument. Consciousness is involved in many types of mental process. Thus the following psychological domains all have complex and different phenomenological aspects—perception, action, language comprehension, language production, the carrying out of routine cognitive operations like mental arithmetic, memory, judgment and choice, error-correction, pretending and other decoupled mental operations (Leslie, 1987), intentions, metacognitive processes as in the 'tip-of-the-tongue state,' imagery, emotions, dreams, and other 'anomalous experiences' (to use the term of Reed, 1972). The very variety of mental states makes single function theories implausible *a priori*. Moreover the looseness of processing to phenomenological correspondence enables theories about consciousness which are apparently quite different to give seemingly quite plausible accounts of the evidence. The moral is that a plausible account of some of the empirical evidence is a quite insufficient basis for giving much credence to a theory of consciousness (see Shallice, 1988b for further discussion).

Rather than considering individual theories, I want to take their common denominator, essentially Mandler's notion of a "consciousness system" and differentiate three different ways in which the term could be interpreted.

Neurological Theories.   On the most reductionist level one could assume that a particular part of the brain contains the consciousness system. Suggestions along these lines have been made by Baars, Gazzaniga, O'Keefe, and Schacter although it is noteworthy that there is little overlap in the regions they select. They stress the thalamus, left hemisphere, hippocampus, and parietal lobes respectively. A theory of this sort would imply that if the particular region lit up with PET scanning this would mean that the subject was experiencing something, and that lesioning the region would lead to loss of awareness even if its outputs to the rest of the brain were artificially recreated. The very variety of anatomical loci suggested does not make this possibility seem plausible.

A Computer Analogy Theory.   The role of the special system could be characterized much more abstractly. The preeminent proposal of this type is Johnson-Laird's (1983) suggestion that the system should be thought of by analogy with the operating system of a computer, with the operating system controlling a hierarchical set of subsystems which can operate in parallel. He arrived at his position through a concern with the computational underpinnings of self-awareness, meta-cognition, intentional decisions, and free will. He argued that these abilities depend on the operating system having access to a model of the self, and the ability to reflect upon it in a recursive way. This self-reflective procedure resembles the recursive embedding of one structure in another and to Johnson-Laird it lies at the heart of meta-cognitive skills and intentional choice. To be more specific, Johnson-Laird views conscious content as the contents of the operating system's working memory.

From a processing perspective I hold to a position with many similarities to Johnson-Laird's. I therefore think the operating system analogy a useful one for higher-level cognitive processing, but there are some problems for Johnson-Laird's particular approach to consciousness:

1. Presumably individual parts of the mental apparatus are either part of the operating system or of the rest of the cognitive system. What grounds are there for assuming working memories are part of the operating system? Most short-term stores would appear to be slave systems for particular types of on-line cognitive operations like scene perception or language comprehension. If such memory stores were made part of the operating system they would be conceptually separated from the processing systems to which they are tightly related

computationally. On the other hand, if the working memory that holds the information corresponding to the contents of consciousness is distinct from them, say Baddeley's (1986) executive store, would it not functionally just reduplicate the slave short-term stores storage functions? Moreover I know of no evidence that there is an executive store which retains specific content information of the sort of which we are aware when viewing a scene, say, and it is not apparent why an operating system should contain such a memory store.

2. Consider a very simple task like naming a set of objects. Once the first object has been named, the processors required to carry out the task remain the same. Given that the operating system specifies what the lower level processors have to do and then allows them to continue and that the systems involved are all highly practiced ones, it would seem that the task would not require continuous use of the operating system and that the subject could carry out the task nonconsciously. Indeed Johnson-Laird (1988) specifically assumes driving, an apparently more complex task, can be carried out nonconsciously. Yet phenomenologically the naming task seems to require one to be aware of the objects. In fact, though, the theory is so abstractly specified that it does not seem possible to be certain what the theory would predict in such a simple situation. The level of task at which one moves from control by a parallel processor only to the requiring of the operating system is unspecified.

3. In the domains where interesting properties are known about the difference between conscious and nonconscious processing such as perception (e.g. Marcel, 1983a) and memory (Gardiner & Java, in press) the theory throws no light.

4. Why should the operating system have the property of being conscious? Johnson-Laird (1988) argues that it derives from the potential for self-awareness: "In self-awareness, there is a need for an element in the model of the current state of affairs to refer to the system itself and to be known so to refer" (p. 365). Making such processes the reason why nonreflective awareness can exist would imply that the processes corresponding to nonreflective awareness that presumably evolved first, initially had no conscious correspondence but, with the development of more elaborate capacities that they do not require, the correspondence developed. This is a logically possible but far from self-evident position.

Thus although Johnson-Laird's is a provocative analogy for describing how a "consciousness system" might function, it is not at all clear how the approach could be developed to deal more concretely with psychological phenomena.

DEVELOPING THE PERSPECTIVES OF MANDLER AND JOHNSON-LAIRD

A More Complex Information Processing Possibility

A third possibility is that the global separation between systems that relate to consciousness and those that do not is appropriate, but that to attempt to characterize either as a single system, other than by contrast with the other is inappropriate. It is fairly clear that the "nonconscious" systems are not appropriately considered a single system. Are there any grounds for thinking this might also be the case for higher-level systems?

I would like to consider this issue from the perspective of two positions. The first is a hypothesis on the primary function of consciousness; namely, that it arises in evolution from the need to control an inherently parallel architecture. This is a view that many have held from William James on, at least as part of their positions on consciousness (e.g., Shallice, Mandler, Johnson-Laird, Umilta).

The second is a model of the control of thought and action developed by Norman and myself with two levels of control. A Supervisory System comes into play in nonroutine situations. It modulates the operation of a second system that, on its own, routinely selects which action or thought schemas are to be operative—Contention Scheduling. Selection of a schema allows it to control whatever special-purpose processing mechanisms it requires and activate any of its "component" or "child" schemas. Contention scheduling is itself a descendant of the mechanism that produced a dominance relation between activated action-systems in my earlier model (see Norman & Shallice, 1986; Shallice, 1988a for discussion). The model was put forward to explain phenomena on attention, the phenomenology of action, and on the neuropsychology of frontal lobe function. It is possible to think of the processing mechanisms on which the schemas "run" as connectionist networks (Norman, 1986)—this is the position I adopt.

This leads to the following processing perspective. Assume that the on-line processing systems consist of a large set of highly specialized networks, which operate in different modes according to the (routine) process they are carrying out. Thus the reading systems and the structures to which they are linked will be in different modes for reading aloud, skimming, proof-reading, memorizing text, etc. Assume also that the mode differences are specified by clamped input from higher levels. When clamping is discussed later it is this process to which I will be referring. This leads to two issues. The first is whether the higher levels are appropriately characterized as a single system and the second is what the relation would be to consciousness.

It seems plausible that there are a variety of higher-level processes that lead to "internal" clamping. The simplest is illustrated by an action-lapse of the capture error sort (Norman, 1981). The clamping is data-driven—that is, there is an "internal" output of the processing nets that predisposes a particular type of clamping to occur and it does so unless actively prevented. This is equivalent to selection in contention scheduling without supervisory control on the Norman & Shallice model, and presumably it occurs very frequently not just in counterproductive action-lapses.

Frequently, however, much more complex processes will be involved. One type are the processes such as error correction, anticipation, preparation, caretaking, checking, and preventing inappropriate responses, which were carried out by the Supervisory System in our earlier model. A standard view in neuropsychology is that the on-line processing systems that are located in posterior cortical structures are controlled or modulated by anterior cortical systems (see e.g., Stuss & Benson, 1986). Indeed the supervisory processes in the Norman/Shallice model were held to be located in prefrontal regions. Current neuroscience evidence raises the possibility that such regions contain a large set of micro-control systems with tighter relations to the more posterior systems they modulate than to each other (e.g., Goldman-Rakic, 1987; Pandya & Barnes, 1987). Thus, even if one considers only processes characterized under the earlier model as "Supervisory," many supranetwork systems seem to be involved.

Qualitatively different processes, however, also contribute to the internal clamping. One is the use of language, which can be viewed as a social process with the function of allowing clamping of one person's processing networks for a second's needs. However the language system of each individual itself contains a very large processing network that transforms the speech signal into an internal output that can be used to control clamping directly. Then there is episodic memory that, it has been argued, has a prime evolutionary function of providing related episodes as a data base when a novel situation occurs (Schank, 1982; Shallice, 1988a). Finally there are the processes related to actions some distance in the future such as planning and intention creation and realization. These are more distant from the direct internal clamping process but have the evolutionary function of contributing to it.

These supranetwork processes have three characteristics:

1. They can critically influence either directly or indirectly the processes carried out in any of the lower-level networks.
2. Many of them use representations that are the same as or can be translated into representations used by others.
3. They can typically operate on only one set of internal network outputs at a time.

Otherwise, one would have to assume that, say, the suppression of an undesired response, the having of a memory, and the creation of an intention could all take place at the same time even when they are not related with each other. An exception would be the type of outputs of the processing networks to higher levels that can be directly used as clamping inputs; these would be the type of "internal" outputs that malfunction when they give rise to capture errors. They can operate in parallel to other higher-level processes.

Why would consciousness arise on such a model? My position would be somewhat related to Johnson-Laird's. Such a system would have a model of its own operation, which would be limited to the representations generally available to the supranetwork systems. These would include those outputs of the processing networks to supranetwork levels that were being used other than to clamp directly the processing networks. The most obvious type of conscious content would then correspond to these outputs of the processing networks used by supranetwork systems. For this set of contents the theory is similar to Schacter's (in press) theory. Conscious contents would also relate to a variety of other sorts of messages sent between supranetwork processors. At the limit these include the mere fact that a particular supranetwork process is active as in contents such as "concentrate on," "trying to remember," "on the tip of the tongue," and so on. The limitations on conscious capacity would stem from the third generalization mentioned earlier.

The problems posed for Johnson-Laird's perspective would be dealt with in the following ways:

1. Working memories can be located within the on-line processing networks. When required, signals from the supranetwork processes can be used to obtain a new output from the networks based on the contents of the stores they contain.

2. Any task which involves the translation of information between the language system and other cognitive systems is held necessarily to involve an internal clamping process. Hence comprehension and speech acts require the supranetwork processes leading to the tight link between being conscious of things and being able to speak about them (see e.g., Dennett, 1969). Thus one would expect naming not to be able to be carried out nonconsciously.

3. As far as perception is concerned, the distinction between the effects of nonexperienced and consciously experienced primes on a subsequent stimulus (Marcel, 1983a) would map on to whether an input to a connectionist net that did not produce an output could have an effect on a subsequent stimulus that was nonzero and differed qualitatively from that of a prime that did produce an output. No appropriate simulation on this issue has yet been reported to my knowledge, but the approach does seem capable of more concrete investigation.

As far as memory is concerned more relevant information is available. It is now widely accepted that there are qualitatively different memory processes, one dimension of difference being whether a memory experience is present (Tulving, 1985; Mandler, 1989). On the present view conscious memories involve retrieval being controlled by a supranetwork process located anteriorly in the brain (see Shallice, 1988a; Tulving, 1989). The other type of memory process just involves within-network changes similar to those by which all weight changes occur in networks, and so is "nonconscious."

4. Consciousness is not seen to be dependent on self-consciousness but rather on the way that many activated representations at the supranetwork level have effects qualitatively different from other states of cognitive system. So if the system could abstractly represent its own internal states to itself it would be expected to differentiate these states from others (see Shallice, 1988b). They would be states that would be translated between a number of different supranet-

work systems in real time. These would not include higher-level representations that were specific to a single supranetwork system. Thus those involved in obtaining a more general schema when a specific one has led to error—presumably a standard error-correction procedure—would not be passed on to other supranetwork systems.

Such an approach to consciousness is of course very speculative. It is a descendent of the positions of Mandler (1975) and Johnson-Laird (1983) in that on this perspective the cognitive system can be viewed globally with the existence of consciousness arising from the distinction between special-purpose processing systems and the systems that control them. However, it can also be viewed from the perspective of theories such as those of Shallice (1972) and Kinsbourne (1988) where consciousness is a property of large parts of the cognitive system, which part depending on the particular subsystems active at the time. Clearly on a model of this sort the best way to characterize consciousness will depend on a more detailed account of the relations between the different supranetwork systems and of what representations they use.

REFERENCES

Allport, A. (1988). What concept of consciousness? In A. J. Marcel & E. Bisiach (Eds.), *Consciousness in contemporary science* (pp. 159–182). Oxford: Oxford University Press.

Atkinson, R. C., & Shiffrin, R. M. (1971). The control of short-term memory. *Scientific American, 224*, 82–90.

Baars, B. J. (1983). Conscious contents provide the nervous system with coherent global information. In R. J. Davidson, G. E. Schwartz, & D. Shapiro (Eds.), *Consciousness and self regulation* (Vol. 3, pp. 45–76). New York: Plenum.

Baddeley, A. D. (1986). *Working memory*. Oxford: Clarendon.

Beauvois, M.-F. & Saillant, B. (1985). Optic aphasia for colours, and colour agnosia: A distinction between visual and visuo-verbal impairments in the processing of colours. *Cognitive Neuropsychology, 2*, 1–48.

Bisiach, E. (1988). The (haunted) brain and consciousness. In A. J. Marcel & E. Bisiach (Eds.), *Consciousness in contemporary science* (pp. 101–120). Oxford: Oxford University Press.

Burnham, J. C. (1968). The new psychology: From narcissism to social control. In J. Braeman, R. Bremner, & D. Brody (Eds.), *Change and continuity in twentieth century America*. Ohio University Press.

Campion, J., Latto, R., & Smith, Y. M. (1983). Is blindsight an effect of scattered light, spared cortex, and near-threshold vision? *Behavioral and Brain Sciences, 6*, 423–486.

Cheesman, J., & Merikle, P. M. (1985). Word recognition and consciousness. In D. Besner, T. G. Waller, & G. E. McKinnon (Eds.), *Reading research: Advances in theory and practice* (Vol. 5, pp. 311–352). New York: Academic Press.

Chomsky, N. (1959). [Review of B. F. Skinner's *Verbal behavior*]. *Language, 35*, 26–58.

Delbecq-Derouesne, J., Beauvois, M.-F., & Shallice, T. (in press). Preserved recall versus impaired recognition: A case study. *Brain*.

Dennett, D. C. (1969). *Content and consciousness*. London: Routledge.

Dennett, D. C. (1978). *Brainstorms*. Cambridge, MA: MIT Press.

Ericsson, K. A., & Simon, H. A. (1985). *Protocol analysis: Verbal reports as data.* Cambridge, MA: MIT Press.

Gardiner, J., & Java, R. I. (in press). Recollective experience in word and nonword recognition. *Memory and Cognition.*

Gazzaniga, M. S. (1985). *The social brain.* New York: Basic Books.

Goldman-Rakic, P. S. (1987). Circuitry of primate prefrontal cortex and regulation of behavior by representational memory. *Handbook of Physiology—The Nervous System* (Vol. 5, pp. 373–417). Baltimore: Williams & Wilkins.

Holender, D. (1986). Semantic activation without conscious identification. *Behavioral and Brain Sciences, 9,* 1–66.

Humphrey, G. (1951). *Thinking: An introduction to its experimental psychology.* Andover, Hants: Methuen.

Jacoby, L. J., Woloshyn, V., & Kelley, C. (1989). Becoming famous without being recognized: Unconscious influences of memory produced by divided attention. *Journal of Experimental Psychology: General, 118,* 115–125.

Johnson-Laird, P. N. (1983). A computational analysis of consciousness. *Cognition and Brain Theory, 6,* 499–508. (A revised version appeared in A. J. Marcel & E. Bisiach (Eds.), *Consciousness in contemporary science* (pp. 357–368). Oxford: Oxford University Press.)

Kinsbourne, M. (1988). Integrated field theory of consciousness. In A. J. Marcel & E. Bisiach (Eds.), *Consciousness in contemporary science* (pp. 239–256). Oxford: Oxford University Press.

Kling, J. W., & Riggs, L. A. (1971). *Woodworth and Schlosberg's experimental psychology* (3rd ed.). Andover, Hants: Methuen.

Koch, S. (1954). Clark L. Hull. In W. K. Estes (Ed.), *Modern learning theory* (pp. 1–176). New York: Appleton–Century–Crofts.

Leslie, A. D. (1987). Pretense and representation: The origins of 'theory of mind.' *Psychological Review, 94,* 412–426.

MacCorquodale, K. M., & Meehl, P. E. (1954). Edward C. Tolman. In W. K. Estes (Ed.), *Modern learning theory* (pp. 177–266). New York: Appleton–Century–Crofts.

Mandler, G. (1975). Consciousness: Respectable, useful and probably necessary. In R. Solso (Ed.) *Information processing and cognition: The Loyola symposium* (pp. 229–254). Hillsdale, NJ: Erlbaum.

Mandler, G. (1984). *Mind and body.* New York: Norton.

Mandler, G. (1989). Memory: Conscious and unconscious. In P. R. Solomon, G. R. Goethals, C. M. Kelley, & B. R. Stephens (Eds.), *Memory—An interdisciplinary approach.* New York: Springer.

Marcel, A. J. (1983a). Conscious and unconscious perception: Experiments on visual masking and word recognition. *Cognitive Psychology, 15,* 197–237.

Marcel, A. J. (1983b). Conscious and unconscious perception: An approach to the relations between phenomenal experience and perceptual processes. *Cognitive Psychology, 15,* 238–300.

Marshall, J. C., & Morton, J. (1978). On the mechanics of Emma. In A. Sinclair, R. J. Jarvella, & W. J. M. Levelt (Eds.), *The child's conception of language.* Berlin: Springer.

Miller, G. A. (1962). *Psychology: The science of mental life.* New York: Harper & Row.

Neisser, U. (1963). The multiplicity of thought. *British Journal of Psychology, 54,* 1–14.

Neisser, U. (1967). *Cognitive psychology.* New York: Appleton–Century–Crofts.

Norman, D. A. (1981). Categorization of action slips. *Psychological Review, 88,* 1–15.

Norman, D. A. (1986). Reflections on cognition and parallel distributed processing. In J. L. McClelland & D. E. Rumelhart (Eds.), *Parallel distributed processing* (Vol. 2, pp. 531–552). Cambridge, MA: MIT Press.

Norman, D. A., & Shallice, T. (1986). Attention to action: Willed and automatic control of behavior. In R. J. Davidson, G. E. Schwartz, & D. Shapiro (Eds.), *Consciousness and self-regulation* (Vol. 4, pp. 1–18). New York: Plenum.

O'Keefe, J. (1985). Is consciousness the gateway to the hippocampal cognitive map: A speculative essay on the neural basis of mind. In D. Oakley (Ed.), *Brain and mind* (pp. 59–98). Andover, Hants: Methuen.

Pandya, D. N., & Barnes, C. L. (1987). Architecture and connections of the frontal lobe. In E. Perecman (Ed.), *The frontal lobes revisited*. New York: IRBN.

Posner, M. I., & Klein, R. M. (1973). On the functions of consciousness. In S. Kornblum (Ed.), *Attention and performance* (Vol. 4, pp. 21–35). New York: Academic Press.

Posner, M. I., & Snyder, C. (1975). Facilitation and inhibition in the processing of signals. In P. M. A. Rabbitt & S. Dornic (Eds.), *Attention and Performance* (Vol. 5, pp. 669–682). London: Academic Press.

Putnam, H. (1960). Mind and machines. In S. Hook (Ed.), *Dimensions of mind* (pp. 138–164). New York: New York University Press.

Reed, G. (1972). *The Psychology of Anomalous Experience*. London: Hutchinson.

Rumelhart, D. E., & McClelland, J. L. (1986). PDP models and general issues in cognitive science. In J. L. McClelland & D. E. Rumelhart (Eds.), *Parallel distributed processing* (Vol. 1, pp. 110–146). Cambridge, MA: MIT Press.

Schacter, D. I. (1989). On the relations between memory and consciousness: Dissociable interactions and conscious experience. In H. L. Roediger III & F. I. M. Craik (Eds.), *Varieties of conscious experience: Essays in honor of Endel Tulving*. pp. 355–390. Hillsdale, NJ: Lawrence Erlbaum Associates.

Schacter, D. L. (in press). Toward a cognitive neuropsychology of awareness: Implicit knowledge and anosagnosia. *Journal of Clinical and Experimental Neuropsychology*.

Schank, R. C. (1982). *Dynamic memory*. Cambridge: Cambridge University Press.

Schwartz, B. (1986). *The battle for human nature: Science, morality and modern life*. New York: Norton.

Shallice, T. (1972). Dual functions of consciousness. *Psychological Review, 79*, 383–393.

Shallice, T. (1978). The dominant action-system: An information-processing approach to consciousness. In K. S. Pope & J. L. Singer (Eds.), *The stream of consciousness: Scientific investigations into the flow of human experience*. New York: Plenum.

Shallice, T. (1988a). *From neuropsychology to mental structure*. Cambridge: Cambridge University Press.

Shallice, T. (1988b). Information-processing models of consciousness: Possibilities and problems. In A. J. Marcel & E. Bisiach (Eds.), *Consciousness in contemporary science* (pp. 305–333). Oxford: Oxford University Press.

Stuss, D. T., & Benson, D. F. (1986). *The frontal lobes*. New York: Raven.

Taylor, D. (1964). *The explanation of behaviour*. London: Routledge.

Tipper, S. P., & Driver, J. (1988). Negative priming between pictures and words in a selective attention task: Evidence for semantic processing of ignored stimuli. *Memory and Cognition, 16*, 64–70.

Tulving, E. (1985). Memory and consciousness. *Canadian Psychology, 26*, 1–12.

Tulving, E. (1989). Memory: Performance, knowledge and experience. *European Journal of Cognitive Psychology, 1*, 3–26.

Umilta, C. (1988). The control operations of consciousness. In A. J. Marcel & E. Bisiach (Eds.), *Consciousness in contemporary science* (pp. 334–356). Oxford: Oxford University Press.

Watson, J. B. (1914). *Behavior*. New York: Holt.

Waugh, N. C., & Norman, D. A. (1965). Primary memory. *Psychological Review, 72*, 89–104.

Weiskrantz, L. (1987). Residual vision in a scotoma. *Brain, 110*, 77–92.

Weiskrantz, L. (1988). Some contributions of neuropsychology of vision and memory to the problem of consciousness. In A. J. Marcel & E. Bisiach (Eds.), *Consciousness in contemporary science* (pp. 183–199). Oxford: Oxford University Press.

Wilkes, K. V. (1988). -, yishi, duh, um, and consciousness. In A. J. Marcel & E. Bisiach (Eds.), *Consciousness in contemporary science* (pp. 16–41). Oxford: Oxford University Press.

16

Question Answering and the Organization of World Knowledge

Arthur C. Graesser
Memphis State University

Sallie E. Gordon
University of Idaho

In the late 1960s an organization theory of memory was advanced by George Mandler (1967, 1972) and a group of other researchers studying memory and cognition (Tulving & Donaldson, 1972). The theory included at least three major assumptions. The first assumption is that knowledge in long-term memory is organized in the form of a hierarchical structure of concept nodes. For example, consider the hierarchical structure that underlies the animal kingdom. The most superordinate node (animal) directly dominates a handful of nodes at a second level (reptile, bird, fish, amphibian, mammal), whereas any given node at the second level (e.g., mammal) dominates a set of nodes at a third level (dog, cat, monkey, etc.), and so on.

A second assumption proposed by Mandler (1967) is that there is a limit to the storage capacity or number of units associated with any given node. Specifically, approximately five units are directly subordinate to any given concept node in a hierarchy. We refer to this as the *limited fanout* assumption. If more than five units are dictated by the world or stimulus material, than a person organizes knowledge to meet cognitive constraints by subdividing a large set of units into subcategories.

A third assumption of organization theory is that the process of learning new material is equivalent to constructing an organized structure of nodes (Mandler, 1967). The recall of old material is accomplished by constructing a retrieval strategy that recovers the contextually specific, organized nodal structure that was assembled when the old material was studied.

The assumption about hierarchical organization is not uniformly accepted in the cognitive sciences. Indeed, knowledge is sometimes organized in the form of a nonhierarchical network or matrix organization (Graesser, Hopkinson, &

Schmid, 1987; Huttenlocher & Lui, 1979; Miller & Johnson-Laird, 1976). Nevertheless, a hierarchical organization appears to predominate in some important domains of world knowledge, as we illustrate later in this chapter. Moreover, there can be costs in processing efficiency to the extent that a knowledge representation deviates from a hierarchical organization. For example, it is easy to become lost when searching a network structure that has a high density of structural loops and that has no root node.

The limited fanout assumption has also been frequently challenged. Most colleagues accept the claim that there are limitations in the span of apprehension, consciousness, and immediate memory (Mandler, 1985). Moreover, few would quibble with the notion that such limitations constrain the course of retrieval in addition to perception, consciousness, and immediate memory. It is well documented that information is retrieved from memory in chunks that are limited to about five items (Graesser & Mandler, 1978). The controversy addresses whether long-term memory per se has a limited fanout. We believe that the debate on this matter has never been adequately resolved.

Aside from empirical tests, it can be argued that there are functional and theoretical grounds for postulating a limited fanout in long-term memory. Dirlam (1972) presented a mathematical proof that there is an optimal chunk size when nodes are searched in a hierarchical structure. Search time is minimized when the fanout is limited to three or four items; this estimate does not depend on the volume of nodes stored in memory and does not appreciably vary with fluctuations in search procedures. A limited fanout in long-term memory would also facilitate interactions with immediate memory. Given that a limited-capacity immediate memory produces new structures in long-term memory, we would expect the new structures in permanent store to be affected by such limitations. Given that immediate memory is continuously activating structures from long-term memory, it would be expedient for the knowledge in long-term memory to fall within the capacity bottleneck of immediate memory.

When organization theory was originally tested in the 1960s and 1970s, the standard stimulus materials consisted of lists of unrelated words, categorically related words, paired associates, and digits. But since that time, we have moved on to the study of more complex and ecologically valid materials, such as stories, instructional text, mathematical systems, and scientific mechanisms. Given this radically different emphasis on the type of material that is stored in memory, we can ask whether the original assumptions of organization theory still hold.

In this chapter we argue that the basic tenets of organization theory continue to be plausible and useful. Organization theory has had a profound, if not permanent, impact on the major theoretical frameworks in such diverse areas as text comprehension, the representation of world knowledge, question answering, planning and problem solving, and computerized expert systems.

One way to test whether a theory of knowledge representation is plausible is to evaluate whether the theory is valid and useful in a wide variety of tasks. The functional utility of Mandler's organization theory is demonstrated in the context of two models that span two radically different phenomena—question answering and problem solving. These models postulate cognitive processes that operate on knowledge structures that are constrained by the hierarchy and limited fanout assumptions of organization theory.

The first model is QUEST, a model of human question answering that has been developed over the past 10 years (Golding, Graesser, & Millis, 1990; Graesser, 1981; Graesser & Clark, 1985; Graesser & Franklin, 1990; Graesser & Murachver, 1985; Graesser, Robertson, & Anderson, 1981). QUEST simulates the answers that adults produce when they answer different types of questions, such as why, how, when, where, what-if, and yes/no verification questions. To answer a particular question, QUEST identifies relevant information sources and systematically taps information within each information source. Each information source is a package of world knowledge that is organized in the form of a "conceptual graph structure" containing nodes and relational arcs. The question answering procedures operate systematically on these structures, pursuing some paths of nodes and arcs but not others, depending on the question category. The success of QUEST in simulating human question answering depends on an appropriate organization of the world knowledge structures as well as an appropriate specification of the question answer procedures that operate on these structures.

The second model accounts for problem-solving activities in specific domains, such as mathematics problems and video recorders (Gordon & Gill, 1989, 1990; Graesser, Gordon, Greer, & Forsythe, in press). This model predicts problem-solving performance by postulating cognitive procedures that operate on conceptual graph structures.

QUEST: A MODEL OF QUESTION ANSWERING

The QUEST model of question answering is more complex than our description in this chapter (see Graesser & Franklin, 1990; Graesser, Lang, & Roberts, 1989). The complete QUEST has four major components. First, QUEST translates the question into a logical form and assigns it to one of several question categories. Second, QUEST identifies the information sources that are relevant to the question. Third, convergence mechanisms narrow the node space from hundreds of nodes among the activated information sources to approximately 10 or fewer answers to a particular question. Fourth, QUEST considers the pragmatic context within which the questioner and answerer are situated, including the goals and common ground of the speech participants. Although the process of question answering is segregated into these four components, we acknowledge that an adequate Q/A model would integrate these components in a highly interactive fashion (Robertson, Black, & Lehnert, 1985). Whereas QUEST is a broad model of question answering, we focus on those components that have an obvious foundation in organization theory.

This section illustrates the systematic features of QUEST in the context of four types of knowledge structures: taxonomic hierarchies, spatial region hierarchies, goal hierarchies, and causal networks. Although the content varies radically among these four types of structures, all of the structures exhibit the hierarchical organization and fanout limitation postulated by Mandler (1967).

Taxonomic Hierarchies

Taxonomic hierarchies organize a set of categories, concepts, and entities that are normally expressed as nouns (see Fig. 16.1). The concept nodes are interrelated by *isa* arcs. This arc denotes a class inclusion relation, specifying that a given set of entities or categories is contained within a more abstract, inclusive category. The structure is hierarchical in the sense that any given node has at most one parent node via the *isa* arc (with few exceptions). The *isa* arc may be segregated into subcategories with finer distinctions (e.g., is a kind of, is an example of, is an instance of), but we are not concerned with these subtleties for the present purposes.

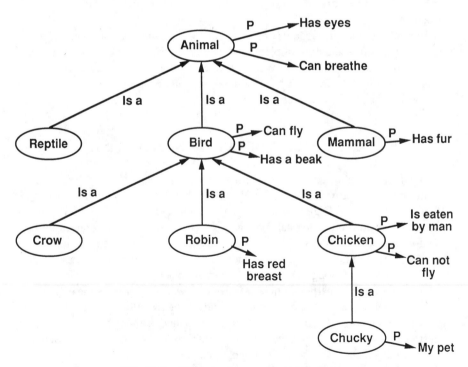

FIG. 16.1.   An example taxonomic hierarchy.

Taxonomic hierarchies have received considerable attention from researchers who have tested theories of memory organization and semantic memory (Battig & Montague, 1969; Bower, 1972; Collins & Loftus, 1975; Graesser & Mandler, 1978; Rosch & Lloyd, 1978; Smith & Medin, 1981). Perhaps this is because most of the nodes can be expressed as simple nouns and because the hierarchical organization is particularly salient in taxonomies.

Each node in a taxonomic hierarchy has a number of properties that are linked to the concept node by property arcs (designated as P). These properties are not haphazardly assigned to the concept nodes; the assignment of a property to a concept must satisfy a "sibling node constraint" that insures that the property is distinctive to that concept. More precisely, when a concept C has a property F, then F is typically true about C but is not typically a property of the sibling nodes of C. For example, a bird can fly, whereas reptiles, mammals, fish, and amphibians rarely fly. A chicken is eaten by people, whereas some of the other types of birds are not eaten by people. It should be noted that the quantifier *typically* is more appropriate than is *never* in our definition of the sibling node constraint; some nonbirds fly, such as bats.

Answers to "class inclusion" questions (e.g., Is an X an F?) are produced by consulting the taxonomic hierarchy. Some of these questions elicit YES answers by virtue of facts directly stored in the hierarchy (e.g., Is a robin a bird?, Is a bird an animal?) However, other YES answers are produced by virtue of a transitivity operator in the Q/A procedure: if A isa B and B isa C, then it follows that A isa C. For all questions of the form "Is an X an F?", the appropriate answer is YES if and only if F is a concept that is superordinate to X via paths of forward *isa* arcs. In Fig. 16.1 there are eight concept nodes and 56 (8 × 7) possible "Is an X an F?" questions. Seven of the 56 questions would be answered YES because of directly stored arcs, whereas five other questions would be answered YES by virtue of the transitivity operator. The other 44 possible questions would receive NO answers (e.g., Is a bird a mammal?, Is a bird a robin?). Therefore, only 22% (12/56) of the total possible questions would receive YES answers.

Answers to "property questions" (i.e., Does X have property F?) can also be produced on the basis of directly stored facts and by inference. There are nine properties directly stored in Fig. 16.1, so nine property questions would directly receive YES answers (e.g., Can a bird fly?, Does an animal have eyes?). Additional YES answers would be generated by an inheritance operator that specifies that a concept X inherits the properties of superordinate concepts (as long as a property of a superordinate concept does not contradict a property of a more subordinate concept). For example, answers to the following questions would be YES by virtue of the inheritance operator: Does a chicken have a beak?, Can a chicken breath?, and Does a chicken have eyes? The answer to the question "Can a chicken fly?" would be NO because the property inherited from bird (can fly) contradicts the property directly stored with chicken (cannot fly). There are 72 possible property questions associated with the example structure because there are eight concepts and nine properties in Fig. 16.1. Nine of the questions would yield YES answers by virtue of directly stored facts and another 22 would yield YES answers by virtue of the inheritance operator. Most of the questions (41/72 = 57%) would receive NO answers.

The taxonomic hierarchy provides a natural organization for answering "definition" questions (i.e., What does X mean? or What is an X?). The QUEST model adopts a genus-differentiae procedure for answering definition questions. This procedure is adopted in most dictionary definitions. The genus-differentiae procedure generates the immediate superordinate node of concept X (via the forward *isa* arc) and the properties directly linked to X (via the forward P arc). The question and answer is articulated as follows:

What is an X?
An X is a ⟨superordinate node⟩ that ⟨property 1⟩,
⟨property 2⟩ . . . ⟨property n⟩.

For example, QUEST produces the following answer to the question "What is a chicken?": A chicken is a bird that is eaten by man and cannot fly.

The taxonomic hierarchy is organized in a way that makes it easy to specify the Q/A procedures of class inclusion, property, and definition questions. There are yet other question categories that have rather simple Q/A procedures which produce sensible answers when applied to the single underlying taxonomic hierarchy:

What is an example of X?
How is X similar to Y?
How is X different than Y?

Therefore, taxonomic knowledge is organized in a special way that coordinates well with the Q/A procedures of many classes of questions.

Spatial Region Hierarchies

Spatial region hierarchies capture the spatial layout of regions and objects in regions. For example, Fig. 16.2 shows how some cities, states, and countries are organized in North America. The region structure is hierarchical with respect to the *is-in* arc. San Diego and Los Angeles are embedded in California, California and Nevada are embedded in the west, and so on. According to organization theory, any given region can directly dominate approximately five subregions without sacrificing a deterioration in perception, memory, and judgment. This explains why the 48 states in North America are segregated into subregions (west, midwest, southeast, northeast) and the subregions are sometimes segre-

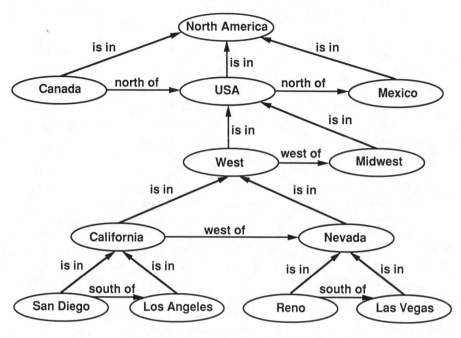

FIG. 16.2.   An example region hierarchy.

gated into sub-subregions (e.g., the west is segregated into the northwest, south-west, and Rocky Mountain states). This also explains why adults can retrieve at most five cities from any given state during a retrieval task. Of course, the state in which a person lives constitutes an exception because there is a rich hierarchy with many intermediate levels of regions.

A region hierarchy also contains a set of directional arcs that designate the relative spatial locations of regions. These arcs include *west-of* (with its inverse *east-of*) and *north-of* (with its inverse *south-of*). The directional arcs are not haphazardly arranged in the region hierarchy. There is a "sibling node constraint" that specifies that any given directional arc can only connect sibling nodes. For example, cities within a state can be related by directional arcs, but cities between states are not connected directly by directional arcs.

One consequence of the sibling node constraint is that inferences must be made when computing the relative location of most regions. For example, inferences must be made when determining that Los Angeles is west of Reno (vs. east of Reno) because there is no directional arc directly connecting these two cousin nodes (see Los Angeles and Reno in Fig. 16.2). In the question "Is Los Angeles west of Reno?" QUEST must arrive at a YES answer on the basis of the following inferential reasoning:

Los Angeles is in California
Reno is in Nevada
California is west of Nevada
Therefore, Los Angeles is west of Reno

The vast majority of adults produce a YES answer to this question even though it is erroneous when a map is carefully examined. An accurate map would clearly reveal that Los Angeles is east of Reno rather than west of Reno. The sibling node constraint therefore explains some interesting errors in spatial judgment. Whenever the spatial region hierarchy (with sibling node constraints) produces output that is incompatible with a Cartesian coordinate system, adults' decisions usually follow the spatial region hierarchy (Stevens & Coupe, 1978).

One might hypothesize that individuals can memorize directional arcs between nodes that are not sibling nodes. However, there would be a large number of such arcs to memorize and there would be very little incremental gain above the information provided by the region hierarchy. We have constructed a spatial hierarchy that contains 100 major cities in the continental United States. The region hierarchy contains approximately 150 *is-in* arcs and 150 directional arcs. This hierarchy with 300 arcs can support thousands of spatial inferences and spatial questions when QUEST's procedures are applied to the structure. Given that there are 100 cities, there are approximately 5,000 pairwise judgments on the north/south direction (e.g., San Diego is south of Chicago) and another 5,000 judgments on the east/west direction (San Diego is west of Chicago), yielding 10,000 judgments. Directly memorizing 10,000 directional relations between cities would of course be quite tedious; we argue that adults would not acquire spatial knowledge by memorizing 10,000 facts. Moreover, the vast majority of these 10,000 relations would be accurately generated when QUEST's inference procedures are applied to our region hierarchy with 300 arcs. When considering the thousands of directional relations between pairs of cities, less than 1% of QUEST's inferred relations are incompatible with a Cartesian map of the United States. Clearly, a region hierarchy admirably satisfies the virtue of cognitive economy.

The region hierarchy can support a vast array of spatial questions. According to QUEST, accurate answers are produced when very simple Q/A procedures operate on the spatial region hierarchy.

Is X in Y?
What ⟨regions⟩ are in X?
Is X north/south/east/west of Y?
What is north/south/east/west of X?
Where is X?

When asked "Where is X?", QUEST samples nodes that (a) are superordinate in the region hierarchy, on paths of forward *is-in* arcs, and (b) directional arcs that radiate from X. For example, when QUEST is applied to the structure in Fig. 16.2, appropriate answers to "Where is San Diego?" are: in California, in the west, in the United States, in North America, and south of Los Angeles. In contrast, QUEST's answers to "What is in X?" questions include nodes on paths of backward *is-in* arcs. When asked "What is in California?", appropriate answers are San Francisco and San Diego, but not the west, the United States, and North America.

Studies by Shanon (1983) have shown that the common ground between questioner and answerer is very critical in the selection of answers to "Where is X?" questions. The answerer first determines a region that constitutes the common ground between the speech participants. Then the answerer produces a region that is slightly more detailed (i.e., one arc away) than the region at the fringe of the common ground. Suppose, for example, that two strangers are in a bar in Los Angeles and one of them asks "Where is San Diego?" The region at the fringe of the common ground is Los Angeles; other regions in the common ground are California, the west, the United States, and North America. An appropriate answer in this scenario would be "south of Los Angeles." Suppose that two strangers are in a bar in Idaho and the same question is asked. In this case, the United States and North America are in the common ground (from the standpoint of the structure in Fig. 16.2) and the west is at the fringe of the common ground. An appropriate answer would be one arc away from the fringe region, which ends up being "in California." If we extend this Q/A procedure, the answer would be "in the United States" when the same question is asked in Toronto and "in North America" when the same question is asked in Warsaw. If the pilots of two spacecrafts had a dialogue in outer space, then the appropriate answer to "Where is San Diego?" would be "on planet earth."

Goal Hierarchies

Goal hierarchies underlie planned action sequences that are executed by animate agents (Card, Moran, & Newell, 1983; Mandler, 1984; Miller, Galanter, & Pribram, 1960; Norman & Rumelhart, 1975; Schank & Abelson, 1977). Each node in a goal hierarchy consists of a goal expression that refers to a state or event desired by the agent.

Figure 16.3 shows an example goal hierarchy for changing a tire on an automobile. The structure is hierarchical with respect to the Reason (R) arc. The reason for a particular goal consists of its superordinate goal, e.g., the reason for getting a lug wrench (Goal 10) is to loosen the bolts (Goal 4). Node 1 (change tire) is the most superordinate goal in the hierarchy, whereas Nodes 10–13 are the most subordinate goal nodes. Therefore, the actions involved in changing a

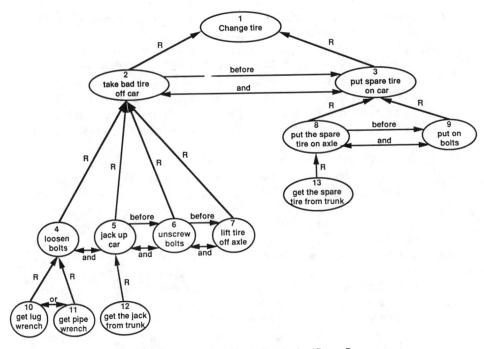

FIG. 16.3.   An example goal hierarchy. R signifies a Reason arc.

tire are not organized along a single associative chain. Instead, the actions are grouped into plans and subplans according to the hierarchical structure depicted in Fig. 16.3 (Bower, Black, & Turner, 1979; Galambos & Rips, 1982). Moreover, any given goal node is directly superordinate to at most five subgoals.

As with the taxonomic hierarchies and region hierarchies, the goal hierarchies include a set of arc categories that interrelate the sibling nodes. First, the sibling nodes are interrelated by bi-directional *and* and *or* arcs. Second, the sibling nodes may be related by *before* arcs when temporal information needs to be conveyed. There is a sibling node constraint that states that only sibling nodes are related by *before* arcs. There is also an implicit temporal relation that specifies that a subgoal must be achieved before its superordinate goal. The fact that unscrewing the bolts (Node 6) precedes putting the spare tire on the car (Node 3) would be inferred from the following temporal relations:

Unscrewing the bolts (6) is a subgoal of taking the bad tire off the car (2) so 6 is *before* 2.

Taking the bad tire off the car (2) occurs *before* putting the spare tire on the car (3)

It should be noted that an adequate temporal calculus for planning is more complicated than what has been illustrated in this example (Allen, 1982). However, the example should convey a general impression of how temporal relations can be derived by applying qualitative reasoning heuristics to the goal hierarchy.

QUEST can account for the following questions that may be asked about goal hierarchies (Graesser, 1981; Graesser & Franklin, 1990; Graesser & Murachver, 1985; Graesser, Robertson, & Anderson, 1981).

Why ⟨goal G⟩?

How is ⟨goal G⟩ achieved?

What are the consequences of ⟨goal G⟩ being achieved?

Is ⟨goal G⟩ achieved before ⟨goal F⟩?

Associated with each of these question categories is a very simple Q/A procedure that systematically searches through the goal hierarchy during the course of fetching answers. For example, answers to why-questions result from sampling (a) superordinate goals on paths of forward Reason arcs and (b) sibling nodes that are connected to the queried goal by a forward *before* arc. The following answers would be legal when QUEST's procedure for why-questions is applied to Fig. 16.3 in answering the question "Why do you unscrew the bolts?".

in order to take the bad tire off the car (Node 2)

in order to change the tire (Node 1)

so the tire can be lifted off the axle (Node 7)

In contrast, Nodes 3, 4, 5, 8, 9, 10, 11, 12, and 13 are illegal answers to this question. That is, for each of these illegal nodes, there is no legal path that connects the node with the queried node. Stated differently, these illegal nodes would never be accessed by the particular question when the Q/A procedure for a why-question is applied to the structure in Fig. 16.3. For goal hierarchies, "what-are-the-consequences" questions have essentially the same Q/A procedure as that of why-questions. The only difference is that the connectives (*in order to, so*) are not expressed.

QUEST's Q/A procedure for how-questions is quite different from that of why-questions. Answers to how-questions sample subordinate goals (on paths of backward Reason arcs). For example, legal answers to "How do you take the bad tire off the car?" (Node 2) are Nodes 4, 5, 6, 7, 10, 11, and 12 whereas illegal answers are Nodes 1, 3, 8, 9, and 13.

Causal Networks

Causal networks underlie the causally driven event chains in physical, biological, and technological systems (e.g., tornadoes, mitosis, and nuclear power, respectively). For example, consider the following event chain on nuclear power.

1. Atoms are split.
2. Energy is released.
3. Water is heated.
4. Steam drives a series of turbines.
5. Turbines produce electricity.

A simple way of representing this event chain is a sequence of event nodes, connected by Cause (C) arcs.

$$[1]—C{\rightarrow}[2]—C{\rightarrow}[3]—C{\rightarrow}[4]—C{\rightarrow}[5]$$

Additional complexity is added when there are structural loops among events. For example, rainfall involves a cycle of events rather than a linear chain. Complexity is also added if a particular event requires a set of enabling states and multiple simultaneous antecedent events. Nevertheless, these levels of complexity can be adequately captured by a causal network that contains a set of event and state nodes connected by C-arcs.

QUEST can account for the answers to a variety of question categories when causal mechanisms are captured by the simple causal networks described earlier. Specifically, answers to why, how, when, and enablement questions are on paths of causal antecedents (i.e., backward C-arcs) whereas answers to consequence and what-if questions are on paths of causal consequences (i.e., forward C-arcs). For example, when asked "How is water heated?" legal answers are Node 1 (atoms are split) and Node 2 (energy is released) but not Nodes 4 and 5. When asked "What are the consequences of water being heated?" legal answers are Node 4 (steam drives a series of turbines) and Node 5 (turbines produce electricity) but not Nodes 1 and 2.

Our description of the Q/A procedures and the causal networks goes a long way toward accounting for the answers that adults give to questions in the context of scientific and technological mechanisms (Graesser, Hemphill, & Brainerd, 1989). Unfortunately, however, the above account is not completely satisfactory (Brown, Burton, & de Kleer, 1982; Forbus, 1984). One problem is that the causal networks can become so large that even a bright adult would be unable to search and operate on the nodes systematically. When there are hundreds of nodes in the causal network, an additional level of structure must be imposed that chunks substructures into natural packages of information. For example, events in a nuclear power plant may be segregated into those that occur in a nuclear fission chamber versus those that occur in chambers that transform steam to electricity. This divide-and-conquer strategy imposes a hierarchical organization on the physical components and events in a mechanism.

Another problem is that most events can be construed from either a macroaggregate perspective or a microparticle perspective. Consider the event *atoms are split*. The macroaggregate perspective refers to a large set of atoms being split, whereas the microparticle perspective refers to the split of a single atom. In some contexts, it is appropriate to adopt a macro perspective, yet in other contexts the micro perspective is needed. For example, a microparticle perspective is needed when deciding that the event "atoms are split" precedes "energy is released"; after the first atom is split, energy begins to be released. The two events are essentially concurrent from the perspective of the macroaggregate level. The fact that each event can be construed from both a macro and micro perspective imposes a hierarchical structure on the representation of causal mechanisms.

A third shortcoming of the original causal networks is that adults frequently impose a goal-oriented, teleological interpretation on event sequences in scientific mechanisms. That is, an Event E occurs for the purpose of achieving subsequent events (e.g., water is heated for the purpose of having steam drive a series of turbines and producing electricity). Indeed, the engineers of a nuclear power plant would design the plant with such goals in mind. Whenever teleological interpretations are imposed on a causal mechanism, a goal hierarchy is superimposed on the causal network and the adult reasons in a goal-oriented manner (Graesser et al., 1989). As a consequence, answers to why-questions end up tapping the goal hierarchy instead of the causal network. When asked "Why is water heated?" adults tend to generate causal consequences as answers: "in order to drive a series of turbines" (Event 4) and "in order to produce electricity" (Event 5). They do not tend to produce causal antecedents as answers: "because atoms are split" (Event 1) and "because energy is released" (Event 2).

Just as a hierarchical organization was at the heart of taxonomic, spatial, and goal-oriented knowledge, a hierarchical organization ends up providing structure and functionality to complex causal networks. There is no intrinsic reason why a hierarchical organization should be imposed on causal systems. However, the cognitive system copes best with a hierarchical organization and a limit of five sibling nodes per nodal chunk.

KNOWLEDGE STRUCTURES AND PROBLEM SOLVING

Our presentation of the QUEST model segregated conceptual graph structures into different classes that were computationally tractable. However, packages of world knowledge actually consist of a hybrid of taxonomic hierarchies, spatial region hierarchies, goal hierarchies, and causal networks. For example, an adult's knowledge of a video recorder would likely include the following information.

1. The VCR would be related to a device taxonomy (e.g., a VCR is a device, a device is an artifact, an artifact is an object).

2. The parts of the VCR are mapped onto a part and region hierarchy (e.g., the play button is on the front panel, the front panel is part of the VCR).

3. The procedures for operating the VCR are organized in the form of action-based goal hierarchies (e.g., the procedure for recording a movie, the procedure for changing a tape).

4. The internal mechanisms of the VCR are organized in the form of a causal network (e.g., pressing the play button causes the tape to play).

The domain knowledge contains arcs from most or all of these types of structures. Moreover, the nodes from one type of structure are integrated systematically with nodes from other types of structure.

We assume that the hybrid knowledge structures have a critical impact on domain-specific problem solving, such as those involved in mathematics or the use of a VCR (Gill, Gordon, Moore, & Barbera, 1988; Gordon & Gill, 1989, 1990; Graesser, Gordon et al., in press). When people learn about a topic, they represent the information as conceptual graph structures that contain a variety of node and arc categories. These structures include procedural action structures, such as those depicted in the goal hierarchy in Fig. 16.3. The conceptual graph structures can represent *rules* that specify how goals are achieved by creating subgoals and by executing action sequences. We also postulate the existence of automatized cognitive processes that are outside the scope of the conceptual graph structures (Anderson, 1983) but such processing components are not the focus of this discussion.

Suppose that an adult wants to solve the problem of videotaping a program on Channel 10. The person has a set of knowledge structures associated with VCRs and similar devices. A subset of the nodes in these conceptual graph structures are activated during problem solving. Some of the nodes are invariantly activated whenever the person uses a VCR. The activation of other nodes depends on the unique context of the particular task and the VCR components that the person perceives. Some actions are directly constructed by virtue of global goals, whereas other actions are triggered by particular VCR controls and display features. Solving a problem is easy when the method of achieving a goal is directly stored in an adult's conceptual graph structure and the nodes from these structures are quickly activated in immediate memory. However, problem solving is slow and effortful when inferences must be generated during the process of constructing a plan.

The process of constructing knowledge-based inferences during problem solving can be very taxing on an immediate memory with limited capacity. Our model of problem solving assumes that people can successfully construct the inferences in route to a critical action (or plan) only when a small number of inferences are sufficient. Gordon and Gill (1990) proposed that adults can successfully generate only two or three inferences when they construct a novel action. These inferences are based on comparatively simple transformations and embellishments of their existing conceptual graph structures. In contrast, adults are unable to construct long chains of reasoning and extensive structural transformations during the course of constructing a novel plan. Gordon and Gill's (1990) model was able to successfully predict 90% of college students' successes and failures in solving a series of tasks involving VCRs and in solving a series of mathematics problems.

Given that world knowledge has an important role in problem solving, it is important for researchers to extract the content of these structures empirically and to map out this content in the form of conceptual graph structures. We have developed a "question probe method" for eliciting the nodes from packages of knowledge in long-term memory. That is, questions are systematically generated and asked in order to elicit adults' knowledge about particular conceptual domains under consideration. The question probe method has been used to elicit knowledge about VCRs (Gordon & Gill, 1990), computers (Eymard, 1988; Graesser & Murray, 1989; Lang, Graesser, & Hemphill, 1990), mathematical systems (Gill et al., 1988; Gordon & Gill, 1990), financial investment (Gordon & Gill, 1989), natural concepts and categories (Graesser & Clark, 1985; Graesser, Magliano, & Tidwell, in press), and text (Graesser, 1981; Graesser & Clark, 1985).

Studies have been conducted to test the validity of the knowledge structures elicited by the question probe method. For example, in addition to the fact that the domain-specific knowledge structures robustly predicted adult problem solving, Gordon and Gill (1990) found that the organization of the conceptual graph structures was quite similar to the organization manifested in the subjects' free recall protocols. In studies on text comprehension, the inferences extracted by the question probe method significantly predicted reading times for words (Graesser, Haberlandt, & Koizumi, 1987), reading times for sentences (Millis, Morgan, & Graesser, 1990), and on-line measures of inference activation (Long, Golding, Graesser, & Clark, 1990).

In closing, it should be obvious that organization theory has had a profound impact on both the cognitive theories and the applied problems that we have pursued during our careers. Without the organization theory of memory, our QUEST model of question answering and our model of problem solving would never have emerged. We also would never have arrived at a satisfactory representation of world knowledge.

ACKNOWLEDGMENTS

This research was funded in part by a grant awarded to the first author by the Office of Naval Research (N00014-88-K-0110) and a grant awarded to the second author by the Air Force Office of Scientific Research (88-0063).

REFERENCES

Allen, J. F. (1982). Modeling events, actions, and time. *Proceedings of the Fourth Annual Conference of the Cognitive Science Society,* Ann Arbor, MI.

Anderson, J. R. (1983). *The architecture of cognition.* Cambridge, MA: Harvard University Press.

Battig, W. F., & Montague, W. E. (1969). Category norms for verbal items in 56 categories: A replication and extension of the Connecticut category norms. *Journal of Experimental Psychology, 80,* 1–46.

Bower, G. H. (1972). A selective review of organization factors in memory. In E. Tulving & W. Donaldson (Eds.), *Organization of memory* (pp. 93–137). New York: Academic Press.

Bower, G. H., Black, J. B., & Turner, T. J. (1979). Scripts in memory for text. *Cognitive Psychology, 11,* 177–220.

Brown, J. S., Burton, R. R., & de Kleer, J. (1982). Pedagogical, natural language, and knowledge engineering techniques in SOPHIE I, II, and III. In D. Sleeman & J. S. Brown (Eds.), *Intelligent tutoring systems* (pp. 227–282). New York: Academic Press.

Card, S. K., Moran, T. P., & Newell, A. (1983). *The psychology of human-computer interaction.* Hillsdale, NJ: Lawrence Erlbaum Associates.

Collings, A. M., & Loftus, E. F. (1975). A spreading activation theory of semantic processing. *Psychological Review, 82,* 407–428.

Dirlam, D. K. (1972). Most efficient chunk sizes. *Cognitive Psychology, 3,* 355–359.

Eymard, L. A. (1988). *The relationship between device knowledge and mental models in children.* Unpublished master's thesis, Memphis State University, Memphis, TN.

Forbus, K. (1984). Qualitative process theory. *Artificial Intelligence, 24,* 85–168.

Galambos, J. A., & Rips, L. J. (1982). Memory for routines. *Journal of Verbal Learning and Verbal Behavior, 21,* 260–281.

Gill, R., Gordon, S., Moore, J., & Barbera, C. (1988). The use of conceptual structures in problem solving. *Proceedings: Annual Meeting of the American Society for Engineering Education, 2,* 583–590.

Golding, J. M., Graesser, A. C., & Millis, K. K. (1990). What makes a good answer to a question?: Testing a psychological model of question answering. *Discourse Processes, 13,* 305–325.

Gordon, S., & Gill, R. (1989). Question probes: A structured method for eliciting declarative knowledge. *AI Applications in Natural Resource Management, 3,* 13–20.

Gordon, S., & Gill, R. (1990). *The role of knowledge structures in domain-specific problem solving.* Unpublished manuscript, University of Idaho, Psychology Department, Moscow, ID.

Graesser, A. C. (1981). *Prose comprehension beyond the word.* New York: Springer-Verlag.

Graesser, A. C., & Clark, L. C. (1985). *Structures and procedures of implicit knowledge.* Norwood, NJ: Ablex.

Graesser, A. C., & Franklin, S. P. (1990). QUEST: A cognitive model of question answering. *Discourse Processes, 13,* 279–303.

Graesser, A. C., Gordon, S., Greer, J., & Forsythe, C. (in press). Design of optimal person-artifact interfaces: Contributions from cognitive science. *Educational Training Technologies.*

Graesser, A. C., Haberlandt, K., & Koizumi, D. (1987). How is reading time influenced by knowledge-based inferences and world knowledge? In B. Britton & S. Glynn (Eds.), *Executive control processes in reading* (pp. 217–251). Hillsdale, NJ: Lawrence Erlbaum Associates.

Graesser, A. C., Hemphill, D. H., & Brainerd, L. E. (1989). Question answering in the context of causal mechanisms. *Proceedings of the Cognitive Science Society,* 621–626.

Graesser, A. C., Hopkinson, P., Schmid, C. (1987). Differences in interconcept organization between nouns and verbs. *Journal of Memory and Language, 26,* 242–253.

Graesser, A. C., Lang, K. L., & Roberts, R. M. (1989). *Question answering in the context of stories.* Unpublished manuscript, Memphis State University, Psychology Department, Memphis, TN.

Graesser, A. C., Magliano, J., & Tidwell, P. (in press). World knowledge, inferences, and questions. In M. Kamil (Ed.), *Multidisciplinary perspectives on literacy research*, Urbana, IL: National Conference on Research in English.

Graesser, A. C., & Mandler, G. (1978). Limited processing capacity constrains the storage of unrelated sets of words and retrieval from natural categories. *Journal of Experimental Psychology: Human Learning and Memory, 4*, 86–100.

Graesser, A. C., & Murachver, T. (1985). Symbolic procedures of question answering. In A. C. Graesser & J. B. Black (Eds.), *The psychology of questions* (pp. 15–88). Hillsdale, NJ: Lawrence Erlbaum Associates.

Graesser, A. C., & Murray, K. (1989). A question-answering methodology for exploring a user's acquisition and knowledge of a computer environment. In S. P. Robertson, W. Zachary, & J. B. Black (Eds.), *Cognition, computing and cooperation* (pp. 237–267). Norwood, NJ: Ablex.

Graesser, A. C., Robertson, S. P., & Anderson, P. A. (1981). Incorporating inferences in narrative representations: A study of how and why. *Cognitive Psychology, 13*, 1–26.

Huttenlocher, J., & Lui, F. (1979). The semantic organization of some simple nouns and verbs. *Journal of Verbal Learning and Verbal Behavior, 18*, 141–162.

Lang, K. L., Graesser, A. C., & Hemphill, D. D. (1990). The role of questioning in knowledge engineering and the interface of expert systems. *Poetics, 19*, 143–166.

Long, D., Golding, J., Graesser, A. C., & Clark, L. F. (1990). Inference generation during story comprehension: A comparison of goals, events, and states. In A. C. Graesser & G. H. Bower (Eds.), *The psychology of learning and motivation: Inferences and text comprehension* (pp. 89–102). New York: Academic Press.

Mandler, G. (1967). Organization and memory. In K. W. Spence & J. A. Spence (Eds.), *The psychology of learning and motivation* (Vol. 1, pp. 327–372). New York: Academic Press.

Mandler, G. (1972). Organization and recognition. In E. Tulving & W. Donaldson (Eds.), *Organization and memory* (pp. 139–166). New York: Academic Press.

Mandler, G. (1985). *Cognitive psychology: An essay in cognitive science.* Hillsdale, NJ: Lawrence Erlbaum Associates.

Mandler, J. M. (1984). *Stories, scripts, and scenes.* Hillsdale, NJ: Lawrence Erlbaum Associates.

Miller, G. A., Galanter, E., & Pribram, K. H. (1960). *Plans and the structure of behavior.* New York: Holt, Reinhart & Winston.

Miller, G. A., & Johnson-Laird, P. N. (1976). *Language and perception.* Cambridge, MA: Harvard University Press.

Millis, K. K., Morgan, D., & Graesser, A. C. (1990). The impact of knowledge-based inferences on reading time for expository text. In A. C. Graesser & G. H. Bower (Eds.), *The psychology of learning and motivation: Inferences and text comprehension* (pp. 197–212). New York: Academic Press.

Norman, D. A., & Rumelhart, D. E. (1975). *Explorations in cognition.* San Francisco: Freeman.

Robertson, S. P., Black, J. B., & Lehnert, W. G. (1985). Misleading question effects as evidence for integrated question understanding and memory search. In A. C. Graesser & J. B. Black (Eds.), *The psychology of questions* (pp. 191–218). Hillsdale, NJ: Lawrence Erlbaum Associates.

Rosch, E., & Lloyd, B. B. (Eds.). (1978). *Cognition and categorization.* Hillsdale, NJ: Lawrence Erlbaum Associates.

Schank, R. C., & Abelson, R. (1977). *Scripts, plans, goals, and understanding.* Hillsdale, NJ: Lawrence Erlbaum Associates.

Shanon, B. (1983). Answers to where-questions. *Discourse Processes, 6*, 319–352.

Smith, E. E., & Medin, D. L. (1981). *Categories and concepts.* Cambridge, MA: Harvard University Press.

Stevens, A., & Coupe, P. (1978). Distortions in judged spatial relations. *Cognitive Psychology, 10*, 422–437.

Tulving, E., & Donaldson, W. (Eds.). (1972). *Organization of memory.* New York: Academic Press.

17

The Unity of Consciousness: A Connectionist Account

Geoffrey E. Hinton
University of Toronto

INTRODUCTION

The main thesis of this chapter is that one of the most puzzling aspects of consciousness can be explained by considering an important limitation of connectionist networks. The puzzle concerns the number of things of which we can be simultaneously aware. In some sense, we are only aware of a single Gestalt at a time. In visual perception, if we attend to one object, we cannot simultaneously attend to other objects. In language understanding, when we comprehend one proposition, we do not simultaneously comprehend other propositions. When solving a complex problem, if we focus on one subtask we cannot simultaneously focus on other subtasks. The puzzle arises because our awareness of a Gestalt presumably involves information about the relationships among the constituents of the Gestalt, so despite the phenomenological evidence for the unity and exclusiveness of consciousness, reason tells us that we must be actively representing several of the constituents of our current Gestalt. So why are we not conscious of those constituents? This puzzle is particularly acute for spotlight theories of attention, because, if an object is under the spotlight, then so are its parts.

The obvious way out of this dilemma is to mistrust or reinterpret the phenomenological evidence and to abandon the idea that we can only attend to (or be aware of) one thing at a time. I propose a quite different solution that respects the phenomenological evidence: The way in which the constituents are represented is very different from the way in which the whole Gestalt is represented. So, if awareness of something corresponds to a particular mode of representation of that thing, our awareness of the Gestalt can involve active representations of the constituents without involving awareness of the constituents. Or to express the same point another way, we can be aware of one entity *as a whole* without being aware of its constituents *as wholes* even though our awareness of an entity as a whole involves awareness of its constituents *as parts*. Being aware of an entity as a part of a larger whole does not constitute consciousness of the entity. This proposal is not just a speculation: It is a natural consequence of implementing cognition in a neural network.

PHILOSOPHICAL PRELIMINARIES

Although our everyday mental concepts and our phenomenological experience are useful evidence for how the mind actually works, they are probably misleading and inconsistent in many respects. Within a limited domain, it is often possible to avoid deciding which of the many properties of a concept like consciousness are really crucial because in that domain the properties nearly always coincide. This confounding of properties may actually be exacerbated by the fact that we tend to choose as concepts precisely those combinations of properties that are highly correlated in our normal experience. New domains, such as simulated neural networks, deconfound the properties and force us to make choices in how we extend the concept. These choices inevitably alter the meaning of the concept in its original domain.

The aim of this chapter is not to explore all the strands that are interwoven in the everyday concept of consciousness. I merely wish to resolve a puzzle about why, in some sense, we are not conscious of the parts of an object of consciousness. In suggesting a technical solution to this puzzle I assume that the relevant aspect of the meaning of the term consciousness can be applied to relatively simple neural networks, even though other important aspects of the term may not be applicable to such simple networks. A geometric analogy may make the methodology clearer. We start with the everyday concept of consciousness, as it applies to human beings, and we project the concept into a simpler domain (a class of neural networks). By examining the shadow of the concept in this simpler domain we can gain insight into some aspects of the full concept in the original domain.

THE BINDING PROBLEM IN NEURAL NETWORKS

Suppose we wish to represent a red square and a blue circle. It is not sufficient to simply activate representations of red, blue, square, and circle. We need to represent what goes with what. Neural networks have three main ways of solving this binding problem:

1. Use dedicated "conjunctive" units that represent conjunctions of properties such as color and shape. Conjunctive units allow many different combinations to be represented simultaneously. However, we need to set aside dedicated conjunctive units for all possible combinations of properties.

2. Use simultaneity. Activate all the properties of one object at the same time, and use the assumption that all the simultaneously activated properties belong to the same object. This requires far fewer units, but we can only represent one object at a time.

3. Use temporary increases of connection strengths between units representing the different properties of an object. This allows a temporary content-addressable memory in which all the properties of an object can be retrieved by activating a subset of the properties. The active representation still involves the assumption that the simultaneously active properties belong to the same object, but the superimposed representations in the temporary connection strengths allow several different sets of bindings to be stored simultaneously in temporary working memory.

Given these three methods of solving the binding problem, how should representations be organized in a neural network? If there are enough units available, it pays to use conjunctive representations because this allows many objects to be represented and processed simultaneously. At first sight, the conjunctive method appears to require n^k units to represent objects that have k different properties each of which has n discriminable values. This exponential explosion can be mitigated by a factor of d^{k-1} by using coarse-coded conjunctive units that have a diameter of d discriminable values along each dimension (Hinton, McClelland, & Rumelhart, 1986). Alternatively, the exponential explosion can be reduced to a mere linear relationship between the number of dimensions and the number of units required if the objects are all in different places. Instead of dedicating a unit to every possible conjunction of property values, we can dedicate a unit to the conjunction of each property value with each spatial location. The different property values of an object are then implicitly bound together by the fact that they share the same location. Notice that this scheme relies on simultaneity to bind together the property values in one location, so it can be viewed as a specialization of either of the first two methods of doing binding. This method of coding seems like a good model of much of visual cortex in which each cortical map represents the conjunction of a few property values with retinotopic location.

However, the method of binding properties together by binding them to location inevitably involves replication of hardware across all locations. This amount of replication seems to be necessary to allow parallel processing without creating contention for access to a central knowledge store, but it is expensive for properties such as complex shape descriptors, of which there may a large number. It also creates problems for learning since it seems to require that every new descriptor must be learned separately for every location. For sufficiently complicated tasks, or for sufficiently complex novel objects, it is not feasible to replicate representations across all possible locations, so the network must substitute time for space and use simultaneity as its method of representing novel combinations.[1] This means that only one novel combination can be represented at a time.

Some of the obvious limitations of only being able to represent one novel combination at a time can be overcome by using fast changing weights to allow several novel combinations to be held in working memory simultaneously, even though only one of these combinations can be actively represented at a time. The contents of working memory would then be rapidly available to consciousness, though they would not themselves be in consciousness.

I assume that the switch to a representation in which only one combination can occur at a time captures an important aspect of what we mean by consciousness,[2] and I show that if this is correct, the phenomenological puzzle about our lack of consciousness of the parts of a Gestalt can be resolved.

If we consider the problem of representing a complex hierarchical object composed of related parts that are themselves composed of related subparts, we get the same trade-off between parallel conjunctive representations and serial representations that rely on simultaneity to represent binding. If we are willing to represent the parts in less detail than we represent the whole, we can represent several parts in parallel by using conjunctive representations and these "reduced descriptions" of the parts can be constituents of the representation of the whole. To make the conjunctive representations of the parts relatively efficient, we can conjoin each property of a part with the relative location of that part within the whole. Alternatively we can use a set of "roles" instead of relative spatial location, and represent constituents of an instantiated schema by activating units that stand for the conjunction of a role and the identity of the role filler (Hinton, 1981).[3]

---

[1]Another difficulty with replicating representations across space is that our motor apparatus is *not* replicated across space, so if we want the representations to control actions there is a problem of contention for the motor apparatus. Of course, motor apparatus *is* replicated across different individuals, so they can simultaneously represent different things without contention—unless they need to act together in which case they may need shared consciousness. The contention for limited motor apparatus is a reason for serial consciousness that is discussed by Shallice (1978). It fits the general pattern that serial consciousness facilitates timesharing—of motor apparatus or of representational apparatus. It may well be that serial consciousness is highly overdetermined by the many different things that can usefully be timeshared.

[2]Other important aspects are *not* captured.

[3]In the perceptual input, several entities can be represented in parallel by conjoining their property values with location or time of occurrence. In more central representations, these spatial or temporal roles may be mapped into non-spatiotemporal roles such as "agent" or "beneficiary." Grammar can be viewed as a set of conventions that allow such mappings to be conveyed correctly from speakers to hearers.

A consequence of representing complex structures in this way is that an object in the world has many different internal representations depending on the focus of attention of the network. If the network focuses on the object as a whole, its major constituents all receive reduced, role-specific representations. If however, the network focuses its attention on one of these constituents, that constituent then replaces the previous object as the current Gestalt and it receives its full canonical representation in which its property values (or its identity) are not conjoined with its role within some larger object. If consciousness of an object corresponds to activating the full canonical representation of the object, the puzzle is resolved.

There is a close relationship between this view of consciousness and the old slogan of the Gestalt psychologists that "the whole is more than the sum of its parts."[4] This has often been interpreted to mean that the whole is the sum of its parts plus some extra emergent properties. What the Gestalt psychologists should have said is that the representation of the whole does not contain the representations of its parts *as wholes*.

SOME NEURO-PSYCHOLOGICAL EVIDENCE

The idea of multiple different representations of the very same external object seems wasteful and implausible if our paradigm for human information processing is the sequential digital computer. We were forced into this apparently clumsy multiplicity by the need to solve the binding problem in a neural network, so it is encouraging that damaged neural networks provide strong evidence in favor of multiple alternative representations of the same external object. In brain-damaged adults, there is a dissociation between two very different types of reading deficit. Some "letter-by-letter" patients lose the ability to read whole words at a single glance, but retain the ability to recognize the individual letters in a word and to piece together the word by sounding out the letters (Shallice, 1988, chapter 4). Other patients can still read whole words quite well, but have grave difficulty in identifying the letters within the word (Warrington & Shallice, 1979). Intuitively, this seems very odd because it is necessary to identify the individual letters in order to correctly identify the whole world.[5] The notion of reduced, role-specific representations makes sense of this kind of deficit. The letter-by-letter readers have lost the reduced, role-specific representations of letters that allow parallel recognition of the whole world, but they retain the

---

[4]A more accurate English translation might have been "the whole is different from the sum of the parts (George Mandler, personal communication).

[5]Experiments using alternating cases for the letters rule out the idea that whole words are primarily recognised by properties such as the shape of their envelope that can be extracted without identifying the individual letters.

canonical representations of letters as wholes. The whole word readers have the opposite problem, so they can use the identities of the letters to recognize the word, but they cannot be aware of the identities of the letters.

RECURSION AND CONSCIOUSNESS

The idea that an object in the world might be given quite different representations depending on the focus of attention gives rise to a way of doing recursion in neural networks. Using some additional control apparatus, and using temporary weight modifications to store previous Gestalts, it is possible to implement two operations that I call *compression* and *uncompression*. Suppose there is an object, O, with a part P. When the system has a Gestalt of O, part of this Gestalt will be a representation of P *as a part*. To focus its attention on P, the system must uncompress the current "reduced description" that encodes P as a part and convert it into a full description that will occupy the whole of the network that is used for encoding the system's current Gestalt. To return from attending to P as a whole to attending to O, the system must compress the Gestalt for P into a reduced description and use additional knowledge (in its temporary weights, long-term weights, or activation of additional units) to reconstruct the rest of the Gestalt.

The processes of compression and uncompression are described in slightly more detail in Hinton (1988). Touretzky (1986) describes a small working system with this flavor. Pollack (1988) describes a method of constructing compressed representations and of learning the operations for compressing and uncompressing them. However, much work remains to be done on efficient ways of compressing and uncompressing representations.

Compression allows the knowledge in the weights of a network to be applied (at different times) to either a whole or a part of that whole. This is important in explaining how people understand sentences like "John was annoyed that Mary found Bill irritating." The very same knowledge about how people interact needs to be applied in understanding the whole sentence and the embedded clause. A system can achieve this by switching from a partially completed Gestalt of the whole sentence to a Gestalt for the embedded clause and then compressing this Gestalt into a reduced description that becomes part of the Gestalt for the whole sentence.

A general mechanism for uncompressing representations would give a neural network the ability to attend to any part of the contents of its consciousness. A general mechanism for compressing representations would allow the neural network to step back from its previous state of consciousness and reflect on it. The previous conscious Gestalt could be compressed into part of a larger Gestalt, thus allowing a network to represent propositions about its own propositional states in the very same hardware that was used for having those states. This view of the neural basis of self-awareness differs significantly from the view that appeals to extra higher-level hardware to support the self-awareness or the monitoring functions of consciousness. Johnson-Laird (1988), among others, has stressed the relationship between recursion and consciousness, and it is therefore interesting that the technical trick that was invoked to explain why we are not aware of the parts of our current Gestalt can also be used to make the representation recursive.

Of course, even if the central hardware can achieve great flexibility by compressing and uncompressing its own representations, it would be sensible to have additional, task-specific hardware to relieve contention for the central hardware. The different pieces of task-specific hardware would have to compete for access to the central hardware, but for routine, overlearned tasks, the central hardware would be unnecessary. This might explain how a person can drive a car without conscious attention.

THE REPRESENTATIONS INVOLVED
IN VISUAL AWARENESS

The idea that attention corresponds to the use of simultaneity to bind property values together is far from new. There is relevant experimental and clinical evidence that corroborates it in the domain of vision. Treisman has greatly enhanced the plausibility of the idea with numerous experiments (Treisman, 1988), Damasio (1989) has argued that it fits neuropsychological data well, and Crick and Koch (1990) have recently suggested that the idea can be related to long range coherent oscillations in the cortex that may trigger temporary changes in connection strengths. But there are some significant differences between the models that these authors seem to be proposing and the ideas presented here (and in Hinton, 1981a, 1981c). The main difference concerns the issue of whether the representations involved in visual awareness are retinotopic. We can contrast two types of model and it seems that Treisman, Damasio, and Crick and Koch are assuming something like the retinotopic model (sketched in Figure 17.1), whereas I am assuming something more like the non-retinotopic model.

A Retinotopic Model of Visual Attention. One model of what happens when a neural network is visually aware of an object is shown in Figure 17.1. There are multiple maps that represent conjunctions of visual properties with retinotopic location, and attending to an object involves simultaneous activation of the same retinotopic location in many different property maps. This model has a major weakness: When the net is aware of the same object in a different retinotopic location, it has a completely different set of activated units. So this model cannot explain what different instances of being aware of the same object have in common. Nor can it explain how we can name a familiar object that occurs in a new retinotopic location.

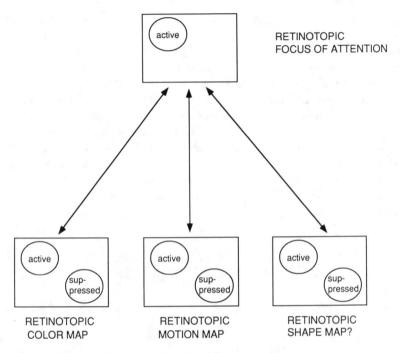

FIG. 17.1.   The representation of the focus of attention interacts with the retinotopic property maps and suppresses all activity in these maps that is not under the spotlight of attention.

A Nonretinotopic Model of Visual Attention.   What we need is a "central" representation in which the location of an object is separated out from its other properties, so that information such as the object's name can be dissociated from the location. Figure 17.2 shows a model of this kind that has a lot in common with the retinotopic model on the input side, but identifies conscious visual awareness with a more central, nonretinotopic representation in which properties such as color are no longer conjoined with their retinotopic location. The idea that attention works via location is still central to the model, but the representation of the selected location is no longer used to alter activity in the retinotopic maps. Instead, the selected location determines which part of each retinotopic property map gains control over the central location-independent representation of that property. The retinotopic maps allow many different objects to be given simultaneous but conjunctive representations. The central representation allows a single object to receive its canonical representation (although this canonical representation may be composed of conjunctive representations of the constituents of the object with their spatial roles within the object). If the same object occurs in a new retinotopic location, its canonical representation will not differ

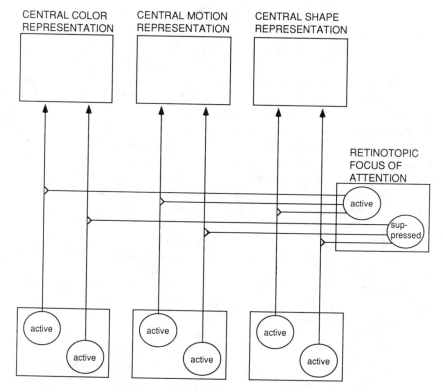

FIG. 17.2.   The representation of the focus of attention does not affect the retinotopic property maps. Instead, it determines which parts of these maps are able to control the central representations. The triangular symbols indicate that activity in the attention system gates the connections between the retinotopic and central representations. The central representations are not maps because they do not need to represent conjunctions of property values with positions.

(apart from the piece that explicitly represents the location). So the name of the object can be associated with the canonical representation.

A Gradual Transition From Space to Time.   The scheme outlined in the previous section assumes a "peripheral" representation that uses retinotopic location to distinguish between properties of different objects and a "central" representation that uses time for the same purpose and is therefore limited to representing one Gestalt at a time. In the peripheral representation, the location of an object determines which units are used to encode it. In the central representation this is no longer true.

Rather than directly recoding the retinotopic representation into a central representation that completely separates retinal location from the other object properties, it may be more efficient to do the recoding in stages. At the bottom level of the hierarchy we use a large number of very small locations so we can only afford a few units per location; we are also restricted to representing just a few simple properties of the object (or object-fragment) in that small location. As we move up the hierarchy we reduce the number of locations by making them larger so we can afford to use more complex and varied properties for the larger object-fragments. We are still restricted to one object-fragment per location because we rely on simultaneity to bind together the various properties within one location, but by using more complex properties we can encode, as a single object-fragment, the multiple simpler object-fragments that occupied several smaller locations. In other words, the shape descriptors of the larger, more complex fragment capture information about spatial layout that is represented at the previous stage by separately representing the positions of the various fragments.

An elaboration of this scheme is to set aside, for each location, several different sets of units so that several qualitatively different objects or object-fragments can be represented at the same time in the same location. Using this three-way conjunction of object-type, object-property-value, and location, the constraint is that only one object of each type can be represented at a time at each location. Mozer (1988) describes an implemented system of this kind, and Zemel, Mozer and Hinton (1990) describe an elaboration of it (called TRAFFIC) that allows much more accurate description and recognition of shapes. For each fragment-type in each location, TRAFFIC uses *activity levels* of units to accurately encode properties such as the retinal position, orientation, and size of the currently present instance of that fragment-type. So location is coded twice: The approximate location determines which set of units is used (so approximate location is used for binding) and the precise location is coded by the activity levels of some of the units in that set. This precise encoding allows the recognition of complex objects (such as a particular face) to make use of detailed metrical information even though the recognition is occurring at a level of the hierarchy at which the locations used for binding purposes are very large.

SUMMARY

For sufficiently complex novel combinations, a neural network cannot afford to set aside conjunctive units in advance, so it is forced to use simultaneity to bind together the various property values of an entity. This leads to a serial bottleneck in which only one Gestalt can be represented at a time, even though this representation can be very rich. The parts of the current Gestalt are represented *as parts,* by using reduced descriptions which conjunctively combine the identity of the part with the role that it plays within the whole Gestalt. This explains why we are not conscious of the parts. By adding the ability to convert Gestalts into reduced descriptions (and vice versa), additional important aspects of consciousness such as self-awareness can be modelled without appealing to separate monitoring hardware.

ACKNOWLEDGEMENTS

I thank George Mandler for encouraging me to take consciousness seriously and for many interesting discussions over the years. Tim Shallice provided many helpful comments on an earlier draft of this chapter.

REFERENCES

Crick, F. & Koch, C. (in press). Towards a neurobiological theory of consciousness. *Seminars in the Neurosciences.*

Damasio, A. R. (1989). The brain binds entities and events by multiregional activation from convergence zones. *Neural Computation, 1,* 123–132.

Hinton, G. E. (1981a). Implementing semantic networks in parallel hardware. In G. E. Hinton & J. A. Anderson (Eds.) *Parallel Models of Associative Memory* (pp. 161–187). Hillsdale, NJ: Lawrence Erlbaum Associates.

Hinton, G. E. (1981b). The role of spatial working memory in shape perception. In *Proceedings of the Third Annual Conference of the Cognitive Science Society,* Berkeley CA.

Hinton, G. E. (1981c). Shape representation in parallel systems. In *Proceedings of the Seventh International Joint Conference on Artificial Intelligence, Vol 2,* Vancouver BC.

Hinton, G. E. (1988). Representing part–whole hierarchies in connectionist networks. In *Proceedings of the Tenth Annual Cognitive Science Society Conference,* 48–54.

Hinton, G. E., McClelland, J. L. & D. E. Rumelhart (1986). Distributed representations. In *Parallel distributed processing: Explorations in the microstructure of cognition.,* (Vol. 1, pp. 77–109). Cambridge, MA: MIT Press.

Johnson-Laird, P. N. (1988). *The computer and the mind.* Cambridge MA: Harvard University Press.

Mozer, M. C. (1988). The perception of multiple objects: A parallel, distributed processing approach. (Report No. 8803). University of California, San Diego: Institute for Cognitive Science.

Pollack, J. (1988). *Recursive auto-associative memory: Devising compositional distributed representations* (Memoranda in computer and cognitive science). Las Cruces, NM: Computing Research Laboratory, New Mexico State University.

Shallice, T. (1978). The dominant action system: An information-processing approach to consciousness. In K. S. Pope & J. L. Singer (Eds.), *The stream of consciousness: Scientiic investigations into the flow of human experience* (pp. 117–157). New York: Plenum Press.

Shallice, T. (1988). *From Neuropsychology to Mental Structure.* Cambridge: Cambridge University Press.

Touretzky, D. S. (1986). BoltzCONS: Reconciling connectionism with the recursive nature of stacks and trees. In *Proceedings of the Eighth Annual Cognitive Science Society Conference.* Cognitive Science Society.

Treisman, A. (1988). Features and objects: The fourteenth Bartlett Memorial Lecture. *Quarterly Journal of Experimental Psychology, 40A(2),* 201–237.

Warrington, E. K. & Shallice, T. (1979). Semantic access dyslexia. *Brain, 102,* 43–63.

Zemel, R. S., Mozer, M. C. & Hinton, G. E. (1990). TRAFFIC: Recognizing objects using hierarchical reference frame transformations. In D. S. Touretzky (Ed.), *Advances in neural information processing systems* (pp. 266–273). San Mateo, CA: Morgan Kaufmann Publishers.

18 Understanding Understanding

David E. Rumelhart
University of California at San Diego

Rumelhart presents a detailed account of a schematic-theoretical model of reading. He cites several studies that have been conducted by himself and others at the Center for Human Information Processing in the processing of stories. His analogy of a reader being like a detective in search of a set of consistent clues to be reconstructed in a logical manner is particularly helpful in understanding some properties of the nature of understanding.

What is understanding? How do we make sense out of what we read or are told? I believe that over the past several years a substantial consensus has arisen in the field of cognitive science about the broad outlines of this process (Fillmore, 1975; Minsky, 1975; Rumelhart, 1977; Rumelhart & Ortony, 1977; Schank & Abelson, 1977). In this paper I wish to sketch the basic features of those outlines and to show how this sketch can be given some reality by a careful analysis of the interpretations people actually make of stories and story fragments.

Consider the following brief fragment of a story.

Mary heard the ice cream truck coming down the street. She remembered her birthday money and rushed into the house.

Upon hearing just these few words most readers already have a rather complete interpretation of the events in the story. Presumably Mary is a little girl who wants to buy some ice cream from the ice cream vendor and runs into the house to get her money. Of course, it doesn't *say* this in the story, there are other possibilities. Mary could be afraid that the ice cream vendor might *steal* her birthday money. Still, most readers find the first interpretation most plausible and retain it unless later information contradicts it.

Consider, in contrast, the following story fragment.

Mary heard the bus coming down the street. She remembered her birthday money and rushed into the house.

Upon hearing a fragment such as this, most people get a rather different notion of what the story might be about. The story fragment is less coherent. For most, Mary is older. Rather than the 4 to 8 year old of the previous paragraph, Mary is now at least a teenager and possibly even an adult. Moreover, the quantity of money is somewhat greater. Almost surely the money is not needed to buy passage on the bus itself—somehow bus fare is too mundane for birthday money.

Consider still another variation on this same story.

Mary heard the ice cream truck coming down the street. She remembered her gun and rushed into the house.

Here we get a rather different interpretation again. Is Mary going to rob the ice cream vendor? Does she fear for her life? Note how the modification of a single word or phrase signals an entirely different interpretation. What sort of process could account for such radical differences? Surely, it cannot be a process which takes word meanings and parlays them into sentence meanings and then into text meanings.

The purpose of this paper is to explore the processes involved in these examples, to give a general account of these processes, and to describe some experiments I have been doing in an attempt to understand them more fully.

To begin, let me lay out a general theoretical account of the comprehension process as I understand it and then turn to some data which help explicate this process.

A Schema-Theoretic Model of Understanding

In my attempts to account for these phenomena I have found it useful to appeal to the notion of *schemata*. Before proceeding with a discussion of comprehension itself, it might be useful to explicate my notion of schemata.

A schema theory is basically a theory about knowledge—a theory about how knowledge is represented and about how that representation facilitates the use of the knowledge in particular ways. According to schema theories all knowledge is packaged into units. These units are the schemata. Embedded in these packets of knowledge, in addition to the knowledge itself, is information about how this knowledge is to be used.

A schema, then, is a data structure for representing the generic concepts stored in memory. There are schemata representing our knowledge about all concepts: underlying objects, situations, events, sequences of events, actions, and sequences of actions. As part of its specification, schema contains the network of interrelations believed to normally hold among the constituents of the concept of question. A schema theory embodies a *prototype* theory of meaning. That is, inasmuch as a schema underlying a concept stored in memory corresponds to the meaning of that concept, meanings are encoded in terms of the typical or normal situations or events which instantiate that concept.

Perhaps the central function of schemata is in the construction of an interpretation of an event, object, or situation—in the process of comprehension. In all of this, it is useful to think of a schema as a kind of informal, private, unarticulated theory about the nature of the events, objects, or situations we face. The total set of schemata we have available for interpreting our world in a sense constitutes our private theory of the nature of reality. The total set of schemata instantiated at a particular moment in time constitutes our internal model of the situation we face at that moment in time or in the case of reading a text, a model of the situation depicted by the text.

Thus, just as the activity surrounding a theory is often focused on the evaluation of the theory and the comparison of the theory with observations we have made, so it is that the primary activity associated with a schema is the determination whether it gives an adequate account for some aspects of our current situation. Just as the determination that a particular theory accounts for some observed results involves the determination of the parameters of the theory, so the determination that a particular configuration of schemata accounts for the data presently available to our senses requires the determination of the values of the variables of the schemata. If a promising schema fails to account for some aspect of a situation, one has the options of accepting the schema as adequate in spite of its flawed account or of rejecting the schema as inadequate and looking for another possibility. Therefore, the fundamental processes of comprehension are taken to be analogous with hypothesis testing, evaluation of goodness of fit, and parameter estimation. Thus, a reader of a text is presumably constantly evaluating hypotheses about the most plausible interpretation of the text. Readers are said to have understood the text when they are able to find a configuration of hypotheses (schemata) which offer a coherent account for the various aspects of the text. To the degree that a particular reader fails to find such a configuration, the text will appear disjointed and incomprehensible.

Schemata are like theories in another important respect. Once they are moderately successful, theories become a source of predictions about unobserved events. Not all experiments are carried out. Not all possible observations are made. Instead, we use our theories to make inferences with some confidence about these unobserved events. So it is with schemata. We need not observe all aspects of a situation before we are willing to assume that some particular configuration of schemata offers a satisfactory account for that situation. Once we have accepted a configuration of schemata, the schemata themselves provide a richness which goes far beyond our observations. Upon deciding that we have seen an automobile, we assume that it has an engine, headlights, and all of the standard characteristics of an automobile. We do this without the slightest hesitation. We have complete confidence in our theory. This allows our interpretations to far outstrip our observations. In fact, once we have determined that a particular schema accounts for some event we may not be able to determine which aspects of our beliefs are based on direct information and which are merely consequences of our interpretation.

On Getting Some Evidence

I have been investigating story comprehension for several years and have developed a story grammar (Rumelhart, 1975) which has proven useful in the analysis of story comprehension and recall. More recently (Rumelhart, 1977), I have recast that original work in the general framework described and have developed a model capable of accounting for the kinds of summaries people give to very simple stories. Although this general approach to story understanding and story memory has proven popular, I have been dissatisfied with the work on two accounts:

1. Although much of the work (including my own) has focused on the process of story understanding, most of the experiments employed postcomprehension measures. Usually the measures have employed story recall and occasionally they have employed summarization. I have wished increasingly for truly "on-line" measures of comprehension.
2. The story grammar approach has tended to focus on abstract features of story comprehension. By its nature, the story schemata I (and most others) have studied offer a very general account of the structure readers see in stories. This generality is a plus in the sense that the schemata are very generally used, but they are a minus in the sense that they ignore the vast amount of other information which subjects can and do bring to bear in understanding stories.

In the series of studies described in this paper, I set out to study this process of hypothesis generation and evaluation during the process of comprehension. Perhaps the simplest way to determine what people are thinking while they are understanding is to ask them.

The basic experimental paradigm involved presenting subjects a series of stories a sentence at a time and, after each sentence, asking them WHO they thought the characters under discussion were, WHAT they felt was going on in the story, WHY the characters behaved as they did, WHEN they think the event described took place, and WHERE they think the story is set. A series of ten pairs of stories and/or story fragments were prepared. Most of the stories were based on initial segments of actual short stories written by well-known authors. The segments were edited slightly so that an alternate version of each story could be created through the modification of one or two words or phrases. The two story versions were designed, like the example story fragments at the beginning of this paper, so that the modification led to a rather different interpretation of the whole story. Each subject read one version of each one of the ten different stories. In order to assess the effects on comprehension of the line at a time interpretation procedure, some subjects were presented the stories two lines at a time, some were presented four lines at a time, and still others were presented the whole story at one time.

Two results emerged immediately from this procedure:

1. The process is very natural. Subjects report that it is very easy to describe the hypotheses that come to mind as they read. Unlike problem solving where the collecting of protocols seems to interfere with the process, our evidence indicates that, if anything, it actually improves comprehension.
2. Subjects show a remarkable degree of agreement. With just three or four subjects the broad outlines of the sorts of results generally obtained become clear.

Perhaps the best way to illustrate the procedure and the kinds of results obtained is by example. Read the following sentence which is the first line from one of my stories.

I was brought into a large white room and my eyes began to blink because the bright light hurt them.

Consider this sentence and what scene comes to mind. There was a good deal of agreement among my subjects. Almost without fail, people belived that this was either an INTERROGATION situation in which the protagonist is being held prisoner, or it is a HOSPITAL scene in which the protagonist is a patient. It is interesting that when asked (after they had finished the story) why they thought it was whatever they thought, almost all reported it was the *bright lights* or the *large white room* which had tipped them off. In point of fact, further experimentation seems to indicate that it was the *was brought* which was the key, putting the protagonist in a passive situation. The large white room and bright lights simply further specify the basically passive situation aroused by the particular construction.

The OIL CRISIS Story

As a second example, consider the following brief passage used in my experiment.

> Business had been slow since the oil crisis. Nobody seemed to want anything really elegant anymore. Suddenly the door opened and a well-dressed man entered the showroom floor. John put on his friendliest and most sincere expression and walked toward the man.

Although merely a fragment, my subjects generated a rather clear interpretation of this story. Apparently, John is a car salesperson fallen on hard times. He probably sells rather large, elegant cars. Suddenly a good prospect enters the showroom where John works. John wants to make a sale and to do that he must make a good impression on the man. Therefore he tries to appear friendly and sincere. He wants to talk to the man to deliver his sales pitch, so he makes his way over to the man. Presumably, had the story continued John would have made the sales pitch and, if all went well, sold the man a car.

How, according to the theory described, do people arrive at such an interpretation? Clearly, people do not arrive at it all at once. As the sentences are read, schemata are activated, evaluated, and refined or discarded. When people are asked to describe their various hypotheses as they read through the story, a remarkably consistent pattern of hypothesis generation and evaluation emerges. The first sentence is usually interpreted to mean that business is slow because of the oil crisis. Thus, people are led to see the story is about a suffering business which is somehow dependent on oil. Frequent hypotheses involve either the selling of cars or of gasoline. A few interpret the sentence as being about the economy in general. The second sentence, about people not wanting elegant things anymore, leads people with the gas station hypothesis into a quandary. Elegance just doesn't fit with gas stations. The gas station hypothesis is weakened, but not always rejected. On the other hand, people with hypotheses about the general economy or about cars have no trouble incorporating this sentence into their emerging interpretation. In the former case, they conclude it means that people don't buy luxury items and, in the latter, they assume it means that people don't buy large, elegant cars much anymore. The third sentence clinches the car interpretation for nearly all readers. They are already looking for a business interpretation—that probably means a SELLING interpretation—and when a *well-dressed man* enters the door he is immediately labeled as someone with MONEY—a prospective BUYER. The phrase *showroom floor* clearly invalidates the gas station interpretation and strongly implicates automobiles which are often sold from a showroom. Moreover, the occurrence of a specific event doesn't fit at all well with the view that the passage is a general discussion of the state of the economy. Finally, with the introduction of John, we have an ideal candidate for the SELLER. John's actions are clearly those stereotypic of a salesperson. John wants to make a sale and his "putting on" is clearly an attempt on his part to "make a good impression." His movement toward the man fits nicely into this interpretation. If he is a salesperson, he must make contact with the customer and deliver the stereotypic "pitch."

Qualitatively, this account fits well with the general theoretical approach I have been outlining. The process of comprehension is very much like the process of constructing a theory, testing it against the data currently available, and as more data becomes available, specifying the theory further—i.e., refining the default values (as perhaps was the case when those holding the "car hypothesis" from the beginning encountered the sentence about nobody wanting anything elegant anymore). If the account becomes sufficiently strained, it is given up and a new one constructed or, alternatively, if a new theory presents itself which obviously gives a more cogent account, the old one can be dropped and the new one accepted.

But where do these theories come from? These theories are, of course, schemata. Presumably, through experience we have built up a vast repertoire of such schemata. We have schemata for car salespersonnel, the kinds of motives they have, and the kinds of techniques they employ. We have schemata for the "oil crisis" and what kinds of effects it has on what kinds of businesses. We have schemata about business people, the kinds of motives they have, and the kinds of responses they make to these motives. The knowledge embedded in these schemata forms the framework for our theories. It is some configuration of these schemata which ultimately forms the basis for our understanding.

But how does a relevant schema suggest itself? Presumably, it is the bottom-up observation that a certain concept has been referenced that leads to the suggestion of the initial hypotheses. The notion that business was slow suggests a schema about business and the economy. Since the slowness was dated from the occurrence of the oil crisis, it is a natural inference that the oil crisis was the *cause* of the slowness. Thus, a BUSINESS schema is activated. The particular TYPE of business is presumably a variable which must be filled. The information about the oil crisis suggests that it may be an oil-related business. Thus, readers are led to restrict the TYPE variable of the BUSINESS schema to oil-related businesses.

At this point, after the bottom-up activation of the high level BUSINESS schema has occurred, this schema would generate a top-down activation of the various possible oil related businesses. Prime candidates for these are, of course, automobile related businesses. Of these, selling gasoline and automobiles are the most salient.

When the second sentence is encountered, an attempt is made to fit it into the schemata currently considered most promising. As discussed, this information could serve to further restrict the TYPE variable in the automobile BUSINESS schema, but doesn't fit well with the gasoline business schema.

The BUSINESS schema presumably has a reference to the BUY or SELL schema. Once activated, these schemata search for potential variable bindings. In the case of the automobile business, the MERCHANDISE variable is bound to be an automobile. The second sentence suggests an elegant automobile. When the third sentence is encountered, the reader has not yet found a candidate for BUYER or SELLER. The sentence about a well-dressed man immediately suggests a potential BUYER. The phrase "showroom floor" offers additional bottom-up support for the automobile hypothesis. In fact, it is a strong enough clue itself that it can suggest automobile sales to a reader who currently considers the alternative schema more likely. We thus have a BUYER and some MERCHANDISE. The well-dressed quality of the BUYER is consistent with our view that the MERCHANDISE is elegant and, therefore, expensive (being well-dressed suggests MONEY). We need only a SELLER—i.e., an automobile salesperson. Readers probably already bring a relatively complete characterization of the "default value" for a car salesperson. We need but little additional information to generate a rather detailed description of goals and motives.

It is, in general, a difficult matter to analyze freeform responses of the sort obtained in this experiment. I have, however, devised a data representation scheme which allows the tracking of a subject's hypotheses through a story. The basic idea is illustrated in Figure 1. At any point in time a subject's hypothesis state can be characterized as a region in a multidimensional hypothesis space in which one dimension is time (or place in the story) and the other dimensions represent the subject's momentary beliefs about WHO the characters are, WHAT is going on in the story, and WHERE the story is set. Just two dimensions, WHERE and WHO, are illustrated in the figure. Each point in the space represents a possible hypothesis at some point in time. A particular subject's sequence of hypotheses can be represented as a path passing through the space. We can imagine that at particularly critical times during the reading of the story the path will turn sharply in several dimensions. At the start, we might imagine that different subjects would occupy a fairly wide region of the space. By the end, all of the paths for the different subjects should have converged on one or two points in the space. The dimensions, other than the dimension of time, are purely

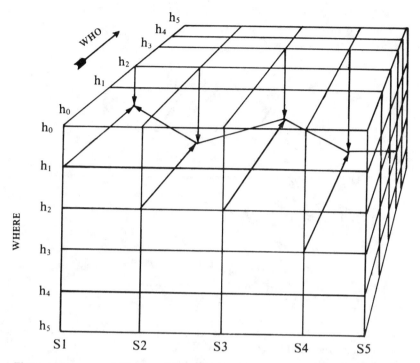

Figure 1. A representation of a subject's shifting hypotheses while reading a story. One dimension represents the sequence of sentences in the story. The other two dimensions represent a subject's hypotheses with respect to WHO the characters are and WHERE the action is taking place. The vector passing through the space represents a possible sequence of hypotheses.

nominal and subjects often hold several hypotheses at once (i.e., they occupy not a point, but a region of the space). Nevertheless, this general representation proves useful in charting subjects' changing hypotheses.

I will illustrate the general form of analysis by looking at some of the results from the "Oil Crisis" story. In order to analyze the data, the responses for each question were categorized and for each subject it was recorded which of the responses was given. For example, there were five different categories of answers to WHERE the story took place. The five categories were:

1. *Indefinite*—when subjects said they had no clear idea.
2. *Gas station*—when subjects believed the action was occurring at a gas station.
3. *Showroom*—when subjects believed the action took place in an automobile showroom.
4. *Luxury store*—when subjects believed the action took place in a luxury store such as a jewelry store or a fancy furniture or clothing store.
5. *Nation*—when subjects believed the story was a general statement about the national economy.

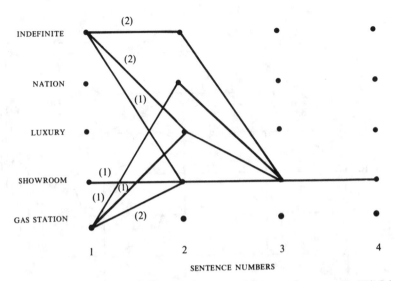

Figure 2. Set of paths through the hypothesis space for the question WHERE the "Oil Crisis" story was taking place.

Figure 2 illustrates the patterns of responses observed from the ten subjects who read this version of the story. Each line on the graph represents a pattern of responses. The number on the lines represents the number of subjects showing that pattern. We can see that five subjects had no clear idea where the events were taking place after the first sentence. One subject thought from the start that it was in an automobile showroom. After the first sentence, four subjects thought the story was taking place in a gas station. We can see that after the second sentence four people thought it was an automobile showroom, three thought it was a luxury store, two were still indefinite, and one thought it was a general discussion of a national economy.

There is not space to illustrate the whole pattern of results for this story, so now I turn to discussion of a second story which shows a more dramatic pattern of results.

The DEAR LITTLE THING Story

Consider the following story used in my experiment.

1. Dear little thing.
2. It was nice to feel it again.
3. She had taken it out of its box that afternoon, given it a good brush, and rubbed life back into its dim little eyes.
4. Little rogue! Yes, she really felt that way about it.
5. She put it on.

6. Little rogue, biting its tail just by her left ear.
7. When she breathed, something gentle seemed to move on her bosom.
8. The day was cool and she was glad she had decided on her little fur.

The results for this story are particularly interesting. As people read the story they form clear impressions of certain aspects of the story, but none of them consider the possibility that the story might be about a fur until the fifth line of the story, and for some, this is not clear until the last line of the story. From the beginning, however, many readers have an impression that the speaker in the story is a woman. Of the twenty people to read the first line of the story, seven mentioned that they thought that it was a woman speaking. In none of my other stories did people spontaneously assign a sex to the speaker after only reading the first sentence. Apparently a number of the readers interpret the pattern of speech here to be typically feminine. This is illustrative of the subtlety of the kinds of clues readers pick up on and that authors count on.

Perhaps the most interesting response was that which subjects made to the WHAT questions. Here we get the clearest picture of their overall assessment of what the story is about. There were six categories of responses given by our subjects. These were:

1. *Clothing*—they thought the woman was talking about a hat or some jewelry.
2. *Fur*—they thought the woman was talking about a fur.
3. *Letter*—they thought someone was writing a letter.
4. *Pet*—they thought the story was about a pet.
5. *Stimulation*—they thought the story was about sexual stimulation.
6. *Toy*—they thought the story was about a stuffed animal or doll.

Figure 3 shows the pattern of hypotheses held by the ten people who read this version of the story. After the opening line, "Dear little thing," people were about evenly split between the possibility that it was about a pet or letter writing. The second line, "It was nice to feel it again," discouraged all but one of the letter writing hypotheses. Some of these decided that the story was about a toy or stuffed animal. Others assumed it was about sexual stimulation or had no clear idea. The third line moved almost everyone who didn't think it was a pet to the view it was a toy. The fourth line offered no new information and people held onto their previous hypotheses. The fifth line, "She put it on," was difficult to assimilate with any of the hypotheses and, as is evident from the figure, nearly everyone switched to the view that it was either a piece of clothing or jewelry or that it was a fur piece. The seventh line strengthened the FUR hypothesis and the eighth line clinched it for everyone.

The figure clearly shows the critical nature of the fifth sentence. We can see subjects, on the basis of such bottom-up information as the use of the word *dear*, determine that it might be a letter or a diminutive reference to a pet. Then, once finding a satisfactory hypothesis, subjects

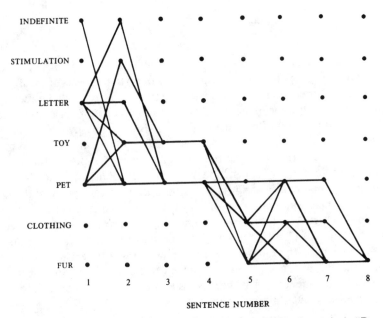

Figure 3. Set of paths through the hypothesis space for the question of WHAT in the "Dear Little Thing" story.

maintain and refine it until disconfirming information is made available. When disconfirmation occurs, subjects search out a new workable hypothesis.

Clearly, in this case, my subjects are behaving according to the hypothesis evaluation mode that I have suggested. But is this the normal way of processing? Doesn't the procedure force them to respond in this way? These are serious questions. Indeed, I believe there is an effect of the procedure. However, I believe it is better categorized as making subjects read more carefully than at modifying the basic procedure. One bit of evidence for this view is that over all of the stories, subjects who interpreted the stories a line at a time more often agreed with one another (and with the experimenters) about the interpretation of the story than subjects who gave an interpretation only after having read the whole story. In addition, a second experiment was carried out to try to get an alternative measure of on-line processing. In this experiment, the subjects were not asked to make any interpretations of the story. Rather, they were presented the story one word at a time and asked to press a button after they read each word to get the next word. The time to read each word was recorded. We can then compare different versions of the same story, one in which we know from the interpretation experiments requires a rather dramatic shift in hypotheses, and another which requires no such shift or a shift at a different place. The "Dear Little Thing" story offers an ideal example. The alternative version of this story differed in three words. Sentence 5 was "She put it down" rather than "She put it on." Sentence 6 ended "by her left ankle" rather than "by her left ear," and sentence 8 ended "take her pet along" rather than "take her fur along." Thus, for the FUR version, subjects probably had to shift hypotheses after line 5. For the PET version, subjects probably already had the correct hypothesis by line 5. Thus, the two stories were identical for the first 49 words and differed in only 3 of the final 38 words.

Since we know from the interpretation experiment that a good deal of reevaluation occurs in the FUR form of the story after line 5 and that a large number of subjects have the PET hypothesis well before line 5, it is reasonable that people would read the last 38 words of the story more slowly in the FUR version. Table 1 shows the average reading time per word for the first 49 and last 38 words for the two versions of the story. The expected difference is apparent in the table. The average reading time for the first half of the story is about the same for the two groups. Those with the FUR version were about 200 milliseconds slower over the last half of the story. Unfortunately, the magnitudes in the table are probably somewhat misleading. There is an average difference of some 20 milliseconds between the groups for the first half of the story. In fact, this average is a mixture of some early slow responses and some later fast responses for the PET group. A better estimate for the difference between the two groups' base line reading speed is 125 milliseconds per word. Thus, the apparent 200 milliseconds per word differences evident in the table is probably closer to a 75 millisecond difference per word. Nevertheless, even with this conservative estimate of the difference between the base reading rate of the two groups, the 75 millisecond per word figure over the 38 words amounts to an average difference of almost 3 seconds longer for the FUR group. Thus, in spite of some difficulties with the data here, it would appear that we have been able to see, in slower reading times, the same hypothesis reevaluation our subjects in the interpretation experiment told us about.

TABLE 1

Mean Reading Time Per Word in Milliseconds

Story Version	First 49 Words	Last 38 Words
FUR	886	1011
PET	864	801

A closer look at the data appears to confirm this conclusion. Much of this effect is already evident on the reading of the last word of line 5. Figure 4 shows the reading times for each word in the line. The most obvious characteristic of these curves is the increased reaction time for the last word of the sentence for both versions of the story. This upswing on the last word of a sentence is normal in all experiments of this sort. It appears to represent some sort of "consolidation" phase of the reading process. More important to the present discussion, however, is the difference in response time between those subjects who heard the word "on" and those who heard the word "down" as the last word of the sentence. Upon hearing *on* the PET and TOY hypotheses are disconfirmed and subjects are forced to begin to reevaluate their hypotheses. This reevaluation apparently takes time. Indeed, as Figure

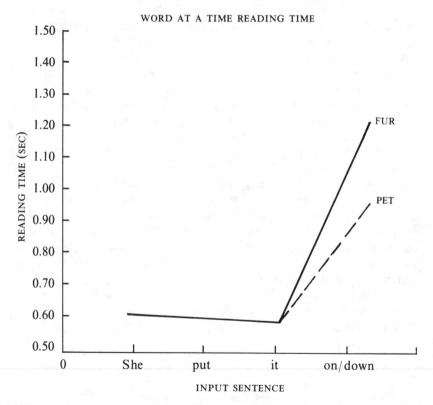

Figure 4. Adjusted word by word reading times for the two versions of line 5 of the "Dear Little Thing" story. Due to overall differences in the reading rates of the two groups, the times for the FUR group were adjusted downward by subtracting 125 msec for each point. This value was chosen so that the two groups showed about the same level of performance over the three words before the two stories diverge.

5 indicates, many of the subjects are apparently still formulating more hypotheses through the following sentence. Notice the time required by the subjects with the FUR version compared with those with the PET version for the word *tail*. Presumably those with the PET version have already hit upon the pet hypothesis and thus the word *tail* fits nicely into their existing interpretation. Many of those in the FUR version have probably chosen the hypothesis that the story is about a piece of clothing or jewelry and thus are not able to integrate "tail" into their existing interpretation—similarly, for the last word of the sentence. The subjects with the PET version have little or no trouble with the pet being near the woman's ankle. The FUR subjects find it difficult to reconcile something with a tail being near the woman's ear.

   Overall, in spite of the unfortunate baseline differences between the two groups, the reading time results do appear to confirm the view

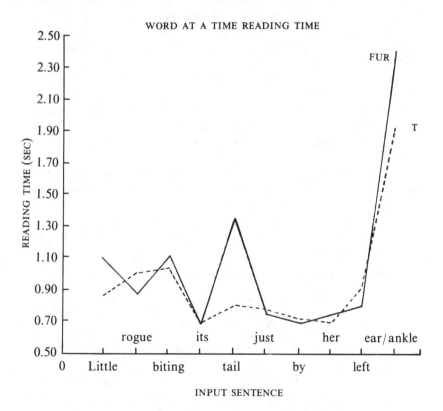

Figure 5. Adjusted word by word reading times for the two versions of line 6 of the "Dear Little Thing" story. Again the times for the PET data represent raw data while the FUR curve has been adjusted downward by 125 msec to adjust for overall differences in reading time between the two groups which was evident before the stories diverged.

that a very different method of gaining access to on-line processing leads to a generally congruent pattern of results.

General Comments

I have tried, in this section, to present a flavor of the results I have been collecting in the context of story comprehension. Due to limitations of space I have been unable to present a complete analysis of all of my data. Nevertheless, these examples should serve to illustrate the major points. When asked to generate interpretations of stories while reading through a story line-by-line, subjects generate hypotheses about the possible contents of the story and evaluate them against the sentences as they read them. If they find the new information confirmatory they maintain and further elaborate their hypotheses. If they find the new information disconfirmatory they eliminate the hypothesis and construct another consistent with the input data. This process seems to involve both top-down and bottom-up processes. Certain words and phrases appear to suggest, from the bottom-up, certain frameworks of interpretation such as the INTERROGATION framework in the first example. Once a particular interpretation has received a moderate degree of support, it can come to guide the processing and interpretation of future inputs. Subjects find it natural to go beyond the specifics of what the input sentences actually say. Their interpretations contain material about aspects of the situation which are totally unaddressed in the input text.

To what degree is this a natural process, as the schema theory sketched in the first section suggests, and to what degree does the procedure force the subjects to behave as the theory suggests they would? This is a difficult question for this approach. It is extraordinarily difficult to get data which bear on this issue. Three approaches have been tried:

1. I have collected word-by-word reading times for subjects not instructed to generate interpretations and have looked for correlations between points in the story where we believe subjects to be evaluating new hypotheses and those where we observe elevated response times. By and large, as the examples presented earlier illustrate, these two measures correlate.
2. I have collected interpretations of subjects after they read the whole story and compared them with those of subjects who read the stories a line at a time. The results showed that subjects who interpreted a line at a time nearly always generated the same interpretations as those who gave us an after-the-fact interpretation. The only discernable difference was that those who gave an interpretation only at the end showed somewhat more variability in their interpretations. It appears that this results from more careless reading on the part of the subjects offering an interpretation only at the end.
3. I have asked a few subjects for retrospective analyses of the processes they went through while reading the stories immediately after reading the stories. Although such subjects mention fewer hypothesis changes than those giving

on-line interpretations, the overall structure of their reports seems to parallel those of the on-line subjects.

None of these methods is really totally convincing in and of itself. Nevertheless, the combination of the fact that the response times seem to follow the hypothesis interpretations, the fact that the interpretation paradigm doesn't seem to affect the final interpretations subjects generate, and the fact that in informal observations subjects' retrospective reports seem very similar to the line-at-a-time results points strongly to the view that the general pattern of hypothesis generation observed in our experiments is present in normal reading.

On Understanding and Misunderstanding

Before concluding, it is useful to consider the application of this general theory to the notion of misunderstanding. On the present account, understanding is the process of finding a configuration of schemata which offers an adequate account of a passage or situation. The analysis given illustrates how such a process is supposed to operate. Clues from the story suggest possible instantiations of schemata which are then evaluated against the successive sentences of the story until finally a consistent interpretation is discovered. Sometimes, a reader fails to correctly understand a passage. There are at least three reasons implicit in schema theory as to why this might occur.

1. Readers may not have the appropriate schemata. In this case they simply cannot understand the concept being communicated.
2. Readers may have the appropriate schemata, but the clues provided by the author may be insufficient to suggest them. Here again readers will not understand the text but, with appropriate additional clues may come to understand.
3. Readers may find a consistent interpretation of the text, but may not find the one intended by the author. In this case, readers will understand the text, but will misunderstand the author.

There are many examples of these three phenomena in the literature. Perhaps the most interesting set of studies along these lines were carried out by Bransford and Johnson (1973). They studied the comprehension of texts in which subjects lacked the appropriate schemata, ones in which the schemata were potentially available, but there were not sufficient clues to suggest the correct ones as well as ones in which subjects were led to choose a wrong interpretation. Consider the following paragraph used in one of their studies.

The procedure is actually quite simple. First you arrange things into different groups. Of course, one pile may be sufficient depending on how much there is to do. If you have to go somewhere else due to lack of facilities that is the next step, otherwise you are pretty well set. It is important not to overdo things. That is, it is better to do too few things at once than too many. In the short run this may not seem important but complications can easily arise. A mistake can be expensive as well. At first the whole procedure will seem complicated. Soon, however, it will become just another facet of life. It is difficult to foresee any end to the necessity for this task in the immediate future, but then one can never tell. After the procedure is completed one arranges the materials into different groups again. Then they can be put into their appropriate places. Eventually they will be used once more and the whole cycle will then have to be repeated. However, that is part of life. [p. 400]

Most readers find this passage, as written, extremely difficult to understand. However, once they are told that it is about washing clothes, they are able to bring their clothes-washing schema to the fore and make sense out of the story. The difficulty with this passage is not that readers don't have the appropriate schemata; rather, it stems from the fact that the clues in the story never seem to *suggest* the appropriate schemata in the first place. The bottom-up information is inadequate to initiate the comprehension process appropriately. Once the appropriate schemata are suggested, most people have no trouble understanding the text.

Although most readers simply find the passage incomprehensible, some find alternative schemata to account for it and thus render it comprehensible. Perhaps the most interesting interpretation I have collected was from a Washington bureaucrat who had no difficulty with the passage. He was able to interpret the passage as a clear description of his job. He was, in fact, surprised to find that it was supposed to be about "washing clothes" and not about "pushing papers." Here we have an example of the third kind of comprehension failure, "understanding the story but misunderstanding the author."

Conclusion

At this point, it might be useful to put this comprehension theory in the context of a theory of communication. I find it useful to think of the general view of comprehension put forth here as suggesting that the problem facing a comprehender is analogous to the problem that a detective faces when trying to solve a crime. In both cases there is a set of clues. The listeners' or readers' job is to find a consistent interpretation of these clues. In so doing, listeners use their own prior experiences and knowledge of the speaker to create a most plausible possibility. Just as the meaning of a particular clue that a detective might find cannot be determined except in relation to the way it fits into the whole situation so, too, the meaning of a particular word, phrase, or even sentence cannot be interpreted except in relation to the way it fits into the whole of the story. Similarly, speakers or writers are to leave trails of clues which, in the opinion of the speakers, will lead readers to make the inferences the speakers wish to communicate. Thus, speakers must use their knowledge of the listener, or at least of the cultural expectations of the listener, to create the set of clues which most reliably and economically leads the listener to the desired hypotheses.

Thus, authors of short stories do not need to spell out every detail. Instead, they provide the reader with subtle clues which they can expect the reader will pick up on. Thus, in the example of the INTERROGATION scene, by subtle use of the passive and the mention of bright lights and a white room, the author has generated in the reader a full-blown image of an entire INTERROGATION scene. The remainder of the story can then play off of these subtle clues and needn't waste time or words setting the scene. Similarly, in the "Dear Little Thing" story, in a single phrase the author has suggested to many that a woman is speaking. I suspect these stories are not at all unusual and that in general all of the inferences we wish to communicate never can be spelled out, and that we must always depend on our ability to draw forth the appropriate schemata in the listener through a large variety of clues.

Finally, let me comment on the direction I wish to push the sort of work I have discussed here. For the past several years, I have been attempting to create a computer simulation system capable of comprehending language according to the kinds of principles just described. I have taken as an empirical goal the attempt to create a program capable of mimicking the experimental results from the interpretation experiments. Obviously, a detailed account of the comprehension process requires a detailed description of the schemata readers have available, as well as an account of the conditions under which certain of these schemata are activated. There is a startling amount of knowledge brought to bear on even the simplest story comprehension task. Nevertheless, I believe that data of the sort I have described will provide a useful data base against which to evaluate models of comprehension.

19 What Every Cognitive Psychologist Should Know about the Mind of a Child

Annette Karmiloff-Smith
MRC Cognitive Development Unit, London

> "Dear Annette,
> in the enclosed paper, you will see where I am now, including the notion
> (which you will like) that consciousness provides the occasion (process?)
> where previously unrelated mental contents can be brought into contact
> and juxtaposition."
> —George Mandler, Personal letter, July 6, 1987.

For a number of years, I have argued that the child is a spontaneous theoretician, that is, the way in which children go about discovering how the world functions (the physical, social, and linguistic worlds) is by building theories, not by simply observing facts (Karmiloff-Smith, 1975, 1979a, 1984; Karmiloff-Smith & Inhelder, 1974/75; see, also, Brown, 1986; Carey, 1985; Gelman & Brown, 1985; Gilliéron, 1982; Gopnik, 1982; Keil, 1988; Leslie, 1988). And children go about their spontaneous discovery task by behaving like the typical scientist. Kuhn (1977) was right in his view that only on the very rare occasions when scientists must actually choose between competing theories do they reason like philosophers or logicians! Both for the child and the adult researcher, scientific progress does not stem from the use of logical criteria on the basis of rational induction from observations. Indeed, as Lakatos (1977) has pointed out, the still widely held opinion that science progresses by repeated overthrow of theories on the basis of observational data is based on two false assumptions: (a) that there is a natural psychological boundary between the theoretical and the observational, and (b) that if a proposition satisfies the psychological criterion of being factual or observational, then it is true. Likewise Quine has argued that the data/theory-confirmation relation is a property of the total system of beliefs in which it is embedded (Quine, 1953).

The tricky psychological boundary between data and theory is now well established. Indeed, so-called observational data are always theory-laden. But here I wish to go further and suggest that fruitful insights about human discovery processes can be drawn from studying the *process* of spontaneous scientific discovery in the child. Before proceeding, let me stress the importance of process rather than content. Most comparisons between child and scientist have hitherto taken a diachronic perspective, emphasizing content and structural change within the history of a particular idea in science compared to children's changing verbal explanations of similar phenomena. Typical examples of this approach can be found in the work of Piaget, Inhelder, and Szeminska (1960) in their study of topological and Euclidean concepts in the history of geometry, as well as the recent work on the history of physics as it relates to ontogenetic stages in child development (Piaget & Garcia, 1983; Garcia, 1987). This does not imply that ontogenesis is a recapitulation of phylogenesis, of course. What Garcia argues is that there are commonalities underlying both individual development and the history of science, and that there are two ways of doing history of science: (a) taking history as the memory of science, which is more or less the Kuhnian method; and (b) taking history as the epistemological laboratory of science, which is the Piagetian school's method, but the focus is on content rather than on process.

My own approach is more synchronic in perspective and concentrates on the processes underlying scientific change in general rather than on the content of any particular concept. I focus on the role of theory building, heuristics, and data in the child's progressive discovery of how the physical world functions. Although the examples are taken from children's developing knowledge of particular aspects of physics, these must be seen as merely illustrative of processes underlying conceptual change in general. Thus, the content of the concepts that I have studied is to some extent irrelevant.

A number of parallels can be drawn between child development and discussions to be found in Kuhn's work (Kuhn, 1962, 1977), but it is important to stress at least one essential difference. Although plunged from the start into a social context, the child is also an individual cognitive organism and much of his or her theory building is endogenously provoked rather than socially mediated. Thus, whilst I am sympathetic to a number of Kuhn's ideas, mine will not link up directly with Kuhn's view of theory building as essentially the result of the social context of a scientific group or community. Nonetheless, the community's commitment to theory and resistance to change in the face of potentially glaring empirical refutation indeed parallel the tenacity of children's theories.

Much of philosophy of science is based on a reconstruction from rationalized verbal reports, and not from actual scientific practice. The opposite holds when working with children, who often have difficulty describing in words what they are doing. This has the advantage of forcing the researcher into devising subtle, non-linguistic means to study children's actual scientific practice. However, focusing on what children *do,* rather than what they *say,* does not preclude the notion of theory. Although it is commonly assumed that a theory must be stateable linguistically, in fact children demonstrate the existence of a theory-in-action (Karmiloff-Smith & Inhelder, 1974), that is, manifest in children's actions are indices of the internal representation of a theory that constrains their overt behavior, even when the children cannot explain the theory verbally. The existence of such theories-in-action can be brought to light in the following way: Hypotheses and counterhypotheses can be tested by being built into the experimental material, thereby revealing the existence of theoretical constraints discernible in children's actions. If one were to rely solely on children's explicit verbal statements, very little would be revealed, particularly because even adults are frequently wrong about what guides their actions (Nisbett & Wilson, 1977) and the capacity of consciousness is limited such that the observational consciousness displaces other contents (Mandler, 1975, 1986, 1987).

Although I shall be using children's overt behavior as data, it is important to stress the difference between behavioral change and representational change, because obviously the same behavior can stem from very different underlying theories. Let us now take three examples to consider the role of theory-building, heuristics, and data for conceptual change.

The first example is from children's implicit knowledge of the law of torque. I shall explain the experimental design very briefly because details can be found elsewhere (Karmiloff-Smith & Inhelder, 1974/1975). Children were asked to balance a series of blocks on a narrow metal support. Some of the blocks had their weight evenly distributed and balanced at their geometric center. Others had been drilled with lead in one end and, although they looked identical to the first type, they actually balanced way off center. I shall henceforth call this type of block "invisibly weighted blocks". The third type had a weight glued visibly on the surface at one end and also balanced off center. These I will call "visibly weighted blocks."

If one were merely to record successful versus unsuccessful balancing, then 4- and 8-year-olds score far better than 6-year-olds. But such data tell us little. A sensitive analysis of microdevelopmental details of behavior reveals much more (see Karmiloff-Smith & Inhelder, 1974/1975, and Karmiloff-Smith, 1984, for full details). Very briefly, it was shown that 4- and 5-year-olds could do this task very easily. They simply picked up each block, moved it along the support until they felt the direction of imbalance, and corrected that by using proprioceptive feedback until the block balanced. By contrast, 6- to 7-year-olds placed every block at its geometric center and were thus incapable of balancing anything but those blocks where the weight was evenly distributed. Finally, 8- to 9-year-olds were able to balance all the types of blocks, as had the youngest subjects.

The results of this study are particularly illuminating with respect to the roles of theory-building and data in the child's progressive understanding of how the physical world functions. The youngest children are very sensitive to information emanating from observable data since, as yet, they entertain no theory about block balancing beyond the idea that objects must be in physical contact horizontally. Each block is treated as a new, different task. Noteworthy is the fact that these youngest subjects made no choice among the different blocks; for example, even if two blocks were identical and the child had just succeeded in balancing one of them, she did not subsequently pick up an identical block to make use of the information just obtained from the previous balancing. Children simply treated the balancing of each of the blocks as a series of isolated problems and their actions were mediated by striving for local, successful goal achievement. In doing so, children were predominantly data-driven, using positive and negative feedback. Information obtained from balancing each block was stored independently and not linked to what had happened in previous attempts nor to what followed. Their processing appeared to be limited to consciousness only of current stimulus-response contingencies that leaves the mental contents of each attempt unrelated (Mandler, 1986). In other words, for the youngest children, the various successful attempts did not lead to new learning; there was as yet no conceptual *domain* of block balancing as such. However, it is essential to recall that, at the behavioral level, these children were successful, but their success depended on piecemeal problem solving.

How can we explain, then, the failure of the more cognitively advanced 6- and 7-year-olds to solve the very same task? Or is it the *same* task? In my view, the reason lies in the fact that these older children become problem generators rather than merely problem solvers. The successful and unsuccessful actions of these children are mediated by a theory. And theory construction responds to goals and concerns that are not exclusively a function of current situations and contexts (Mandler, 1986). These somewhat older subjects thus go beyond the successful goal attainment of the younger children, build a theory to explain how blocks balance, and thereby create a conceptual domain of block balancing. But in building their theory on the basis of retrieval of previously stored information, these older children simplify the domain and thereby unify and render coherent their theory about it. By their overt actions of attempting to balance all blocks at their geometric center, 6- and 7-year-olds show that they have indeed built a theory—the "things-balance-in-the middle" or "geometric center" theory—and that they rigidly apply their theory to all their block-balancing attempts. All subsequent behavior is mediated by this theory. Thus, they no longer use the positive and negative proprioceptive feedback of the direction of imbalance of a block, the current stimulus-response contingencies so useful to younger children's successful balancing. The 6- to 7-year-old treats negative feedback as if she, the *child*, were in difficulty, not as if the theory were at fault. Indeed, the theory goes unquestioned for a long time. These children do exactly what Kuhn (1962) has argued scientists do. Children do not abandon their theory despite glaring counter-examples! Instead, they look for an error in the procedure. So when a weighted block placed at the geometric center falls, children put it back on the support again at the geometric center but very much more gently!

Finally, when these children can no longer treat the failure as an error in the procedure, they simply push aside any unevenly weighted block as impossible to balance, that is, as an anomaly that they can ignore. The data are rejected as irrelevant! But as we shall see, these theory-building children are wise to ignore data. As Feyerabend (1981) has argued, in science progress is made by following a theory, not by observation. In other words, progress is frequently achieved by rearranging the data about the world so as to fit our theoretical assumptions. I hate to think how true this is, of course, of the cognitive developmentalist!

Where does the child's initial theory come from, simplified and incorrect as it is? The theory as such is not of course out there in the physical world. It is in the child's mind, in the child's stored internal representations. In my view, children's theories are built on the basis of intensional properties and not on the theory's extension, that is, not with respect to the real world situation that it covers. There are three ways that the theory can be built up in the child's mind (Karmiloff-Smith, 1990). First, knowledge may be specified innately. Such knowledge does not, in my view, have the status of a theory because it remains embedded in an effective procedure for operating in the physical world. To have theoretical status for the cognizer, it must be re-represented. A second step toward gaining knowledge is to interact with the external world and pay attention to information gained locally. This is indeed what the youngest children do, in using proprioceptive feedback. However, a third way to gain knowledge is to pay attention to certain aspects of the information that is already stored internally and, if necessary, ignore new information. This involves a process of redescription and explicitation that I have detailed elsewhere (Karmiloff-Smith, 1986, 1990). It is not by looking for further information in the external environment that the child builds a theory. Rather, he or she has to work on internal representations of previously independently stored entries and generate the theory from relevant patterns across the stored entries (e.g., many objects in the world do balance at their geometric center). The child must mark internally what is common across the relevant entries, and find a generalization parsimonious enough to encompass a sizeable number of events.

When, finally, by 8 or 9 years of age, children are able to balance the unevenly weighted blocks, their *successful behavior* is similar to that of the youngest children. But clearly the *representations* underlying the behavior are very different. And words like *weight* and *middle* change meaning as they become embedded into a broader theoretical framework. Indeed, as Gopnik (1982) has argued, lexical terms are always theoretical terms for the child from the outset. Thus, as the child's theory changes so do the meanings of the terms. The relationship between the changing lexicon and theory has been extensively explored by Kuhn (1987) in his analysis of the concept of *motion* from Aristotlean to present-day physics.

Why do children change their simple geometric-center theory? First, because of an accumulation of anomalies that themselves require explanation and cannot be fitted into the original theory. But it is essential to stress that the recognition and re-evaluation of anomalies as having the status of counter-examples depend crucially on a prior, very firm commitment to a theory. This takes time developmentally because clearly, all the information was potentially available from the start. Interestingly also, the accumulation of anomalies does not induce the child to go on immediately to build a more comprehensive theory to encompass all the data. Rather, children keep their geometric-center theory based on length alone for one set of blocks, create a new theory based on weight alone for the set of visibly weighted blocks, and continue to reject as anomalies fitting neither theory the invisibly weighted blocks. Thus, it is as if for one set of blocks they believe "here there's length but no weight" and for the other set of blocks they believe "here there's weight but no length"! At first, then, children temporarily create two domains rather than trying to explain all the data within a single domain. But in doing so, they lose both the unity of the potentially broader domain and the simplicity of their previous single geometric-center theory. This creates a new inner tension that is finally resolved when the child develops his or her correct, naive version of the law of torque.

This developmental progression demonstrates how the same stimuli represent different data for children at different ages. In other words, when a weighted block balances off center, this represents positive feedback for the younger children because it meets their goal. However, the very same stimulus (a weighted block balancing off-center) represents negative feedback for older children holding the geometric center theory. And, when a block placed off-center falls, this represents negative feedback for the younger children, whereas the same stimulus represents positive feedback for the somewhat older children because it confirms their geometric-center theory. Similarly, Kuhn (1977) has argued that members of different scientific communities are presented with different data by the very same stimuli. It is important to differentiate between, on the one hand, goal failure (or what might be thought of as "desire" failure) and, on the other hand, expectation failure (what might be thought of as "belief" failure).

Let us now take another example. We have just seen that children ignore potentially important observable data when they are committed to a particular theory. By the same token, children actually invent observables to meet their theoretical commitments. An experiment was carried out on action and reaction as compensating forces (Piaget, Karmiloff-Smith, & Bronckart, 1978; see Karmiloff-Smith, 1984, for a reinterpretation of the data). Children were asked to explain what happens when a number of items are placed on top of others. For instance, when a piece of wood is placed on a sponge, the sponge becomes slightly indented. What is happening? When the same piece of wood is placed on a table, no visible effect occurs. Why is this? What is happening? We asked children such questions with a series of items and surfaces made of iron, sponge, wood, polyethylene, and so on. The results were briefly as follows. The youngest children provided a series of isolated explanations. Each item was seen as a separate problem. Thus, when a piece of wood was placed on sponge and it became slightly indented, children explained that the wood pushed on the sponge because the wood was heavy. When the same piece of wood was put on a table and nothing visible happened, this was explained by the fact that the wood was light. In other words, children described the very same piece of wood as "heavy" in one situation and "light" in another. When the wood was placed on polyethylene and no visible effect occurred, the children explained that it was because polyethylene "like to stay flat," and so forth. A series of different, but locally applicable and plausible explanations was provided by the child that had no internal coherence for the adult observer. But there is no contraindication from the child's vantage point because, in fact, the child is not linking the different events and explanations into a coherent whole, that is, does not yet consider them as part of a single domain. They are merely processing each current stimulus-response contingency without conscious processing of the relationship between the different events (Mandler, 1986). The sequence of explanations are contradictory only if we, as adults, consider them as competing explanations for the same problem. Young children consider them as a series of different problems.

Older children, by contrast, do view this as a single domain. The older child has developed a theory that everything exerts force on something on which it is placed. And he or she finds it easy to hold this theory when anything heavy is placed on the sponge that becomes visibly indented. But the child is also constrained by another, temporarily more powerful theory, more powerful because it is held for much longer developmentally: that all causes must have *observable* effects. One might therefore expect the placing of something on the table with no observable effects to be a threat to the child's theory of action and reaction. Not so! To explain the force exerted by the wood on the surface of the table, children argued that they saw the table flinch a little and then quickly re-flatten, but that the experimenters were not able to see the effects because they did not look carefully enough!

Finally, of course, children subsequently relax the belief that all causes must have observable effects and they accept that, in all cases, action and reaction are exerting compensatory forces. But prior to this, children, like scientists, shape the data to fit the theory and, to maintain their theory, they go as far as to invent *observable* data!

This developmental pattern is important in that it demonstrates not only that the child ignores data that ought to refute a theory, but also that they inadvertently *invent* data to fit the theory to which they are deeply committed. And, as the reader will readily recognize a feeling of déjà-vu, obviously children are not alone in this!

Let us now go on to a discussion of children's use of general heuristics as they go about discovering how the physical world functions. Heuristics can be used in two ways. They are used unconsciously (algorithmically) or, in some circumstances, they are used consciously (explicitly) as promising paths for search, along the lines of Simon's "weak methods" (Langley, Simon, Bradshaw, & Zytkow, 1987). Spatial representations are a good example of these two uses. Take the case of symmetry. Symmetry is often used simply as an algorithm of which children are unaware. This was clear from the examples of block balancing when children start to use spatial symmetry. However, in other cases, symmetry is used as an explicit heuristic. This is certainly to be seen in adult scientific practice. For instance, mineralogists explicitly use symmetry as a discovery process even when they know that the object under study is not symmetrical (Nicolle, 1965). In problem-solving tasks, one can observe children purposely spreading out a symmetrical spatial layout to see whether the new spatial pattern suggests anything to them (Karmiloff-Smith, 1979b).

Another example of the way in which heuristics can be used both algorithmically and explicitly can be found in quantification. Just as children search for spatial patterns, so they search for numerical patterns as a promising path for discovery. For example, one can observe children counting elements in a physics problem-solving task, to see if the result will give them an idea (Karmiloff-Smith, 1984). They are obviously consciously probing their knowledge of number patterns to potentiate their search.

But quantification can be also an impediment to discovery. Another study relating to the physical law of torque, but with a new design using an unusual balance scale (Karmiloff-Smith, 1975, 1984; Piaget & Karmiloff-Smith, in press), looked *inter alia* at the function of quantification as a heuristic for children. The task set for the children was different from the way in which previous researchers have used conventional balance scales, that is, with fixed fulcrum and pegs at equal intervals along an arm, on which disks of equal weight are placed (Inhelder & Piaget, 1958; Klahr & Siegler, 1978; Stavy, Strauss, Orpaz, & Carni, 1982). In those studies children were asked to anticipate which way the arm would tilt for a series of items in which the experimenter combined different distances and weights. By contrast, in my study, the children manipulated the materials on their own. The materials were much richer in design than the conventional balance scale. First, the fulcrum of the arm was mobile; it could be fixed by the child not only in the center but also at any one of the 15 holes along the arm, excluding each extremity where a metal peg was attached on which to hang weights. Second, the weights were not disks of equal size. Rather, they were in the form of plastic numbers, from 1 to 9, increasing in weight by 1 unit per number (for example, with a centered fulcrum, number 5 on one end would be in balance with numbers 2 and 3 hung on the other end). There was a duplicate for each of the numbers 1 through 5, but numbers 6 through 9 were singletons, forcing children into numerical compositions. By such a design, it was hoped to observe the child actively solving balance problems by using a variety of types of representation (physical, numerical, spatial, kinaesthetic) and to explore the role of quantification as a heuristic in children's understanding of physics.

The most interesting results came from the items where the fulcrum was decentered and, to place the bar in balance, the child had to hang a large number of elements on the shorter end and one or even no elements on the long end. First, children use symmetry in their actions. Once they hang something on one end (the short end that is tilted upward), they then automatically hang something on the other end (the long end, despite the fact that it is already tilted downward!). Thus, children do not only use symmetry as a heuristic in space, they also use symmetry as a heuristic in their actions.

However, with time, children begin to use rather elaborate multiplication procedures to work out the relationship between length and the weights, and finally they manage to get the arm with the decentered fulcrum in balance. Once they had achieved balance, with lots of numbers on the short end and one number on the long end, children were then asked to add two more objects to the now balanced arm. Obviously they should have taken, say, a 1 to hang on the long end and, say, a 9 to hang on the short end. But this is not what children did. They hung two identical objects, one at each end, and were absolutely astounded to see the longer arm tilt downwards. And, instead of then using the quantification procedure employed to get the bar in balance originally, they took off the two objects and put back the identical two on each end much more slowly and carefully. They clearly considered something in the procedure to be at fault rather than the underlying theory. What is even more interesting is that 20 adult subjects, intelligent but naive in the science of physics, did exactly the same and showed the same surprise! It seems as if, once subjects have learned to use quantification, this blocks them from developing a deeper semantic understanding of the law of torque. Moreover, they seem to be guided by a very strong theory that once the world is empirically in balance, nothing is happening any longer with respect to the dynamics of compensating forces.

We are reminded here of the experiment on action and reaction discussed above. As long as something became indented, then children understood that there were dynamic compensating forces at work, but once no effects were observable, younger children thought the world was static. I believe something similar is interpretable in this balance scale experiment where, once the arm has been brought into balance with the decentered fulcrum, the resulting physics are then considered static. This also probably explains why children take a long time developmentally to seek an explanation of simpler cases of balance, because balance is not considered to be the result of dynamic interactions and thus, paradoxically, because there are no *observable* cause/effect relations, children consider nothing is happening physically and thus there is nothing to explain! But we have seen that even adults have problems with equilibrium in more complex tasks. It would thus seem that states of *equilibrium* are frequently conceptualized by nonexperts in physics as *static* rather than as constantly involving dynamic interactions and compensating forces.

To summarize, children are clearly not just problem solvers. They rapidly become problem generators, and they move from local, successful goal-mediated actions to theory-mediated actions. Children first exploit information in the environment. As Mandler has argued, children's conscious attention is probably limited to current stimulus-response contingencies whose mental contents remain unrelated in the internal representations (Mandler, 1986). If ever children are empiricists, it is only very briefly as they first approach a new domain. But subsequently they exploit the information that they have already stored in their internal representations. At this point, consciousness may serve to bring previously isolated mental contents into juxtaposition and contact (Mandler, 1986).

And clearly children are not falsificationists. They constantly develop theories and create domains, carving and re-carving nature at new joints. And they simplify and unify incoming data to make them conform to their theories. This of course both potentiates and curtails learning (Karmiloff-Smith, 1990). The theories give the child predictive control, because they refer coherently and stably to several events in a domain. But in order to hold on to their theories, children treat what should be counter-examples as mere anomalies, and they initially judge their own procedures as faulty rather than question their theory. Theories about the static nature of equilibrium and the necessity for observable effects resulting from causal events curtail conceptual change in children and adults. Some very powerful heuristics, such as symmetry and quantification, both potentiate and impede conceptual change. It is highly likely that some aspects of both symmetry and number are built-in capacities of the human mind (Gelman, 1986; Starkey, Spelke, & Gelman, 1983; Spelke, 1985) and they subsequently get used as algorithms in children's actions and visuo-spatial interpretations of the world. But to be used consciously as purposeful heuristics suggesting promising search paths in problem solving, these capacities have to be redescribed to become eventually available to conscious access (Karmiloff-Smith, 1986, 1990). In this sense, consciousness is neither epiphenomenal nor an executive system; it is an emergent property of the cognitive system ontogenetically and operates, as Mandler (1986) has cogently argued, as a necessary constituent of human mental activity.

ACKNOWLEDGMENTS

First presented at the Society for Philosophy and Psychology Annual Meeting, University of California at San Diego, June, 1987, and subsequently published in *Mind & Language* (1988) under the title "The child is a theoretician, not an inductivist." This is a modified version adapted as a tribute to my very dear friend and colleague, George Mandler.

REFERENCES

Brown, A. L. (1986). Analogical learning and transfer: What develops? In S. Vosniadou & A. Ortony (Eds.), *Similarity and Analogical Reasoning* pp. 369–412.
Carey, S. (1985). *Conceptual change in childhood*. Cambridge, MA: MIT Press.

Feyerabend, P. K. (1981). *Realism, Rationalism and Scientific Method. Philosophical Papers Volume 1.* Cambridge University Press.

Garcia, R. (1987). Sociology of Science and Sociogenesis of Knowledge. In B. Inhelder, D. de Caprona, & A. Cornu-Wells (Eds.), *Piaget Today* (pp. 127–140). Hillsdale, NJ: Lawrence Erlbaum Associates.

Gelman, R. (1986). *First principles for structuring acquisition.* Presidential address to Division 7 of the American Psychological Association. *Newsletter of Division 7 APA.*

Gelman, R., & Brown, A. L. (1985). Changing views of cognitive competence in the young. In N. J. Smelser & D. R. Gerstein (Eds.), *Knowledge in the Social and Behavioural Sciences: Discovery and trends over fifty years* (Proceedings of a Commemorative Symposium on the Fiftieth Anniversary of the Ogden Report, *Recent Social Trends in the United States*) (pp. 175–207). New York: Academic Press.

Gilliéron, C. (1982). Conservation: Forty-five years later. *Journal of Structured Learning, 7,* 167–174.

Gopnik, A. (1982). Words and Plans: Early language and the development of intelligent action. *Journal of Child Language, 9,* 303–318.

Inhelder, B. & Piaget, J. (1958). *The Growth of Logical Thinking from Childhood to Adolescence.* New York: Basic Books.

Karmiloff-Smith, A. (1975). *Les metaphores dans l'action chez les enfants de 5 et de 12 ans.* Paper presented at the Symposium of the International Center for Genetic Epistomology, Geneva.

Karmiloff-Smith, A. (1979a). *A Functional Approach to Child Language.* Cambridge University Press.

Karmiloff-Smith, A. (1979b). Problem-solving procedures in children's construction and representations of closed railway circuits. *Archives de Psychologie,* XLVII (1807) 37–59.

Karmiloff-Smith, A. (1984). Children's problem solving. In M. E. Lamb, A. L. Brown, & B. Rogoff (Eds.), *Advances in Developmental Psychology, Volume III* (pp. 39–90). Hillsdale, NJ: Lawrence Erlbaum Associates.

Karmiloff-Smith, A. (1986). From metaprocesses to conscious access: Evidence from children's metalinguistic and repair data. *Cognition, 23*(2), 95–147.

Karmiloff-Smith, A. (1988). The child is a theoritician, not an inductivist. *Mind & Language, 3,* 183–195.

Karmiloff-Smith, A. (1990). Innate constraints and developmental change. In S. Carey & R. Gelman (Eds.), *Structural Constraints on Development.* Hillsdale, NJ: Lawrence Erlbaum Associates.

Karmiloff-Smith, A. & Inhelder, B. (1974/5). If you want to get ahead, get a theory. *Cognition, 3*(3), 195–212.

Keil, F. C. (1988). *Promiscuous realism and the problem of original similarity on the emergence of theoretical beliefs as constraints on concept acquisition.* Paper presented to the Eighteenth Annual Symposium of the Jean Piaget Society: Biology and Knowledge: Structural Constraints on Development, Philadelphia.

Klahr, D. & Siegler, R. S. (1978). The representation of children's knowledge. In H. W. Reese & L. P. Lipsitt (Eds.), *Advances in Child Development* (Vol. 12, pp. 61–116). New York: Academic Press.

Kuhn, T. S. (1962). *The Structure of Scientific Revolutions.* Chicago: University of Chicago Press.

Kuhn, T. S. (1977). *The Essential Tension: Selected Studies in Scientific Tradition and Change.* Chicago: University of Chicago Press.

Kuhn, T. S. (1987). Guest Lecture series, University College, London.

Lakatos, I. (1977). *The Methodology of Scientific Research Programmes. Philosophical Papers Volume 1.* Cambridge: Cambridge University Press.

Langley, P., Simon, H. A., Bradshaw, G. L., & Zytkow, J. M. (1987). *Scientific Discovery: Computational Explorations of the Creative Process.* Cambridge, MA: MIT Press.

Leslie, A. M. (1988). The necessity of illusion: Perception and thought in infancy. In L. Weiskrantz (Ed.), *Thought without Language* (pp. 185–210). Oxford: Oxford University Press.

Mandler, G. (1975). Consciousness: Respectable, useful, and probably necessary. In R. Solso (Ed.), *Information processing and cognition: The Loyola symposium* (Also in: Technical Report No. 41, Center for Human Information Processing, University of California, San Diego. March, 1974.) Hillsdale, NJ: Lawrence Erlbaum Associates.

Mandler, G. (1986, December). The function of consciousness in psychological theory. *Aspects of consciousness and awareness*, Symposium conducted at the Center for Interdisciplinary Research, University of Bielefeld.

Mandler, G. (1987). Problems and directions in the study of consciousness. In M. Horowitz (Ed.), *Conscious and unconscious mental processes*. Chicago: University of Chicago Press, 1987.

Nicolle, J. (1965). *La symétrie*. Paris: Presses Universitaires de France.

Nisbett, R. E., & Wilson, T. D. (1977). Telling more than we can know: Verbal reports on mental processes. *Psychological Review, 84, 3,* 231–259.

Piaget, J., & Garcia, R. (1983). *Psychogenèse et Histoire des Sciences*. Paris: Flammarion.

Piaget, J., Inhelder, B., & Szeminska, A. (1960). *The Child's Conception of Geometry*. London: Routledge and Kegan Paul.

Piaget, J., Karmiloff-Smith, A. & Bronckart, J. P. (1978). Généralisations relative à la pression et à la réaction. In J. Piaget (Ed.), *Recherches sur la Généralisation* (pp. 169–191). Paris: Presses Universitaires de France.

Quine, W. (1953). Two dogmas of empiricism. In W. Quine (Ed.), *From a Logical Point of View* (pp. 20–46). Cambridge, Mass.: Harvard University Press.

Spelke, E. S. (1985). *Object perception and the object concept in infancy*. Paper presented at the Minnesota Symposium on Child Development, Minneapolis.

Starkey, P., Spelke, E. S., & Gelman, R. (1983). Detection of intermodal correspondences by human infants. *Science, 222,* 179–181.

Stavy, R., Strauss, S., Orpaz, N., & Carni, G. (1982). U-shaped behavioural growth in ratio comparison. In S. Strauss & K. R. Stavy (Eds.), *U-Shaped Behavioural Growth* (pp. 11–36). London: Academic Press.

V EMOTION

Nancy Stein
University of Chicago

A TRIBUTE TO GEORGE MANDLER: MAKING SENSE OUT OF EMOTION

When I was asked to write a chapter in tribute to George Mandler, I did not have much work to do. My research on children's understanding and representation of emotion has been heavily influenced by George's approach to both emotion and life. With regard to George's theory of emotion, I have been most influenced by three of his ideas: his constructivist approach to understanding the relationship between thought and emotion; the concept of discrepancy with reference to both eliciting and understanding emotion; and his observations of how people use information about emotion to make decisions about everyday events. Thus, a discussion of these three issues is interleaved throughout our chapter: *Making Sense Out of Emotion: The Representation and Use of Goal-Structured Knowledge.*

What we have shown in several different studies of emotional understanding is the following. First, the meaning of an event and the subjective feeling of experiencing an emotion are always dependent on the prior knowledge, beliefs, and goals of the person involved in the situation. No event has only a single interpretation. To the extent that people in a culture develop shared knowledge systems about the importance and value of an event, then, their memories and interpretations will overlap. But, memory and knowledge for emotional events will always be the result of making sense out of the incoming information, and this process is always dependent on the individual's structure of values, goals, and beliefs about the world.

We show in several studies that different emotions are experienced in response to a single event. For example, some individuals experience one emotion such as sadness, and others experience another emotion such as anger. The critical variables in predicting these two different emotional experiences are inferences made about the probability of reinstating the goal, the causes of the precipitating event, and the outcomes that result from the event. Specifically, when anger is experienced, people have made the inference that a goal can be reinstated and that the event was most likely caused by an animate agent. Anger also results when the outcome of a situation results in an aversive state that continues over time, despite the fact that inanimate events can cause these negative states. Aversiveness of an outcome often regulates the experience and expression of anger as much or more than initial inferences about goal reinstatement or the cause of the event. One reason for the powerful influence of aversiveness is that the ongoing pain caused by the outcome situation causes a re-evaluation of the possibility of re-instating the goal. Aversiveness forces a reinterpretation of beliefs about goal reinstatement, even when inferences have been made that reinstatement is not possible. Sadness results when people conclude that the goal under consideration cannot be reinstated, that the cause of the loss was accidental rather than intentional, and that the resulting negative outcome will be detrimental to other goals in addition to the current one under consideration.

Our model of emotional understanding is not only constructive in nature, but we also assume that understanding emotion presupposes a continual updating of beliefs, depending upon how current conditions are perceived to benefit or harm the individual. Although George's theory of emotion addresses these issues, we have attempted to clarify and speak more directly on the issue of process during the understanding and experience of emotion. By this, I mean that we actively attempt to describe the sequence of content-based inferences that are made during an emotional experience and we also attempt to delineate how these inferences differ as a function of experiencing different emotions. Furthermore, we focus on the goals, plans, and actions that arise during emotional experience. We begin the test of our content-driven model by addressing issues of development and learning as well as issues related to the structure and representation of knowledge about emotion.

Perhaps it is in our efforts to describe content-based inferences related to different emotional experiences that we begin to differ from the position that George adopts. In both of his books on emotion (Mandler, 1975, 1984), George contends that not very much can be learned from studying the folk psychology of emotion, specifically in reference to the language used to talk about and label emotional experience. Our approach has been based on the assumption that language and talk about emotion can tell us as much as any other approach to emotion. Furthermore, it is in the talk about and the conceptualization of emotional experience that the organization and structure of this knowledge becomes exceedingly clear. Often, the fuzziness of criteria and definitions used to understand the language of emotion is due to the lack of adequate knowledge about both emotion and language rather than any inherent difficulty with language per se.

We also rely on a goal-based approach to the structure of emotion knowledge more seriously than George does. Although we would be the first to admit that a goal-based approach does not describe all the important aspects of emotional experience, we would argue that this approach affords a powerful method for assessing the representation of emotional events in everyday social interaction. Planning for the future, reviewing the past, and assessing ongoing situations in terms of their beneficial nature describes many activities undertaken in interpersonal interaction (Heider, 1958). Thus, conceptualizing a theory of emotion in terms of goals, plans, actions, and outcomes has proven highly beneficial (Stein & Jewett, 1986; Stein & Levine, 1987, 1989; Stein & Trabasso, 1989).

More importantly, using a goal-based approach to the study of emotion allows us to describe and illustrate the importance of discrepancy in the regulation of emotional experience and expression (Stein & Trabasso, 1989). The notion of discrepancy or novelty has been a seriously misunderstood aspect of George's theory. The difficulty most people have with discrepancy is that they can theoretically generate many situations where the outcome of an event is totally predictable and yet a strong emotional reaction is experienced.

In our chapter, we bring data to bear on just this issue. We attempt to show that in real life people are not very accurate in their predictions about future events. In fact, their memory for past events in terms of predicting how they will respond in the future is often faulty. What people think will happen and what happens are two different things. Although some aspects of an event are predictable, other dimensions are more uncertain. Unexpected outcomes occur with great frequency. Moreover, some aspects of an event are not well understood. When a stable representation of the event is formed, the poorly understood parts are often not included. It is precisely when incoming information pertains to some aspect of an event that was not expected or not understood that an emotional response is experienced. We discuss how this hypothesis is supported by our data.

Specifically, we show that shifts in emotional intensity or the quality of an emotional response are always accompanied by reference to a novel aspect of the precipitating event. In presenting our data, we argue that the difficulty in understanding notions of discrepancy stem from a basic misconception about the nature of representation. In order to understand how expectations are formed about the predictability of an event, studies of emotion must deal more directly with the concepts of probability, certainty, and decision making. By focusing on these dimensions and by assuming that people continually *update and change* their representations of an event, the necessity of including notions of novelty and discrepancy in describing emotion becomes apparent.

Thus far, I have written only about George's influence on my thinking with regard to theories of emotion. In reality, he has influenced me in many other aspects of my life. I was never a "formal" student of George's. When I was at LaJolla as a postdoctoral fellow, I worked primarily in collaboration with Jean

Mandler. However, George was never far away, and he was always available when it came to discussing ideas or the intellectual promise of a particular theory. In fact, over all the years I have known George, I have never seen him turn away anyone who had a cogent or innovative approach to a problem, despite the fact that he might have a severe disagreement with the approach. The seeking of ideas, turning them around, breaking them down, reflecting on their psychological (as well as their historical and philosophical) importance was the focus of discussion.

Several characteristics of George immediately come to mind when I think of his influence on me: His searing honesty, his unwavering accuracy in making predictions about both the personal and intellectual life of a person, his ability to judge whether or not an idea had any worth, his ability to go on a hunch or intuition in formulating a problem, his ability to see through to the guts of an issue and cut out the dross, and his ability to foster creativity in the best possible manner.

For me, one of the most pervasive qualities that defines George is his honesty. Whenever I ask George for an opinion, I know that some of what he says I will not want to hear. George always sees beyond the immediate, and consequently, focuses on long-range gain and pain rather than short-range pleasure. Thus, if you want to hear about the problems that you will face, or the choices you will have to make, either personally or intellectually, George's opinions are invaluable. His accuracy is unfaltering. However, take his advice with a good stiff drink, because the level of self-awareness and self-reflection required to digest what George says is often great and the experience quite humbling.

On the other hand, I have never met a more nurturant and concerned individual, who really does care and does give a damn, not only *if* you survive but how well you survive. Quality and goodness are important to him. George's ability to explain and teach, especially if he senses a reciprocal honesty, is brilliant. For those who have experienced these interactions, their lives have been enriched and enhanced. He is a mentor and friend of the best kind. But reciprocating with commitment, humor, and the lack of pretense are essential. For again, one thing that George values is a vision that goes beyond the here and now.

It is George's wisdom and humor, combined with his ability to describe and predict the lay of the land, that I think I will remember the best. After once complaining to him that some of my work on emotion was passed over by a colleague, with only a footnote mentioning our current work, George told me that I should be glad because at least my name was spelled correctly in the footnote. He had had experiences where even his name was misspelled. Another time, Jean and I were revising a paper for publication. Because we had to deal with what we thought were unfair editorial comments, I became quite frustrated and very agitated. George tactfully (or not so tactfully) reminded me that the goal was not to get even but to get the paper published. And under these circumstances, what the editor wanted the editor got, unless it compromised my moral integrity or decency. And he felt I had a long way to go before that happened.

Finally, his advice and concern for dealing with what I know to be my worst personal characteristics have been unique and uplifting. As honest as George is, he also has the capacity to understand, accept, and forgive. And for this I am grateful. We all can think of individuals, without whom our lives would not have had the quality of goodness and enrichment that we desire. For me, George is one of those people, and I walk around with a little piece of George serving as a homunculus, to remind me to be aware, to be more at ease, and to enjoy the present as much as possible.

20 Making Sense Out of Emotion: The Representation and Use of Goal-structured Knowledge

Nancy L. Stein
Linda J. Levine
University of Chicago

This chapter focuses on the representation of emotional experience and the way in which emotion and thought are interrelated. We present a model that specifies the type of knowledge acquired about emotion, the way in which this knowledge is organized, and how it is used to regulate behavior. We describe the thinking that occurs during emotion episodes and the way in which thought and emotion influence each other. We also illustrate how emotional behavior is perceived and understood by both children and adults, and we show how differences in values and beliefs lead to variation in emotional responses. As such we address issues related to both learning and development.

Our model of emotion is based on a goal-directed, problem-solving approach to the study of personal and social behavior. We assume that much of behavior is carried out in the service of achieving and maintaining goal states that ensure survival and adaptation to the environment. A basic tenant underlying this belief (Stein & Levine, 1987, in press) is that people prefer to be in certain states (i.e., pleasure) and prefer to avoid other states (i.e., pain). A second assumption is that when people experience unpleasant states, they attempt to regulate and change them. One way of achieving this change is to represent a state, called a goal. A goal state can then be used to initiate action or thinking that results in the desired internal state change.

A critical dimension in defining and describing emotional experience, therefore, focuses on the concept of change. Representing and evaluating change with respect to how valued goals have been affected is seen as a necessary prerequisite for experiencing and regulating emotion. As such, our theory is oriented toward a specification of the process by which changes in goal states are detected and emotions are elicited. We also focus on the way in which emotion-eliciting events are represented and the type of thinking that occurs throughout an emotion episode. Thus, the encoding and retrieval processes that occur during emotional understanding become germane.

Given our focus on the importance of changing conditions, a distinguishing characteristic of emotional experience is an effort to assimilate some type of new information into current knowledge schemes (Mandler, 1975, 1984). We (Stein & Levine, 1987) contend that people constantly monitor their environment in an effort to maintain preferred states. To succeed at this task, pattern-matching procedures are used to analyze and compare incoming data to what is already known. When new information is detected in the input, a mismatch occurs, causing an interruption in current thinking processes. Attention then shifts to the novel or discrepant information. With the attentional shift comes arousal of the autonomic nervous system and a focus on the implications new information has for the maintenance of valued goals. Thus, emotional experience is almost always associated with attending to and making sense out of new information.

Consequently, learning almost always results during an emotional episode. In an attempt to understand the nature of changing conditions, people revise and update their beliefs about the conditions necessary for maintaining their goals. For example, people encode many different aspects of the conditions that cause a goal to be achieved or to fail. Furthermore, people often change the value associated with a set of particular goals; that is, in attaining or failing to attain a goal, the value associated with that and other goals may increase or decrease in strength. As a result, people often forfeit their goals as a function of failure or they may intensify their efforts to achieve their goal.

We assume that people have a built-in mechanism that allows them to represent action–outcome sequences in relationship to the maintenance of goals (Gallistel, 1985; Piaget, 1981; Stein & Levine, 1987, in press). Individuals are able to infer and represent the causal conditions that must be operative in order to produce actions that result in certain outcomes, and they are able to use this knowledge to achieve goals. Thus, when a change in goal maintenance occurs and emotions are experienced, plans become operative. Being able to access a plan that specifies the conditions necessary to achieve a goal provides an opportunity for coping with goal failure. Similarly, constructing and carrying out a plan enables the maintenance of a goal, once it has been achieved.

There are situations, however, where little planning occurs or where plans cannot be accessed and retrieved. Intense emotional experience often precludes access to certain types of information, and under these conditions, critical inferences about the emotion situation are not made. Thus, intensity of an emotional experience along with the sensory and physiological feedback associated with such responses become important dimensions in predicting the thinking, decision making, and quality of planning that occur during emotional experience.

Because we are dealing with very young children as well as adults, we discuss some changes that occur in emotional awareness as a function of development and learning. Approaching this issue is thorny at best, for often developmental differences are more a function of the type of knowledge acquired or the degree to which children have been exposed to a task rather than to any general process pertaining to development per se. With due respect to this potential confound, however, certain developmental differences in emotional processing must be considered.

The debates concerning development revolve around which aspects of emotion are innate and which are learned. A second issue concerns the nature of the changes that occur in children's knowledge of emotion and the way in which development affects the organization of emotion. We begin by considering some of the regulatory processes present at birth and some that develop as a function of maturation and experience. Then we present an analysis of the specific processes and types of knowledge that are acquired and used during emotional experience. Finally, we present data that bear on the validity of our model, with respect to both developmental and individual differences in emotion knowledge.

THE DEVELOPMENT OF EMOTIONAL EXPERIENCE

The first issue we consider is whether preferences are innate. At birth, the infant's repertoire includes a set of behaviors for responding to different types and intensities of stimulation. Many are reflexive in nature (i.e., the startle, orienting, blinking, and sucking reflex). Some involve an affective response to the nature of stimulation. For example, certain events precipitate distress responses, consisting of volatile activity, crying, and particular facial expressions. Other events elicit a quieting response, with the absence of volatile activity and expression. A few researchers have held that these responses are evidence for assuming that the infant has innate preferences for being in certain states and preferences for avoiding others. For example, Zajonc (1980) argues that initial preferences need no cognitive input for their elicitation and that they drive all other forms of emotional development.

We do not question the existence and importance of preferences, for they are critical to the experience and expression of emotion. But we take issue with the claim that newborns have acquired full-blown preferences such as desires to be in certain states or desires to avoid others. The fact that infants experience pleasure and distress does not mean that they prefer or desire to shift from one state to another. Having preferences requires the ability to represent, compare, and choose between two different states, where a desire to orient more toward one state than another is expressed. To carry out this type of thinking, a person must have acquired the ability to represent a state that does not currently exist. Although newborns can experience pleasure or distress in response to different events, they have yet to acquire the capacity to represent internal or external states different from those currently directing their behavior.

One reason that young infants experience difficulty in representing hypothetical states such as goals is that they have yet to acquire enough knowledge to construct stable representations of their environment. Being able to construct organized representations permits an infant to understand the causal constraints that make events predictable; that is, when infants have enough exposure to and experience with a specific situation such that they are able to construct a stable representation, they form expectations whereby they understand that certain actions and events result in certain outcomes. In other words, they learn that certain conditions must be present for specific actions and events to occur. In conjunction with this type of understanding, young infants also learn that their own actions can control or change the conditions that lead to certain outcomes. The result of acquiring an adequate knowledge of the world is that young infants engage in decision making about the value of particular experiences, and they can actually determine whether or not to pursue a particular objective.

Although much of this learning occurs rapidly, it does not appear to be present in the newborn infant. The critical period appears to be the first 4 to 5 months of life. During this time, several significant changes occur. First, the infant's ability to habituate to different classes of events increases. Evidence of habituation signals that infants can form predictable representations of a phenomenon and that they experience some type of discrepancy (or dishabituation) when novel stimuli are introduced. Second, infants attend more systematically to external events so that they appear to consciously engage in an appraisal process (Campos, this volume; Emde, 1980; Sroufe, 1979). In other words, these young children begin to evaluate an event in terms of how it will affect them. This evaluation requires that the infant understand that a given event results in a specific outcome and that the outcome results in a particular affective state. If the affective state is aversive or unpleasant, the infant must then be able to understand and represent a state that is not unpleasant. Third, children begin to construct plans that enable them to change their current affective state, and they become more skilled in regulating their motor behavior so that they can carry out and accomplish their plans.

From an analysis of current literature on infant development (e.g., Fernald, 1984; Mandler, 1988), these skills seem to cohere and become integrated somewhere during the 4th to 7th month of life. When infants can bring to bear all these skills, we would say that a true emotional reaction can be experienced. In making this claim, we are distinguishing between the more general class of affective versus the more specific class of emotional responses. Affective responses are those that include distress or quieting behaviors where changes in the level of autonomic nervous system arousal occur without an evaluative component being accessed. These types of reactions occur frequently in the young infant and less frequently in the adult. Emotional reactions are those that involve the autonomic nervous system as well as higher order thinking processes. In the following discussion, we lay out the processes and components involved in our model of emotional experience and understanding.

EVALUATION PROCESSES UNDERLYING EMOTIONAL EXPERIENCE

A necessary feature in our theory is the presence of a representational system that monitors subjective states and bodily reactions. Monitoring is carried out in the service of moving toward states that are beneficial for survival and moving away from environments that are harmful. The primary function of this system is to access knowledge that allows the evaluation of an event, action, object, or state in regard to its value (see also Mandler, 1982, 1984). This representational system must include information about states that are pleasurable and preferred and states that are aversive and to be avoided. The system also contains information about the conditions that lead to specific goal states, and it contains information about the relative ordering of goals in terms of their necessity for maintaining or avoiding certain states (i.e., preferences).

Given these properties, a value system has three primary characteristics. First, it is hierarchical in nature such that a series of goals can be represented with regard to the causal conditions that embed and connect one goal to another. Second, preference trees can be constructed such that certain goals are considered more valuable than others. And third, this system is dynamic in nature such that some preferences and some parts of a goal hierarchy (i.e., the conditions linking goals together) can be changed. As a result of incorporating new information about conditions leading to the attainment of valued goals, the structure of the hierarchy undergoes continued construction and reorganization. Goals that have a high value on one occasion often decrease in value on another, depending on the operating conditions. Similarly, goals that are unfamiliar or lacking in value often increase in worth as new connections are made between these new goals and other valued familiar goals. The important point is that, like all other schemata, value systems are both stable and dynamic. Some parts of the value system remain constant and other parts change.

The existence of a value system is fundamental to emotional behavior (Lazarus & Folkman, 1984; Mandler, 1984; Stein & Levine, 1987) because it alerts individuals to those situations that bring pleasure and pain. With such a system operating, two primary tendencies exist: the desire to attain or maintain a valued state and the desire to get out of or avoid an aversive state. As we previously stated, a value system becomes operative when an individual is in one particular state, can imagine the existence of another one, and has an understanding that the imagined end state leads to a more pleasurable outcome.

Thus, a second component critical to our model is the ability to detect change in the environment as well as in one's own internal states. Moreover, the change must be assessed with respect to maintaining current values and goals. Here, we describe the different processes that occur when emotional reactions are experienced. We begin by describing baseline activities that occur immediately before the onset of a precipitating event. Four are of interest: (1) the type of ongoing

299

cognitive activity, (2) the level of physiological arousal, (3) the emotional state of the participant, and (4) the type of ongoing overt activity. These variables are important because our model assumes that an emotional reaction always causes a change in the first three processes and often causes a change in overt actions as well (Ekman, 1977). Thus, our model is a state change model where all properties change in some specific way when an unexpected precipitating event occurs.

Precipitating events emerge from three different sources: the environment (i.e., a physical event such as a rain storm, a fire, the formation of a rainbow, or the action of another person, such as the giving of a gift or the violation of a promise), one's own actions, or the result of memory retrieval of past events. For an emotional response to occur, the precipitating event must be encoded and accessed during the evaluation process. In the case of retrieving an event from memory, the initial encoding has already taken place, but the event must be accessed and placed in working memory. Then, a meaning analysis has to be performed on the focal information.

The meaning analysis can be broken down into different processes. Of primary interest are those that facilitate the integration of incoming information into current knowledge structures. Assuming that different pattern-matching procedures underlie most attempts to integrate new information into current knowledge stores, it is important to discriminate between those where a match results and those where a discrepancy occurs. If incoming information is congruent with information in existing knowledge stores, then it is readily assimilated into current knowledge schemes. Under these conditions, individuals are often unaware of the processes associated with encoding and understanding.

When a mismatch occurs, however, information cannot be immediately assimilated into current working schemes. By definition, some of this information is novel or unexpected; that is, some aspect of the incoming information is incongruent with what was expected, given the current state of a person's knowledge. Mismatches cause an interruption of ongoing thinking, give rise to subsequent evaluation processes, and cause subsequent changes in states of ANS arousal (Mandler, 1975, 1984). When both ANS arousal and cognitive evaluation occur, an emotional reaction occurs. As we stated before, precipitating events often cause ANS arousal leading to an affective or reflexive response. However, we do not consider these affective responses to belong to the class of emotional responses, because no evaluation of current goal states is made. It is when both autonomic arousal and evaluation occur that an emotional reaction occurs.

When the evaluation process is initiated, an assessment is first made as to whether an adequate representation of the precipitating event exists. Many instances occur where only part of an event is understood because the information is so novel. In these cases, surprise and a sense of curiosity is evoked. This indicates that the first cognitive activity of the individual is to form a representation of the event in the service of understanding the new information; that is, many precipitating events require that new categories get formed or that beliefs are updated so that the event can become known and predictable. Then an evaluation can be made as to whether the event has any significance with respect to changing, blocking, or facilitating the attainment of valued goals.

Separating the process of forming an adequate representation from the process of evaluation is difficult because frequently the two occur in close temporal proximity. However, the formation of a representation always precedes the evaluation process. Moreover, different affective reactions should occur when representations are being formed than when changes in goal maintenance are being assessed. Surprise, curiosity, and interest are indicative of the formation of new representations, whereas happiness, anger, sadness, and fear are indicative of those emotions that occur when an event is being assessed with respect to the maintenance of valued goals.

The fact that surprise is often reported in conjunction with happiness, anger, or distress lends support to the notion of separating the understanding process from the evaluation process. When surprise occurs in close proximity to other emotions, surprise normally precedes other emotions. As an example, we provide dialogue from a recent study we (Stein & Trabasso, 1989) have carried out with 5-year-old children. On one occasion, a kindergarten student was told that her teacher was going to let all the children paint as part of the normal course of activities in the classroom. The child was then told that painting would occur on a daily basis, and she was asked how she would feel if she were allowed to paint everyday in her classroom. Her responses to this question were that she really liked painting (value) and that she felt it made her really happy (emotional response), especially when she could paint whatever she wanted.

This child was then told that today when she got through painting, her teacher was going to give her all the paints to take home. As a result, she would be able to paint at home as well as in school. The child was then asked to describe her thoughts and feelings in response to this event. She began by saying: "Do you really mean that she (the teacher) is going to let me take all the paints home? Am I the only one who gets to do this? Is this a present for me? Does she want me to paint everyday?"

If we had videotaped the facial expression of this child, we would have seen a look of surprise followed by a look of concern as she began to talk. First, this child did not quite believe that the teacher would give her a gift. Thus, to respond to this event, she first had to change her belief about the relative improbability of the event occurring. If we had asked her whether or not she thought her teacher would ever give her a gift of paints, we would probably be able to show that this child judged the event as highly unlikely. Approximately 70% of all the children in this study (Stein & Trabasso, 1989) actually said: "I don't believe it. Can you believe it? Why would she do that?" Apparently, teachers are not thought of as givers of gifts, and the act of a teacher giving a child a gift to take home violated these children's conceptions of what a teacher does. For children to evaluate the event in terms of their own goals, however, they first had to accept the fact that the teacher was indeed giving them a gift with which they could do whatever they wanted. Once the children accepted this fact, almost all of them expressed extreme happiness.

Thus, in our example, children first attempted to discern the truth value associated with the occurrence of a precipitating event. They then attempted to understand exactly why the teacher was giving them a paint set and what she wanted them to do with the set. The general act of one person giving another a gift was not an unfamiliar event to these children. In fact, this transaction is highly familiar, and children considered it a very pleasant experience. Therefore, most of the children encoded the event correctly the first time they heard about it. However, disbelief was still expressed because of the ambiguity inherent in the event. A teacher could give children paint sets for many reasons other than the one expressed in the text. The children were not initially convinced that the stated reason was in fact the one that the teacher had in mind. For these children, teachers are not associated with gift giving as much as they are associated with setting up tasks that must be accomplished. Thus, the novel element for these children was the act of their teacher giving them a gift.

The familiar combined with a novel dimension is often the factor that causes the greatest surprise, shock, or horror when such an event occurs. Examples of tragedies are those instances where a horrible event occurs, such as a plane crash or an earthquake, where the victim loses a loved one and does not believe that such an event could ever happen to him or her. The familiarity of such an event (i.e., knowing that such an event could happen and perhaps witnessing the grim reality of others having to cope with such a disaster) allows the victim to experience horror or grief. Moreover, shock and an air of unreality set in almost immediately or often precede the feeling of terror and grief. The ability to accept the fact that the event really has occurred and cannot be changed is the critical variable that regulates whether or not the consequences of the event will be processed. If doubt surrounds the occurrence of an event, attention will be focused first on determining the certainty of the event. For if there is any doubt that such an event occurred, most likely all possible resources will be devoted to ascertaining the reality of the event.

Surprise and interest are different from emotional responses in that they indicate an effort to construct new representations of novel information in a precipitating event. These affective responses are not directly associated with an evaluation of how a precipitating event affects the accomplishment of goals. The degree to which a precipitating event is considered possible or understood will predict whether surprise or interest is expressed. If the implications of the precipitating event are not evaluated in terms of whether valued goals have been threatened, blocked, or attained, then surprise should be expressed. Attempting to understand how precipitating events affect valued goals should be associated with states of interest or curiosity. However, as soon as the event is understood in terms of a valued goal, specific emotional responses should be present.

We now turn our attention to a description of the process of thinking and planning associated with four emotional responses. Most investigators studying the conceptual organization of emotional knowledge have simplified the thinking processes associated with emotional responses. Although emotional responses can indeed be rapid, occurring almost in an automatic fashion (Ekman, 1977), the delay between a precipitating event and an emotional response can also be quite long. We know of few on-line processing studies that have actually documented the variations in the time delays of emotional responses, nor do we know of any studies that have described the multiple changes that occur during attempts to understand the meaning of a precipitating event. Although we illustrate how four different emotional responses occur, our focus is on the process of experiencing and thinking about emotion.

THINKING AND REASONING ABOUT HAPPINESS, ANGER, AND SADNESS

When we talk about happiness as opposed to pleasure, or when we refer to anger, sadness, and fear, as opposed to pain, distress, or a startle response, we need to include additional evaluative processes that focus on the recognition of changes in maintaining or attaining a valued state (see Sroufe, 1979, for a cogent analysis of this shift). Pleasure, pain, interest, distress, and startle can occur without many of the dimensions associated with the causes of happiness, anger, sadness, or fear. These latter emotions do not occur independent of a context. We are happy or sad about something that happened; we are angry at something, we are afraid of something. These emotions occur because evaluations have been made about how a particular event will affect valued goals.

Before presenting a process analysis of these emotions (see Stein & Jewett, 1986; Stein & Levine, 1987, for an extended analysis), we draw attention to three problematic issues associated with the study of emotion. The first concerns the belief that some type of novel information must be detected for any emotion to be experienced. The second focuses on the disruption of thought and the disorganized nature of thinking and behavior that supposedly occur as a function of experiencing an emotion. The third pertains to whether positive and negative emotions have differential effects on thinking, planning, and decision making (see Isen, this volume, for a review of this literature; see Schwarz, 1988, for a somewhat different analysis).

For some reason, the claim that emotional responses occur in response to processing new or discrepant information has been one of the more misunderstood assertions associated with cognitive theories of emotion (Isen, 1984; Scherer, 1984; Sroufe, 1979). Positive emotions, in particular, are seen as not requiring the processing of novelty and are thought not to result in the interruption of ongoing cognitive activity. Moreover, positive emotions are thought to differ from negative emotions in being facilitative rather than disruptive of ongoing thought and behavior (see Isen, this volume; or Averill, 1979; Sroufe, 1979; for a discussion of these claims).

In a recent theoretical paper (Stein & Levine, 1987), we argued that both classes of emotional responses result from the processing of novel information. Moreover, both positive and negative emotions could be seen as facilitative or disruptive of ongoing thinking, depending on the context in which the emotion is experienced. Some of the variables regulating thinking once an emotion has been experienced are: the importance of attaining or maintaining the goal under consideration, whether or not plans have been formulated to cope with goal failure or success, whether or not immediate action is required; whether or not all goal-related activities have been accomplished; and whether or not the full implications of the goal–outcome relationship have been understood. These dimensions not only regulate attention and thinking during emotional experience, but they also regulate the intensity with which an emotion is experienced.

To say that negative emotions disrupt thinking or that positive emotions facilitate thinking is to conclude that the class of positive emotions versus those of negative emotions have some general property in common that would serve to influence subsequent thinking and planning. Moreover, the experience of positive versus negative emotion would be independent of the context that evoked the emotion. Although positive emotions are associated with reactions to goal success whereas negative emotions are evoked in response to goal failure, the thinking and reasoning in positive and negative emotional episodes is significantly constrained by the importance of the goal being considered and by the quality of inferences made about a goal in relation to other goals.

We now describe the evaluation and planning processes associated with the emotions happiness, sadness, anger, and fear (a more detailed description can be found in Stein & Levine, 1987). We have chosen to focus on only four emotions in order to give an in-depth description of each emotion. Our goal is to advance a theory about the process of experiencing an emotion and to speak to issues concerning the thinking and reasoning during an emotional episode.

We begin with a description of happiness to illustrate how it depends on the recognition of discrepant information, and how different types of "happy" experiences can either disrupt or facilitate thought and behavior. Moreover, we discuss the somewhat contradictory claims of Isen (this volume) and Schwarz (1988), who on the one hand claim that happiness leads to more creativity (Isen, this volume) and on the other assert that happiness leads to mindless, less analytical behavior (Schwarz, 1988). Finally, we show how an analysis of goal hierarchies and goal conflict is essential to understanding the representation of this emotion.

HAPPINESS

For a person to experience happiness, four dimensions must be detected or inferred from a precipitating event: First, some aspect of the event must be perceived as novel with respect to the ability to maintain, attain, or avoid a particular goal state; second, the inference must be made that a valued state has been achieved; third, an inference must be made about the certainty of attaining or maintaining the goal; that is, the person must believe that goal attainment is certain or that goal attainment has already occurred such that no further obstacles can hinder goal success; and fourth, a person must believe that enjoyment of the goal state or goal maintenance will follow from the outcome.

A prototypical way of thinking about the experience of happiness is to envision the transition from a negative to a positive state. Before the precipitating event occurs, the baseline thinking and behavior of an individual must be described. If we take those situations where people begin an emotion episode in a negative emotion state, several dimensions characterize their state. First, they have not yet attained the valued goal under consideration or they believe that a valued goal is threatened. Moreover, they believe that the probability of attaining the goal is not high.

A precipitating event then occurs causing or enabling the goal to be achieved. Happiness results when the following inferences are made. First, the event is encoded and seen as discrepant from what is known or believed. When an individual begins the emotion episode in a negative state, the discrepancy occurs because of the belief that goal achievement was not very likely. The fact that the goal has been attained or that goal attainment is virtually guaranteed violates expectations; that is, something unusual or unexpected has occurred. Attention is then focused on two different dimensions. First, an assessment is made as to whether or not the event was encoded properly, and second an appraisal is made about the relative certainty that a particular goal has been attained.

An example from one of our studies (Stein & Trabasso, 1989) illustrates this point. Five-year-old children were initially asked to imagine that their mother was not going to be able to read them a story before bedtime. They were told that they would just have to go to bed by themselves. Children were then asked: (a) how they would feel if this happened to them, (b) how intense their feelings would be (rating intensity on a 5-point scale), and (c) how sure they would be that their mother would not read them a bedtime story. In 92% of the cases, children said that they would feel sad because they could not hear a story and would have to go to bed alone. Their feelings were very intense, 4.5 out of 5. In rating the certainty of the fact that they were not going to get a story read to them, the average score was 1.5, with 1 being certain that no story would be read and 5 being certain that a story would be read to them.

After answering these questions, children were then told that their mother had thought about it again and that she was going to read them a story because she was able to get more of her chores done than expected. Children were asked what their first thoughts were about this event. Approximately 96% of the children said they would feel really happy because they loved stories and were glad that their mother changed her mind. Thus, for the clear majority of children there was a rapid shift from believing that goal attainment was at a very low probability (1.5) to believing that they would really attain their goal (4.5).

The other 4% of the children did not experience as significant a shift in certainty ratings. Their scores went from 1.6 to 3.5 on the certainty scale. These children first focused on whether or not their mother would really be able to get her chores done in time for the story. Thus, once the uncertainty of goal attainment was established in the beginning of the episode, a few children did not automatically believe that goal attainment was certain. When explicitly asked about how they felt when their mother said she would read them a story, these children said they felt okay but would wait to see if she really read them a story. None spontaneously expressed happiness, and when pressed explicitly about their feelings, most said they felt nervous or "jittery" or didn't know how they felt.

These data illustrate that happiness is expressed when expectations about the probability of goal success are violated. However, children must also update their beliefs about the certainty of goal success if they are to experience happiness. If they are able to change their beliefs, then happiness will be expressed. And when they talk about being happy, children almost always focus on being able to enjoy the activities associated with goal fulfillment. If children do not believe that goal attainment is certain, then a low-level anxiety response is evoked. Thus, the perception of certainty appears to be a necessary component to the expression of happiness.

Happiness does not necessarily require that people initially be in a negative emotion state. Individuals can make the transition to a happy state by first being in a more neutral state or by experiencing surprise or interest, signaling the formation of a new representation. However, once the representation is constructed and inferences are made about the success and the certainty of goal attainment, happiness is experienced.

Situations also exist where the experience of happiness intensifies. For example, suppose a person has just achieved an important goal and experiences a state of happiness. Suddenly, another event occurs to ensure the achievement of other valued goals. In this case, the emotion of happiness should intensify. The increase in intensity is due to the unexpected attainment of additional desired goals, some of which may be more valued than those originally attained. For example, in one of our studies, (Stein & Trabasso, 1989), 5-year-old children were told that they were to imagine that their teacher brought a new toy to class every week and that they got an hour to play with it by themselves. Children responded to this initial situation by giving almost unanimously happy responses, with an average of 4.3 on a 5-point intensity rating scale.

The children were then told that the teacher decided that they could take the toy home and keep it, because she knew how much they liked the toy. After acknowledging their surprise at such an event, 94% of the children expressed happiness about being able to take the toy home. The average intensity rating rose to from 4.3 to 4.9. Moreover, when asked if they were just as happy after getting the toy to take home, more happy, or less happy, 96% responded with more happy. When asked whether or not they expected the teacher to give them a toy, 94% said that they never thought she would do such a thing.

What we have shown so far is that fulfilling goals unexpectedly is sufficient to evoke happiness. Accomplishing additional goals unexpectedly increases the intensity of happiness. The question remains, however, as to whether novelty is *necessary* to induce happiness once inferences have been made about the achievement of a valued goal. In an attempt to answer this question, we asked 5-year-old children to respond to situations where habitual positive activities were repeated. Children were probed about their feelings and expectations the first time the teacher brought a new toy, the second time, and the third time. In all these instances, the children were told to remember that each time the teacher brought a toy, it would be different from the one before. In these situations, 80% of the children gave the same emotional response (happiness) over all three situations, and their intensity ratings remained the same (4.5). When asked why they would feel happy, over 98% explained their emotion by saying they would get to play with a new toy. Thus, the introduction of a new toy each time served to maintain the initial intensity rating of these children.

Children were then asked how they would feel if their teacher brought the same toy to class the first week, the second week, and the third week. In collecting this data, we took care to introduce the events sequentially as they would occur in a real-world environment. Again, 92% of the children said they would be happy the first time, with a mean intensity score of 4.7. After trial two, 75% said they would be really happy, with a mean intensity score of 3.5. On the third trial, only 20% said they would be really happy, with a mean intensity score of 2.8. Those children who did not express happiness said that they wouldn't feel anything or that they would become bored. The reason given for these affective responses (or lack of a response) was that sometimes they got tired of playing with the same toy and they needed to switch to another one.

Thus, we propose that when continued exposure to an event results in an emotional response at the same intensity level as the initial response, some degree of novelty is still being processed. However, as people incorporate the novel aspects of a stimulus and build a more stable representation of the event (i.e., the event becomes predictable and responses to it automatic), the emotional response decreases in intensity, eventually resulting in a state where attention is no longer focused on the event. These changes are similar to those described in studies of habituation and adaptation to a stimulus, where subjects become immune and almost unaware of certain sensations. Although our studies are still in the preliminary stages of development, they speak to the necessity of considering more seriously the role of repeated exposure on ratings of novelty, predictability, pleasure or pain, emotion, and intensity of the felt emotion. It is in the further understanding of adaptation phenomema that we will be able to determine whether or not novelty is necessary for the evocation of an emotional response.

Positive emotions do not necessarily facilitate thinking any more than negative emotions. Many studies have attested to the fact that positive mood states provoke more divergent thinking than negative emotions (see Isen, 1984, 1987, this volume), but that negative mood states, such as anger, lead to a greater degree of vigilance and analytical thinking than positive emotions. Thus, both positive and negative moods have been shown to facilitate thinking, depending on the nature of the thinking processes measured.

Our interpretation of these findings, however, is somewhat different from those of Isen (this volume) and Schwarz (1988). Although both these investigators have established robust findings with regard to how mood state affects subsequent thinking, we argue that both positive and negative emotions can be used to induce divergent or analytical thinking, and both classes of emotion can facilitate or hinder subsequent processing of new information. The important variables are the understanding and decision-making processes associated with the event that caused an emotional response and the thinking focused on coping with the emotion (see Folkman & Lazarus, this volume, on emotion-focused coping). We argue that the contextual constraints surrounding the induced mood state are as important as the particular valence of the mood.

Recent studies exploring the effect of mood state on subsequent thinking and decision making have focused largely on determining the effects of mood on subsequent thinking (Isen, 1984, 1987; Johnson & Tversky, 1983), without describing the thinking and decision-making processes that occur as a function of experiencing a particular emotion. The thinking that precedes a particular emotion, along with the intensity of the emotional experience, are powerful determinants of the ability to shift attention to new incoming information. For example, certain classes of "positive" events, like winning 40 million dollars in a lottery, are truly disruptive, as well as exhilarating. The probability of ever attaining this goal is small, and the number of life goals affected is enormous. If this event occurred before the presentation of some other cognitive task, we doubt we would see any facilitative effects of the happy state, including divergent thinking. In fact, we doubt that an experimenter could even get a subject's attention were this event to occur. However, if the event resulting in a positive emotion did not relate to other important life conditions and did not require continued attention to the emotion-eliciting event, then the focus of attention could readily shift to a new task.

Similar comments can be made about negative emotions. Thinking about a newly introduced task will be facilitated or disrupted depending on the type of prior goal obstructed, the value of the goal, and the complexity of the planning activities that result as a function of goal failure. In fact, if the experimental task required finding a solution to the problem that elicited the emotion in the first place, negative emotions might well facilitate performance on the task, especially in regard to divergent thinking. For example, one of the first steps in a problem-solving sequence is often devoted to "brainstorming" or generating many possible alternatives that might lead to a solution. The activation of this strategy is often the direct result of goal failure on the first attempt at a solution.

The important point in regard to the effects of happiness on subsequent thinking is that individuals typically construct plans to maintain the goal that has been achieved. They also attempt to maintain the positive emotion state associated with the successful outcome. The structure and content of some positive outcomes, however, are simpler than others. Figures 3.1 and 3.2 illustrate the different planning sequences accompanying two different positive outcomes. The first example is taken from the Stein (1988) corpus of stories children have generated in response to different stems. The second is taken from several newspaper articles about the Chicago winner of the 40 million dollar lottery. In the first example (Fig. 3.1), the plan is simply to participate in an activity that ensures the maintenance of the accomplished goal. We see this type of plan generated by young children when we give them a toy that they really desire. Their primary plans are to play with the toys and keep them close by for future play. In these situations, the outcome does not lead to consideration of any other goal except one of enjoyment.

In other situations, the achievement of the first goal is simply the first step in achieving more important goals. There are times when a person must accomplish a series of subgoals to achieve the superordinate goal. Happiness may be associated with the attainment of each subgoal. However, knowledge that the positive state is transitory unless other conditions are fulfilled results in attention to the new conditions that must be fulfilled.

Figure 3.2 illustrates the complexity associated with winning a lottery. Discovering that you hold the winning ticket in a lottery is only the first step in receiving the money. Although hearing your number broadcast over the radio results in surprise and a shock-like response, intense happiness does set in. In fact, the feeling by a recent Illinois lottery winner was described as one of disbelief and then sheer joy, especially as the increasing number of goals that could be accomplished was reviewed.

However, soon after the initial expression of happiness, disbelief again sets in. The number is confirmed again by calling the radio station to verify that the number was heard correctly. Joy is again expressed but short-lived because instructions are then given about claiming the money. These procedures involve accomplishing certain subgoals, like not losing the ticket, meeting the deadline for turning in the ticket, and showing care in driving to the radio station. The effect of activating these subgoals is to evoke anxiety over losing the ticket or not making the deadline. The complexity of the scenario continues even when the

INITIAL STATE
Johnny lost favorite toy
Won't be able to play with toy car after dinner
Won't be able to play "Racer" with Mike

WISH ASSOCIATED WITH STATE
Wishes he could find it

FEELING STATE
Feels sad about loss

REACTION
Go to sandbox to "mope"

ACTION
Discovers toy underneath sandcastle he built

OUTCOME
Now he can play with the car
Now he can play "Racer" with Mike

EMOTION STATE
Feels happy

PLAN OF ACTION
To play with car after dinner
To play "Racer" with Mike

ACTION
Carries out plans of action

OUTCOME
Successful

EMOTION STATE
Maintains state of happiness

FIG. 20.1.   Simple episode.

ticket is handed in and the winner confirmed. The lottery winner's parents are contacted because they put up some of the money for the ticket, and decisions need to be made as to how the winnings will be divided. Again, happiness in interleaved with attention to other goals that need to be accomplished as a result of winning. Thus, the question of context or framing becomes an important concern in making predictions about the effect of different emotions or mood states on subsequent thinking.

Our position also differs from that of Bower (Bower & Cohen, 1982), who proposed that the induction of specific mood states results in the activation of memories highly similar to the one induced by the emotion. From this point of

INITIAL STATE
Mike bought lottery ticket
So did one million others
Does not expect to win

↓

WISH ASSOCIATED WITH STATE
Wants to win lottery
Would not have to work
Could go to college
Could get married
Could buy house for parents
Could start own business

↓

PLAN OF ACTION
To find out if he won

↓

ACTION
Listens to radio

↓

OUTCOME
Numbers match his ticket

↓

EMOTION STATE
Happiness, combined with surprise and startle

LIST OF GOALS AND EVENTS THAT ARE EMBEDDED IN LEARNING OF WIN

1. Check ticket again to make sure of accuracy
2. Find out how to claim money
3. Find out how ticket can be protected until money is claimed
4. Be careful driving to lottery site so you won't get into an accident
5. Check with parents and brothers to see how winnings will be divided
6. Decide how many of you are going to the lottery board to claim the money
7. Go down to board to claim prize

PROBLEMS ARISING AS A FUNCTION OF THE LOTTERY WIN

1. Discord between parents and brothers as to how money should be distributed
2. Arguments with IRS about legality of dividing lottery win
3. Arguments with lawyers about the necessity of a prenuptial agreement concerning lottery money
4. Discord at work because of status change and availability of new resources
5. Problems in starting a new business because of lack of skill in any particular area

GOAL COMPLETION AS A FUNCTION OF LOTTERY WIN

1. Got married
2. Split money with parents and brothers
3. Bought parents new house

FIG. 20.2.   Complex episode.

view, when in a sad state, thinking reflects a series of associations related to the notion of sadness per se and not to the situation. Although we can think of instances where associative chaining occurs, a primary assumption underlying our model is that the experience of emotion is goal driven and problem focused. Moreover, when an emotion is experienced, attention is directed toward being able to maintain or reinstate a goal. Instead of running off an associative network that is driven by the emotion per se, people try to achieve a better understanding of the conditions that would lead to goal maintenance or reinstatement. Therefore, thinking subsequent to an emotional experience is likely to focus on the conditions that caused the emotional reaction, past experiences that allow predictions to be made about the probable consequences of the event, memories of successful strategies adopted in response to similar situations in the past, and an assessment of the outcome of those strategies.

We also assume that as people succeed or fail to attain valued goals, they learn more about the conditions that lead to the outcome. They also change their beliefs and feelings about the people who took part in their emotional experiences. For example, as a function of winning the 40 million dollar lottery, Mike changed his feelings about many of his friends. A few of them decided to ask Mike for backing in a financial venture. When Mike refused, they reacted by completely ignoring him. The result was that Mike learned that they did not consider him a friend unless he would support them financially. Moreover, they tried to harm him by rejecting him. Mike felt devastated at the loss of these friendships, but at the same time the value of these friendships decreased. Mike no longer trusted any of them.

From these newspaper and magazine accounts, we developed a scenario that explained Mike's feelings and reactions to the lottery in terms of the goals he wanted to accomplish before the lottery and after winning the lottery. The scenario contained the feelings Mike expressed and the plans that he actually carried out. Then we asked eight students to rank the importance of Mike's goals before and after the lottery. We predicted a significant change in almost all importance scores given before and after the lottery. Before winning the lottery, the average ratings assigned to each of five goals on a 10-point importance scale, with 10 being the most important, were as follows:

1. Get Married: 7
2. Go to college: 8
3. Stop work: 9
4. Buy a house for parents: 5
5. Start own business: 4

Once the lottery was won, however, certain goals became more important and others became less important. For example, our scenario included the fact that Mike decided that the first thing he wanted to do was to get married, so his rating of getting married went from 7 to 10. He then decided that he didn't have to go to college because he had enough money so that he didn't have to worry about education or his future. Thus, the rating of going to college went from 8 to 2. Buying a house for his parents became very important as did his concern about their general welfare. The importance rating went from a 5 to a 9. Before the lottery, he was so preoccupied with his own growth and survival that he rarely devoted the time or effort into thinking about his parents except in a rather automatic "caring" fashion. Starting his own business stayed at a medium low level because being accepted as a "regular" guy became more important as a function of winning the lottery. Mike perceived that people at work began to treat him differently. He now had access to resources that few of them did. Moreover, he received a great deal of publicity about his win, including being written about in "People" magazine and "Good Housekeeping." Thus, Mike felt a dramatic change in the feelings and attitudes people had toward him. His response to this change was to place a greater degree of importance on maintaining his present job, so the importance rating for stopping his job went from 9 to 3.

Thus, an event like winning a lottery changed the perceived importance attached to several different goals. Certain goals became more important in the sense that Mike really wanted to achieve these goals, and others became less important in that he did not have an immediate desire to see them accomplished. Some goals, like going to college, became very unimportant. In fact, for those goals that shifted dramatically in their level of importance, we must consider another issue: whether their value also changed.

Although the degree of importance and the degree of value overlap considerably, these dimensions are not isomorphic. In collecting our rankings, importance was defined by the question, "How much does Mike really want to accomplish this goal? How important is it that he accomplish this goal?" Although positive value would probably be imputed to most of Mike's goals (i.e., "How much does he like doing this?"), this does not always have to be the case. Accomplishing a subgoal can be very important in maintaining a higher order goal, but true displeasure can be expressed in terms of how much the subgoal is valued. For example, before winning the lottery, Mike asserted that he hated his job and would do anything he could to quit. After the lottery, winning the acceptance of his friends became very important to him, and he chose to do it by maintaining contact with them through his job. However, he still hated his job. The problem was that he could not generate any other plan of action that would accomplish the superordinate goals that were important to him.

Although we are just beginning to describe the nature of value construction and that of shifting values, both these factors are important for theories of emotional understanding. The value imputed to a goal and the importance of achieving it organize and determine in part whether an emotional response is experienced and the plan of action associated with the emotional response. As we turn now to a description of anger and sadness, we illustrate again the centrality of values, value construction, and learning from negative outcomes. Moreover, we again show that when people experience loss or aversive states, the number of goals affected can vary dramatically. Thus, the consequences can be major in that several different goals are affected, or they can be minor in that one or two goals are affected.

Given that anger and sadness are similar in this regard, what differentiates them? According to our model (Stein & Levine, 1987, 1989) anger occurs when a person responds to a loss or aversive state by inferring that the obstructed goal can be reinstated. More specifically, people firmly believe that they can somehow initiate a plan to restore the original conditions that existed before a loss or an aversive state occurred. In these circumstances, attention is often focused on understanding the cause of the loss or aversive state so that an effort can be made to change the conditions resulting in the undesired state. Thus, anger often carries with it a desire not only to reinstate the goal but also to remove or change the conditions that led to goal blockage in the first place.

Unlike many other analyses of anger (Averill, 1979; Roseman, 1979, 1984; Weiner, 1985), in our analysis the perception of intentional harm or the presence of an animate agent is not necessary to invoke anger. Anger is expressed because a person experiences an unexpected loss, failure, or aversive state and refuses to accept being in the resultant state. Refusal here means that the person believes that somehow the conditions surrounding the loss or aversive state can be changed so that the unpleasant state no longer exists. Thus, almost any type of loss or aversive state can evoke anger when a belief about goal reinstatement exists.

The intentional harm component associated with anger may be a function of socialization. In most societies, anger is not condoned because the plan accompanying anger is often destructive and harmful to others. In some societies, actions carried out under the influence of anger are often thought to indicate insanity (Averill, 1979; Tavris, 1982) or the lack of the ability to reason. Therefore certain forms of anger are acceptable only in young children who have not yet been accorded the status of a reasoning and thinking person (Lutz, 1985a, 1985b). However, when children reach the age of 6 or 7, they are taught that anger is a permissible emotion, but only under certain conditions. The distinguishing dimension that is used to teach children when anger can be expressed is directly associated with intentional harm (Lutz, 1985a, 1985b). In fact, in the Ifaluk society, two different words are used to talk about anger. One refers to anger evoked without reason, and the other refers to justifiable anger cause by an agent who meant intentional harm.

Although sadness and anger often occur in response to the same event, sadness is different from anger in two respects. Sadness is experienced when a person believes that a goal cannot be reinstated. Although people who experience sadness often desire to reinstate a failed goal (much like anger), the plan of action associated with sadness is one of goal abandonment or goal substitution. Here we make a distinction between the wishes that accompany an emotion and the plans of action that are activated by goal failure. When people suffer major losses such that they no longer have access to a valued state, such as the loss of a loved one, they soon recognize that no possibility exists for them ever to reinstate their goal (e.g., to regain the relationship in the literal sense). Under these conditions, however, the desire to reinstate the goal does not necessarily recede or become less important. Because a multitude of memories are associated with loved ones, the desire to have them back or to interact with them again often remains ever present. A good example of this desire was expressed by the comedian George Burns (1988), who confessed to the fact that once a month when he visited Gracie Allen's grave he sat and talked to her about everything that was happening to him. In fact, he admitted that he had been doing this for 24 years, since Gracie had died. This is not uncommon behavior on the part of many individuals (Worden, 1982). The social condemnation that goes along with it, however, inhibits most individuals from expressing their real desires and thoughts.

In many instances, the uniqueness of a love object determines whether the desire to reinstate the goal abates. If the love object is deemed irreplaceable, the desire to recreate the original conditions before the loss remains strong. Although this type of desire is deemed unrealistic (i.e., the focus of attention is on the recreation of conditions that are no longer possible), positive value can be attributed to this type of thinking. By recreating previous situations that were highly valued, an opportunity exists to examine exactly what it was about the situation that proved to be so important. By focusing on these critical features, wishes and plans can gradually be constructed to substitute a goal for the permanently blocked goal.

Wishes and plans to abandon the goal can also occur. Many times, goal failure results in such intense distress, as well as sadness, that the goal is abandoned without a desire to reinstate or substitute a similar goal. For example, in many athletic competitions, the athletes who lose will not try to compete again. They feel that they've given the competition their best shot and interpret their losing as irrevocable under any condition. Thus, the goal to become the top athlete is permanently abandoned, and no future attempts are made.

So far, we have described the evaluation and planning processes associated with anger and sadness. One more phenomenon with respect to these two emotions deserves discussion. Not only do the same events provoke these two emotions, but often both emotions are expressed in reaction to a loss or aversive state. In our model, the expression of more than one emotion to a precipitating event is not only feasible but increasingly likely, especially as a function of development. The reason for the occurrence of multiple emotions is that a precipitating event can change the probability of attaining or maintaining more than one goal. Anger can be expressed in regard to one goal and sadness to another.

The prototypic context in which both emotions are expressed is one of loss, where the loss is brought about by intentional harm (Stein & Levine, 1989). For example, when Johnny found out that his friend smashed his favorite toy to pieces, at least three different emotional responses could be expressed: Johnny could be sad, angry, or both sad and angry. On the one hand, Johnny is sad because his favorite toy has been destroyed, and he feels that it is irreplaceable. Thus, even though he would like the toy fixed, he knows that it's impossible to repair it, so sadness is expressed. On the other hand, Johnny feels really angry because he recognized that his friend intentionally destroyed his favorite toy. In doing this, his friend violated either an unwritten or explicit code about what friends are and are not allowed to do. Moreover, the violation of this code resulted in direct harm, and Johnny perceived this act as a threat to other important goals. He also felt that his friend could repeat the harmful act in other situations.

Thus, loss caused by an agent intending harm generates changes in the status of several goals. One set of changes focuses on the loss of a valued object and the goals associated with its reinstatement. Another set of changes focuses on the relationship between Johnny and his friend. The violation of the "friendship" code results in the realization that Johnny cannot trust his friend in other situations. Moreover, the fact that his friend was responsible for breaking the toy evoked a desire to have the friend recompensate him in some way. It is interesting to note that anger responses to irrevocable loss often involve getting the harmful agent to engage in some kind of behavior that promotes the substitution of a goal by the injured party. For example, Johnny's response to the loss of his toy was to demand that his friend reimburse him for the cash amount of the toy. According to Johnny, the only way the friendship could ever be restored was for his friend to pay for the broken toy. Moreover, his friend had to "promise" that he would never again engage in another harmful act directed toward Johnny.

There are many instances of anger where the primary goal of the injured party is simply to destroy the agent who caused intentional harm. However, this is not necessarily the prototypic anger response (Tavris, 1982). For revenge strategies to be initiated, specific inferences must be made about the aggressor. The first concerns the value the victim places on the aggressor, and the second focuses on the degree of harm the aggressor can still inflict on the victim. If the victim believes that the aggressor will actively seek to carry out harmful acts in the future and if the victim believes that the aggressor's behavior cannot be changed, then the solution of destroying the aggressor or destroying the aggressor's power might emerge. Indeed, we can generate many examples of these solutions by examining intense family conflict, where the majority of violent acts are committed. In the prototypic anger situation, however, the goal of the victim is to reinstate the original conditions that existed before the loss or aversive state occurred (Stein & Jewett, 1986). The restoration of conditions focuses on both those that pertain to the loss (if possible) and to the relationship that exists between the victim and the aggressor.

To test many of these ideas, we (Stein & Levine, 1989) carried out an empirical study with 3- and 6-year-old children as well as a group of college students. The task for all subjects was to respond to several different events by thinking out loud and by answering questions that focused on the causes of three different emotions: happiness, sadness, and anger. The events used to elicit these three emotions were constructed to mirror four different types of goal–outcome relationships: (a) the attainment of valued states; (b) the avoidance of undesirable states; (c) the loss of a valued state; and (d) failure to avoid an undesired state. The valued states focused on acquiring or losing a favorite toy car or a puppy. Unpleasant states focused on having to eat a disliked food (spinach) or having to be outside when it was very cold. The type of event that caused these states also varied such that the end states resulted as a function of: (a) another person intentionally causing the outcome, (b) another accidentally causing the outcome, or (c) a physical event causing the outcome.

All subjects were asked a series of questions regarding their feeling states, their first thoughts after the event occurred, the reasons for their feelings, the type of wish they would have in response to coping with the situation, the plans they would devise to carry out, and explanations for their choice of actions. In other words, each subject was guided through all the parts of an emotion episode related to a causal theory of emotional understanding. Although many investigators have described theoretical constructs for examining the process of emotional experience, the specific processes that are actually carried out with respect to the encoding, representation, and retrieval of information have yet to be described. Thus, we chose to structure our interview to reflect the various processes associated with the sequence of representing and understanding emotional experience.

Figure 3.3 contains the proportion of anger responses reported in each causal condition (physical event, animate agent causing intentional harm, animate agent causing unintentional harm) for each type of negative outcome (loss versus aversive state). Anger was chosen more frequently in all conditions when the

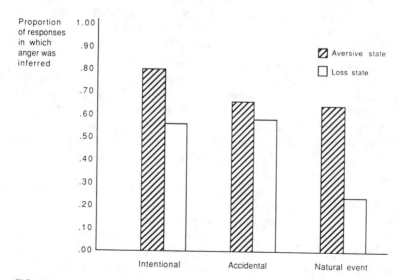

FIG. 20.3   Proportion of responses in which anger was inferred in each causal condition and in episodes ending in loss and aversive states.

episodes ended with an aversive rather than a loss state. The type of causal agent, however, did affect the proportion of anger responses.' When an animate agent intentionally or unintentionally caused the story protagonist to suffer a loss, anger responses were more frequent than when a natural event caused the loss. Thus, the mere presence of an animate agent was enough to increase the frequency of anger responses in loss states. When an intentionally harmful agent put the story protagonist into an aversive state, the frequency of anger responses increased significantly in proportion to the frequency in aversive conditions where accidental harm resulted. Thus, the concept of agency is important in ascribing anger to others, but the type of goal failure is also a powerful predictor of anger. Thus, our results are similar to those of Berkowitz and Heimer (1989), who contend that aversive events indeed prime anger, irritation, and hostility across a variety of contexts.

If anger is elicited by the perception that harm has occurred and that an unpleasant state exists, then the immediate goal will be to focus on the removal of the unpleasant state. Desiring a change in the existing conditions should be especially true in situations of an aversive painful nature. In fact, our results supported this hypothesis. When aversive states resulted and the emotion inferred was one of anger, over 76% of all subjects desired to reinstate the goal. However, the plans of action adopted were often associated with abandoning the goal rather than reinstating it. For example, in one of our scenarios, subjects were told that a protagonist would have to eat spinach for dinner because there was no other food in the house. Under these circumstances, the clear majority of subjects expressed anger at having to eat a food that was intensely disliked. On the other hand, most adopted plans of action where the protagonist ate the disliked food. When spinach was all there was to eat in the house, many subjects stated that the thought of not eating anything was worse than eating the spinach. Thus, in actuality plans to abandon the goal were enacted.

These data strongly suggest that the planning process associated with specific emotions is more complex than originally described. Although anger and sadness carry definite wishes of goal reinstatement, the plans that accompany the two emotions are often constrained by an assessment of how the desired plan of action will affect the achievement of other goals. If the desired plan will result in a more general failure experience such that more goals become unattainable, then the normal plan associated with an emotion will not be enacted. Thus, reasoning about possible conflict among goals becomes an important concern in future work on emotional experience.

Furthermore, what needs to be examined is the effect of repeated anger in situations where the aversive state continues over time. In our study, subjects had to make predictions about other people's behavior when aversive states were experienced on a one-time basis. For example, our scenarios had protagonists having to eat spinach because of a snow storm or because one's mother forgot to buy a favorite food at the store. Although these aversive states were permanent, in the sense that, for the moment, subjects chose to tolerate them in order to avoid other unpleasant states, it is unclear what would happen if subjects were exposed to aversive states on a continual basis. If someone had to eat spinach everyday and initially disliked it, the ensuing response might change from one of toleration to one where specific action was taken to end the aversive state. If no action could be taken, the option of not maintaining other important goals might be made. Under these conditions, anger responses could easily become ones of sadness.

CONCLUSIONS

The approach we are advocating in the study of emotion is one where the achievement of specific goals are tracked over time in order to assess how success or failure of one goal affects the maintenance of other goals. Moreover, the way in which subjects react to repeated success or failure must be assessed. Something is learned each time a person attempts to achieve a goal and either succeeds or fails. If subjects succeed at attaining a valued goal, the initial focus of attention is typically on the positive consequences that ensue from success. Moreover, a feeling of relaxation often accompanies positive feeling states because effort is no longer needed to plan for successful goal attainment. In fact, Schwarz (1988) proposes that happy states lead to rather mindless behavior. Happy people are not as evaluative of other people's actions as angry people are. Moreover, assessing the conditions that led to goal success does not appear to be as frequent as when failure occurs.

These findings may hold for the initial period immediately following goal success. However, success also requires maintenance activities. When subjects realize that an effort has to be made to maintain valued goals, then an analysis of the conditions that led to goal success should be of central importance. If goal-related activities have not been successful, the initial focus of attention should be on attempts to understand and control the conditions that might lead to goal success. If, however, repeated attempts at goal attainment end in failure, the typical reaction might be one of assessing the consequences of failure rather than focusing on conditions that led to failure. What we are suggesting is that the degree of uncertainty associated with goal maintenance might regulate the type of thinking carried out subsequent to an emotional reaction rather than the valence of the expressed emotion.

Furthermore, different negative emotions such as sadness, anger, and fear have very different effects on subsequent thinking and reasoning activities. Although each of these emotions is defined as negative, each carries with it a different plan of action (Stein & Jewett, 1986; Stein & Levine, 1987). Anger and fear are both active emotions in that plans are oriented toward goal reinstatement or maintenance. However, the two are different. Anger tends to orient people toward an assessment of the conditions that would result in a reinstatement of the goal. This desire often leads people to assess the conditions that actually caused goal failure so that any obstacle can be removed. Thus, thinking about angry situations tends to promote backward thinking.

Fear, on the other hand, is oriented toward maintaining valued goal states (Stein & Jewett, 1986). Specifically, self-preservation, either psychological or physical, is at stake. Thus attention is focused primarily on methods to ensure self-preservation. Often, this desire leads to a plan of removing the self from the threatening situation. Therefore, the conditions that led to the threatening situation are not assessed. Rather, plans for preventing harm are central. Given that the focus of attention is different for fear and anger, we are curious as to how each of these emotions would affect subsequent thinking on tasks unrelated to the experience of the emotion. Moreover, we would ask how the immediacy of formulating a plan of action in each emotion state would affect subsequent thinking and reasoning.

And finally, the intensity of the emotional reaction should be an important predictor of thinking and reasoning. Intensity, as it is currently defined (Mandler, 1975, 1984), is most often associated with the importance of the goal at stake. However, the amount of effort that needs to be expended in carrying out goal activities, as well as the necessity to act quickly, may also be pertinent in assessments of intensity. The important point, however, is that the intensity of an emotional reaction restricts the amount of attention that can be given to subsequent thinking activities. As Rachman (1978) has noted, the intensity of a fear response precludes processing any extraneous information to a great extent. Rather, attention becomes narrowed to specific dimensions of the situation related to expected impending harm.

REFERENCES

Averill, J. R. (1979). Anger. In H. E. Howe & R. A. Dienstbier (Eds.), *Nebraska Symposium on Motivation: Human Emotions* (Vol. 26, pp. 1–80). Lincoln: University of Nebraska Press.

Berkowitz, L., & Heimer, K. (1989). Aversive events and negative priming in the formation of feelings. In L. Berkowitz (Ed.), *Advances in experimental social psychology.* New York: Academic Press.

Bower, G., & Cohen, P. R. (1982). Emotional influences in memory and thinking: Data and theory. In M. S. Clark & S. T. Fiske (Eds.), *Affect and Cognition: 17th Annual Carnegie Symposium on Cognition.* Hillsdale, NJ: Lawrence Erlbaum Associates.

Burns, G. (1988). Gracie: A love story. New York: Putnam.

Ekman, P. (1977). Biological and cultural contribution to body and facial movements. In J. Blocking (Ed.), *Anthropology of the body.* London: Academic Press.

Emde, R. (1980). Levels of meaning in infant development. In W. A. Collins (Ed.), *Minnesota Symposium on Child Psychology* (Vol. 13). Hillsdale, NJ: Lawrence Erlbaum Associates.

Fernald, A. (1984). The perceptual and affective salience of mothers' speech to infants. In L. Feagans, C. Garvey, & R. Golinkoff (Eds.), with M. T. Greenberg, C. Harding, & J. Bohannon, *The origins and growth of communication.* Norwood, NJ: Ablex.

Folkman, S., and Lazarus, R. S. (in press). Coping and emotion. In N. L. Stein, B. Leventhal, & T. Trabasso (Eds.), *Psychological and biological approaches to emotion*. Hillsdale, N.J.: Lawrence Erlbaum Associates.

Gallistel, C. R. (1985). Motivation, intention, and emotion: Goal-directed behavior from a cognitive neuroethological perspective. In M. Frese & J. Sabini (Eds.), *Goal-directed behavior: The concept of action in psychology*. Hillsdale, NJ: Lawrence Erlbaum Associates.

Isen, A. (1984). Toward understanding the role of affect in cognition. In R. Wyer & T. Srull (Eds.), *Handbook of social cognition* (Vol. 3, pp. 179–236) Hillsdale, NJ: Lawrence Erlbaum Associates.

Isen, A. (1987). Toward understanding the role of affective cognition. In R. S. Wyer & T. S. Srull (Eds.), *Handbook of social cognition* (Vol. 3). Hillsdale, NJ: Lawrence Erlbaum Associates.

Johnson, E. J., & Tversky, A. (1983). Affect, generalization, and the perception of risk. *Journal of Personality and Social Psychology, 45*, 20–31.

Lazarus, R. S., & Folkman, S. (1984). *Stress, appraisal, and coping*. New York: Springer.

Lutz, C. (1985a). Ethnopsychology compared to what? Explaining behavior and consciousness among the Ifaluk. In G. M. White & J. Kirkpatrick (Eds.), *Person, self, and experience: Exploring pacific ethnopsychologies*. Berkeley: University of California Press.

Lutz, C. (1985b). Cultural patterns and individual differences in the child's emotion meaning system. In M. Lewis & C. Saarni (Eds.), *The socialization of affect* (pp. 161–186). New York: Plenum Press.

Mandler, G. (1975). *Mind and emotion*. New York: Wiley.

Mandler, G. (1982). The structure of value: Accounting for taste. In M. S. Clark & S. T. Fiske (Eds.), *Affect and cognition: 17th Annual Carnegie Symposium on Cognition*. Hillsdale, NJ: Lawrence Erlbaum Associates.

Mandler, G. (1984). *Mind and body: Psychology of emotion and stress*. New York: Norton.

Mandler, J. (1988). How to build a baby: On the development of an accessible representation system. *Cognitive Development, 3*, 113–136.

Piaget, J. (1981). *Intelligence and affectivity*. Palo Alto, CA: Annual Reviews.

Rachman, S. J. (1978). *Fear and courage*. San Francisco: W. H. Freeman.

Roseman, I. J. (1979). *Cognitive aspects of emotion and emotional behavior*. Paper presented at the American Psychological Association Meetings, New York.

Roseman, I. J. (1984). Cognitive determinants of emotions: A structural theory. In P. Shaver (Ed.), *Review of personality and social psychology: Emotions, relationships, and health* (Vol. 5, pp. 11–36). Beverly Hills: Sage.

Scherer, K. R. (1984). On the nature and function of emotion: A component process approach. In K. R. Scherer & P. Ekman (Eds.), *Approaches to emotion*. Hillsdale, NJ: Lawrence Erlbaum Associates.

Schwarz, N. (1988, August). *Happy but mindless*. Paper presented at the Symposium: Affect and Cognition, 24th International Congress of Psychology, Sydney, Australia.

Sroufe, A. (1979). Socioemotional development. In J. Osofsky (Ed.), *The handbook of infant development*. New York: Wiley.

Stein, N. L. (1988). The development of storytelling skill. In M. B. Franklin & S. Barten (Eds.), *Child language: A book of readings*. New York: Cambridge University Press.

Stein, N. L., & Jewett, J. (1986). A conceptual analysis of the meaning of negative emotions: Implications for a theory of development. In C. E. Izard & P. Read (Eds.), *Measurement of emotion in infants and children* (Vol. 2, pp. 238–267). New York: Cambridge University Press.

Stein, N. L., & Levine, L. J. (1987). Thinking about feelings: The development and organization of emotional knowledge. In R. E. Snow & M. Farr (Eds.), *Aptitude, learning, and instruction: Cognition, conation and affect* (Vol. 3, pp. 165–198). Hillsdale, NJ: Lawrence Erlbaum Associates.

Stein, N. L., & Levine, L. J. (1989). The causal organization of emotional knowledge: A developmental study. *Cognition and Emotion*, Special Issue on the Development of Emotion.

Stein, N. L., & Trabasso, T. (1989). Children's understanding of changing emotion states. In C. Saarni & P. L. Harris (Eds.), *Children's understanding of emotion*. New York: Cambridge University Press.

Tavris, C. (1982). Anger: The misunderstood emotion. New York: Simon & Shuster.

Weiner, B. (1985). An attributional theory of achievement motivation and emotion. *Psychological Review, 92* (4), 548–573.

Worden, J. W. (1982). *Grief counseling and grief therapy.* New York: Springer.

Zajonc, R. (1980). Feeling and thinking: Preferences need no inferences. *American Psychologist, 35*, 151–175.

21 The Emotion-in-Relationships Model: Reflections and Update

Ellen Berscheid
University of Minnesota

Mandler interruption theory

My invitation to participate in this volume celebrating the redoubtable scholarship of George Mandler stems, no doubt, from my application and slight extension of his "interruption theory of emotion," as he originally outlined it in *Mind and Emotion* (1975). The application was to emotion as it occurs, or sometimes inexplicably and disappointingly fails to occur, in the context of a close relationship with another person and the extension (i.e., the "completion hypothesis") was intended to account better for positive emotions (Berscheid, 1983).

In the few pages allotted to me to pay my respects to George Mandler and his works, I should like, first, to sketch the background events that led to my discovering *Mind and Emotion* a decade or so ago. Second, I shall adumbrate the emotion-in-relationships (E-in-R) model and discuss the indirect influence it and George's theory of emotion had upon the very conception of what a close relationship is, and thus the approach many of us are now taking to the systematic study of interpersonal relationships. And, finally, I will describe some of our efforts to test the E-in-R model and the validating findings that have accrued to its credit—and so also to the credit of its "grandfather," interruption theory. It is this last account, of course, that is most important because true homage to another's intellectual contribution to the scientific enterprise is always paid in that most valuable of coins, empirical elbow grease.

SEARCHING FOR ANSWERS ABOUT LOVE AND RELATIONSHIPS IN THE SWAMP OF EMOTION

In the late 1970s and early 1980s, one could discern only faint glimmers of the surge of emotion theory and research that was shortly to take place and that continues in intensity and volume to the present day. Emotion was still regarded by many as an impenetrable swamp into which certain scholars had wandered over the years of psychology's history, some never to return (see Berscheid, 1990). Even with Stanley Schachter as an impressive role model, the chances of a social psychologist making a quick foray into that jungle, capturing something worthwhile to help illuminate interpersonal relationships, and then getting out clear-eyed seemed to be slim to none.

I had at that time, however, two strong reasons to overcome my pessimistic view of the benefits of an immersion in the emotion literature of the day. The first reason was personal and involved William Proxmire, the then-Senator from Wisconsin and member of the committee that made appropriations for the National Science Foundation. He issued a press release just before Valentine's Day in 1976 that, in effect, told the world (truly the world—a friend shopping in GUM's department store in Moscow at the time heard my name and Proxmire's over the loudspeaker but could not decipher the remainder of this urgent radio bulletin) that I was studying romantic love with federal monies. It also mentioned that rather than wasting taxpayer money on an insoluble puzzle, the matter should be left to Elizabeth Barrett Browning and Irving Berlin. Study of the Alaskan brown bear and other National Science Foundation (NSF) funded projects were also strongly criticized but, luckily for the bear, only the love portion of the release captured widespread public interest.

Far more disconcerting than the peculiar mixture of death threats and proposals of marriage subsequently received from numerous unsavory persons were the bushels of letters that arrived from scholars all over the world. Only Red China was silent, as always at that time—virtually every other country on the world map, even little Albania of James Bond fame, was heard from. They all asked that I please tell them, by express return mail, all that I had discovered about romantic love. Unfortunately, the funded research Proxmire had attacked was actually generic interpersonal attraction research; it examined the antecedents and consequences of "liking," more properly classified as an evaluation than an emotion, using Simon's (1984) proposed terminological convention for emotion scholars. In the text of my proposal, however, I had speculated briefly about the phenomenon of romantic love and this was represented by a fatal line or two in the proposal's abstract.

And, so, I had little useful to say to the world about romantic love. In fact, I knew next to nothing about love. Hatfield and I (Berscheid & Walster, 1974) had previously attempted to explain some instances of the feeling of passionate love, but the Schacterian misattribution-of-arousal process theorized to be involved in these instances could reasonably account for only a small fraction of instances in this category of emotions. Thus, our theoretical effort properly belonged in the misattribution-of-arousal literature; it certainly was not the simple and sovereign theory of romantic love that it was enthusiastically, but mistakenly, taken by some to be.

I found myself, then, in the worst of all possible worlds: pilloried, on the one hand, for studying a topic I actually was not, and, on the other, politely considered either a numbskull or a charlatan by scholars world-wide who quickly discovered I could not answer their questions about love. I realized quickly that if I had the name and notoriety, I may just as well have the game—and I suspected that the game had to be lurking somewhere in that forbidding thicket of emotion theory and research.

There was a second reason for burying myself—temporarily, I hoped—in the emotion literature of the time. I had been invited to join a group of psychologists of different stripes whose mission was to develop a conceptual framework that would facilitate the systematic study of close relationships. Close relationships was a topic whose time had come given the erosion of the American family unit by divorce and serial marriage and by the growing popularity of such "alternative" life styles as cohabitation. Ominously, we were to be funded by the NSF.

Close relationships and emotion are soul mates, of course. Most of the questions people have about close relationships actually have to do with the emotions and feelings they experience within those relationships, or, in association with the partner. For this reason, no one interested in relationships can fail to be interested in emotion. Conversely, the most intense and dramatic of the emotions are experienced in relationships with other people, especially close relationships; interpersonal relationships, in fact, are generally agreed to be the context in which emotions and feelings of any kind are most frequently experienced. One might expect, then, that emotion theorists and researchers would keep a weather eye out for the implications of their propositions and findings for interpersonal relationships. This, I was to discover, is rarely true; scholars of emotion tend to be interested in relationships primarily when searching for illustrative examples to revive their readers' flagging attention to the specifics of their theory or to the phenomena under investigation. Rather, I was to learn that scholars devoted to solving the mysteries of human emotion were doing very nicely, thank you, with their rats and chickens and lesioned apes, with their facial musculature and their brain circuitry, and that other than for the person whose experience of emotion was being dissected (and, possibly, the anonymous other who might attempt to "decode" the identity of the emotion), the emotion theoretical landscape was remarkably unpopulated.

I learned all this when I finally sat down to work. On one side of the room was a formidably large mound of papers and books about emotion that I had bought, borrowed from colleagues, or purloined from the library; on the other side, there was an equally large collection of questions that any reasonably complete theory of emotion should have been able to answer about the emotions as people actually experience them in their daily lives. These were questions frequently asked by undergraduate and graduate students, by marital, family, and other relationship counselors and clinicians, by media reporters and columnists who interview "love researchers," as well as by the man and woman on the street. Together, they composed what I came to think of as the "paradoxes, conundrums, and sad facts about emotion in close relationships" (for a listing of some of these questions, see Berscheid, 1982).

The answers to the questions, I believed, had to be somewhere in that big pile of books and papers about emotion. Fortunately, the pile included Mandler's *Mind and Emotion;* unfortunately, the book was thicker than the others as well as forbidding of mien and so it kept sinking to the bottom. It thus was not until after I had spent many months of reading about how emotions are "blended" with each other in a kaleidoscope of ways, of reading historical accounts about the discouragingly difficult problem of emotion in psychology, and of plowing through lengthy tracts that, in the end, put all the answers to questions about emotion somewhere in the hippocampus (or was it the hypothalamus?), that I picked up Mandler's book.

All, or at least almost all, the answers seemed to be lying there in Mandler's theoretical framework. Moreover, Mandler had style! The only claim he made for his theory was that it seemed to him to be "more right than wrong"; what he had to say was not incompatible with what other sensible people were doing at other levels, and in other areas, of analysis; and, most importantly for me and my mission, Mandler, unlike the other theorists I had read, gave full attention to the fundamental question that, I now realized, permeated those commonly asked questions about emotion in relationships: "*When* do people experience emotion?" (or, its mirror image: "Why *don't* they experience emotion—even though they think they should and even though they would like to?").

Mandler's hypothesis that interruption, by his definition an *unexpected* event, is a sufficient and possibly necessary condition for the experience of emotion was clearly the key that could open the doors to understanding emotion in the context of close relationships. Mandler maintained that when an individual experiences emotion, an interruption of some ongoing activity—either an organized behavior sequence or a higher-order plan—has probably occurred. Most other theorists were content to examine and to dissect virtually all of the elements involved in emotional experience except the one that puts the whole fascinating and complex apparatus in motion—the nature of the events that trigger emotional experience.

EMOTION-IN-RELATIONSHIPS

What does the interruption hypothesis have to do with interpersonal relationships? The answer now seems obvious. As a student of social psychology would put it, people are "action centers"—they do things (or, unexpectedly, they fail to do the things we counted on them to do) that have the result of interrupting what we are in the process of doing, often performing organized behavior sequences or progressing toward the goals of higher-order plans. Other people are "emotogenic stimuli," as Albert Ellis once put it, because they can thus be potent sources of unexpected help when what they do, or stop doing, facilitates the resumption of previously interrupted behavior sequences or plans *or* when their actions bring us to our goals sooner and easier than we had anticipated. Similarly, they can be sources of unexpected harm.

The specific application and elaboration of Mandler's interruption theory to close relationships now seems relatively straightforward. At the time, however, it did not unfold as easily as it might have had our group's conception of a "close relationship" been, at the start of our deliberations, what it evolved to be at the end (see Kelley et al., 1983). When we began our efforts to develop a conceptual framework that would facilitate the study of close relationships, we, like everyone else, defined a close relationship with reference to the positivity of the "bonds," "feelings," "emotions," or the "affect" experienced in association with the relationship partner. Close relationships are so permeated with strong positive feelings and emotions (see, for example, Attridge & Berscheid, in prep.) that it is hard not to define a close relationship with reference to these very visible and positively valued phenomena.

At the end of our deliberations, however, a close relationship was defined only with respect to the degree of *interdependence* between two persons' activities, where the term *activities* was meant to include cognitive and physiological activities as well as more easily observable verbal and molar behavioral activities. Thus, we (Kelley, et al., 1983) viewed two people as being in a "relationship" with each other to the extent that a change in the state (or the activities) of one person causes a change in the state of the other (the common means of determining whether *any* two entities are in relationship with each other). A "close" relationship was viewed as one in which: (a) a change in the state (or the activities) of one person *frequently* causes a change in the state of the other; (b) the change that is caused is *strong* (perhaps as evidenced by a short latency of response, or a high amplitude of response, or by a long chain of responses); (c) the change is true for *diverse* kinds of activities (or the partner has influence over many of the individual's behavior domains); and (d) this pattern of high interdependence in the activities of the partners has been characteristic of the relationship for a relatively long *duration* of time.

Or, to put it another way, and as illustrated in Figure 21.1, the basic descriptive data of relationships are the activities of two people placed over the same time line so that the causal linkages between the two person's activities can be determined (see Levenson & Gottman, 1983, for an illustration of such a sequential analysis of time series data in marital relationships). The relationship lies in the causal interconnections between the activities of two persons; no causal connections, no relationship (no matter what the participants might like to think). A relationship is revealed to be a *close* one by frequent, strong, and diverse interconnections between the two activity chains over a long time duration. The pattern of causal interconnections between two individuals' activity chains taken

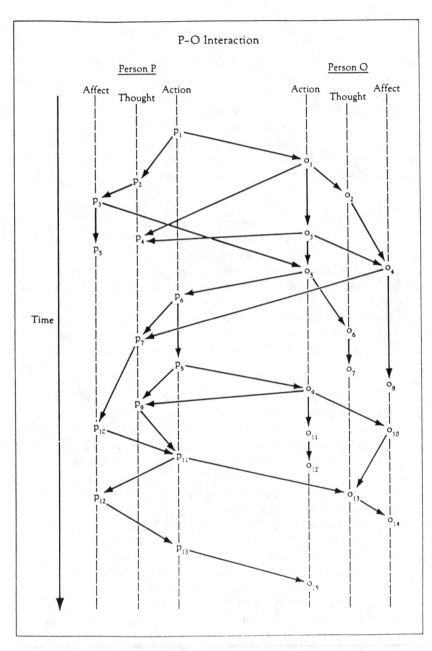

FIG. 21.1. The basic data of a dyadic relationship. Each person has a chain of events, each chain including affect, thought, and action. The events are causally connected within each chain (shown by arrows from one p to another or from one o to another) and the two chains are causally interconnected (shown by arrows from a p to an o or from an o to a p). The interchain connections constitute the essential feature of interpersonal relationships. (From Kelley et al., 1983)

over the same time line thus forms the basic infrastructure of the relationship, and it is from that infrastructure that emotional experience "in" the relationship (or in association with the partner) springs.

The answers to many of the puzzles about emotion in close relationships appear to unwind in straightforward fashion from this basic framework. In addition to determining the causal linkages between the individuals' activity patterns, however, it is also necessary to know, within each partner's activity chain, which portions of the chain of activities form organized action sequences of behavior and which of these are part of higher-order plans, and, especially, which of the partners' organized action sequences are "meshed" with each other (as illustrated in Figure 21.2). The ability individuals in close relationships have to interrupt each other (either by unexpectedly doing something they should not, or, equally likely, by not doing something they should), and thus to be the source of emotional experience, can readily be appreciated.

I can here do no more than sketch the bones of the E-in-R model as it was originally described and subsequently elaborated upon (Berscheid, 1983; Berscheid, Gangestad, & Kulakowski, 1984; Berscheid, 1986), and thus also can

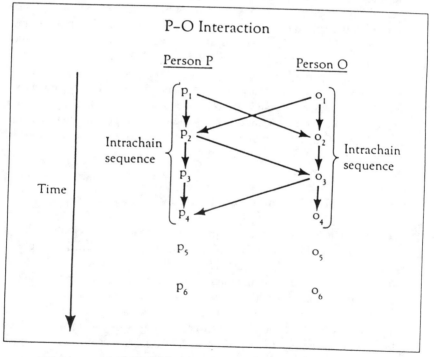

FIG. 21.2.   Illustration of meshed intrachain sequences. The P-to-O causal interconnections facilitate O's intrachain sequence and vice versa. (From Kelley et al., 1983)

do no more than hint of my excitement upon reading *Mind and Emotion*. On a personal level, I have felt gratitude that George made an honest woman of me—I believe I now have something sensible to say about emotion to those who once accused me of knowing something about romantic love. On a professional level, the debt of scholars who hope to understand close relationships may prove to go beyond what George has directly contributed on the emotional front, for I suspect that it was the availability of his theory that helped influence how many of us now view the quality of "closeness" in relationships. That is, when one defines a close relationship as characterized by strong, positive affective ties (as many people still do), one soon runs into tight knots of paradox. At the least, for example, it becomes difficult to understand relationships that are predominantly unhappy and unhealthy but that endure for lifetimes, as well as relationships in which the emotions the partners experience upon irrevocable separation are greater than those they ever experienced within the relationship itself. Without having an easily traversed bridge between the close relationship and the emotions experienced in it, a bridge the interruption hypothesis provides, I wonder if we would have had the courage to define a close relationship without reference to the emotions and feelings the participants experience in association with each other.

Although the absence of feeling and emotion in the core definition of a close relationship was easily the most controversial aspect of our conceptual framework when it was originally presented, the separation of closeness, or interdependence, from affect is increasingly seen to be one of its strengths. It has turned out to be a strength partially because it allows one to treat emotion as a dependent variable—or as the *focus* of analysis, rather than simply as a "classificatory" variable that aids in understanding other phenomena—and partially because banishing affect from our conception of closeness may be helping us and others to predict some of the outcomes that relationship researchers have traditionally wanted to predict, as I shall discuss next.

THE VALIDITY OF THE E-IN-R MODEL

The ease with which Mandler's theory of emotion translates into emotion as it is experienced in the context of relationships with others should rack up several points for it on that great "validation scoreboard" in the sky for emotion theories. That is, if it is true that emotion is most frequently experienced in the context of our relationships with others, then any theory of emotion developed without specific reference to relationships (as Mandler's was) should, if it is a "correct" theory as God views it, translate easily to the situation in which emotions are most frequently experienced. There is, however, more concrete information on the validity of the E-in-R model that, in turn, indirectly supports the grandfather theory. I will use my remaining space, then, to describe briefly the Relationship Closeness Inventory (RCI), which was developed by me, Mark

Snyder, and Allen Omoto (1989), to help test hypotheses about emotion in relationships.

To predict emotion and other relationship phenomena, we believed it would be useful to have an instrument that would allow us to get a "quick fix" on a specific relationships's degree of closeness. Accordingly, and using the Kelley et al. framework as a heuristic, the RCI assesses the interdependence of a relationship by means of three subscales. The first of these is a *Frequency* subscale which simply assesses the amount of time the two people spend together alone on a daily basis (i.e., with other people not present). Although spending time alone together is neither a necessary nor a sufficient condition for two people to have impact on each other, it is probably the single most facilitative condition for interpersonal influence. The second measure, called the *Diversity* subscale, contains an exhaustive listing of all the activities it is possible for two people in the target population (e.g., and in the original case, young adults) to do together or to do in the presence of the partner. The individual's score on this scale is the number of *different*—not the sheer number of—activities the two persons have done together in the past week. The reasoning behind this index is that the greater the number of different activities two people do together, the wider their domain of potential influence upon each other (and thus, of course, the greater their vulnerability to interruption from the partner and the lower their likelihood of quickly finding a "substitute partner" to help them resume interrupted activities). The third measure is called the *Strength* subscale. It assesses the degree of perceived influence the partner has on a number of daily activities (what programs are watched on TV, for example) as well as the partner's influence on higher-order plans. After transformation of the first two subscale scores so that all three are on the same metric, they are summed to form a "closeness" score.

What is unusual about the RCI is that questions about the individual's feelings for his or her partner—how much he or she "likes" and how much he or she "loves" the partner, for examples—are nowhere to be found. Nor does the RCI assess the amount of conflict two people experience in their relationship with each other (as do many marital satisfaction scales, for example, including the venerable Locke-Wallace). Moreover, the RCI does not attempt to assess the quality and frequency of the emotions the individual typically experiences in association with the partner. For many people, including many relationship researchers, such questions would form the very core of an instrument that hoped to assess closeness. We, too, ask such questions of our respondents, but the answers play no part in our estimation of the closeness of the relationship.

After determining that the RCI possesses certain desirable psychometric properties, is reliable, and discriminates between relationships the individual designates as close and those he or she regards as not close, we sought to examine the RCI's predictive validity with a sample of romantic relationships that also had been previously designated by the individual as his or her closest relationship. Our predictive criteria were two relationship outcomes in which relationship researchers traditionally have been interested: (a) relationship stability; and (b) the amount of emotional distress the individual experiences if and when the relationship dissolves.

To make a very long (about 4 years long) story short, in the predictive sweepstakes we put our RCI up against, first, a subjective index of closeness that assessed the individual's *own* beliefs about the closeness of the relationship. Second, we asked the RCI to perform against an Hedonic Emotional Tone Index that assessed the positivity of the emotions and feelings typically experienced in the relationship, with the frequency of negative emotions subtracted from the positive such that higher numbers on this index reflected happier relationships. We also put the RCI up against the "Longevity" of the relationship, or the length of time the relationship had already endured. The stability of these romantic relationships that were also the individual's closest was examined 3 months after the initial RCI assessment and then again 9 months later.

What we found is that, first, the Subjective Closeness Index did not predict much of anything, and it certainly did not predict whether these romantic relationships would dissolve; how close the individual believed the relationship to be was not associated with its stability. Nor did the individual's own estimate of the stability of the relationship prove to have even a modicum of accuracy. The Hedonic Emotional Tone Index was no better a predictor of dissolution; happier relationships were not more stable than less happy relationships. And Longevity, at least in this sample of relationships of young adults, did not predict dissolution either. Only our emotionless and affectless (or "heartless," as it has been called) RCI predicted whether the relationship would dissolve. Moreover, the RCI made its prediction in a relatively precise way: Those individuals who broke up within 3 months had lower RCI scores than whose relationships were dissolved at 9 months, and the RCI scores of these people, in turn, were lower than those whose relationships were intact at the 9-month mark.

We had also administered an Affect Index that assessed how much the individual "liked" and "loved" the partner. As one might expect, the closer the relationship as assessed by the RCI, the higher the individual's Affect score. More interestingly, however, the scores on the Affect Index were more highly correlated (significantly so) with the Subjective Closeness Index than with the RCI. How close a relationship *feels* has a great deal to do with an individual's evaluations of the other; if the individual likes and loves the other, he or she tends to believe the relationship is close. But how close the relationship truly is has more to do with interdependence than affect. Or, to put this another way, interdependence predicts what the construct of "closeness" is supposed to predict, in this case, the likelihood that the relationship will dissolve, with closer relationships being more stable.

We also examined the amount of emotional distress people experienced after the dissolution of those relationships that broke up. Other things being equal, the greater the interdependence, the greater the amount of interruption there should be when the relationship is dissolved and, so, the greater the emotional distress that should be experienced. Studies examining this point with the RCI have, so far, supported this hypothesis (e.g., Simpson, 1987; Creed, Attridge, Simpson, & Berscheid, in preparation). In the particular study described above (where the romantic relationships were also the individual's closest), the emotional distress effect was in the right direction but only marginally significant (while Longevity of the relationship *did* significantly predict distress at break-up). The "weasel factor" here is the availability of substitute partners (who reduce the severity of interruption upon loss of a partner and allow the quick resumption of organized activities and plans) which we, unfortunately, failed to assess in this study.

The availability of substitute partners—or at least the individual's perception that other partners would be available should the present relationship dissolve—was assessed, along with the RCI score, in a recent study of romantically involved couples conducted by Creed et al. (in preparation). The predictions of the association between closeness, substitute partner availability, and break-up, as well as between these and the degree of emotional distress in instances of dissolution, are straightforward. The higher an individual's dependence on the relationship, and the lower the goodness of perceived alternatives to the current relationship partner, the greater the stability of the relationship should be. If, however the relationship should dissolve, it is these individuals—those who are highly dependent on the partner and who also have few available substitute partners—who should experience the most emotional distress.

It should be noted that these hypotheses were tested for individuals, not couples, although both relationship partners participated in the study. Relationship partners, it appears, are rarely symmetrical in their degree of closeness, at least as closeness is assessed by the RCI. Correlations between partners' RCI scores run from about .40 to .50, giving credence to the view that there is "her" relationship, there is "his" relationship, and then there is "their" relationship as viewed by an outside observer, where the symmetricality of closeness, or dependence, is an important datum.

Examination of the data revealed extremely strong support for the break-up hypothesis. Men who had relatively low closeness scores but high goodness-of-alternative scores were three times more likely to break up with their partners than those with high RCI scores and low Alternatives scores. The results for women were even stronger: Those with low RCI scores and high Alternatives scores were *six* times more likely to break up than those who were not only close to their partners but also perceived that they had few good alternatives to their current partner. Both the individual's RCI scores and his or her Alternatives scores were each significantly correlated, in the predicted direction, with break-up for men and for women.

About one-third of the sample of couples dissolved their relationship within the period of time we followed them. The degree of emotional distress the men experienced upon dissolution of their relationships also was in strong accord with our hypotheses; both the man's RCI score and his Alternatives score were significantly associated, in the predicted directions, with the degree of distress he reported experiencing (RCI $r = .38$; Alt $r = -.41$). But the degree of emotional distress the women said they experienced upon relationship dissolution was not explained by our independent variables. Neither their RCI scores nor their Alternatives scores were associated with the amount of distress they reported (although, it will be recalled, both of these variables were significantly associated with relationship stability for women). For women, however (but not for men), the degree of distress they said they experienced was significantly associated with whether they or their partner initiated the break-up; those whose partners terminated the relationship reported significantly more emotional disruption than those who terminated the relationship themselves or who jointly agreed with their partners to end the relationship. Why there should be these sex differences in factors associated with emotional distress, we do not yet know. Overall, it should be noted, both men and women experienced about the same amount of emotional disruption when the relationship dissolved, so differential amount of emotional disruption on the part of men and women does not help explain why women do not show an association between closeness, availability of substitute partners, and distress.

The E-in-R model is not an easy one to test, nor is Mandler's interruption theory of emotion. One needs to know the individual's organized sequences of behavior as well as his or her hopes and dreams and, to test the E-in-R model, how another person fits into these. Such things are hard to engineer in the laboratory, and it is harder still to experimentally—and ethically—manipulate their facilitation or interruption. (See, however Pfenning, Clore, & Ortony, in preparation, for a clever "natural experiment" approach to the problem.) Our nonexperimental approach, through the development of the RCI, has been slow and laborious. Moreover, we have only the bluntest of instruments to show for our efforts. But at least we are in the real world, and in real relationships, which is where the emotion action is. And, so far, the validation news is good.

Come the millennium, then, when the trumpets are sounded to summon all emotion theorists to account for themselves (and especially to account for the amount of time other people have spent reading and testing their theories, not to mention the forests that were felled throughout history to print the words of emotion theorists), I am confident that George Mandler will be able to add to his impressive list of scholarly good works, the illumination of many phenomena in close interpersonal relationships.

REFERENCES

Attridge, M., & Berscheid, E. (in prep.). Emotion and closeness: Descriptive profiles of romantic, friend, and family relationships. University of Minnesota.

Berscheid, E. (1982). Attraction and emotion in interpersonal relationships. In M. S. Clark & S. T. Fiske (Eds.), *Affect and cognition* (pp. 37–54). Hillsdale, NJ: Lawrence Erlbaum Associates.

Berscheid, E. (1983). Emotion. In H. H. Kelley, E. Berscheid, A. Christensen, J. H. Harvey, T. L. Huston, G. Levinger, E. McClintock, L. A. Peplau, & D. R. Peterson. *Close relationships*. New York: Freeman and Company.

Berscheid, E. (1986). Emotional experience in close relationships: Implications for child development. In Z. Rubin & W. Hartup (Eds.), *The effects of early relationships upon children's socioemotional development*. Hillsdale, NJ: Lawrence Erlbaum Associates.

Berscheid, E. (1990). Contemporary vocabularies of emotion. In Bert S. Moore & A. M. Isen (Eds.), *Affect and social behavior* (pp. 22–38). Cambridge, England: Cambridge University Press.

Berscheid, E., Gangestad, S. W., & Kulakowski, D. (1984). Emotion in close relationships: Implications for relationship counseling. In S. D. Brown & R. W. Lent (Eds.), *Handbook of counseling psychology*. New York: Wiley.

Berscheid, E., Snyder, M., & Omoto, A. M. (1989). The Relationship Closeness Inventory: Assessing the closeness of interpersonal relationships. *Journal of Personality and Social Psychology, 57*, 792–807.

Berscheid, E., & Walster, E. (1974). A little bit about love. In T. L. Huston (Ed.), *Foundations of interpersonal attraction*. New York: Academic Press.

Creed, M., Attridge, M., Simpson, J. A., & Berscheid, E. (in prep.). The stability of romantic relationships: A test of couple and individual level factors. University of Minnesota.

Kelley, H. H., Berscheid, E., Christensen, A., Harvey, J. H., Huston, T. L., Levinger, G., McClintock, E., Peplau, L. A. & Peterson, D. R. (1983). *Close relationships*. New York: Freeman and Company.

Levenson, R., & Gottman, J. (1983). Marital interaction: Physiological linkage and affective exchange. *Journal of Personality and Social Psychology, 45*, 587–597.

Mandler, G. (1975). *Mind and Emotion*. New York: Wiley.

Pfenning, J., Clore, G. L., & Ortony, A. (in prep.). The role of goal importance in the experience of naturally occurring emotions. Northwestern University.

Simon, H. A. (1984). Affect and cognition: Comments. In M. S. Clark & S. T. Fiske (Eds.), *Affect and cognition*. Hillsdale, NJ: Lawrence Erlbaum Associates.

Simpson, J. A. (1987). The dissolution of romantic relationships: Factors involved in relationship stability and emotional distress. *Journal of Personality and Social Psychology, 53*, 683–692.

22

Value and Emotion

Andrew Ortony
Northwestern University

In some remote causal way, I am writing this piece as a result of the fact that my first serious introduction to the psychology of emotion was George Mandler's book *Mind and Emotion* (Mandler, 1975). My initial reaction upon reading it was, I recall, rather mixed. I felt it was interesting and largely believable, but I also found it frustrating and incomplete. I began corresponding with George on a number of issues raised by *Mind and Emotion,* and soon, with considerable encouragement from him, I got going on the study of emotion. I started doing what George felt somebody, but not he, should be doing, namely, I started thinking about the cognitive antecedents of the different emotions. My colleagues and I worked on this problem for nearly ten years, finally publishing our efforts in a book entitled *The Cognitive Structure of Emotions* (Ortony, Clore, & Collins, 1988). One of the main themes of that work was the idea that there are three classes of emotions. This first class consists of emotions resulting from appraisals rooted in goals, the second from appraisals rooted in standards and norms, and the third from appraisals grounded in tastes and attitudes.

In the early 1980s, George began to devote serious attention to the notion of value. This interest was primarily stimulated by his belief that value plays a central role in emotion, an opinion with which I am in strong agreement. Indeed, at least the last two of the three classes of emotions that my colleagues and I proposed clearly implicate what George thinks of as values. But the view that values are central to emotions does not appear to be one that is widely held by emotion theorists—certainly, it is difficult to find books on emotion with index entries for "value," and coherent discussions of the psychological, especially cognitive, foundations of value are few and far between. George was disturbed by this neglect.

In taking on the problem of value, George was grappling with an immensely difficult and understudied topic. In *Approaches to a Psychology of Value* (Mandler, 1989) he bemoans the fact that psychologists have paid so little attention to the issue. He wrote, referring to his earlier efforts to bring some ideas about it into the public forum: "The purpose [of Mandler (1982)] was in part to expose some budding ideas to public inspection, but also to invite and generate some discussion on the problem itself. The invitation was apparently declined. Psychology in general is still valueless (though, of course, *not* value free). I shall now try again."

In this chapter, I shall present a few of my own preliminary thoughts on the issue of value. In doing so, perhaps I can contribute in some small way to George's hope that the field begin to take the question of value more seriously. I shall take George's concluding remarks in his aforementioned work at face value: "I started by reasserting my attempt to move psychologists to discuss seriously and in a principled way the sources and conditions of value. I certainly do not claim any kind of completeness for this account, nor any certainty for the propositions advanced here. I do hope that they will be the beginning of a study of value—even if it begins by questioning what I have tried to do here" (Mandler, 1989, p. 22). George knows me well enough to know that it is inevitable that I should begin by questioning what he has tried to do!

George's primary focus is on values as preferences, as likes and dislikes, rather than as moral beliefs and opinions. In this sense, values need (and often can be given) no justification. I cannot (and normally am not expected to) justify the fact that I like baseball or that I like strawberries, although sometimes it is possible to explain such an attitude. In general, however, I just like what I like, and dislike what I dislike. Of course, my liking of strawberries need not be innate—perhaps I did not like them as a child. But acquired or not, my liking of strawberries is a matter of taste (no pun intended), not of adopted choice. Such values, George wants to argue, contribute to emotional experience. On the other hand, and this is important in the present context, values do not, he asserts, arise out of emotion.

If values do not arise from emotions, where do they come from? What leads people to evaluate objects and events positively or negatively? George's basic answer to this question is in terms of schema theory—in terms of schema conformity and discrepancy (see Figure 22.1). With some caveats, George's proposal is that there are three unambiguous sources of positive affect.

First, as a limiting case, we have the situation in which some object or event (which I shall call an experience, for simplicity) is congruous with some existing schema. In this case we have positive value with, curiously, zero intensity. The next, slightly more intense case of positive value arises when the experience is slightly incongruous but, because it is only slightly so, it is readily assimilated to an existing schema. The third unambiguously positive case arises when there is severe incongruity between an input and an active schema that can be resolved by

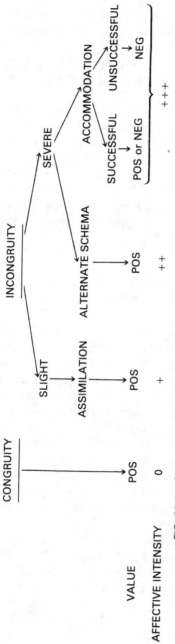

FIG. 22.1. Several possible outcomes of schema congruity and incongruity in terms of both values and affective intensity. The resultant value is shown as either positive (POS) or negative (NEG). Degree of affective intensity is shown to vary from zero to +++ (from Mander, 1982).

assimilating it to an alternate schema. There remain two other cases. The first of these involves successful accommodation. That is, the experience can be assimilated only to a *changed* schema. This can give rise to either positive or negative value. In either case, George maintains that the resulting intensity is quite high. However, the most intense case is, according to George, the negative case in which a severely incongruous experience cannot be assimilated even after accommodation.

There is much more to George's approach to value than I have described; however, this structural account lies at the heart of his view, and has done so since he started seriously thinking about the issue. In the rest of this chapter I want to focus on three questions. The first is whether or not the general account that George proposes can do what he intends, the second concerns George's supposition that the relation between values and emotions is unidirectional— from values to emotions, and the third is a proposal for a model that might move us toward an account of the relation between emotions and beliefs, values, and experience.

IS SCHEMA CONFORMITY AND DISCREPANCY ENOUGH?

I agree with George that there are many occasions upon which positive and negative reactions arise as a result of the kind of schema matches and mismatches that he describes. The question that I want to address first is whether all such reactions result from the mechanisms that George proposes and whether all such mechanisms lead to such reactions. I think that the answer to both may be "no." My reason is based on the idea, which I shall elaborate in the next section, that representations often, indeed usually, include affective information (Fiske, 1982). For example, my ARMED-BURGLAR schema surely includes my distaste for such people. It is not, nor can it be, a representation that incorporates only stereotypic factual (i.e., affect-free, non-evaluative) information about things like what it is that armed burglars do and how and why they do it. The most compelling real-world reason for believing that this must be the case is the existence of prejudice.

To see the implications of affective information in schemas, it may be easier to operationalize schema conformity and discrepancy in terms of realized and violated expectations. I suspect that George would be willing to accept this, at least as an analogy. So, imagine you are lying in bed at night. You know that there have been a number of occasionally violent burglaries in your neighborhood recently. You think you hear the sound of an intruder in your house and become increasingly frightened. You listen, motionless, ever more convinced that you have the right explanation for what you hear. Suddenly, a change in the way the moonlight is illuminating the door of your bedroom leads you to realize that the door is being slowly opened. You quietly pull the bedcovers over your head while peeking out to see who is coming in. As you peek, you are overcome with the fear that if you can see the intruder, he can see you. When you finally see the figure of a person wearing a ski mask with a gun in hand your suspicions that you have an armed burglar in your room are unambiguously confirmed. Your heart is pounding—you think you are going to die.

Meanwhile, back at the (cognitive) ranch, you have a perfect schema fit. Total congruity. You have no difficulty assimilating what you see to your active ARMED-BURGLAR schema. If I understand George's view correctly, this means that there ought to be positive affect resulting from this confirmed expectation. But such a conclusion does not seem credible. Surely, the only outcome that could possibly produce positive affect in such a situation would be a violation of the expectation. But if I am right that successful assimilation by the active ARMED-BURGLAR schema would lead to negative rather than positive affect, it follows that not all cases of successful assimilation to an active schema lead to affectively positive reactions. Although I shall not pursue this now, it is presumably possible to find comparable cases in which the schema congruity and incongruity conditions that George describes in fact generate affective reactions that differ in valence relative to the predictions of the model. The part of George's model that is, I think, correct, is the quantitative part concerning the relative intensity of the associated reactions, but it seems to me that we need to rethink the qualitative aspects that concern the origin of positive and negative valence. We will have to acknowledge that representations can come with affect already in them, in which case we are left with a new problem, namely, that of explaining the origin of value in schemas, and that is what this chapter is all about.

EMOTIONS, VALUES, AND TRAITS

I mentioned earlier that George believes the relation between values and emotions is unidirectional—from values to emotions. He writes (Mandler, 1989): "I have become convinced that the problem of value is at the heart of human emotional experience. I do not assert the converse, that emotion is at the heart of the problem of value. Values, even simple preferences, do not arise out of emotion; rather, they contribute to emotional experiences" (p. 4). Unfortunately, George does not explain why values do not arise out of emotions, and because his intuitions and mine diverge on this point, I shall try to make a case for the claim that in addition to values being an important source of emotions, emotions are an important source of values and, more specifically, that they can be the source of value in schemas.

Imagine that you are introduced to a man whom you have no particular desire to meet. As you learn his name and what he does, you go through the motions of being interested in meeting him. But your initial reaction is in fact one of indifference—you neither like him nor dislike him. Maybe you build a skeletal schema for him, but because he appears to have no interesting or salient characteristics, no such characteristics are incorporated into your representation of him. Now suppose that the person starts talking and behaving in a way that you find offensive. He persists, and you become irritated, and as he continues you find yourself increasingly disliking him. Let us now compare your original attitude of indifference to your new attitude of dislike. Such a change in attitude must surely have concomitants in your representation of him. Your schema for him must contain the material necessary for this new, negative attitude—it did not have it before, but it has it now. This material might include the trait-based information that the person is very unfriendly and very aggressive, as well as the emotional information that he caused you to be upset.

The first point that I want to make is that values assigned to trait variables are direct manifestations of our values. If I do not value friendliness as a characteristic of people, then even if I can scale people (or their behaviors) on a friendly–unfriendly dimension, such a scale value cannot contribute to my dispositional liking of them. The second point is that insofar as trait representations do in fact represent values, representations of individuals in terms of traits are representations that incorporate values. The third point is that the particular constellation of traits (and the values on them) that are represented in the schema for some particular target can result from emotional interactions with the target. And finally, I want to suggest that one's dispositional liking for an individual is normally determined by one's emotional interactions with that person, independent of trait representations. In other words, if somebody makes me angry, and if a consequence of this can be that it changes my dispositional liking for that person, then assuming that dispositional liking is part of my value system, we have to conclude that emotions can influence values.

Not surprisingly, our discussion of value has already brought us into the realm of traits. This suggests that an obvious place to look for some serious discussion of value would be in the literature of social cognition, especially the part that has to do with impression formation. Unfortunately, this turns out not to be the case. The level of analysis that we need lies below that on which this literature usually focuses. Research on impression formation, person perception, and person memory, insofar is it deals with the issue of where attitudes come from, usually comes to rest on ideas such as that evaluative judgments are determined by the affective value of (currently) salient beliefs (e.g., Fishbein & Ajzen, 1975), or that they are the result of some sort of algebraic combination of weighted scale values on a set of traits (Anderson, 1971). The problem with the first kind of analysis is that it does not offer an account of the ultimate origin of the affective value of a belief. If my attitude toward or evaluation of somebody is negatively affected by learning that he is a Republican, this can only be explained if I have an explanation of why I have a negative attitude toward Republicans. The problem with the second approach is that values on attributes are simply not sufficient to explain everyday facts. I can have scale values for a set of attributes about a person I have never met, and yet not know whether I like him.

Recent work by Srull and Wyer (e.g., Wyer & Srull, 1986; Srull & Wyer, 1989) perhaps comes closest to dealing with the issue, although they tend to view impression formation as a goal of social information processing rather than as a spontaneous product of it. Their general view is that trait information is assembled at the time that an evaluative judgment is first made by classifying behaviors in terms of the most accessible applicable traits that they exemplify. This leads to the construction of a general evaluative concept, likeableness, that becomes associated with the target and that can be used later to make an evaluative judgment without reference to the specific behaviors from which it was constructed. Srull and Wyer (1989) suggest that the mechanism for generating a general evaluative concept of an individual from trait-behavior clusters is probably similar to that proposed by Anderson (1971, 1981).

Comprehensive as their proposals are, I have a number of problems with the Srull and Wyer model. Many of these have to do with the kind of data that the model seeks to accommodate. The data are generally derived from a research paradigm that lacks ecological validity. In the typical experiment in person perception research, subjects read descriptions of the characteristics and activities of (usually fictitious) individuals and then are required to make a judgment, for example, about how likeable such an individual would be. However, because the targets are rarely real people who are personally significant to the subjects, there is no reason to suppose that subjects care one way or the other about them (Berscheid, 1982); they neither like nor dislike those about whom they are making judgments or recalling behaviors. Maybe this is why subjects are typically asked to give likeableness ratings (rather than liking ratings). Unfortunately, likeableness ratings are usually treated as surrogates for liking ratings (see, for example, Fiske & Pavelchak, 1986; Srull & Wyer, 1989). The problem is that the general evaluative concept of likeableness is nothing more than a very general trait. Although it might on occasion be the underlying representation for dispositional liking, it is not always so, and quite possibly is not even normally so. Insofar as trait information enables likeableness judgments, it enables predictions or expectations about liking. But predicting that one will like somebody is not the same as liking them. Predictions can be wrong. Furthermore, there is nothing contradictory about asserting that, for example, Ronald Reagan is likeable but that one does not like him, and it is certainly not unheard of for people to like individuals while evaluating them negatively on their most salient traits (we might call this the "you're a bastard but I love you" syndrome).

Another problem I have with the Wyer and Srull model (and many other accounts of person perception) is that they seem to presuppose a stability of social judgments that I suspect is not so common in the real social world. Thus, it is possible to interpret their model as proposing that a global evaluative social judgment (e.g., of likeableness) is a read-out of what appears to be a relatively stable evaluative concept of the target. Now this might be an unfair criticism, but I think Wyer and Srull would acknowledge that their model does not focus on the dynamic aspects of person representation or social judgment. This is something of a problem because, as Berscheid (1982) points out, in moving from the laboratory to naturalistic settings, "the focus radically changes from accounting for stability and constancy in affective behaviors towards [a target] to accounting for instability and inconstancy" (p. 42f.).

My final discomfort with the Srull and Wyer model is that it treats traits as categorical rather than continuous constructs—a target is viewed as either friendly or unfriendly, pleasant or unpleasant. Perhaps they do not believe that traits are categorical, but their model in no way exploits them as continuous. In the model that I am about to sketch, this aspect of traits turns out to be quite important, at least at the level of representation if not at the level of conscious awareness.[1]

A MODEL OF PERSON REPRESENTATION

The main purpose of the last section's brief excursion into impression formation was to set the stage for a more detailed examination of the relationship between values and emotions in which we pay more attention to the issue of how mental representations of value-laden objects might be structured. Because I find it an interesting topic in its own right, I shall restrict myself to some proposals about how we might consider individual people to be represented, rather than worrying about the representation issue with respect to objects, events, or categories.

Clearly, because we are able to make evaluative judgments about other people, our representations of those people must contain information that will enable the construction of such evaluations. It may be that in some cases, we really do directly store such an evaluation so that a specific judgment really is a simple read-out of the (current, or most recently computed) value of how much one likes (or dislikes) the target. However, we still need an account of how such stored values change and of where they come from. Central to my proposals is the idea that they do not necessarily always come from the same sort of information.

It seems to me that we need to distinguish three types of information that can, in principle, be part of a representation of a person (and possibly of other things too). One of the three parts of person representations contains the accumulated

---

[1]In fact, the treatment of traits as categorical rather than continuous constructs appears to have been an almost intentional decision by the field. My claim is not that the internal representation of trait information is literally quantitative, but that it qualitatively represents the approximate shape of the distribution. A categorical equivalent of this would be to treat, for example, "extremely aggressive" as a different trait from "somewhat aggressive," and so on.

value-free facts (including observed behaviors) held to be true of the individual. I shall call this aspect of the representation the *fact* component, and I view it as relatively stable, normally changing only by accretion. For example, someone's representation of Margaret Thatcher might initially contain only the beliefs that she is female, in her 60s, married, and the British prime minister. These are all matters of (putative) fact, not matters of value; they are not represented as being good or bad. This is not to say that they cannot have evaluative implications, but only that if they do, these implications are not part of the fact component.

Important evaluative implications that factual knowledge may have are represented in the value-laden component of the representation, a component that I shall call the *value* component. For example, the fact that Margaret Thatcher is the British prime minister might, for some individuals, imply that because she is a politician she is likely to be very unscrupulous and ambitious. These would be inferences to traits inherited from the stereotype of a category to which Thatcher had been assigned (Fiske & Neuberg, 1990). Thus, the resulting representation might contain relatively extreme initial assignments on the evaluative dimensions scrupulous–unscrupulous and ambitious–unambitious. In the case of person representations, I envision the value component as being comprised of a set of evaluative dimensions, which we usually call traits, to which values have been assigned on the basis of inferences from directly or indirectly acquired propositional information or observed behaviors.

Whereas the value component of the representation of some individuals contains trait-based information, I think it may be helpful to suppose that at any point in time only a few trait dimensions are represented here. Specifically, I have in mind that the value component contains information pertaining to only the currently most diagnostic traits for that individual. I take a trait to be diagnostic with respect to a target if there is a history of extreme values, high variability, or if some current observation seems extreme with respect to it. So, if Smith is one of the most selfish people I know, my value component for Smith might include the selfish–generous dimension. And if I view him as sometimes (to some people, in some situations) quite friendly, and sometimes (to the same or other people, in other situations) rather unfriendly, then the friendly–unfriendly dimension might be represented in the value component. Finally, if I view Smith as being neither particularly intelligent nor particularly stupid, but suddenly he does something that causes me to think he must be remarkably stupid, then the intelligent–unintelligent dimension could become (at least temporarily) diagnostic. Such highly diagnostic information is readily accessible, and it is accessible not simply as trait identities that are particularly strongly associated with the target, but also as distributional information. Indeed, it is by virtue of their distributional properties that traits get into the value component in the first place. They get in because the distributions are unimodal but highly skewed, or bimodal or multimodal; none of them is normal (even in the case of a trait inconsistent behavior such as Smith's surprisingly stupid act, there is the beginning of a bimodal distribution). This is why I think it helpful to view traits as continuous rather than as categorical constructs. Furthermore, their distributional properties will surely play a role in the construction of social judgments (see also Kahneman & Miller, 1986).[2] What drives the system is deviations from normalcy. In all cases, however, I think it reasonable to suppose that some points on the distribution may be related to specific retrievable entries in the fact component.

The idea that some of the information we have encoded about individuals is fact-based and some trait-based is not particularly new, even though the constraints that I have proposed for trait representations may be. But it is the third aspect of person representations that is the most distinctive feature of the model I am proposing. This aspect is what I call the *affective experience* component. It is curious that social psychologists who deal with attitudes and impression formation have devoted so little attention to the role of affective experience induced by the target (although see Berscheid & Walster, 1978, and Clore, 1975). Perhaps the recent neglect is a consequence of the typical research paradigm that I criticized earlier—fictitious people of no personal significance tend not to induce affective experiences in us. In any event, many of the things with respect to which we have attitudes are things that directly or indirectly give rise to emotional reactions in us. People talk to us, or do things to us or for us, or we observe or otherwise come to know about what they do or did or what happened to them. In some cases, the emotions we have in response to such events are immediate feelings of (momentary) liking or disliking, emotions that Ortony, et al. (1988) call attraction emotions. In other cases, attraction emotions arise indirectly, as a result of an initial experience of a more specific emotion. So, for example, we often find ourselves (momentarily) disliking somebody who is making us angry. In either case, what is important in the current context is the idea that we end up with relatively undifferentiated emotions of momentary liking or disliking. What I am proposing is that the affective experience component contains a summary record of the liking and disliking experiences that the target person has induced in us, again in the form of something like a frequency distribution of positive and

---

[2]There is a complex issue lurking here. Imagine you meet somebody who engages in the courageous act of climbing up a dangerous cliff in order to save somebody's life. If, in Kahneman and Miller's (1986) terms, one recruits ordinary people as the norm or contrast set, then courage would certainly be diagnostic for this individual and thus, according to the model, the relevant dimension ought to be incorporated into the value space. But now suppose that you see someone else doing exactly the same thing but you know that he is a stunt man in a movie that is being shot. The same observed behavior evaluated with respect to stunt men could seem quite normal. There are several ways of dealing with this. One, which is not very parsimonious, but which might still be right, is multiple representations—one for each major role the person fills, with the context activating the appropriate one. A simpler solution would be to use an exception marker. This would involve thinking of the dimensions in the value space as being tagged with the names of any category with respect to which the dimension was known *not* to be diagnostic. In this scheme, we would have an extreme value on the courageous–fearful dimension with a tag such as "not as stunt man."

negative feelings of different intensity. This is not a record of the particular emotions induced, but only a record of the magnitude and sign of the undifferentiated affect (see Diener, Larsen, Levine, & Emmons, 1985 for the relevance of frequency of undifferentiated positive and negative affect for subjective well-being). I am assuming that the event itself along with the facts pertaining to its particular emotional impact are represented in and, in principle, recoverable from the fact component.

When we come to ask what is "dispositional" liking, we might imagine that it is primarily determined by a temporally weighted frequency function from the affective experience component, perhaps modulated by some sort of summary assessment of currently salient information in the value component. The value component associated with the representation of a person is influenced by changes in both the fact and the affective experience components. In other words, the attributions that I make with respect to individuals are influenced both by things that I (come to) believe to be true of them, and by the quality of my emotional experiences with respect to them. For example, if I learn that Smith, whom I was previously disposed to like, was once convicted and imprisoned for child abuse, I might introduce some (even many) dimensions into the value component that were previously not explicitly represented—I might now think him very dishonest, untrustworthy, insincere, and cruel whereas previously I just viewed him as normal along these dimensions.

The interesting and more difficult case is the one in which there already is an explicitly represented dimension, let us say one with a positively skewed distribution of trustworthy behaviors, and I then observe a highly inconsistent behavior. In such a situation, it seems reasonable to suppose that the behavior is located in the appropriate place on the dimension in the value component. But how would we respond if asked how trustworthy we thought the target was? Different answers could result from different processes. One answer might be "I used to think he was very trustworthy, but now I'm beginning to have doubts." Another might be "Moderately," and yet another "Very." These are interestingly different. The first is a qualitative response perhaps based on the realization that a bimodal distribution might be emerging. It reflects uncertainty as to how to construct a summary value. The second commits to a summary value, but gives great weight to the inconsistent information.[3] The third possibility would be one that essentially discounted the inconsistent behavior as an aberration having no noticeable effect on the central tendency. There is no a priori reason to believe that different individuals treat such cases in the same way, or that the same individual resolves different cases in the same way. This is an empirical question.

---

[3]There is evidence that attitudes are strongly governed by primacy (e.g., Anderson, 1965; Asch, 1946; Dreben, Fiske, & Hastie, 1979). I do not know the extent to which this effect interacts with familiarity with the target. It might be, for example, that the effect is strong for relatively unfamiliar targets, but that recency plays a larger role with familiar targets. This is a complex issue beyond the scope of the present chapter.

GLOBAL JUDGMENTS AND PERSON REPRESENTATIONS

In the last section I outlined a tripartite model of person representation. I want now to consider how the kind of representations that I have suggested might be used in making global social judgments and how they change over time.

I shall start by discussing the question of global judgments of liking, because these judgments are presumably based on what George calls "simple preferences." So, imagine you have a colleague, Fred, and you are asked "How much do you like Fred?" The simplest way in which the representation you have of Fred can provide a basis for a response is through the affective experience component. Recall that this component encodes a distribution of the frequency of undifferentiated positive and negative feelings of different intensity. If the current shape of the distribution reflects the fact that Fred has induced mainly negative and moderately intense emotions in you, you could simply retrieve some measure of central tendency and transform it into a response indicating moderate (or considerable, or whatever) dislike. At the same time, however the central tendency is determined, it would seem desirable that it be capable of being sensitive to highly salient recent information.[4] If Fred's most recent actual or reported behaviors have been drastically out of character and have generated positive feelings in you, one might sometimes expect the judgment to reveal a dispositional liking that is more positive than it used to be.

What I am proposing is that the primary source of information in a person representation for making liking judgments is the affective experience component. In a nutshell, what I am suggesting is that dispositional liking is primarily determined by the history of momentary liking and disliking, and that momentary liking and disliking (themselves emotions) can have their roots in other emotions. The bottom line here is that the primary source of dispositional liking (i.e., simple preferences) is emotion.

Now, even though the primary determinant of how much one likes or dislikes (i.e., one's attitude toward) somebody is the history of affective experience induced by that person, it seems reasonable to suppose that in some evaluative judgments the contribution of the affective experience component is modulated or even eliminated. Of particular interest here is the possibility that it plays a much less central role in judgments of likeableness. These judgments might well be based primarily on information in the value component, by somehow integrating diagnostic trait information. The contribution of information from the affec-

---

[4]A simple way in which recency effects could be modeled would be for the current summary value to be computed by taking an increment away from the previous summary value in the direction of the most recent value. The size of this increment would affect the sensitivity to recent information. I am indebted to Bill Revelle for this observation.

tive experience component might then be modulatory rather than constitutive. It could be eliminated if one made the liking judgment while in the midst of an emotional state, possibly even an emotional state not induced by the target.

I now want to summarize what I think might be the different roles of and interconnections between the three components in a person representation. First, the most important claim is that the affective experience component is the primary source of attitudes. Because the affective experience component is always updated in response to the emotions induced by the target, attitudes are subject to change, sometimes, as in rapidly evolving close relationships, quite quickly and quite dramatically. Second, the value component is the primary source of likeableness judgments, and the primary source of predictions and explanations about the (especially interpersonal) behavior of the target. The contents of this component are subject to change in two main ways. One is through the introduction of new diagnostic traits inferred from newly encountered extreme behaviors (coded in the fact component) that are out of character with respect to the existing trait structure in the value component. The second way in which the value component can change is generally more gradual and involves a change in shape of the distribution on a trait dimension.

My third main point is that observations and beliefs about the target are coded in the fact component and are sometimes relatable to particular points in distributions in both the affective experience and the value components. And finally, the affective experience component can be an information source for the fact component. For example, I can represent the fact that the target made me angry yesterday, or that the target often makes one angry, and this can lead to an evaluative inference (e.g., the target is exceptionally aggressive, annoying, uncooperative, etc.) that is manifested by a change in the value component.

The claim that liking judgments are normally determined by the affective component rather than the value component seems intuitively plausible. It amounts to saying that you like someone, say Mary, because most of your encounters with her have made you feel good rather than because you find her intelligent, attractive, and trustworthy, even though she is not very punctual and not very generous. Furthermore, by eschewing reliance on traits as the basis for liking judgments, we can explain the difficulty of making liking judgments about unknown others. Suppose I tell you that I have a female friend who is novelist. I tell you that she is uncommonly beautiful, intelligent, sensitive, and warm. On the basis of this information (and more like it) you could obviously construct both a fact component and a value component. However, there would be nothing in the affective experience component. In such a case, there is something odd about my asking you how much you like her. Your response would be "She sounds terrific, but I don't know whether I like her. I haven't met her." (Indeed, it is almost a joke to say "I like her already"—before even meeting her.) So, with respect to dispositional liking, we generally have no opinion if we have no corresponding affective experience. On the other hand, the value component is often the source of *predictions*. You might confidently expect that you would like her when you met her.

One way of viewing the difference between the affective experience component and the value component is to say that the former contains first order and the latter contains second order affective information. The second order information is very important because it allows the incorporation of affective expectations by inference in cases where we have had no direct experience (as well as in cases where we have). Few of us have actually had an encounter with an armed burglar, yet we all know that we do not like the idea. When we think we are encountering a particular armed burglar, our dislike of the idea is presumably based on inferences from a stereotype that lead us to expect the individual to be selfish, unkind, ruthless, dangerous, and so on. We infer (perhaps from expected behaviors, perhaps directly) extreme values on dimensions corresponding to such characteristics, and consequently, we expect to experience negative emotions in an encounter. In the example of the nighttime intruder that I gave earlier, all we need is for the generic ARMED-BURGLAR schema to contain this kind of affective information. From the theoretical perspective, this amounts to saying that we have a value component for social categories as well as for individuals, and in fact, there seems to be no reason why categories should not have something like an affective experience component too.

There are some empirical data that can be interpreted as providing at least mild support for aspects of the model I am proposing. Abelson, Kinder, Peters, and Fiske (1982) reported the results of some analyses of data from national surveys relating to political person perception. In particular, they looked at the relationship between two kinds of independent variables on summary evaluations of and preferences for well-known political figures. Their independent variables were, first, affective experiences induced by the politicians and, second, trait ratings. In other words, they examined the relationship between aspects of what we would call the affective experience component and (no doubt, at least to some extent) the value component on (summary evaluative) liking judgments.[5] The results were clear. Judgments based on self reports about whether targets had induced emotions (e.g., fear, anger, pride) in subjects were better predictors of summary evaluative judgments than were the ratings on a set of traits (e.g., dishonest, weak, knowledgeable). Furthermore, there appeared to be no differential effect for individual emotions over and above the fact that they induced positive or negative feelings. All of this is consistent with the idea that emotions induced by a target leave relatively simple affective traces that are the primary source of summary evaluations of liking or disliking. In other words, the study

---

[5]The reason I hedge a little here on whether this really constitutes pitting the affective experience space against the value space is that for the traits examined to appear in the value space, it would be necessary, on my account, for them to have the right kind of distributional properties. In fact there is no reason to believe that this was generally true.

not only suggests a separable representational difference between what Abelson et al. (1982) called affective and semantic information, but subjects were also making their evaluative judgments by giving more weight to the affective information, that is to the fact that targets had induced emotions (derived from the affective experience component) than to semantic information, that is, their trait representations (derived at least in part from the value component).

Finally, I want to consider briefly the possibility that values in a broader sense than simple preferences might arise from emotions. How, for example, might one explain the fact that most of us value helpfulness so that helpful–unhelpful becomes a dimension that can potentially play a role in the value component? With some caveats having to do with social and cultural sanctions, I think we can answer this by supposing that the affective experience component is developmentally prior to the value component. In other words, children first learn to value something (including people, objects, and types of behavior) because they like it, and they like it because it makes them feel good. Consider a child who notices that every time that he needs help and gets it, he has a positive feeling toward the helper and a positive feeling vis-à-vis his or her improved situation. Let us further suppose that the child realizes that when he or she gives help to someone else, the other behaves in a way that is also suggestive of positive feelings. These positive feelings, perhaps along with those that arise from the general social sanctioning the child receives and sees for helping behavior, might well lead the child to believe that there is something intrinsically good about helping. Presumably, in some such way, the child comes to value the attribute of helpfulness; that is, helpfulness comes to be viewed as a value-laden attribute rather than as a value-free one.

CONCLUSION

I have tried to show that emotions are indeed a source of value. Primarily, I have focused on this in the sense of values as simple preferences, trying to show that it is the affective residue of distinct emotions induced by someone that constitutes the primary source of dispositional liking for that person. I think the same sort of model could be used to explain liking outside the interpersonal domain. I am sure that my proposals are inadequate in many ways. There are many complex factors at work. Nevertheless, I think that there is a fertile research ground here. And if I am right about this, and if we start to cultivate it, no one will be happier than George Mandler.

ACKNOWLEDGMENTS

Preparation of this article was supported in part by grants from the National Science Foundation, BNS 8318077 and BNS 8721853, and in part by Andersen

Consulting through Northwestern University's Institute for the Learning Sciences. I am grateful to Gerald Clore for helpful comments on a draft of this chapter.

REFERENCES

Abelson, R. P., Kinder, D. R., Peters, M. D., & Fiske, S. T. (1982). Affective and semantic components in political person memory. *Journal of Personality and Social Psychology, 42,* 619–630.

Anderson, N. H. (1965). Primacy effects in impression formation using a generalized order effect paradigm. *Journal of Personality and Social Psychology, 2,* 1–9.

Anderson, N. H. (1971). Integration theory and attitude change. *Psychological Review, 78,* 171–206.

Anderson, N. H. (1981). Foundations of information integration theory. New York: Academic Press.

Asch, S. E. (1946). Forming impressions of personality. *Journal of Abnormal and Social Psychology, 41,* 258–290.

Berscheid, E. (1982). Attraction and emotion in interpersonal relations. In M. S. Clark & S. T. Fiske (Eds.), *Affect and cognition* (pp. 37–54). Hillsdale, NJ: Lawrence Erlbaum Associates.

Berscheid, E., & Walster, E. H. (1978). *Interpersonal attraction* (2nd ed.). Reading, MA: Addison-Wesley.

Clore, G. L. (1975). *Interpersonal attraction: An overview.* Morristown, NJ: General Learning Press.

Deiner, E., Larsen, R. J., Levine, S., & Emmons, R. A. (1985). Intensity and frequency: Dimensions underlying positive and negative affect. *Journal of Personality and Social Psychology, 53,* 767–774.

Dreben, E. K., Fiske, S. T., & Hastie, R. (1979). The independence of item and evaluation information: Impression and recall order effects in behavior-based impression formation. *Journal of Personality and Social Psychology, 37,* 1758–1768.

Fishbein, M., & Ajzen, I. (1975). *Belief, attitude, intention and behavior: An introduction to theory and research.* Reading, MA: Addison-Wesley.

Fiske, S. T. (1982). Schema-triggered affect: Applications to social perception. In M. S. Clark & S. T. Fiske (Eds.), *Affect and cognition* (pp. 55–78). Hillsdale, NJ: Lawrence Erlbaum Associates.

Fiske, S. T., & Neuberg, S. L. (1990). A continuum of impression formation, from category-based to individuating processes: Influences of information and motivation on attention and interpretation. In M. P. Zanna (Ed.), *Advances in experimental social psychology* (Vol. 23) (pp. 1–74). New York: Academic Press.

Fiske, S. T., & Pavelchak, M. A. (1986). Category-based versus piecemeal-based affective responses: Developments in schema-triggered affect. In R. M. Sorrentino & E. T. Higgins (Eds.), *Handbook of motivation and cognition: Foundations of social behavior* (pp. 167–203). New York: Guilford.

Kahneman, D., & Miller, D. T. (1986). Norm theory: Comparing reality to its alternatives. *Psychological Review, 93,* 136–153.

Mandler, G. (1975). *Mind and emotion.* New York: Wiley.

Mandler, G. (1982). The structure of value. In M. S. Clark & S. T. Fiske (Eds.), *Affect and cognition* (pp. 3–36). Hillsdale, NJ: Lawrence Erlbaum Associates.

Mandler, G. (1989). *Approaches to a psychology of value.* Unpublished manuscript.

Ortony, A., Clore, G. L., & Collins, A. (1988). *The cognitive structure of emotions.* New York: Cambridge University Press.

Srull, T. K., & Wyer, R. S. (1989). Person memory and judgment. *Psychological Review, 96,* 58–83.

Wyer, R. S., & Srull, T. K. (1986). Human cognition in its social context. *Psychological Review, 93,* 322–359.